Through the
Eyes of
the Child

THROUGH THE EYES OF THE CHILD

Obtaining Self-Reports from Children and Adolescents

ANNETTE M. La GRECA
University of Miami

ALLYN AND BACON
Boston   London   Sydney   Toronto

Series Editor: Susan Badger
Editorial-Production Service: York Production Services
Cover Administrator: Linda K. Dickinson
Manufacturing Buyer: Tamara Johnson

Library of Congress Cataloging-in-Publication Data

Through the eyes of the child : obtaining self-reports from children
  and adolescents / [edited by] Annette M. La Greca.
     p.   cm.
  Includes bibliographical references.
  ISBN 0-205-12340-6
  1. Self-perception in children.   2. Self-perception in teenagers.
3. Self-perception in children—Testing.   4. Self-perception in
teenagers—Testing.   I. La Greca, Annette M. (Annette Marie)
BF723.S28T49   1989
155.4′1828—dc20   89-28181
                                                             CIP

Printed in the United States of America

10 9 8 7 6 5 4 3 2 1   95 94 93 92 91 90

This book is dedicated with much admiration, affection, and love to my parents.

Contents

Preface

The purpose of the present volume is to provide an overview of procedures for assessing children's perceptions of themselves and others. Although much attention has been devoted to issues in child intellectual, observational, educational, and personality assessment, it is only recently that vigorous interest has emerged regarding the assessment of children's perceptions of their own internal, psychological states, as well as their perceptions of themselves, their family, and their peers.

This relatively new emphasis on children's reports is long overdue, as psychologists have made extensive use of children's self-reports in clinical and research settings for many years. Despite the importance of obtaining information from children, via interviews or self-report measures, at the time this volume was prepared no edited books on this topic could be found. As someone who has been involved with graduate instruction in the area of child assessment for many years, this void has been a source of some personal frustration. In an attempt to remedy this situation, the present volume is intended to provide current information on a variety of self-report formats (interviews, pencil and paper self-report measures, ratings of peers) that have been used with children and/or adolescents in clinical or research settings.

Although there is no one theoretical orientation that predominates in this text, the measures described herein clearly reflect objective, rather than projective, approaches to child assessment. In this sense, the text is problem-focused and largely influenced by developmental, cognitive, and behavioral perspectives on the assessment process. Moreover, the term *children* is used generically to refer to youngsters of elementary school age and to adolescents, although the predominant emphasis is on preadolescent youth. Specific references to preschool age children are noted within several of the chapters as are special considerations relevant to adolescents. The emphasis is on providing overviews of several important conceptual, developmental, and methodological issues, as well as detailed information on a selective sampling of interviews and instruments commonly used in clinical and research settings, rather than an exhaustive and comprehensive compilation of all existing self-report measures employed with children and adolescents.

The first main section of the book is intended to raise some general issues and to provide basic background information regarding developmental (Chapter 2) and psychometric (Chapter 3) considerations relevant to obtaining child self-reports. These themes are later echoed in the chapters on specific interviews and self-report measures.

The second major section contains information on interviewing children and establishing rapport (Chapter 4), as well as specific research applications of structured interview formats (Chapters 5 and 6). While providing practical information, these chapters also illustrate some of the complexities of developing and validating interview formats for research purposes.

The chapters in Part III survey measures for assessing children's perceptions of their own internal psychological states (Chapters 7 and 8 on depression, anxiety, and fears), their peers (Chapter 9), and their self-concepts (Chapter 10). What these areas have in common is their focus on phenomena that are difficult to assess without children's input; consequently, they represent perhaps the most common clinical and research applications of children's self-reports at the present time. The extensive development of child report measures in these areas reflects the difficulty of obtaining adequate information on children's internalizing states, self-concepts, and peer status using alternate assessment formats or exclusive input from other informants.

The final section of the text is devoted to special applications of children's self-reports that are relatively new, innovative, and important. The increasing use of children's reports in court testimony (Chapter 11) and the necessity of obtaining information from children in situations of alleged sexual abuse (Chapter 12) raise special concerns about obtaining valid and accurate reports from young children and require that examiners develop considerable expertise in relevant assessment strategies. Health care settings (Chapter 13) represent yet another domain in which children's reports are essential components of the assessment process.

Throughout this volume, contributors have considered clinical and empirical issues relevant to child self-reports whenever possible. This dual sensitivity is demonstrated, for instance, in the chapters on childhood depression (Chapter 7) and children's self-concepts (Chapter 10). Other chapters are, by necessity, more directly oriented toward clinical issues,

such as those on the interview process (Chapter 4) and investigatory interviews for suspected victims of child sexual abuse (Chapter 12). Information
contained in these chapters, however, also should be of benefit to
researchers who must gain the cooperation and interest of their young
subjects if they are to obtain accurate and reliable child reports. In contrast,
other authors report on measures that have been used primarily in research
settings, such as the Type A interview (Chapter 6).

I personally wish to extend my sincere thanks to the contributors of
this volume for the very high quality of their chapters and for their responsiveness to suggestions and editorial feedback. In all cases, the contributing
authors have had extensive applied and/or research expertise with the
instruments reviewed.

Finally, it is my hope that the present volume will prove to be a useful
reference for graduate students, researchers, and clinicians in the fields
of clinical child, developmental, and health psychology, who frequently
confront issues of how to obtain reliable, accurate, and meaningful self-
reports from children.

A.M.La G.

Contributors

STEPHEN R. BOGGS
Department of Clinical and
  Health Psychology
University of Florida

JAN NEAL COOLS
Department of Psychiatry
Duke University Medical Center

LYNNDA M. DAHLQUIST
Division of Pediatric Psychology
Texas Children's Hospital
Baylor College of Medicine

SHEILA EYBERG
Department of Clinical and
  Health Psychology
University of Florida

A.J. FINCH, JR.
Department of Psychiatric and
  Behavioral Sciences
Medical University of
  South Carolina

RANDALL C. FLANERY
Eating Disorders Program
Lutheran General Children's
  Medical Center

TERENCE A. GERACE
Department of Epidemiology and
  Public Health
University of Miami School
  of Medicine

SUSAN HARTER
Department of Psychology
University of Denver

KAY HODGES
Department of Psychology
Eastern Michigan University

ALAN E. KAZDIN
Department of Psychology
Yale University

ANNETTE M. LA GRECA
Department of Psychology
University of Miami

STEVEN LANDAU
Department of Psychology
Illinois State University

KATHLEEN L. LEMANEK
Division of Child Development
    and Rehabilitation
Children's Hospital of
    Philadelphia

JULIA A. McINTOSH
Department of Psychology
University of South Carolina

RICHARD MILICH
Department of Psychology
University of Kentucky

KAREN SAYWITZ
Division of Child and Adolescent
    Psychiatry
Harbor/UCLA Medical Center

JOHN C. SMITH
Department of Health Promotion
Springfield College

WENDY L. STONE
Department of Pediatrics
Vanderbilt University School
    of Medicine

C. EUGENE WALKER
Department of Psychiatry
College of Medicine
The University of Oklahoma

MARY M. WELLMAN
Mill Ward Road
Charlton, MA

SUE WHITE
Department of Psychiatry
Case Western Reserve University
    School of Medicine
Cleveland Metropolitan
    General Hospital

PART I

General Conceptual Issues

CHAPTER 1

Issues and Perspectives on the Child Assessment Process

ANNETTE M. LA GRECA

INTRODUCTION

Current views of the assessment process recognize the importance of obtaining information from children and adolescents (Bierman, 1983; La Greca, 1983; Mash & Terdal, 1988). Regardless of theoretical orientation, professionals working with children and families, as well as researchers in the areas of child development, developmental psychopathology, and pediatric behavioral medicine, often must obtain information directly from children and adolescents and cannot rely predominantly or exclusively upon observational assessments or reports from significant others in youngsters' lives.

   Among the formats used to assess youngsters' perceptions of themselves and others, interviews and self-report measures are the most common; they will be the focus of this chapter and text. More specifically, this chapter reviews several aspects of the child assessment process and highlights several concerns germane to obtaining youngsters' reports in clinical and research settings.

Interviews

Although far more attention has been devoted to the interview process with adults than with children, this position is changing (La Greca, 1983). Historically, the relative paucity of information on child interviews reflected difficulties in obtaining accurate, reliable, and valid information from children (Yarrow, L. J., 1960 and Yarrow, M. R., 1960), issues that were complicated by the cognitive and verbal demands imposed by an interview assessment. Recent developmental research has expanded our awareness of young children's capabilities and sharpened our skills in obtaining reports from children. In particular, evidence confirming that children as young as seven years of age could provide accurate and reliable reports when questions were phrased in a manner that young children could understand and demands for verbalizations were minimized (Herjanic, Herjanic, Brown, & Wheatt, 1975), spurred interest in developing interview formats for children.

Interviews are critical for obtaining information, appreciating children's unique perspectives, and establishing rapport (La Greca, 1983). Consequently, both the content (i.e., the specific information to be gathered) as well as the process of the interview (e.g., establishing a positive, cooperative relationship) become issues of concern for clinicians and researchers alike. Information relevant to the content and process of child interviews may be derived from a variety of sources, including the literature on empirically oriented structured interviews, psychodynamic approaches to child treatment, and developmental research.

Structured diagnostic interviews first gained attention in the late 1960s with the Isle of Wight studies (Rutter & Graham, 1968) of child and adolescent psychopathology. Since that time, several structured interview formats, such as the Child Assessment Schedule (Hodges, Kline, Fitch, McKnew, & Cytryn, 1981; Hodges, Kline, Stern, Cytryn, & McKnew, 1982), the Diagnostic Interview Schedule for Children (Costello, Edelbrock, Dulcan, & Kalas, 1984), and the Diagnostic Interview for Children and Adolescents (Herjanic & Campbell, 1977; Herjanic et al., 1975), have been developed for use in epidemiological and clinical research and have applicability to clinical practice as well. For the most part, these structured diagnostic interviews comprehensively assess children's social, emotional, and behavioral functioning with the intent of deriving DSM-III (or DSM-III-R) diagnoses, although more specialized interviews also have been designed to evaluate specific aspects of psychological functioning (e.g., depression) or behavior (e.g., Type A behavior pattern). Structured interviews have contributed to our knowledge of the content as well as the process of interviewing children. (Chapters 5 and 6 review several structured interview formats currently used in clinical and health research.)

Psychodynamic contributions are most apparent in writings related to the clinical *process* of interviewing children (e.g., Axline, 1947; Gardner, 1971; Greenspan, 1981; Rich, 1968; Simmons, 1974; Werkman, 1965). This is not surprising, given that the predominant focus of traditional child treatment has been the establishment of a positive therapeutic relationship between the therapist and the child. (See Chapters 2, 4, and 12 for discussions of the interview process with children and adolescents.)

Finally, a wealth of developmental research in areas such as person perception, understanding of the self, memory skills, language development, and understanding of temporal relationships has further expanded our awareness of how to conduct interviews in ways that are sensitive to youngsters' cognitive, social, and emotional capabilities. In particular, Chapters 2, 10, and 11 delineate some of these developmental sequences, and their relevance to obtaining self-reports from children. Also of interest are Chapters 4 and 12, which provide specific examples of clinical applications of the child interview process.

Self-Report Instruments

Assessing children's perspectives has been a long-standing priority for psychologists of medical, psychodynamic, psychometric, or otherwise "traditional" clinical orientations (Achenbach, 1985). Psychologists of the psychodynamic tradition historically emphasized the use of projective measures for assessing children's personality, such as the Rorschach (Ames, Learned, Metraux, & Walker, 1952), Thematic Apperception Test (Murray, 1943), Children's Apperception Test (Bellak & Bellak, 1952), and Rosenzweig Picture Frustration Study (Rosenzweig, Fleming, & Rosenzweig, 1948). Although the underlying assumptions and psychometric properties of such measures have been seriously questioned (Achenbach, 1982; French, Graves & Levitt, 1983; O'Leary & Johnson, 1986), many clinicians use these instruments in an informal manner to obtain an idiographic picture of the child's personality (Achenbach, 1982).

Disillusionment with the psychometric properties of projective techniques contributed to the development of objective self-report measures, such as the children's form of the Manifest Anxiety Scale (Casteneda, McCandless, & Palermo, 1956) and the Piers-Harris Children's Self

Concept Scale (Piers & Harris, 1969). Initial objective self-report measures assessed specific "traits" in children, or feelings and self-perceptions that could not easily be assessed in other ways. For the most part, these instruments were modeled closely on adult self-report measures (Achenbach, 1982).

With increasing psychometric sophistication in clinical and developmental research, use of factor analytic procedures, and interest in multivariate assessment procedures, self-report measures that were developed in the 1950s and 1960s met with skepticism from many researchers and clinicians. Newer instruments, such as the Self-Perception Profile for Children (Harter, 1985; also see Chapter 10 of this volume), or revisions of measures, such as the (Revised) Children's Manifest Anxiety Scale (Reynolds & Richmond, 1978; see Chapter 8), have supplanted earlier scales and demonstrate greater sensitivity to psychometric and developmental issues.

In contrast with a traditional assessment approach, behaviorally oriented psychologists initially eschewed the use of children's self-reports. However, more recent formulations of the child and family behavioral assessment process recognize the value of obtaining children's perceptions of themselves and others (Bierman, 1983; Mash & Terdal, 1988). This new position reflects an acknowledgment of the limitations inherent in other behavioral assessment methods, such as direct observation (Nelson, 1983), as well as an awareness that children's perceptions can influence their behavior and mediate the effects of treatment (Mash & Terdal, 1988; Phillips & Bierman, 1981). Moreover, difficulties surrounding the assessment of youngsters' covert, internal states and rarely occurring events via other assessment methods (e.g., teacher and parent report, direct observation), have prompted behaviorally oriented clinicians and researchers to seek reliable, accurate, and developmentally appropriate means for obtaining information from children.

In view of these concerns emanating from a variety of theoretical perspectives, the underlying assumption of this volume is that children's thoughts and feelings about themselves and others are critical to the scientific and clinical understanding of the child. As this volume attests, the availability of children's self-report measures with satisfactory psychometric properties has expanded considerably in recent years. This growth is at least partly related to concerns with individual differences in children's emotional, social, and psychological development. To a large extent, the most widely used self-report instruments assess aspects of children's internal psychological states (e.g., fear, anxiety, depression, pain) and self-perceptions (e.g., self-concept), and are the focus of the present volume. However, instruments are now available for a broad range of children's interpersonal, behavioral, and affective functioning (e.g., life stress, coping skills, social skills, medical compliance, perceived behavior problems).

NATURE OF THE ASSESSMENT PROCESS WITH CHILDREN

Multiperson Perspective

The first basic characteristic of the child assessment process is that it usually involves multiple persons in the child's environment (La Greca, 1983). In addition to information provided by the child, other significant individuals such as parents, teachers, and peers contribute in important ways to our understanding of youngsters' behavior. Children's self-reports generally must be viewed in the context of the broader picture that evolves from independent reporting sources. This multiperson perspective contrasts sharply with the adult assessment process, which often involves only the adult in question. Several factors contribute to this differing perspective with children.

First, children are under the social control of others in their environment (Mash & Terdal, 1988). As a consequence, children's behavior often is situation specific. Hyperactive behavior in the classroom, for example, may not be predictive of overactivity in home or clinic settings (Klein & Gittelman-Klein, 1975). Given this situational specificity, it becomes important to evaluate the broader social context within which the child functions. The actions of parents, teachers, and peers will affect and be affected by the child.

Second, the nature of the intervention process with children is such that significant others in the child's life are usually involved in treatment. Since intervention efforts incorporate multiple persons, the assessment process must respect these multiple perspectives as well.

It is also the case that children typically are referred for treatment by others, usually a parent or teacher. This necessitates obtaining the perspective of the adults who are distressed by the child or the situation and adds further complexity to the assessment process, as individuals can have markedly divergent perspectives. Mothers and fathers, as well as teachers and parents, often disagree about the presence or degree of child behavior problems (e.g., Jacob, Grounds, & Haley, 1982; Mattison, Bagnato, & Strickler, 1987; Webster-Stratton & Hammond, 1988).

These factors underscore the need for assessing others' perspectives, in addition to the child's, and coordinating these multiple sources of information to provide an integrated, comprehensive picture of the child's functioning. (See Reich & Earls, 1987, for a discussion of integrating information from multiple informants.)

Multimethod Assessment

A second basic tenet of child assessment (and assessment in general) is that multiple methods are desirable. Although this volume is devoted to children's self-reports, a broader assessment strategy is essential for an accurate clinical or research understanding of the child.

Multiple assessment methods are desirable due to the limitations inherent in any one procedure. Parent interviews, for example, may provide valuable information regarding child and family functioning, yet parents' retrospective accounts have shown little stability over time and tend to distort children's behavior in the direction of precocity (Hetherington & Martin, 1979). Furthermore, a parent's psychological state may influence reports of child behavior (Forehand & Brody, 1985; Webster-Stratton & Hammond, 1988). Depressed mothers, for instance, report more behavioral disturbance in their children relative to nondepressed moms (Webster-Stratton & Hammond, 1988). Behavioral observations, on the other hand, may appear to provide more objective information; however, problems associated with reactivity of measurement, observation of low frequency behaviors, and interrater reliability are common (Kent & Foster, 1977; Mash & Terdal, 1988). In order to minimize the limitations of any one assessment procedure, a comprehensive, multimodal approach is advocated. (See Chapter 7, for example, for a discussion of multiple measures and multiple informants in the assessment of childhood depression.)

Developmental Framework

Given the rapid and uneven developmental change that is characteristic of children (Evans & Nelson, 1977; Mash & Terdal, 1988), a developmental perspective is critical to understanding youngsters and their behavior. A knowledge of "age appropriate" functioning is a prerequisite for identifying many childhood problems. For instance, nocturnal bed-wetting may be common among three-year-olds, but represents a significant problem for a seven-year-old. Moreover, on a conceptual level, models of child psychopathology must adopt a developmental framework; adult models of psychopathology cannot adequately be extrapolated to children (Yule, 1981).

Throughout this volume, authors have presented a wealth of information regarding the interface between youngsters' development and the child assessment process. In particular, Chapter 2 reviews research on children's language skills and perceptions of themselves and others, drawing implications for the use of child interviews and self-reports. Similarly, Chapter 11 describes current developmental research relevant to obtaining reports from child witnesses.

Importance of the Child's Perspective

One of the consequences of children being referred for treatment by adults is that some youngsters may not be experiencing subjective distress or comprehend the nature of the problem and the reasons for assessment (Evans & Nelson, 1977; Mash & Terdal, 1988). In order to engage children in the assessment process, therefore, one must solicit their input and perspective. Furthermore, in the case of internalizing problems, such as feelings of depression or anxiety, children's perceptions are paramount to the assessment process.

Whether in a research or clinical setting, the assessment of internalizing problems in children poses difficulties that are not apparent for more obvious, externalizing childhood disorders, such as conduct problems and hyperactivity. Emotional discomfort, low self-esteem, subjective feelings of distress, and negative self-statements, which are central aspects of internalizing problems, may be difficult for parents and teachers to identify accurately and reliably (Quay & La Greca, 1986). In fact, parent and teacher reports of internalizing problems in children have not been found to correspond well with children's self-reports (see Chapter 7), except for fears and phobias which often are accompanied by specific avoidance behaviors.

Childhood depression, in fact, may be the most difficult internalizing problem for adults to identify in children. Many of the cognitive and affective components of depression, such as guilt, self-blame, feelings of rejection, and negative self-image (Kaslow, Rehm, & Siegel, 1984; Poznanski & Zrull, 1970; Rutter & Garmezy, 1983; Sandler & Joffe, 1965), are difficult to observe. Consistent with this view, Rutter has indicated that adolescents' reports of severe depression may go undetected by parents and teachers (Rutter, 1979; Rutter & Garmezy, 1983). Even reports from independent adult observers correspond poorly with each other. For instance, Rutter and Graham (1968) found considerable disagreement among psychiatrists on their ratings of youngsters' depression.

On the other hand, while often aware of emotional discomfort, children may experience difficulty in labeling, defining, or verbally communicating their subjective state (Quay & La Greca, 1986). Systematic input from children and adolescents must be obtained in a manner that minimizes demands for verbal expression and is sensitive to the youngsters' capabilities and developmental status. Fortunately, several structured diagnostic interviews (see Chapter 5) and self-report measures (see Chapters 7 through 10) have been developed that are sensitive to these issues.

Much less attention has been accorded to obtaining self-reports from children with externalizing types of problems, such as inattention, hyperactivity, and aggressive behavior, yet the need for systematic input from these youngsters may be critical as well. Ideas about and attributions for the effects of stimulant medications may contribute to the behavior of children with attention deficit disorders (R. Milich, February 1989, personal communication). Furthermore, individual differences in youngsters' social or emotional functioning may predict treatment responsiveness among aggressive youth. Along these lines, Lochman and associates (Lochman, Lampron, Burch, & Curry, 1985) found that aggressive boys (fourth- to sixth-graders) with poor pretreatment levels of social problem-solving skills demonstrated a greater decrement in disruptive and aggressive behavior as a result of intervention than aggressive boys with good pretreatment skills. Interestingly, when untreated aggressive boys were considered, those with high levels of self-esteem and good problem-solving skills displayed the greatest spontaneous improvement in aggressive behavior over the school year. This kind of research illustrates the potential utility of children's self-reports in studies of individual characteristics predictive of treatment outcome and behavior change.

SPECIFIC ISSUES IN THE USE OF CHILD REPORTS

Special Populations

For the most part, the interviews and self-report measures described in this text were developed for use with "normal" school children or specific clinical populations and may not be applicable or generalizable to some special children encountered in clinical or research settings. (See Chapters 3 and 10 for extended discussions of this issue.) This concern is particularly relevant for the assessment of youngsters with cognitive or academic deficits (e.g., learning disabilities, mental retardation). Such youngsters may not possess the skills to complete structured interviews or self-report measures as intended. Deviations from standard administration procedures (e.g., having the items read to the child; defining specific vocabulary words) may be necessary to adapt the demands of the instrument, or its response requirements, to the individual child.

Of further concern is the validity of the data obtained when a measure is used with a special group that was not represented in the initial standardization sample or subsequent psychometric research. Inferences and conclusions drawn from such data can be erroneous or misleading. For example, Susan Harter (see Chapter 10) has raised this issue with respect to the Self-Perception Profile for Children (SPPC), as she and her colleagues (Renick, 1985; Renick & Harter, 1988) found that the factor structure of the SPPC differed for youngsters with specific learning disabilities, as compared with their normal achieving schoolmates. Their data indicated that learning disabled (LD) youth drew clear distinctions between their academic competence (e.g., how well they could read) and their cognitive competence (e.g., how smart they were), whereas for most elementary school children, academic and cognitive self-perceptions were closely intertwined. As a result of these findings, the SPPC has been revised for use with LD youngsters, so that their academic and cognitive self perceptions are assessed independently rather than as one unified factor of scholastic competence. Without this information, using the standard SPPC, one might draw the wrong conclusions regarding the cognitive self-perceptions of LD youth.

In summary, considerable caution must be exercised when using self-report measures with exceptional populations. (See Chapter 3 for a further discussion.)

Ethical Concerns

Numerous ethical issues arise in the course of assessing youngsters and families. Although a detailed coverage of ethics is beyond the scope of this chapter, the interested reader is referred to several excellent sources for further information, including Koocher (1986), the ethical standards of psychologists (American Psychological Association, 1981) and child researchers (Society for Research in Child Development, 1973), as well as Standards for Educational and Psychological Testing (American Psychological Association, 1985). In addition, ethical concerns and confidentiality are discussed in Chapters 4, 7, and 9 of this volume. Of interest to the present discussion, however, are two issues that are specific to the use of self-report assessments in research settings.

Perhaps the major issue of concern facing clinical researchers is the identification of "at risk" children in nonclinical samples. When interviews or self-report measures are used in community research settings, it may be possible to identify youngsters who are in need of professional assistance, such as children who obtain extreme scores on measures of depression or peer rejection or who report evidence of parental abuse during a structured interview. How should such disclosures be handled? Ethical guidelines adopted by the American Psychological Association (1982) and the Society for Research in Child Development (1973) indicate that investigators have a responsibility to effect assistance for research participants whose welfare is judged to be at serious risk. If this is the case, what are the limits of confidentiality for child self-reports?

Burbach, Farha, and Thorpe (1986) recently surveyed researchers who had administered self-report inventories of depression in community samples and found that very few investigators had anticipated or planned for the identification of severely depressed or suicidal children. These authors discuss the ethical concerns associated with the use of children's self-reports of depression, taking the position that information on "high risk" youngsters should be shared with individuals who can act on the information (e.g., teacher, parent). They advocate informing children of the limits of confidentiality prior to conducting any assessments, so that investigators are free to take action, when appropriate. As these authors note, careful phrasing of child consent forms may be necessary, such as:

> "If a child's responses show that he/she might have a problem, we will talk to the child's parents to see if we can help." (p. 586).

More appropriately worded, but parallel, statements should be included in parental consent forms as well. This strategy for handling the identification of youngsters at risk for depression or suicide clearly is applicable to other research uses of youngsters' self-reports.

Another concern that arises in research settings is the emotional impact of the assessment process. For instance, will youngsters become psychologically distressed as a result of answering questions about depression, fears, and worries, or their peer relations? Apparently, there is little empirical data on this particular issue. Burbach et al. (1986) note that there is no evidence to support a causal link between the use of self-report questionnaires and depression or suicide in children. Yet, investigators have reported difficulties in gaining acceptance of research protocols from institutional research review boards when self-report measures of depression are included (Burbach et al., 1986). (Landau and Milich, in Chapter 9, similarly note the paucity of data regarding the negative impact of peer rating and peer nomination measures.) Clearly, further investigation of the emotional impact of self-report assessment procedures would be desirable.

Bias in Self-Reporting: Social Desirability

A major objection to the use of children's self-reports has been their subjective bias. To the extent that youngsters' reports reflect their own, unique perspectives, these subjective impressions are valuable. However, in an effort to please adult examiners, youngsters may react to the demand characteristics of the assessment situation by responding in socially desirable ways. Therefore, to facilitate obtaining accurate reports from children, efforts to limit socially desirable responses are of interest. Interviews and self-report measures can be designed to minimize social desirability by the way questions are phrased. (See Chapter 12 for a discussion of problematic questioning strategies in children's interviews and Chapter 10 for a discussion of social desirability in children's self-report measures.) Assessing social desirability directly and independently from other measures may be another way to determine the extent to which children's reports are biased in this direction. In addition, some measures, such as the Revised Children's Manifest Anxiety Scale (Reynolds & Richmond, 1978; also see Chapter 8) include a "Lie Scale" as part of the instrument to evaluate youngsters' tendency toward socially desirable reporting. In other instances, carefully worded test instructions (e.g., there are no right or wrong answers) may prompt youngsters to be more forthright in their answers. Careful attention to the issue of social desirability will help to insure more accurate child reports.

SUMMARY

This introductory chapter highlighted the current clinical and empirical interest in obtaining self-reports from children and adolescents. A brief review of historical trends in the development of structured interviews and self-report measures was provided, as well as several guidelines relevant to the child assessment process. Finally, issues such as the use of self-report measures with special populations, ethical concerns in research settings, and problems associated with socially desirable responding were described.

The general issues raised herein are addressed further in subsequent chapters. Thoughtful consideration of the issues presented in this chapter, and throughout the text, should enable researchers and clinicians to make the most of their efforts to obtain accurate, reliable, and meaningful self-reports from children and adolescents.

REFERENCES

Achenbach, T.M. (1982). Assessment of taxonomy of children's behavior disorders. In B.B. Lahey & A.E. Kazdin (Eds.), *Advances in clinical child psychology.* (Vol. 5). (pp. 1–38). New York: Plenum.

Achenbach, T.M. (1985). *Assessment and taxonomy of child and adolescent psychopathology.* Beverly Hills, CA: Sage.

American Psychological Association. (1981). Ethical principles of psychologists. *American Psychologist, 36,* 633–638.

American Psychological Association. (1982). Ethical principles in the conduct of research with human participants. Washington, DC: Author.

American Psychological Association. (1985). *Standards for educational and psychological testing.* Washington, DC: Author.

Ames, L.B., Learned, J., Metraux, R.W., & Walker, R.N. (1952). *Child Rorschach responses.* New York: Hoeber-Harper.

Axline, V. (1947). *Play therapy.* New York: Balantine Books.

Bellak, L., & Bellak, S.S. (1952). *Children's Apperception Test.* (2nd ed.) New York: CPS.

Bierman, K.L. (1983). Cognitive development and clinical interviews with children. In B.B. Lahey & A.E. Kazdin (Eds.), *Advances in clinical child psychology.* (Vol. 6). (pp. 217–250). New York: Plenum.

Burbach, D.J., Farha, J.G., & Thorpe, J.S. (1986). Assessing depression in community samples of children using self-report inventories: Ethical considerations. *Journal of Abnormal Child Psychology, 14,* 579–589.

Castaneda, A., McCandless, B.R., & Palermo, D.S. (1956). The children's form of the Manifest Anxiety Scale. *Child Development, 17,* 317–326.

Costello, A.J., Edelbrock, C.S., Dulcan, M.K., & Kalas, R. (1984). Testing of the NIMH Diagnostic Interview Schedule for Children (DISC) in a clinical population (Contract No. DB-81-0027). Final report to the Center for Epidemiological Studies, National Institute for Mental Health. Pittsburgh: University of Pittsburgh.

Evans, I.M., & Nelson, R.O. (1977). Assessment of child behavior problems. In A.R. Ciminero, K.S. Calhoun, & H.E. Adams (Eds.), *Handbook of behavioral assessment.* (pp. 603–681). New York: Wiley.

Forehand, R., & Brody, G. (1985). The association between parental personal/marital adjustment and parent-child interactions in a clinic sample. *Behavior Research and Therapy, 23,* 211–212.

French, J., Graves, P.D., & Levitt, E.E. (1983). Objective and projective testing of children. In C.E. Walker & M.C. Roberts (Eds.), *Handbook of clinical child psychology.* (pp. 209–247). New York: Wiley.

Gardner, R. (1971). *Therapeutic communication with children: The mutual story telling technique.* New York: Science House.

Greenspan, S.I. (1981). *The clinical interview of the child.* New York: McGraw-Hill.

Harter, S. (1985). *The Self-Perception Profile for Children: Revision of the Perceived Competence Scale for Children.* Manual, University of Denver.

Herjanic, B., & Campbell, W. (1977). Differentiating psychiatrically disturbed children on the basis of a structured interview. *Journal of Abnormal Child Psychology, 10,* 307–324.

Herjanic, B., Herjanic, M., Brown, F., & Wheatt, J. (1975). Are children reliable reporters? *Journal of Abnormal Child Psychology, 3,* 41–48.

Hetherington, E.M., & Martin, B. (1979). Family interaction. In H.C. Quay & J.S. Werry (Eds.), *Psychopathological disorders of childhood.* (2nd ed.) (pp. 247–302). New York: Wiley.

Hodges, K., Kline, J., Fitch, P., McKnew, D., & Cytryn, L. (1981). The Child Assessment Schedule: A diagnostic interview for research and clinical use. *Catalogue of Selected Documents in Psychology, 11,* #56.

Hodges, K., Kline, J., Stern, L., Cytryn, L., & McKnew, D. (1982). The development of a child assessment instrument for research and clinical use. *Journal of Abnormal Child Psychology, 10,* 173–189.

Jacob, T., Grounds, L., & Haley, R. (1982). Correspondence between parents' reports on the Behavior Problem Checklist. *Journal of Abnormal Child Psychology, 10,* 593–608.

Kaslow, N.J., Rehm, L.P., & Siegel, A.W. (1984). Social-cognitive and cognitive correlates of depression in children. *Journal of Abnormal Child Psychology, 12,* 605–620.

Kent, R.N., & Foster, S.L. (1977). Direct observation procedures: Methodological issues in naturalistic settings. In A.R. Ciminero, K.S. Calhoun, & H.E. Adams (Eds.), *Handbook of behavioral assessment.* (pp. 279–328). New York: Wiley.

Klein, D.F., & Gittelman-Klein, R. (1975). Problems in the diagnosis of minimal brain dysfunction in the hyperkinetic syndrome. *International Journal of Mental Health, 4,* 45–60.

Koocher, G.P. (1986). (Ed.), *Children's rights and the mental health professions.* New York: Wiley.

La Greca, A.M. (1983). Interviewing and behavioral observations. In C.E. Walker & M.C. Roberts (Eds.), *Handbook of clinical child psychology.* (pp. 109–131). New York: Wiley.

Lochman, J.E., Lampron, L.B., Burch, P.R., & Curry, J.F. (1985). Client characteristics associated with behavior change for treated and untreated aggressive boys. *Journal of Abnormal Child Psychology, 13,* 527–538.

Mash, E.J., & Terdal, L.G. (1988). Behavioral assessment of child and family disturbance. In E.J. Mash and L.G. Terdal (Eds.), *Behavioral assessment of child disorders.* (2nd ed.) (pp. 3–65). New York: Guilford Press.

Mattison, R.E., Bagnato, S.J., & Strickler, E. (1987). Diagnostic importance of combined parent and teacher ratings on the Revised Behavior Problem Checklist. *Journal of Abnormal Child Psychology, 15,* 617–628.

Murray, H.A. (1943). *Thematic Apperception Test manual.* Cambridge: Harvard University Press.

Nelson, R.O. (1983). Behavioral assessment: Past, present, future. *Behavioral Assessment, 5,* 195–206.

O'Leary, K.D., & Johnson, S.B. (1986). Assessment and assessment of change. In H.C. Quay & J.S. Werry (Eds.), *Psychopathological disorders of childhood.* (3rd ed.) (pp. 423–454). New York: Wiley.

Phillips, J.S., & Bierman, K.L. (1981). Clinical psychology: Individual methods. *Annual Review of Psychology, 32,* 405–438.

Piers, E., & Harris, D. (1969). *The Piers-Harris Children's Self Concept Scale.* Nashville, Tennessee: Counselor Recordings and Tests.

Poznanski, E.O., & Zrull, J.P. (1970). Childhood depression: Clinical characteristics of overtly depressed children. *Archives of General Psychiatry, 23,* 8–15.

Quay, H.C., & La Greca, A.M. (1986). Disorders of anxiety, withdrawal, and dysphoria. In H.C. Quay & J.S. Werry (Eds.), *Psychopathological Disorders of Childhood.* (3rd ed.) (pp. 73–110). New York: Wiley.

Reich, W., & Earls, F. (1987). Rules for making psychiatric diagnoses in children on the basis of multiple sources of information: Preliminary strategies. *Journal of Abnormal Child Psychology, 15,* 601–616.

Renick, M.J. (1985). Examining the self-perceptions of learning disabled children and adolescents: Issues of measurement and a model of global self-worth. Doctoral dissertation, University of Denver.

Renick, M.J., & Harter, S. (1988). The Self-Perception Profile for Learning Disabled Students: Manual. University of Denver.

Reynolds, C.R., & Richmond, B.O. (1978). "What I Think and Feel": A revised measure of children's manifest anxiety. *Journal of Abnormal Child Psychology, 6,* 271–280.

Rich, J. (1968). *Interviewing children and adolescents.* London: Macmillan.

Rosenzweig, S., Fleming, E.E., & Rosenzweig, L. (1948). *The children's form of the Rosenzweig picture-frustration study.* St. Louis: Author.

Rutter, M. (1979). *Changing youth in a changing society.* London: Nuffield Provincial Hospitals Trust.

Rutter, M., & Garmezy, N. (1983). Developmental psychopathology. In E. M. Hetherington (Ed.), *Handbook of child psychology: Socialization, personality, and social development.* (Vol. IV). (pp. 775–911). New York: Wiley.

Rutter, M., & Graham, P. (1968). The reliability and validity of the psychiatric assessment of the child. I. Interview with the child. *British Journal of Psychiatry, 114,* 563–579.

Sandler, J., & Joffe, W. (1965). Notes on childhood depression. *International Journal of Psychoanalysis, 46,* 88–96.

Simmons, J.E. (1974). *Psychiatric examination of children.* (2nd. ed.). Philadelphia: Lea & Febiger.

Society for Research in Child Development. (1973). *Ethical standards for research with children.* Chicago: Author.

Webster-Stratton, C., & Hammond, M. (1988). Maternal depression and its relationship to life stress, perceptions of child behavior problems, parenting behaviors, and child conduct problems. *Journal of Abnormal Child Psychology, 16,* 299–315.

Werkman, S. (1965). The psychiatric diagnostic interview with children. *American Journal of Orthopsychiatry, 35,* 764–771.

Yarrow, L.J. (1960). Interviewing children. In P.H. Mussen (Ed.), *Handbook of research methods in child development.* New York: Wiley.

Yarrow, M.R. (1960). The measurement of children's attitudes and values. In P.H. Mussen (Ed.), *Handbook of research methods in child development*. New York: Wiley.

Yule, W. (1981). The epidemiology of child psychopathology. In B.B. Lahey & A.E. Kazdin (Eds.), *Advances in clinical child psychology*. (Vol. 4). (pp. 1–51). New York: Plenum.

CHAPTER 2

Developmental Issues in Children's Self-Reports

WENDY L. STONE
KATHLEEN L. LEMANEK

INTRODUCTION

Although self-report techniques have long been considered a critical component of the adult assessment process, their utility in child assessment has been recognized only recently. It is generally accepted that most adults are capable of providing valuable information about themselves through interview procedures or self-report measures. In contrast, children have historically been viewed as unreliable perceivers and reporters of events. Doubts about children's capacity to present accurate information, combined with easy access to adult sources of information (i.e., parental reports), resulted in the under-utilization of self-report assessment data.

Developmental limitations also restricted the use of self-report techniques with children in the past. Self-report instruments used for adults were not well-suited to the reading ability, vocabulary level, or life experiences of young children. Moreover, the use of interview techniques required adaptations to the developmental characteristics of children, such as their limited attention span and language skills.

18

Recent years, however, have seen renewed interest in obtaining self-report information from children. This has been reflected in several trends: the development of child versions of many adult self-report measures, the development of a number of new structured interview schedules designed for children, and increased research exploring reliability issues as they pertain to children's self-reports. Moreover, the developmental literature has contributed to a greater understanding of children as dynamic, changing organisms, with unique experiences and capabilities at different ages.

The purpose of this chapter is to review the developmental issues that affect the use of self-report techniques with children. Issues pertaining to clinical interview situations as well as pencil-and-paper inventories will be discussed. The developmental literature from preschool through adolescence will be reviewed, with special attention paid to empirically based conclusions.

COGNITIVE-DEVELOPMENTAL ISSUES

Whether answering questions in an interview situation or circling responses on a pencil-and-paper measure, the accuracy of children's self-reports will depend on their acquisition of certain cognitive and social-cognitive skills. Among these skills are children's level of communication development and their ability to understand themselves and others in their environment. This section will review specific cognitive-developmental factors that underlie children's ability to provide accurate self-reports. Information presented in this section is summarized in Tables 2.1 and 2.2

Concept of Self

One assumption underlying the use of self-report measures with children is that children possess a coherent sense of their "selfhood" that would render their reports meaningful. The focus of this section is to explore children's emerging understanding of themselves as unique individuals with physical and mental dimensions. Specific questions that will be addressed include the following:

What are the limits of self-understanding at different developmental levels?

How does the concept of the self change with age?

On what basis do children come to differentiate themselves from others?

TABLE 2.1   Summary of Major Developmental Trends in Three Areas of Social-Cognitive Functioning

	Social-Cognitive Area		
Age (in years)	Concept of Self	Person Perception	Understanding of Emotions
Birth to 3	Visual self-recognition.		Differentiation between facial expressions.
	Description of own physical and mental states.		Communication about simple emotions.
4 to 6	Concrete self-descriptions, based on physical appearance, behaviors and activities.	Description of others in concrete, observable, global terms.	Accurate identification of happiness from facial expressions and situational cues.
	"All-or none" conceptualization of personal traits.	Explanations of others' behaviors infrequent, based on situational factors.	Use of body cues and situational cues to understand own emotions.
	"Self" viewed as part of body.		No awareness of simultaneous experience of different emotions.
7 to 11	Self-descriptions incorporate psychological characteristics and social comparisons.	Description of others in terms of behavioral dispositions and personal characteristics.	Accurate recognition of negative emotions. Use of mental cues to understand own emotions.
	Awareness of different components of self, situationally based.	No awareness that others can possess both negative and positive qualities.	Understanding of simultaneous experience of different emotions.
	Differentiation between mental and physical aspects of self.	Explanations of others' behaviors more common, beginning use of dispositional factors.	

(continued)

TABLE 2.1 (*Continued*)

Age (in years)	Social-Cognitive Area		
	Concept of Self	Person Perception	Understanding of Emotions
12 to 16	Abstract self-descriptions, based on psychological constructs, dispositional characteristics, beliefs, and values.	Description of others in terms of complex, abstract, stable characteristics.	Understanding of discrepancy between inner feelings and outward expressions.
	Integration of disparate aspects of self to form consistent self-identity.	Spontaneous explanations of others' behaviors, based on situational and dispositional factors.	Causal reasoning about others' emotions.
	Self conceptualized primarily in mental terms, as processor of experience, capable of self-reflection and self-monitoring		

*No available literature for this age.

Several investigators have provided empirical data outlining the development of self-understanding at various ages. This information can be pieced together to create a rough sketch of the emerging sense of self from infancy through adolescence. Since a detailed review is beyond the scope of this chapter, the interested reader is referred to excellent reviews by Damon and Hart (1982) and Harter (1983) for more comprehensive coverage of this topic.

Substantial evidence has accumulated to indicate that a sense of one's physical self begins in infancy. Self-awareness in infants is conceptualized as visual self-recognition and is assessed by examining infants' responses to their mirror images, photographs, and other visual representations of themselves. Investigations have revealed that infants as young as 9 to 12 months demonstrate early aspects of self-recognition. However, self-awareness at this age is action-based; it is limited to the understanding that their own physical movements are causally related to their moving visual images (Lewis & Brooks-Gunn, 1979). Self-recognition on the basis of static elements of their physical appearance is first seen at 15 to 18 months; at this age infants are able to differentiate between pictures of themselves and others on the basis of facial features associated with gender and age (Amsterdam, 1972; Lewis & Brooks-Gunn, 1979).

TABLE 2.2   Summary of Early Language Development

Age (in years)	Area of Language		
	Phonology	*Syntax*	*Semantics*
One to two	50-word vocabulary	Telegraphic speech, two- to three-word sentences.	Basic understanding of many words referring to concrete objects.
Two to three	900-word vocabulary	Use of plurals, irregular verb endings, possessives, and other morphemes. Use of negatives and questions.	Concept development characterized by overextension and underextension of word meanings.
Three to five	2000-word vocabulary	Overgeneralization of grammatical rules such as irregular verb endings.	Idiosyncratic speech, such as creating new words.
Five to seven	Over 2600-word vocabulary	Refinement of grammar, such as relearning of irregular verb endings and constructing more complex and varied sentences.	Concept development reflects beginning understanding of general and specific characteristics of objects within and across categories.

The emergence of language skills in children enables us to further understand their level of self-knowledge. Studies of the spontaneous speech of toddlers reveal that children between the ages of 18 and 24 months begin to refer to themselves by name, use personal pronouns, and make self-descriptive statements (Harter, 1983; Kagan, 1981). By 28 months toddlers demonstrate the capacity to spontaneously describe their own internal mental states; for example, children in this age group use language to indicate their perceptions (e.g., "see," "taste"), emotions (e.g., "funny," "scared"), cognitions (e.g., "know," "think"), and physiological states (e.g., "thirsty," "tired") (Bretherton & Beeghly, 1982; Shatz, Wellman, & Silber, 1983).

More direct investigations of self-concept development have utilized verbal interviews with children as young as three and four years. Information obtained from open-ended interviews has revealed that young children conceptualize themselves primarily in physical terms throughout the preschool years (Broughton, 1978; Selman, 1980). The self is thought to be part of the body, and little understanding of a distinction between inner experience and overt behavior is evidenced. Analysis of young children's self-descriptions also reveals their physicalistic conceptions of the self. Young children have been found to describe themselves most commonly in terms of their physical attributes (e.g., "I have brown hair"), possessions (e.g., "I have a dog"), overt behaviors (e.g., "I watch TV"), and preferred activities (e.g., "I like to swim") (Keller, Ford, & Meacham, 1978; Livesley & Bromley, 1973; Secord & Peevers, 1974). Moreover, young children also make differentiations between themselves and others primarily on the basis of observable behaviors and characteristics, rather than internal experiences (Guardo & Bohan, 1971).

Many dramatic changes in the concept of the self begin between the ages of seven and eight years. In general, middle childhood is a period of increasing specificity in children's understanding of themselves. Their self-understanding becomes more situationally based, as they come to appreciate that there are many components of their "self," and that they may feel or act differently in dissimilar situations. One aspect of differentiation occurs with respect to children's use of trait labels in self-descriptions. Harter (1986a) describes a change in children's use of trait labels that progresses from "all-or-none" thinking to a greater ability to distinguish between one situation and the next. For instance, regarding the trait of intelligence, young children tend to think of themselves as "all smart" or "all dumb." However, at around the age of eight years they come to understand that they can be smart in some areas (e.g., math) and dumb in others (e.g., spelling). It is not until the age of 10 or so that children realize that they can be both smart and dumb in the same domain (Harter, 1986a).

Although children continue to describe themselves primarily in terms of their activities and physical characteristics, psychological conceptions of the self are also seen in middle childhood. At the age of seven or eight, children begin to distinguish between mental and physical aspects of the self. They can explain their distinctness from others in terms of different thoughts and feelings, as well as their individual physical and material attributes (Broughton, 1978; Guardo & Bohan, 1971). Moreover, children at this age begin to recognize the possibility of discrepancies between psychological experience and outer physical appearance (i.e., a person can act one way and feel a different way). Thus they become conceptually aware of the possibilities of putting on a facade and intentionally deceiving others (Elliott, 1982; Selman, 1980). Children at this age show an emerging awareness that they have better access to their thoughts than others do (Selman, 1980); however, the understanding that they know themselves better than their parents know them does not become prominent until adolescence (Rosenberg, 1979).

A sense of the social self also emerges more clearly in middle childhood. Children begin to use social comparisons in forming their self-evaluations and identity. For example, Livesley and Bromley (1973) found that, with increasing age, children's self-descriptions included more frequent comparisons with others. Similarly, Ruble (1983) found that children over seven years old use information about their own performance as well as that of their peers in forming self-evaluations. Experimental investigations have also revealed that accuracy in judging one's own abilities increases at this age. Whereas younger children tend to have overly positive perceptions of their abilities, despite feedback to the contrary, seven- and eight-year-old children begin to adjust their self-perceptions according to feedback and past experiences with success or failure (Nicholls, 1978, 1979; Parsons & Ruble, 1977; Stipek, 1981).

In adolescence, the concept of the self increases in complexity and abstractness. The self-descriptions of adolescents reveal a much higher proportion of psychological constructs and interpersonal characteristics relative to those of younger children (Bernstein, 1980; Montemayor & Eisen, 1977; Rosenberg, 1979). Once concrete and behaviorally-based, self-descriptions now incorporate abstract conceptions such as temperament and disposition (e.g., "I'm easygoing"), and beliefs, attitudes, and values (e.g., "I'm a pacifist") (Bernstein, 1980; Livesley & Bromley, 1973; Montemayor & Eisen, 1977; Secord & Peevers, 1974). The self is now conceptualized primarily in mental—rather than physical—terms. Keenly aware of their inner thoughts, feelings, and wishes, adolescents embrace a new dimension of self-awareness. The self is now seen as an active processor of experience, one that is capable of self-reflection, self-monitoring, and self-evaluation (Broughton, 1978; Selman, 1980). Moreover, a major developmental task of adolescence is the conceptual integration of the self-system. Now that disparate aspects of the self are recognized, adolescents strive to organize them into an internally consistent self-identity (Bernstein, 1980; Grotevant & Adams, 1984; Harter, 1986a,b; Waterman, 1982).

In summary, children's self-understanding progresses along a developmental continuum from concrete, physicalistic, and situation-specific views of the self to abstract, psychological, and trait-like self-definitions. Before the age of seven or eight, children's self-understanding is limited to isolated pieces of information about observable characteristics and actions; little ability to integrate or organize this information is present (Harter, 1983). As a consequence, interview and self-report measures with preschool and early elementary-aged children should employ concrete and action-oriented questions (e.g., "Do you cry?" instead of, "Are you sad?"). Moreover, in light of the difficulty that young children have making realistic judgments about themselves (Harter & Pike, 1984), it is important to supplement their self-report information with material obtained from other sources, such as teachers and parents. At around the age of eight years, however, children first become aware of their "personness" and acquire a more global sense of the self (Harter & Pike, 1984). After this age, children's self-reports become considerably more meaningful, as they are better able to report on their thoughts and feelings, and to provide more accurate information regarding diverse experiences and situations. However, the increased use of social comparison processes and the greater psychological awareness of elementary-aged children may contribute to a tendency toward socially appropriate responding. This possibility suggests the importance of including social desirability scales on self-report measures and of continuing to obtain confirmatory information from other individuals close to the child. With adolescents, interview and self-report measures can delve into new depths, as individuals acquire the ability to evaluate their own thoughts and behaviors critically and to analyze others' reactions to their behaviors.

Person Perception

The developmental processes involved in understanding oneself and in understanding others appear to be intricately interwoven. Various theories (e.g., Damon & Killen, 1982; Mead, 1934) have emphasized the importance of obtaining feedback from social interactions and social experiences in the development of self-perception. In turn, a basic assumption in person perception research is that social interactions are strongly influenced by one's conceptualizations of others (Shantz, 1983). Conceptualizations of others are further assumed to be affected by both cognitive structures of the perceiver and characteristics of the perceived (Shantz, 1983). A study by Dornbusch, Hastorf, Richardson, Muzzy, and Vreeland (1965) helps to illustrate this last assumption. In this study, 9- to 11-year-old children were requested to describe a few of their tent-mates at summer camp. All descriptions were coded into one of 69 categories for comparison (e.g., physical aggression, mental abilities). The authors found a 45% overlap between categories used when two children described the same person, indicating a common effect of the perceived. The overlap increased to 57% when one child described two other people, highlighting the perceiver's cognitive structure as a factor in perceptions. Although research on person perception stems from diverse theoretical and methodological perspectives (Shantz, 1983), certain developmental trends can be delineated (Barenboim, 1981) and are reviewed in the following section.

The literature suggests that before the age of seven, children are better able to describe the behavior of others than offer explanations of it (Flapan, 1968; Wood, 1978). Preschool- and early elementary-aged children describe others primarily in terms of concrete, observable characteristics, such as their appearance (e.g., "Anne has brown eyes"), possessions (e.g., "Michael has a red bike"), or specific behaviors (e.g., "Maria hits me") (Barenboim, 1981; Livesley & Bromley, 1973; Peevers & Secord, 1973; Scarlett, Press, & Crockett, 1971). Global evaluative phrases (e.g., kind, good, unkind, bad) are also used occasionally and reflect young children's tendency to dichotomize people into two classes: those who please and those who do not (Watts, 1944). This use of observable, physical terms in describing others is similar to that seen in children's self-descriptions.

Children's ability to explain the behavior of others is dependent upon their understanding of the differences between intended and accidental acts (Heider, 1958; Jones & Davis, 1978). Children at age four are not able to make this distinction, and assume that all acts, as well as their outcomes, are intended (King, 1971; Smith, 1978). Five- and six-year-olds improve considerably in their ability to differentiate intended from accidental acts (King, 1971; Smith, 1978). They are also beginning to distinguish between intended and accidental outcomes, but tend to infer desirable outcomes as intended and undesirable ones as accidental (King, 1971; Smith, 1978). During the early school years, children's understanding of the intentions of others in both simple and complex situations becomes more finely tuned (Shantz, 1983).

Similarly, young children have difficulty distinguishing cause and effect as related to another child's academic success. Children in preschool through first grade do not yet understand that one's effort and one's ability both influence the outcome (i.e., success or failure). They tend to equate effort with ability, regardless of outcome (i.e., hard workers are smart, no matter what scores they get) (Nicholls, 1978; Shaklee, 1976).

Although young children do not often make causal attributions about the behavior of others, when they do, their explanations tend to stress situational rather than dispositional factors (Flapan, 1968; Wood, 1978). For example, Newman, Ruble, and Rholes (1987) found five- and six-year-olds to be more likely than their eight- and nine-year-old counterparts to consider situational factors in predicting the future behavior of others. Specifically, younger children based their predictions of future generosity on the situations in which it was to occur, whereas older children were more likely to use information regarding past performance to make predictions. It should be noted, however, that young children can use dispositional information in certain instances. In predicting future athletic performance, for example, both groups based their responses on the other's past performance. During the preschool to early school years, children also move from attributing their own viewpoint to others to recognizing that others have different thoughts, feelings, and visual experiences; however, they still assume that those in similar situations will have similar perceptions (Flavell, Everett, Croft, & Flavell, 1981; Selman, 1980).

During middle childhood (i.e., approximately 7 to 12 years of age), children begin to use psychological constructs in describing others. Psychological constructs generally refer to inferred, internal, fairly stable personal characteristics (e.g., "Susan is so stubborn") or behavioral dispositions (e.g., "Alex always shares his school supplies") (Barenboim, 1981). Between seven and eight years of age, the number and type of psychological constructs that children use to describe others increase dramatically (Barenboim, 1981; Livesley & Bromley, 1973; Peevers & Secord, 1973; Scarlett et al., 1971). This increased use of dispositional features in children's description of others coincides with their use of trait labels in self-descriptions.

At this time children's descriptions are typically either positive or negative in emotional tone and do not reflect an awareness that others can possess both good and bad attributes (Watts, 1944). In fact, only about half of 13- and 14-year-olds understand that others simultaneously possess desirable and undesirable attributes (Watts, 1944). Elementary-age children are able to supplement their descriptions with explanations of current behavior, predictions of future behavior, and mention of dispositional factors (Flapan, 1968; Livesley & Bromley, 1973; Newman et al.,

1987). For instance, compared to preschoolers, seven-year-old children have a clear understanding that effort influences outcome. At the age of 10 their understanding deepens, as they come to recognize that dispositional factors (i.e., ability) are also causally related to outcome (Nicholls, 1978). Between 6 and 12 years of age, children also are able to reflect on their own thoughts and feelings from another's perspective (Selman, 1980).

Whether any significant changes in person perception occur specifically between the ages of 8 and 12 years is still in question. Several studies (Livesley & Bromley, 1973; Sprague, Beauregard, & Voelker, 1987; Yarrow & Campbell, 1963) have not found age differences in the number or type of categories used when describing the behavior and characteristics of others. However, other investigators (Barenboim, 1981; Peevers & Secord, 1973; Scarlett et al., 1971) have shown differences between these ages in the application of psychological constructs as a basis for comparing others. For example, Barenboim (1981) examined the sequence of three person perception processes in children ranging in age from 6 to 16 years. Results indicated that the use of behavioral comparisons (i.e., describing and comparing others along behavioral dimensions) increased between six and eight years of age and then decreased between ages 9 and 11. In contrast, the frequency of psychological constructs rose sharply between ages 7 and 11, and the use of psychological comparisons increased most dramatically between the ages of 10 and 12 years. In general, it appears that differences within this age group are reported when utilizing abstract process categories (e.g., psychological constructs) versus specific "personality" categories (e.g., sociability).

During adolescence (i.e., between 12 and 16 years of age) significant alterations in person perception occur. The behavior of others is now viewed as an interaction between personal characteristics and situational factors (Shantz, 1983). There is a decrease in the use of general information categories (e.g., age, sex, residence) to describe others (Livesley & Bromley, 1973) and an increase in the use of psychological comparisons and categories reflecting consistent traits (e.g., "Linda is more generous than Joy"), interests and abilities (e.g., "Steven is smarter in math than most ninth graders"), and beliefs (e.g., "David is lazier today than usual") (Barenboim, 1977, 1981; Livesley & Bromley, 1973; Peevers & Secord, 1973). This more complex and abstract description of others is consistent with how adolescents describe themselves.

Adolescents, especially around age 13, frequently offer spontaneous explanations of others' behavior and emphasize dispositional factors as causal (Flapan, 1968; Livesley & Bromley, 1973). This focus on dispositional factors helps to support the position that adolescents are developing an understanding of how personal characteristics relate to each other and what causative effect these characteristics have on future behavior (Barenboim, 1981). At this time, adolescents also typically differentiate between specific causes of behavior (e.g., effort versus ability) as well as clearly associate ability with outcome (Karabenick & Heller, 1976; Weiner & Peter, 1973). Finally, adolescents are now able to describe, explain, and predict others' behavior from mutual perspectives and generalized society-based concepts (e.g., morality) (Selman, 1980).

Now that we have reviewed developmental trends related to person perception, let's look briefly at the research on sex differences and on characteristics of the perceived. Although Wood (1978) found no sex differences in describing characters in films, many studies employing a free description methodology have reported differences. In general, girls have been shown to emphasize such categories as interpersonal skills and social relationships (e.g., Peevers & Secord, 1973; Sprague et al., 1987), whereas boys use such categories as physical aggression, interests, and academic ability (e.g., Dornbusch, Hasdorf, Richardson, Muzzy & Vreeland, 1965; Peevers & Secord, 1973). Consistent sex differences have been identified when making causal attributions about the behavior of others (Shantz, 1983). That is, boys attribute failure to a lack of effort and girls attribute it to a lack of ability (Dweck, 1978). The development changes outlined above pertain equally well to children's perceptions of people who they know and don't know (Shantz, 1983). In addition, there is general agreement that as children get older, they use more and different categories to describe liked same-sex and opposite-sex peers compared to disliked peers (Peevers & Secord, 1973; Scarlett et al., 1971; Sprague et al., 1987). However, the specific ages at which these changes occur is still unclear.

In summary, children's understanding of the behavior of others progresses along a similar continuum as that reported for children's self-understanding. This continuum reflects a shift from viewing others in terms of concrete, observable characteristics to an increased understanding of others in terms of abstract, personal characteristics. Greater refinement is also seen in children's ability to describe and explain the behavior of others, to attribute causes of behavior to situational and dispositional factors, and to generate inferences about the intentions, abilities, and feelings of others (Shantz, 1983).

This review suggests that individuals interested in preschool-aged children's perceptions of others should be prepared for concrete responses that are based on observable features such as physical appearance and specific behaviors. Although preschoolers can describe the behavior of others, they cannot yet provide accurate causal explanations for behavior; for example, behaviors resulting in good outcomes are viewed as intended, while those resulting in negative outcomes are seen as accidental. The most dramatic changes in person perception occur at around seven or eight years of age. After this age, children are better able to understand the perspective of others and describe "why" they do things. However, until adolescence, explanations tend to emphasize situational rather than dispositional causes of behavior. Interview and self-report measures tapping adolescents' perceptions of others can be expected to yield considerably more complex and psychologically sophisticated responses.

Children's Understanding of Emotions

In many instances, self-report techniques are geared toward obtaining information about children's feelings. Whether assessing a child's reaction to his parents' divorce or evaluating the presence of depression in a withdrawn child, researchers and clinicians often ask children to describe their own feelings or interpret those of others. For this reason, it is important to understand the development of children's understanding of their own feelings as well as their ability to recognize and interpret the emotional state of others.

It has been demonstrated that by the time they are three years old, children have already acquired a general understanding of themselves and others as emotional beings and have developed the ability to communicate about simple emotions in everyday situations. They are often able to label basic feeling states of themselves and others, make simple causal interpretations of feelings, and engage in pretend play involving emotional expression (Bretherton, Fritz, Zahn-Waxler, & Ridgeway, 1986). Throughout the childhood years, the understanding of emotion becomes more refined, as children learn to make more complex causal inferences, acknowledge mental aspects of emotions, and appreciate the possibility of feeling two conflicting emotions at the same time.

Investigators employing interview approaches have generally found marked shifts in children's conceptions of emotions to occur between the ages of six and eight or nine years. In identifying their own emotions, children 6 years old and younger are more apt to use idiosyncratic body cues (e.g., a smile) or situational cues (e.g., a birthday party), whereas eight- to nine-year-olds rely more on their own inner experiences and mental cues (Carroll & Steward, 1984; Harris, Olthof, & Terwogt, 1981). Moreover, children 8 years and older demonstrate a greater awareness that one can exercise control over one's emotions using mental strategies. That is, they are beginning to understand that they can change and hide their feelings (Carroll & Steward, 1984; Harris et al., 1981). In identifying the emotions of others, Harris and colleagues (1981) found that only older children (i.e., 11 years and above) recognized that outward expressions may not match inner feelings; however, this study did not include children between the ages of 6 and 11 years.

The ability to understand the possibility of having two different feelings at the same time also shows developmental variations. Preschoolers tend to deny the presence of simultaneous emotions, and six- to eight-year-olds can accept the possibility of different feelings only if they are separated temporally (e.g., feeling scared in a haunted house and then happy after you get out) (Harter, 1986a). It is only between the ages of 8 and 12 that children come to accept the simultaneous co-occurrence of two emotions (e.g., feeling happy and sad at the same time) (Carroll & Steward, 1984; Harris, 1983; Harter, 1986a).

Interestingly, children's understanding of their parents' emotions has been found to lag behind their self-understanding by about one year (Harter, 1986a). The ability to make appropriate causal inferences about one's parent's emotions shows a developmental progression. In the preschool years, children assume that the same events causing their own emotional reactions are also the sources of their parents' emotions. Between six and ten years old, children are able to identify causes of emotions that are more appropriate to their parents, but they see themselves as the primary cause of parental emotions. At the age of 10 to 12 years, children recognize that sources of their parents' emotions can include people and events unrelated to themselves (Harter, 1986a).

Experimental studies investigating children's understanding of others' emotions have generally focused on two different types of affective knowledge: the identification of facial expressions and the inference of affect from situational cues. The ability to distinguish between different categories of facial expressions has been demonstrated in infants as young as seven months (Caron, Caron, & Myers, 1982; Nelson, 1987). Infants at this age can generalize their recognition of certain emotions (e.g., happiness) across different models (Ludemann & Nelson, 1987) and various facial features of the expression (e.g., "toothy" versus "nontoothy" expressions of joy) (Phillips, Wagner, Fells, & Lynch, 1987). Furthermore, 12-month-old infants have been found to use expressive information conveyed in their mothers' faces to guide their behavior (e.g., cross a visual cliff) (Sorce, Emde, Campos, & Klinnert, 1987).

Most studies have revealed that accuracy in recognizing emotions from facial expressions varies as a function of the specific affect (e.g., Felleman, Barden, Carlson, Rosenberg, & Masters, 1983; Field & Walden, 1982a) as well as the age of the child (e.g., Cunningham & Odom, 1986;

Odom & Lemond, 1972; Walden & Field, 1982). Happiness is the earliest emotion to be reliably identified; children as young as four to five years old are able to identify facial expressions of happiness at 86% to 92% accuracy (Felleman et al., 1983; Reichenbach & Masters, 1983). Preschoolers can also identify sad and angry expressions at greater-than-chance frequencies, though their accuracy is compromised by a tendency to confuse the two (Felleman et al., 1983; Reichenbach & Masters, 1983). Recognition of more difficult emotions, such as fear and disgust, improves through the childhood years (Field & Walden, 1982b; Odom & Lemond, 1972).

The ability to recognize facial expressions has been associated with certain personality characteristics. For example, Field & Walden (1982b) found extraverted children to be more accurate decoders of emotions. Moreover, children who are high self-monitors (i.e., concerned with the situational appropriateness of their interpersonal behavior) also tend to be more accurate in their recognition of others' facial expressions (Edwards & Eder, 1987; Leone, 1987).

The ability to infer emotions from situational cues also improves with age. Again, happiness is the most easily recognized emotion; by the age of three to three and one-half, most children can identify a protagonist's feelings of happiness based on situational cues presented in stories (Borke, 1971, 1973). Negative emotions (i.e., sadness, fear, and anger) can be identified at frequencies above chance level by the age of four, though accuracy in identifying these feelings increases considerably between the ages of four and seven years. Interestingly, judgments of emotion based on situational cues are more accurate than those based on facial expressions (Reichenbach & Masters, 1983).

Children's ability to coordinate situational and expressive information has been assessed by presenting stimuli containing incongruous facial and situational cues (e.g., a picture of a frowning child at a birthday party). Whereas younger children (i.e., preschoolers and first-graders) tend to base their judgments of affect on facial expressions, older children (i.e., third- and sixth-graders) are more likely to rely on situational and contextual cues (Gnepp, 1983; Reichenbach & Masters, 1983). Gnepp (1983) found that the ability to create a story reconciling the inconsistent cues also increased with age; whereas preschoolers were able to do this less than half of the time, the corresponding figure for sixth-graders was 80%. Children in all age groups tended to resolve the inconsistency by reconstructing the situation (e.g., he's sad because his best friend isn't at the birthday party). However, sixth-graders were the most likely to reconcile the inconsistency by suggesting that the protagonist was not displaying his true feelings (Gnepp, 1983).

Indeed, the increased understanding of display rules (i.e., guidelines for regulating the appropriateness of expressive behavior in social situations) in late childhood may account for older children's reliance on situational, rather than facial, cues (Reichenbach & Masters, 1983). Saarni (1979) found ten-year-olds to surpass six- and eight-year-olds in their understanding that internal emotional experiences and external affective expressions need not correspond. Although an emerging understanding of this concept may be seen in children as young as four years, the differentiation between real and apparent emotions is made more systematically, and judged more accurately, by older children (Harris, Donnelly, Guz, & Pitt-Watson, 1986). A related finding is that older children (i.e., eight- and ten-year-olds) are more likely than younger children (i.e., five-year-olds) to use covert cues in judging a story protagonist's feelings (Westerman & Donaldson, 1987).

Older children also benefit more than their younger counterparts from the provision of information regarding the story character's personality and past experiences and behaviors. Whereas children as young as five to six years old can use this knowledge to infer the protagonist's subsequent emotional reactions, this information is used more systematically by children between the ages of 7 and 11 years (Gnepp, 1987; Gnepp & Chilamkurti, 1987). This pattern is consistent with that found for other aspects of person perception, described in the previous section.

Two additional conclusions regarding children's understanding of others' emotions are particularly relevant to this review. First, children's ability to decode emotions seems to improve as a function of the degree of similarity between the target person and the child. Specifically, children are better decoders when they are judging others of the same sex and similar age (Felleman et al., 1983; Shantz, 1983). Second, the ability to understand another's feelings has been found to relate to other aspects of children's social functioning. Good decoders demonstrate higher rates of prosocial behavior, receive more positive peer sociometric ratings, and obtain higher peer and teacher ratings of interpersonal competence (Denham, 1986; Rothenberg, 1970; Spence, 1987).

In summary, the above review suggests that children are not able to provide accurate reports of their own emotions until the age of eight to nine years, when their affective self-understanding comes to be based on internal, mental cues. Before this age, young children are likely to rely on situational or body cues in identifying their own feelings. Individuals attempting to elicit information about young children's feelings through interview or self-report measures might benefit from focusing questions on specific physical cues (e.g., a smile, a frown, a tummy ache) that might be associated with certain emotions; however, this information is likely to be idiosyncratic and not generalizable from one child to another. After the age of eight, children's increasing reliance on mental cues enables them to provide more accurate and sophisticated self-report information. For example, at this time children come to realize that they have control over their emotions (e.g., they can change and hide their feelings) and that they can experience two different feelings simultaneously.

Interviewers should also be aware that a child's understanding of his/her own emotions is likely to exceed his/her understanding of the feelings of others. Although preschool-aged children can reliably recognize happiness in others, they may confuse the emotions of sadness and anger. Preschoolers tend to take others' emotions at "face value;" they do not yet understand that feelings can be disguised. Throughout the preschool and elementary years, children's causal reasoning about other people's (i.e., their parents') emotions remains egocentric; in fact, it is not until adolescence that individuals come to recognize that others can have feelings that are unrelated to themselves. It remains an empirical question whether children's causal attributions of the emotions of others closer in age (i.e., peers) develop earlier.

Language Skills

The quality and quantity of information obtained from a child during an assessment partly depends on the communication skills of that child. Before we can even begin to understand how these skills influence self-report information, knowledge of the developmental acquisition of communication skills is needed. The following section highlights the progression of communication skills from infancy through adolescence with a focus on the three areas of language development: phonology (i.e., system of sounds that form words), syntax (i.e., grammar), and semantics (i.e., meaning of words). The interested reader is referred to texts written by Dales (1972) and Akmajian, Demers, and Harnish (1984) for more extensive coverage of language development and linguistics.

In any type of interaction, communication not only involves knowing what to say, but how and when to say it (Liebert, Wicks-Nelson, & Kail, 1986). Research on the development of communication indicates that the basic linguistic skills are acquired between one and five years of age. The changes in communication that are observed during the elementary school and adolescent years appear to be more a refinement of these basic skills than a learning of new skills (Bee & Mitchell, 1980). Changes in vocabulary skills, syntactic skills, and semantics do not occur, however, in a haphazard fashion. Language acquisition and refinement proceed in a regular and fixed order in all children (Hetherington

& Parke, 1975). Such a sequential order will be evident in the following description of the three areas of language development. This information is summarized in Table 2.2

Phonology
During the prelinguistic phase, from birth to approximately one year of age, language development progresses from crying, to cooing, to babbling, to patterned speech. Some distinguishing features of children's babbling include echolalia, or the repetition of consonant-vowel combinations (e.g., "dadadada"), and the appearance of intonational patterns. Although children who are approaching their first birthday are able to utilize word-like sounds to refer to objects, people, or events, they continue to use nonword utterances for six months or more (Bee & Mitchell, 1980). During this time (i.e., between 11 and 18 months), children also start to communicate with gestures (e.g., pointing, waving) (Bates, Benigni, Bretherton, Camaioni, & Volterra, 1979) and to comprehend what others say to them (Liebert et al., 1986).

Children's first meaningful words are spoken anywhere from 8 to 18 months of age. These early words appear to be used for communicating in one of two ways: to label objects (e.g., "cookie") or to express a whole sentence through a single word (Bee & Mitchell, 1980). Animals (e.g., "doggie"), food (e.g., "milk"), and toys (e.g., "ball") are the three categories typically represented in children's first ten words (Nelson, 1973). In addition, most of the early words are action-oriented (e.g., "go") and refer to one's own actions rather than the behavior of others (Huttenlocher, Smiley, & Charney, 1983). The size of children's vocabulary increases quickly during the preschool years, growing from 50 words at age one and one-half, to about 900 words at age three, to over 2000 words at age five (Smith, 1926).

Syntax
The development of syntactic skills, or the ability to combine words into functional sentences, seems to occur in two stages (Bee & Mitchell, 1980). Stage 1 generally begins at around 18 months of age and is characterized by two- or three-word sentences. These sentences are either statements of fact (e.g., location of object) or requests (e.g., for action) (Brown, 1973). Children's speech during this stage is referred to as telegraphic, in that only "content" words are included when constructing sentences (i.e., nouns, verbs, modifiers). For example, a two-year-old child may express the fact that his dog is sitting near the back door by saying, "Doggie sit door." The rules that children use to construct their sentences

may be based on either the position of the words (Braine, 1976) or the function that the words serve (e.g., possessive) (Bloom, 1970).

Approximately one year later, Stage 2 begins with the appearance of different grammatical morphemes (i.e., strings of sounds that convey meaning, such as articles and inflections). The emergence of different morphemes takes place in a fairly predictable sequence: (1) plurals, prepositions ("on"), and irregular verb endings; (2) articles ("a"), possessives (-'s), and auxiliary verbs ("do"); and (3) verb contractions ("I'm") (Block & Kessell, 1980; Brown, 1973). As children are adding morphemes to their speech, they are also asking questions and using negatives. The form of "Wh-" questions that children ask emerges in a distinct order (i.e., what, where, why, how); these words are simply placed at the beginning of a declarative sentence (Wootten, Merkin, Hood, & Bloom, 1979). Early negative sentences are also formed by consistently attaching one negative word (e.g., "no") to affirmative sentences (e.g., "No more milk") (Hetherington & Parke, 1975). At some point within this stage all children overgeneralize the grammatical rules they learn. For example, once children learn the rule of adding "-ed" to form the past tense, this rule is overgeneralized to all verbs and the correct forms of irregular verbs are no longer used (e.g., "went" reverts back to "goed") (Ervin, 1964). Overgeneralization is particularly common in three- to five-year-olds (Kuczaj, 1978). Stage 2 continues throughout the school years as syntax grows in complexity and children's speech becomes less qualitatively different from that of adults (Hetherington & Parke, 1975).

Semantics

Semantic development involves generating functional categories or concepts and then identifying words that fit those concepts (Liebert et al., 1986). Children as young as one and two years of age seem to possess a basic understanding of words and larger classes, if these words refer to objects that can be acted on (e.g., pieces of clothing) (Liebert et al., 1986; Nelson, 1974). However, children at this age frequently overextend the meaning of a word, i.e., calling all round objects "ball" or all adult males "Daddy" (Bowerman, 1976; Clark, 1975). The majority of overextensions may, in fact, stem from the limited vocabularies of young children and not from inaccurate concept formation (Clark, 1977). For example, a child may recognize that a fire engine is not a car, may not know the word for it, and, therefore, says "car."

In addition to overextensions, toddlers often underextend words such that the word "doll" may only mean the one that has red hair and talks (Bloom, 1973). Two other interesting elements of toddlers' and preschoolers' speech include: creating words to describe new experiences (e.g., "Happy Turkey Day" to describe Thanksgiving) (Mendelsohn, Robinson, Gardner, & Winner, 1984) and relying on characteristic features of objects to define concepts (e.g., dirty shirts are found only at a laundromat) (Keil & Batterman, 1984). These semantic qualities make it difficult to interpret the meaning of young children's idiosyncratic utterances, especially if taken out of context (Hetherington & Parke, 1975). The development of adult-like semantics is a lengthy process and seems to proceed less systematically than other linguistic skills (Bee and Mitchell, 1980).

Although children's language by age five or six is similar to that of adults', changes in phonology, syntax, and semantics continue to occur during the elementary school years (Hetherington & Parke, 1975). These changes consist of increases in vocabulary (e.g., over 2600 words by age seven), relearning irregular verbs, using sentences more varied in structure, slowly constructing a greater number of passive versus active sentences, and understanding the unique versus general features of concepts by age eight or nine (Chomsky, 1969; Ervin, 1964; Landau, 1982; Smith, 1926).

While language development progresses in a series of steps, the rate of development varies significantly between children (Bee & Mitchell, 1980). Thus far, our discussion has centered on age differences in the acquisition of linguistic skills. Current data do not support sex differences in vocabulary or syntax among infants and preschoolers. However, during adolescence, females are generally superior to males on most measures of linguistic skills (e.g., reading comprehension, spelling) (Bee & Mitchell, 1980). Research on social class differences indicates that middle-class children show advanced vocabularies compared to lower-class children throughout the preschool and elementary school years (Stodolsky & Lesser, 1967). In contrast, there appear to be no social class differences in the development of syntactic skills (Shriner & Miner, 1968).

Pragmatics

As stated earlier, communication not only involves linguistic skills and nonverbal signs, but also implicit rules between the speaker and listener. Infants begin to learn these implicit rules by observing their parents model turn-taking in conversations (Liebert et al., 1986). During the preschool years, children acquire most rules of conversation, such as replying to a comment with a relevant remark or behavior (Garvey & Hogan, 1973) and prompting a response from others by repeating or paraphrasing their remarks (Garvey & Berninger, 1981). Children's conversational styles are similar to adults' by around the age of five (Liebert et al., 1986). Finally, associated with developing perspective-taking skills, children continue to improve the efficiency of their messages by considering characteristics of the setting and of the listener (Liebert et al., 1986).

In summary, children's language development follows a progression from a concrete, action-oriented focus to a more flexible, complex, and conceptual understanding and use. Unlike the other social-cognitive areas reviewed above, the basic dimensions of language development are well-established by the age of five. However, further refinements in vocabulary development, grammatical usage, and concept development continue throughout childhood. Discussion of the implications of a child's level of language development for the use of interview techniques and self-report measures can be found in the following section.

DEVELOPMENTAL ASPECTS OF SELF-REPORTS AND INTERVIEWS

The following section will address developmental issues that relate more specifically to the use of interview strategies and self-report inventories with children of different ages. Characteristics of self-report measures and interview situations will be discussed first, with particular attention paid to strategies for facilitating accurate reporting in children. The literature on the reliability of children's self-reports will then be reviewed.

Characteristics of Self-Report Inventories

A child's ability to comprehend and respond appropriately to self-report inventories is much more limited than that of an adult. Children's language, reading, and writing skills are less well-developed, their attention span is more restricted, and their life experiences are considerably more limited in scope. As a consequence, adaptations in test materials and administration procedures are necessary. The younger the child, the more extensive these adjustments need be.

This section will explore developmental issues as they affect a child's ability to respond accurately to self-report instruments. Although there has been little empirical research bearing directly on this subject, its implications extend to clinicians and researchers who are involved in the selection, administration, or interpretation of children's self-report measures.

To investigate this subject, we must turn to the literature on the development of self-report instruments for children. Many of the measures currently used with children (e.g., locus of control, anxiety, and depression scales) have been adapted from adult instruments. In describing the scale development, authors often detail the changes that were felt to be necessary to accommodate the special needs and capabilities of children. However, their discussions, in large part, focus on children as differentiated from adults; little attention is directed toward the developmental changes that occur within the broad range of what are considered to be the childhood years. Nevertheless, interesting information can be gleaned from examining this literature.

For elementary school-aged children, one of the most important requisites for test construction is the use of language suitable to children's vocabulary and reading abilities. Most self-report instruments for children are geared toward the third grade reading level. Whereas researchers in the past have had to rely on the opinion of teachers or reading specialists regarding the suitability of test items, more recently "readability formulas" have been developed to serve just that purpose. Information regarding the reading levels required for specific self-report measures, such as that reported by Prout & Chizik (1988), can be invaluable to clinicians or researchers seeking to utilize the inventories. However, it is interesting to note that many investigators advocate reading the instruments aloud to elementary school-aged respondents (e.g., Crandall, Katkovsky, & Crandall, 1965; Nowicki & Strickland, 1973; Reynolds & Richmond, 1978).

For younger children (i.e., preschoolers through second-graders), self-report questionnaires are generally read aloud; the testing situation thus more closely resembles that of a structured interview. For children this young, circumventing short attention spans and specific response sets becomes increasingly important. In particular, test developers need to be cognizant of the liabilities inherent in various response formats. For example, Mischel, Zeiss, & Zeiss (1974) reported that preschoolers in their pilot sample tended to respond to yes-no questions in the affirmative. Moreover, they found forced-choice formats to present difficulties of another sort: Children were more likely to endorse the last stated alternative. Crandall and colleagues (1965) reported similar problems using forced-choice items; they found that even first- and second-graders had difficulty keeping both response alternatives in mind. These problems have led to many creative solutions, such as reading each response alternative twice, reversing the order during the second reading (Mischel et al., 1974); providing picture cues to facilitate comprehension and memory (Harter & Pike, 1984; Nowicki & Duke, 1974); and having children rate the degree to which an alternative is true for them, instead of forcing a choice between true and false (Harter, 1982).

Attracting and maintaining the interest and attention of young children (i.e., under seven years of age) can also present a challenge in the self-report situation. In many cases, a pictorial format utilizing cartoon drawings has been used to generate interest in the task (e.g., Harter & Pike, 1984; Nowicki & Duke, 1974). Moreover, pictures also serve the important function of clarifying and concretizing the verbal material. Another method for engaging the interest of young children is the use of specific, relevant, age- and gender-appropriate questions. For example, Harter and colleagues developed separate versions for their Pictorial Scale of Perceived Competence and Social Acceptance (Harter & Pike, 1984); one version is for use with preschool and kindergarten-aged children, and the other is for first- and second-graders. Moreover, different sets of picture stimuli are used for boys and girls. Mischel and colleagues (1974) asked their preschool subjects introductory questions as a "warm-up" to each item (e.g., "Are you happy sometimes?") in order to involve the children as well as to make each stimulus situation as vivid as possible.

Many of the same techniques used to help young children adjust to interview situations are also used to help the child feel more comfortable during the administration of self-report measures. For example, Mischel et al. (1974) utilized a sequence of activities that included bringing children to a "surprise room" containing a box of toys, engaging in an initial play period to establish rapport, introducing the task as a "question and answer game," and following through with a promise to play again after completing the measure. Further discussion about useful techniques for interview situations can be found in the following section.

Characteristics of Child Interviews

Most, if not all, clinicians and researchers would agree that different strategies are required when interviewing children compared to adults. While there is much research on the specific interview behaviors and skills that enhance communication with adults, research on the interview process with children is rather sparse (Kanfer, Eyberg, & Krahn, 1983; La Greca, 1983). Fortunately, during the past twenty years clinicians have begun to identify specific interviewing strategies and clinic situations that characterize child interviews (Greenspan & Greenspan, 1981; Kanfer et al., 1983). This section will look at these strategies and situations as they relate to the developmental issues previously reviewed. While the focus of this section will be on comparing child and adult interviews, reference to specific developmental levels will be made where data are available. The interested reader is referred to chapters written by Bierman (1983) and Sattler (1988) for additional information on child interviews, as well as to Chapters 4 and 5 of this volume.

In general, a more active role is taken in child interviews relative to adult interviews. The interviewer needs to structure and direct the interview session to a greater degree, with the child's behavior and verbalizations serving as a guide (Kanfer et al., 1983). An accepting and neutral attitude should be conveyed toward the child's communications, and personal biases should not interfere with the interview (La Greca, 1983). Although children should be encouraged to express their thoughts and feelings readily, limits should be placed on their behavior (La Greca, 1983). Instances of inappropriate behavior (e.g., aggressive, destructive), aimed at either property or the interviewer, usually can be handled by reiterating the rules of the situation, redirecting the child towards an incompatible behavior, or praising occurrences of appropriate behavior (Kanfer et al, 1983). Interviews with younger children differ from those of older children, in that the sessions are generally shorter and their parents are more likely to remain in the room during the interview. As with adult interviews, it is important to remember that the relationship between the interviewer and the child is a professional one, in which physical contact and nurturant behaviors should be kept to a minimum (Kanfer et al., 1983).

Establishing rapport and eliciting cooperation are essential if information about how children perceive themselves, their environments, and their problems is to be obtained (Kanfer et al., 1983). Making appropriate introductory remarks is the first step in establishing rapport. Waiting for the parents to introduce the child is preferable when meeting younger children, whereas introducing yourself is recommended with older children (Kanfer et al., 1983). Other strategies have been suggested to aid in establishing rapport with children of varying ages. Rapport can be established with preschool children by showing a toy or playing a game before the interview, or visiting the nursery school or home to increase familiarity (Yarrow, 1960). In fact, the entire interview with preschool children can be conducted in a playroom to assist in the expression of thoughts and feelings through toy play (e.g., using paper, crayons, clay, dolls, animal puppets, books). Playing a competitive board game (e.g., Othello, checkers) with children approximately 5- to 11-years-old can help in establishing rapport (Sattler, 1988). Rapport with adolescents can be achieved through open communication about the importance of their input in decision-making and about the limits of confidentiality (Sattler, 1988). Communication with children and adolescents can be enhanced if clinicians and researchers stay in touch with current interests and trends such as Saturday morning cartoon heroes, "fad" clothing, and popular musical groups (Kanfer et al., 1983). The fact that children are brought to the interview by their parents may result in confusion regarding the reason for referral and what to expect. Children may express these concerns verbally (e.g., "Can I go home with my Mom?") or behaviorally (e.g., refusal to speak). These concerns should be addressed early in the initial interview through direct questions and comments, so that they do not interfere with the interview process (Sattler, 1988).

Inducing and maintaining cooperation from children in interview situations can be achieved with such strategies as making descriptive comments about the child's appearance, behavior, and demeanor; using reflective statements (i.e., echoing or rephrasing child's remarks); offering frequent praise for participation (with less demonstrative praise for older children); and avoiding the use of critical statements about the child's behavior or verbalizations (Kanfer et al., 1983). These strategies serve the purposes of: (1) providing attention to the child, (2) organizing the child's behavior, thoughts, and feelings, (3) prompting ongoing behavior to continue, and (4) directing the discussion toward specific areas of interest (Kanfer et al., 1983).

One of the most important strategies for establishing rapport and cooperation is the use of age-appropriate communication. For young children such communication may involve using simple vocabulary and short sentences that contain only one idea (e.g., few qualifying phrases), emphasizing specific questions that require concrete answers (e.g., "What is your favorite subject?") rather than open-ended questions that may produce vague replies (e.g., "Tell me about school"), and avoiding the use of "why" questions and silences longer than a few seconds so as not to engender frustration or defensiveness (Bierman, 1983; Kanfer et al., 1983; La Greca, 1983). With children who are reluctant to speak about certain topics, the following techniques can be helpful in maintaining cooperation: (1) use hypothetical questions (e.g., "Let's pretend that . . ."), (2) recount the details of a problematic situation, (3) comment on a topic that is being avoided, and follow up with questions based on the child's verbal or behavioral responses, (4) present two acceptable alternatives, and (5) allow a positive response to be given before requiring one that is negative or critical (Bierman, 1983; Sattler, 1988; Yarrow, 1960).

The extent of children's responses to interview questions is related to their level of development and cognitive abilities. Somewhat lengthier, more detailed responses can be expected from older children, whereas shorter, global responses are typically provided by younger children. When children refuse to speak or evidence distress responses (e.g., screaming, crying), prompts can be continued in the form of descriptive and reflective statements germane to their behavior, a period of parallel play or free play can be initiated, or children can be asked to respond nonverbally, such as pointing to pictures or drawing (Bierman, 1983; Kanfer et al., 1983; Sattler, 1988). As Reisman (1973) stated, only on rare occasions should the interview be rescheduled if cooperation is not obtained.

These interviewing strategies should be effective in obtaining information spanning diverse areas of life. The following list is a sample of topical areas most often assessed in child and adolescent interviews: (1) referral problem (e.g., what the child thinks the problem is), (2) home (e.g., sibling fighting), (3) school (e.g., grades), (4) peers (e.g., activities with friends), (5) interests (e.g., hobbies or sports), (6) fears/worries (e.g., things the child is scared of), (7) somatic concerns (e.g., headaches), (8) self-concept (e.g., what the child likes least about him/herself), (9) thought disorder (e.g., hearing voices), (10) aspirations (e.g., career), (11) heterosexual relations (e.g., dating activities), and (12) drug/alcohol use (La Greca, 1983; Sattler, 1988). Obviously, not all topics should be covered in every child interview; for example, the latter two categories are usually reserved for adolescents. In addition, certain topics may be more effective in reducing the initial apprehension of young children versus older children. Questions related to things they know and like (e.g., age, pets, TV shows) are preferred topics for younger children, whereas questions that focus on friends, school, or social activities are useful with older children (Kanfer et al., 1983).

Reliability of Child Reports

The question of whether children and adolescents are capable of reliably and accurately reporting their behavioral and emotional problems has been investigated extensively over the last 10 years. An over-reliance on information provided by adults when assessing children stemmed from the belief that children were limited in their ability to perceive and/or report problems because of developmental features (Mokros, Poznanski, Grossman, & Freeman, 1987). However, as more and more assessment measures were developed to account for these features (e.g., employing pictorial formats and situationally based versus general items), the discrepancy between children's and adults' reports became evident. The question has thus shifted from "Are children reliable reporters?" to "How well do children, adults, and peers agree?" and "Whose report is more accurate?" Answers to these questions appear to depend on a variety of factors including the informant used, the assessment method employed, the population studied, the content of the measures, and the age and gender of the subjects. This section presents data on the agreement between children's and adults' reports of the child's psychopathology based on these factors.

Agreement between various combinations of children's, parents', teachers', and peers' reports has been examined by comparing the responses to interviews and/or rating scales. Comparisons generally have been made between the presence versus absence of symptoms (i.e., interviews) or between the severity ratings of symptoms (i.e., rating scales and questionnaires). Studies on agreement have included both clinical populations (e.g., psychiatric inpatients and outpatients) and nonclinical populations (e.g., regular education classrooms). A wide age range of children also has been sampled (i.e., ages 5 to 18), through the focus has been on the elementary school and junior high school years (e.g., ages 6 to 16).

Equivocal results have been obtained when examining the agreement between child and parent interviews. Moderate-to-high agreements have been found for the Diagnostic Interview for Children and Adolescents (DICA) regarding overall ratings (i.e., 80%) (Herjanic, Herjanic, Brown, & Wheatt, 1975), certain diagnoses (e.g., Conduct Disorder, Attention Deficit Disorder) (e.g., Welner, Reich, Herjanic, Jung, & Amado, 1987), and questions referring to symptoms that are objective, severe, or unambiguous (e.g., takes medicine, repeated a grade, wets the bed) (Herjanic & Reich, 1982; Reich, Herjanic, Welner, & Gandhy, 1981). In comparison, low but significant correlations have been reported for other interviews, such as the Schedule for Affective Disorders and Schizophrenia for School-Age Children (K-SADS) (e.g., Angold et al., 1987; Weissman et al., 1987) and the Diagnostic Interview Schedule for Children (DISC) (e.g., Edelbrock, Costello, Dulcan, Conover, & Kalas, 1986), and inconsistent correlations have been found for the Anxiety Disorders Interview Schedule for Children (ADIS-C) subscales across groups (i.e., total, gender, age) (Nelles, Eisen, & Silverman, 1987).

Studies comparing interviews with rating scales and those comparing different rating scales also have obtained mixed results. The correspondence between children's and parents' reports for both internalizing behaviors (e.g., depression, anxiety) and externalizing behaviors (e.g., aggression, hyperactivity) has been in the high range (Romano & Nelson, 1987), in the moderate range (Moretti, Fine, Haley, & Marriage, 1985; Treiber & Mabe, 1987), and in the low-to-moderate range (Kazdin, Esveldt-Dawson, Unis, & Rancurello, 1983a; Weissman, Orvaschel, & Padian, 1980). However, several studies (Kazdin, French, & Unis, 1983b; Kazdin, French, Unis, & Esveldt-Dawson, 1983c) have reported correlations in the moderate-to-high range for the same raters (e.g., children, mothers) across scales. While some investigations have shown that both children's and parents' reports discriminate among diagnostic groups (Kazdin et al., 1983a; Romano & Nelson, 1987), others have found that children's ratings are more consistent with their diagnosis (Moretti et al., 1985), and still others have reported that only parent ratings differentiated children with and without a psychiatric diagnosis (Kazdin et al., 1983c; Weissman et al., 1980).

In terms of agreement between children's, teachers', and peers' ratings, studies have reported a positive relationship between self-perception profiles and teachers' ratings of classroom behavior and achievement (Kowalski, 1987), as well as moderate correlations between self-competence ratings and teachers' ratings of competence, and peer ratings of likability (Wojcik & Glenwick, 1987). However, other research generally has found higher agreement between peer/teacher ratings of psychopathology (e.g., depression, withdrawal, aggression) compared to self/peer and self/teacher ratings (Ledingham, Younger, Schwartzman, & Bergeron, 1982; Sacco & Graves, 1985). Finally, the following results have been obtained when comparing children's, teachers', and parents' reports: (1) moderate correlations between self/parent, self/teacher, and mother/teacher ratings of depression (Leon, Kendall, & Garber, 1980; Reynolds, Anderson, & Bartell, 1985); (2) moderate-to-high correlations between self-reports of negative peer interactions and negative peer ratings, and adults' reports of behavioral problems (Bierman & McCauley, 1987); and (3) moderate correlations between self-reports of positive peer interactions and parents' reports of social competence, and positive peer ratings (Bierman & McCauley, 1987).

Several trends have emerged from the data in this area. For example, children generally report significantly more subjective symptoms (e.g., variable appetite, worries about parents), whereas parents report more objective, behavioral symptoms (e.g., throws things when mad, pesters other children) (Herjanic et al., 1975; Herjanic & Reich, 1982). Furthermore, children endorse a greater number of symptoms for all disorders (e.g., Moretti et al., 1985; Weissman et al., 1987), except for conduct disorders, where parents' reports about their children are greater (Edelbrock et al., 1986; Kashani, Orvaschel, Burk, & Reid, 1985).

Slightly different results have been found concerning severity ratings and specific areas of agreement. In comparison to parents, teachers, and peers, children tend to rate their symptoms as less severe on various disorders and to give higher ratings on measures of social and academic competence (Kazdin et al., 1983a,b; Ledingham et al., 1982; Treiber & Mabe, 1987). However, Mokros et al. (1987) have suggested that severity ratings may be sample dependent. That is, clinically referred children seem to give less severe ratings to questionnaire and interview items than their parents, whereas children used for control purposes provide more severe ratings than their parents. Specific areas that have shown fairly good agreement, though not consistently across all children-parent-teacher comparisons, include aggressive behavior (e.g., Ledingham et al., 1982), school problems (e.g., school phobia) (e.g., Nelles et al., 1987) and suicidal ideation/attempts (e.g., Angold et al., 1987). Finally, the effects of age and gender on agreement have been inconsistent. Studies have either reported no effects on agreement (e.g., Moretti et al., 1985) or better agreement between parents and young children (e.g., Edelbrock, Costello, Dulcan, Kalas, & Conover, 1985), older children (e.g., Herjanic & Reich, 1982), girls (e.g., Nelles et al., 1987), and boys (e.g., Angold et al., 1987).

Various hypotheses have been proposed to explain the discrepancy between children's and others' reports: (1) children's perceptions are accurate, but they do not report certain behaviors (e.g., subjective symptoms) to others; (2) perceptions are different, but they reflect actual behavioral differences in specific settings; (3) dissimilar reports are a function of symptom type (e.g., overt, ideational) and disorder (e.g., conduct disorder, depression), and (4) parental responses are influenced by a "negative halo" effect whereby parents tend to endorse many negative characteristics of their children (Kazdin et al., 1983b; Ledingham et al., 1982; Leon et al., 1980; Treiber & Mabe, 1987). Although each hypothesis has helped to clarify some of the conflicting findings in the literature, none can account for all of them.

Perhaps children's and others' reports should be viewed as reflecting different but equally reliable and valid perceptions of behavior (Kazdin et al., 1983b; Leon et al., 1980). For instance, parents and teachers may be considered more sensitive reporters of objective, behavioral symptoms, though their estimate of symptom severity may be somewhat high (Leon et al., 1980; Weissman et al., 1987). On the other hand, children may be regarded as more accurate reporters of their subjective symptoms, though they give lower estimates of symptom severity and inflated ratings of adaptive behavior (Kazdin et al., 1983b; Ledingham et al., 1982; Weissman et al., 1987). As such, there is a consistent recommendation that until more conclusive evidence is obtained indicating that one informant is more reliable, information should be collected from multiple informants (e.g., Leon et al., 1980; Weissman et al., 1987). When, and if, conflicting information is obtained, some clinicians and researchers (e.g., Angold et al., 1987) state that children's reports should be used as the criteria by which to judge the accuracy of adults' reports, whereas others (e.g., Puig-Antich & Gittelman, 1982) set adults' reports as the criteria. Unfortunately, there are currently no firm guidelines on how to resolve discrepant information and on whose report should be given the most weight in the assessment process (Angold et al., 1987, Weissman et al.,

1987). (See also Chapters 3, 5, and 10 of this volume for discussions of this issue.)

CONCLUSIONS

This chapter has reviewed a number of developmental issues that affect the use of self-report techniques with children. The initial sections outlined specific cognitive and social-cognitive skills believed to underlie children's ability to produce accurate self-report information. Developmental changes in their ability to form a consistent self-identity, to perceive and interpret the behavior of others, to understand their own emotions as well as others' emotions, and to comprehend and produce language were reviewed in light of current empirical findings. It is hoped that such a review will underline the importance of considering developmental features, as well as provide useful information for clinicians and researchers using self-report assessments.

The second part of this chapter presented information pertaining more directly to the self-report and interview situations. Its purpose was to familiarize the reader with techniques and strategies for eliciting accurate and reliable information from children at different ages and to provide a review of the current empirical findings regarding the reliability of children's self-reports. Although the research in the latter area yields few definitive conclusions, it does highlight a number of issues critical to the use of self-report techniques with children and underscores the need for continued research in this area.

REFERENCES

Akmajian, A., Demers, R.A., & Harnish, R.M. (1984). *Linguistics: An introduction to language and communication* (2nd ed.). Cambridge, MA: M.I.T. Press.

Amsterdam, B. (1972). Mirror self-image reactions before age two. *Developmental Psychobiology, 5*, 297–305.

Angold, A., Weissman, M.M., John, K., Merikangas, K.R., Prusoff, B.A., Wickramaratne, P., Gammon, G.D., & Warner, V. (1987). Parent and child reports of depressive symptoms in children at low and high risk of depression. *Journal of Child Psychology and Psychiatry, 28*, 901–915.

Barenboim, C. (1977). Developmental changes in the interpersonal cognitive system from middle childhood to adolescence. *Child Development, 48*, 1467–1474.

Barenboim, C. (1981). The development of person perception in childhood and adolescence: From behavioral comparisons to psychological constructs to psychological comparisons. *Child Development, 52,* 129–144.

Bates, E., Benigni, L., Bretherton, I., Camaioni, L., & Volterra, L. (1979). *The emergence of symbols: Cognition and communication in infancy.* New York: Academic Press.

Bee, H.L., & Mitchell, S.K. (1980). *The developing person: A life-span approach.* New York: Harper & Row.

Bernstein, R.M. (1980). The development of the self-system during adolescence. *The Journal of Genetic Psychology, 136,* 231–245.

Bierman, K.L. (1983). Cognitive development and clinical interviews with children. In B.B. Lahey & A.E. Kazdin (Eds.), *Advances in clinical child psychology* (Vol. 6). (pp. 217–250). New York: Plenum.

Bierman, K.L., & McCauley, E. (1987). Children's descriptions of their peer interactions: Useful information for clinical child assessment. *Journal of Clinical Child Psychology, 16,* 9–18.

Block, E.M., & Kessell, F.S. (1980). Determinants of the acquisition order of grammatical morphemes: A re-analysis and re-interpretation. *Journal of Child Language, 7,* 181–188.

Bloom, L.M. (1970). *Language development: Form and function in emerging grammar.* Cambridge, MA: M.I.T. Press.

Bloom, L.M. (1973). *One word at a time: The use of single word utterances before syntax.* The Hague: Mouton.

Borke, H. (1971). Interpersonal perception of young children: Egocentrism or empathy? *Developmental Psychology, 5,* 263–269.

Borke, H. (1973). The development of empathy in Chinese and American children between three and six years of age. *Developmental Psychology, 9,* 102–108.

Bowerman, M. (1976). Semantic factors in the acquisition of rules for word use and sentence construction. In D.M. Morehead & A.E. Morehead (Eds.), *Normal and deficient child language* (pp. 99–179). Baltimore: University Park Press.

Braine, M.D.S. (1976). Children's first word combinations. *Monographs of the Society for Research in Child Development, 41,* (Serial No. 164).

Bretherton, I., & Beeghly, M. (1982). Talking about internal states: The acquisition of an explicit theory of mind. *Developmental Psychology, 18,* 906–921.

Bretherton, I., Fritz, J., Zahn-Waxler, C., & Ridgeway, D. (1986). Learning to talk about emotions: A functionalist perspective. *Child Development, 57,* 529–548.

Broughton, J. (1978). Development of concepts of self, mind, reality, and knowledge. *New Directions for Child Development, 1,* 75–100.

Brown, R. (1973). *A first language: The early stages.* Cambridge, MA: Harvard University Press.

Caron, R.F., Caron, A.J., & Myers, R.S. (1982). Abstraction of invariant face expressions in infancy. *Child Development, 53,* 1008–1015.

Carroll, J.J., & Steward, M.S. (1984). The role of cognitive development in children's understanding of their own feelings. *Child Development, 55,* 1486–1492.

Chomsky, C. (1969). *The acquisition of syntax in children from 5 to 10.* Cambridge, MA: M.I.T. Press.

Clark, E.V. (1975). Knowledge, context, and strategy in the acquisition of meaning. In D.P. Dato (Ed.), *Georgetown University round table on languages and linguistics, 1975. Developmental psycholinguistics: Theory and application* (pp. 77–98). Washington, D.C.: Georgetown University Press.

Clark, E.V. (1977). Strategies and the mapping problem in first language acquisition. In J. MacNamara (Ed.), *Language learning and thought* (pp. 147–168). New York: Academic Press.

Crandall, V.C., Katkovsky, W., & Crandall, V.J. (1965). Children's beliefs in their own control of reinforcements in intellectual-academic achievement situations. *Child Development, 36,* 92–109.

Cunningham, J.G., & Odom, R.D. (1986). Differential salience of facial features in children's perception of affective expression. *Child Development, 57,* 136–142.

Dales, P.S. (1972). *Language development: Structure and function.* Hinsdale, IL: Dryden Press.

Damon, W., & Hart, D. (1982). The development of self-understanding from infancy through adolescence. *Child Development, 53,* 841–864.

Damon, W., & Killen, M. (1982). Peer interaction and the process of change in children's moral reasoning. *Merrill-Palmer Quarterly, 28,* 347–367.

Denham, S.A. (1986). Social cognition, prosocial behavior, and emotion in preschoolers: Contextual validation. *Child Development, 57,* 194–201.

Dornbusch, S.M., Hastorf, A.H., Richardson, S.A., Muzzy, R.E., & Vreeland, R.S. (1965). The perceiver and perceived: Their relative influence on categories of interpersonal perception. *Journal of Personality and Social Psychology, 1,* 434–440.

Dweck, C.S. (1978). Achievement. In M.E. Lamb (Ed.), *Social and personality development.* New York: Holt, Reinhart, & Winston.

Edelbrock, C., Costello, A.J., Dulcan, M., Kalas, R., & Conover, N.C. (1985). Age differences in the reliability of the psychiatric interview of the child. *Child Development, 56,* 265–275.

Edelbrock, C., Costello, A.J., Dulcan, M.K., Conover, M.C., & Kalas, R. (1986). Parent-child agreement on child psychiatric symptoms assessed via structured interview. *Journal of Child Psychology and Psychiatry, 27,* 181–190.

Edwards, L.A., & Eder, R.A. (1987, April). *Individual differences in young children's sensitivity to social cues: The emergence of self-monitoring.* Paper presented at the meeting of the Society for Research in Child Development, Baltimore, MD.

Elliott, G.C. (1982). Self-esteem and self-presentation among the young as a function of age and gender. *Journal of Youth and Adolescence, 11,* 135–153.

Ervin, S. (1964). Imitation and structural change in children's langauge. In E.H. Lenneberg (Ed.), *New directions in the study of language* (163–189). Cambridge, MA: M.I.T. Press.

Felleman, E.S., Barden, R.C., Carlson, C.R., Rosenberg, L., & Masters, J.C. (1983). Children's and adults' recognition of spontaneous and posed emotional expressions in young children. *Developmental Psychology, 19,* 405–413.

Field, T.M., & Walden, T.A. (1982a). Production and discrimination of facial expressions by preschool children. *Child Development, 53,* 1299–1311.

Field, T.M., & Walden, T.A. (1982b). Production and perception of facial expressions in infancy and early childhood. In H. Reese & L. Lipsitt (Eds.), *Advances in child development and behavior: Volume 16* (pp. 169–211). New York: Academic Press.

Flapan, D. (1968). *Children's understanding of social interaction.* New York: Teachers College Press.

Flavell, J.H., Everett, B.A., Croft, K., & Flavell, E.R. (1981). Young children's knowledge about visual perspective: Further evidence for the Level I - Level 2 distinction. *Developmental Psychology, 17,* 99–103.

Garvey, C., & Berninger, G. (1981). Timing and turn taking in children's conversations. *Discourse Processes, 4,* 27–59.

Garvey, C., & Hogan, R., (1973). Social speech to social interaction: Egocentrism revisited. *Child Development, 44,* 562–568.

Gnepp, J. (1983). Children's social sensitivity: Inferring emotions from conflicting cues. *Developmental Psychology, 19,* 805–814.

Gnepp, J. (1987, April). *Children's understanding of emotional reactions: Inferring appraisals from prior experience and behavior.* Paper presented at the meeting of the Society for Research in Child Development, Baltimore, MD.

Gnepp, J., & Chilamkurti, C. (1987, April). *Children's use of personality attributions to predict behavior and emotion.* Paper presented at the meeting of the Society for Research in Child Development, Baltimore, MD.

Greenspan, S.I., & Greenspan, N.I. (1981). *The clinical interview with children.* New York: McGraw-Hill.

Grotevant, H.D., & Adams, G.R. (1984). Development of an objective measure to assess ego identity in adolescence: Validation and replication. *Journal of Youth and Adolescence, 13,* 419–438.

Guardo, C.J., & Bohan, J.B. (1971). Development of a sense of self-identity in children. *Child Development, 42,* 1909–1921.

Harris, P.L. (1983). Children's understanding of the link between situation and emotion. *Journal of Experimental Child Psychology, 36,* 490–509.

Harris, P.L., Donnelly, K., Guz, G.R., & Pitt-Watson, R. (1986). Children's understanding of the distinction between real and apparent emotion. *Child Development, 57,* 895–909.

Harris, P.L., Olthof, T., & Terwogt, M.M. (1981). Children's knowledge of emotion. *Journal of Child Psychology and Psychiatry, 22,* 247–261.

Harter, S. (1982). The Perceived Competence Scale for Children. *Child Development, 53,* 87–97.

Harter, S. (1983). Developmental perspectives on the self-system. In E.M. Hetherington (Ed.), P.H. Mussen (Series Ed.), *Handbook of child psychology: Vol.*

4. *Socialization, personality, social development* (pp. 275–385). New York: Oxford University Press.

Harter, S. (1986a). Cognitive-developmental processes in the integration of concepts about emotions and the self. *Social Cognition, 4,* 119–151.

Harter, S. (1986b). Processes underlying the construction, maintenance, and enhancement of the self-concept in children. In J. Suls & A. Greenwald (Eds.), *Psychological perspectives on the self: Vol. 3* (pp. 136–182). Hillsdale, NJ: Lawrence Erlbaum.

Harter, S., & Pike, R. (1984). The Pictorial Scale of Perceived Competence and Social Acceptance for Young Children. *Child Development, 55,* 1969–1982.

Heider, F. (1958). *The psychology of interpersonal relations.* New York: Wiley.

Herjanic, B., Herjanic, M., Brown, F., & Wheatt, J. (1975). Are children reliable reporters? *Journal of Abnormal Child Psychiatry, 3,* 41–48.

Herjanic, B., & Reich, W. (1982). Development of a structured psychiatric interview for children: Agreement between child and parent on individual symptoms. *Journal of Abnormal Child Psychology, 10,* 307–324.

Hetherington, E.M., & Parke, R.D. (1975). *Child psychology: A contemporary viewpoint.* New York: McGraw-Hill.

Huttenlocher, J., Smiley, P., & Charney, B. (1983). Emergence of action categories in the child: Evidence from verb meanings. *Psychological Review, 90,* 72–93.

Jones, E.E., & Davis, K.E. (1978). From acts to dispositions: The attribution process in person perception. In L. Berkowitz, *Cognitive theories in social psychology* (pp. 283–303). New York: Academic Press.

Kagan, J. (1981). *The second year: The emergence of self-awareness.* Cambridge, MA: Harvard University Press.

Kanfer, R., Eyberg, S.M., & Krahn, G.L. (1983). Interviewing strategies in child assessment. In C.E. Walker & M.C. Roberts (Eds.), *Handbook of clinical child psychology* (pp. 95–108). New York: Wiley & Sons.

Karabenick, J.D., & Heller, K.A. (1976). A developmental study of effort and ability attributions. *Developmental Psychology, 12,* 552–560.

Kashani, J.H., Orvaschel, H., Burk, J.P., & Reid, J.C. (1985). Informant variance: The issue of parent-child disagreement. *Journal of the American Academy of Child Psychiatry, 24,* 437–441.

Kazdin, A.E., Esveldt-Dawson, K., Unis, A.S., & Rancurello, M. (1983a). Child and parent evaluations of depression and aggression in psychiatric inpatient children. *Journal of Abnormal Child Psychology, 11,* 401–413.

Kazdin, A.E., French, N.H., & Unis, A.S. (1983b). Child, mother, and father evaluations of depression in psychiatric inpatient children. *Journal of Abnormal Child Psychology, 11,* 167–180.

Kazdin, A.E., French, N.H., Unis, A.S., & Esveldt-Dawson, K. (1983c). Assessment of childhood depression: Correspondence of child and parent ratings. *Journal of the American Academy of Child Psychiatry, 22,* 157–164.

Keil, F.C., & Batterman, N. (1984). A characteristic-to defining shift in development of word meaning. *Journal of Verbal Learning and Verbal Behavior, 23,* 221–236.

Keller, A., Ford, L.H., & Meacham, J.A. (1978). Dimensions of self-concept in preschool children. *Developmental Psychology, 14,* 483–489.

King, M. (1971). The development of some intention concepts in young children. *Child Development, 42,* 1145–1152.

Kowalski, P.S. (1987, April), *The relationship between profiles of self-perception and classroom achievement behavior.* Paper presented at the meeting of the Society for Research in Child Development, Baltimore, MD.

Kuczaj, S. (1978). Children's judgments of grammatical and ungrammatical irregular past-tense verbs. *Child Development, 49,* 319–326.

La Greca, A.M. (1983). Interviewing and behavioral observations. In C.E. Walker & M.C. Roberts (Eds.), *Handbook of clinical child psychology* (pp. 109–131). New York: Wiley & Sons.

Landau, B. (1982). Will the real grandmother please stand up? The psychological reality of dual meaning of representations. *Journal of Psycholinguistic Research, 11,* 47–62.

Ledingham, J.E., Younger, A., Schwartzman, A., & Bergeron, G. (1982). Agreement among teacher, peer, and self-ratings of children's aggression, withdrawal, and likability. *Journal of Abnormal Child Psychology, 10,* 363–372.

Leon, G.R., Kendall, P.C., & Garber, J. (1980). Depression in children: Parent, teacher, and child perspectives. *Journal of Abnormal Psychology, 8,* 221–235.

Leone, C. (1987, April). *Individual differences in the recognition of emotions: Self-monitoring in children.* Paper presented at the meeting of the Society for Research in Child Development, Baltimore, MD.

Lewis, M., & Brooks-Gunn, J. (1979). *Social cognition and the acquisition of self.* New York: Plenum.

Liebert, R.M., Wicks-Nelson, R., & Kail, R.V. (1986). *Developmental psychology,* (4th ed.). Englewood Cliffs, NJ: Prentice-Hall.

Livesley, W.J., & Bromley, D.B. (1973). *Person perception in childhood and adolescence.* New York: Wiley & Sons.

Ludemann, P.M., & Nelson, C.A. (1987, April). *Generalized recognition of positive and negative facial expressions.* Paper presented at the meeting of the Society for Research in Child Development, Baltimore, MD.

Mead, G.H. (1934). *Mind, self, and society.* Chicago, IL: University of Chicago Press.

Mendelson, E., Robinson, S., Gardner, H., & Winner, E. (1984). Are preschoolers' renamings intentional category violations? *Developmental Psychology, 20,* 187–192.

Mischel, W., Zeiss, R., & Zeiss, A. (1974). Internal-external control and persistence: Validation and implications of the Stanford preschool internal-external scale. *Journal of Personality and Social Psychology, 29,* 265–278.

Mokros, H.B., Poznanski, E., Grossman, J.A., & Freeman, L.N. (1987). A comparison of child and parent ratings of depression for normal and clinically referred children. *Journal of Child Psychology and Psychiatry, 28,* 613–627.

Montemayor, R., & Eisen, M. (1977). The development of self-conceptions from childhood to adolescence. *Developmental Psychology, 13,* 314–319.

Moretti, M.M., Fine, S., Haley, G., & Marriage, K. (1985). Childhood and adolescent depression: Child-report versus parent-report information. *Journal of the American Academy of Child Psychiatry, 24,* 298–302.

Nelles, W., Eisen, A.R., & Silverman, W.K. (1987, November). *Degree of diagnostic agreement between parent and child using a semi-structured interview.* Paper presented at the meeting of the Association for Advancement of Behavior Therapy, Boston, MA.

Nelson, C.A. (1987). The recognition of facial expressions in the first two years of life: Mechanisms of development. *Child Development, 58,* 889–909.

Nelson, K. (1973). Structure and strategy in learning to talk. *Monograph of the Society for Research in Child Development, 38,* (Serial No. 149).

Nelson, K. (1974). Concepts, word, and sentence: Interrelations in acquisition and development. *Psychological Review, 81,* 267–285.

Newman, L.S., Ruble, D., & Rholes, W.S. (1987, April). *Children's understanding of the causes of behavior.* Paper presented at the meeting of the Society for Research in Child Development, Baltimore, MD.

Nicholls, J.G. (1978). The development of the concepts of effort and ability, perception of academic attainment, and the understanding that difficult tasks require more ability. *Child Development, 49,* 800–814.

Nicholls, J.G. (1979). Development of perception of own attainment and causal attributions for success and failure in reading. *Journal of Educational Psychology, 71,* 94–99.

Nowicki, S., & Duke, M.P. (1974). A preschool and primary internal-external control scale. *Developmental Psychology, 6,* 874–880.

Nowicki, S., & Strickland, B.R. (1973). A locus of control scale for children. *Journal of Consulting and Clinical Psychology, 40,* 148–154.

Odom, R.D., & Lemond, C.M. (1972). Developmental differences in the perception and production of facial expressions. *Child Development, 43,* 359–369.

Parsons, J.E., & Ruble, D.N. (1977). The development of achievement-related expectancies. *Child Development, 48,* 1075–1079.

Peevers, B.H., & Secord, P.F. (1973). Developmental changes in attribution of descriptive concepts to persons. *Journal of Personality and Social Psychology, 27,* 120–128.

Phillips, R.D., Wagner, S.H., Fells, C.A., & Lynch, M. (1987, April). *Do infants recognize emotion in facial expressions?: Categorical and "metaphorical" evidence.* Paper presented at the meeting of the Society for Research in Child Development, Baltimore, MD.

Prout, H.T., & Chizik, R. (1988). Readability of child and adolescent self-reporting measures. *Journal of Consulting and Clinical Psychology, 56,* 152–154.

Puig-Antich, J., & Gittelman, R. (1982). Depression in childhood and adolescence. In E.S. Paykel (Ed.), *Handbook of affective disorders* (pp. 379–392). New York: Guilford.

Reich, W., Herjanic, B., Welner, Z., & Gandhy, P.R. (1981). Development of structured psychiatric interview for children: Agreement on diagnosis comparing child and parent interviews. *Journal of Abnormal Child Psychology, 10,* 325–336.

Reichenbach, L., & Masters, J.C. (1983). Children's use of expressive and contextual cues in judgments of emotion. *Child Development, 54,* 993–1004.

Reisman, J.M. (1973). *Principles of psychotherapy with children.* New York: Wiley.

Reynolds, C.R., & Richmond, B.O. (1978). What I think and feel: A revised measure of children's manifest anxiety. *Journal of Abnormal Child Psychology, 6,* 271–280.

Reynolds, W.M., Anderson, G., & Bartell, N. (1985). Measuring depression in children: A multimethod assessment investigation. *Journal of Abnormal Child Psychology, 13,* 513–526.

Romano, B.A., & Nelson, R.O. (1987, November). *The assessment of childhood depression: Discrimination and concurrent validity.* Paper presented at the meeting of the Association for Advancement of Behavior Therapy, Boston, MA.

Rosenberg, M. (1979). *Conceiving the self.* New York: Basic Books, Inc.

Rothenberg, B.B. (1970). Children's social sensitivity and the relationship to interpersonal competence, intrapersonal comfort, and intellectual level. *Developmental Psychology, 2,* 335–350.

Ruble, D.N. (1983). The development of social-comparison processes and their role in achievement-related self-socialization. In E.T. Higgins, D.N. Ruble, & W.W. Hartup (Eds.), *Social cognition and social development: A sociocultural perspective* (pp. 134–157). New York: Cambridge University Press.

Saarni, C. (1979). Children's understanding of display rules for expressive behavior. *Developmental Psychology, 15,* 424–429.

Sacco, W.P., & Graves, D.J. (1985). Correspondence between teacher ratings of childhood depression and child self-ratings. *Journal of Clinical Child Psychology, 14,* 353–355.

Sattler, J.J. (1988). *Assessment of children* (3rd ed., pp. 400–471). San Diego, CA: Jerome M. Sattler, Pub.

Scarlett, H.H., Press, A.N., & Crockett, W.H. (1971). Children's descriptions of peers: A Wernerian developmental analysis. *Child Development, 42,* 439–453.

Secord, P.F., & Peevers, B.H. (1974). The development and attribution of person concepts. In T. Mischel (Ed.), *Understanding other persons* (pp. 117–142). Oxford, Eng.: Basil Blackwell.

Selman, R.L. (1980). *The growth of interpersonal understanding: Developmental and clinical analyses.* New York: Academic Press.

Shaklee, H. (1976). Development in inferences of ability and task difficulty. *Child Development, 47,* 1051–1057.

Shantz, C.U. (1983). Social cognition. In P.H. Mussen (Ed.), *Handbook of child psychology: Vol. 3* (pp. 495–555). New York: Wiley.

Shatz, M., Wellman, H.M., & Silber, S. (1983). The acquisition of mental verbs: A systematic investigation of the first reference to mental state. *Cognition, 14,* 301–321.

Shriner, T.H., & Miner, L. (1968). Morphological structures in the language of disadvantaged and advantaged children. *Journal of Speech and Hearing Research, 11,* 605–610.

Smith, M.C. (1978). Cognizing the behavior stream: The recognition of intentional action. *Child Development, 49,* 736–743.

Smith, M.E. (1926). An investigation of the development of the sentence and the extent of vocabulary in young children. *University of Iowa Studies in Child Welfare, 3.*

Sorce, J.F., Emde, R.N., Campos, J.J., & Klinnert, M.D. (1987). Maternal emotional signalling: Its effects on the visual cliff behavior of 1-year olds. *Developmental Psychology, 21,* 195–200.

Spence, S.H. (1987). The relationship between social-cognitive skills and peer sociometric status. *British Journal of Developmental Psychology, 5,* 347–356.

Sprague, D.J., Beauregard, D., & Voelker, S.L. (1987, April). *Person perception in children: The effects of age, sex, and popularity.* Paper presented at the meeting of the Society for Research in Child Development, Baltimore, MD.

Stipek, D.J. (1981). Children's perceptions of their own and their classmates' ability. *Journal of Educational Psychology, 73,* 404–410.

Stodolsky, S., & Lesser, G. (1967). Learning patterns in the disadvantaged. *Harvard Educational Review, 37,* 556–593.

Treiber, F.A., & Mabe, P.A. (1987). Child and parent perceptions of children's psychopathology in psychiatric outpatient children. *Journal of Abnormal Child Psychology, 15,* 115–124.

Walden, T.A., & Field, T.M. (1982). Discrimination of facial expressions by preschool children. *Child Development, 53,* 1312–1319.

Waterman, A.S. (1982). Identity development from adolescence to adulthood: An extension of theory and a review of research. *Developmental Psychology, 18,* 341–358.

Watts, A.F. (1944). *The language and mental development of children.* London: Harrap & Co.

Weiner, B., & Peter, N. (1973). A cognitive-developmental analysis of achievement and moral judgments. *Developmental Psychology, 9,* 290–309.

Weissman, M.M., Orvaschel, H., & Padian, N. (1980). Children's symptoms and social functioning self-report scales: Comparison of mothers' and children's reports. *Journal of Nervous and Mental Disease, 168,* 736–740.

Weissman, M.M., Wickramaratne, P., Warner, V., John, K., Prusoff, B.A., Merikangas, K.R., & Gammon, G.D. (1987). Assessing psychiatric disorders in children: Discrepancies between mothers' and children's reports. *Archives of General Psychiatry, 44,* 747–753.

Welner, Z., Reich, W., Herjanic, B., Jung, K., & Amado, H. (1987). Reliability, validity, and parent-child agreement studies of the Diagnostic Interview for Children and Adolescents (DICA). *Journal of the American Academy of Child and Adolescent Psychiatry, 26,* 649–653.

Westerman, M.A., & Donaldson, S.K. (1987, April). *Children's use of overt and covert cues to infer emotions in others.* Paper presented at the meeting of the Society for Research in Child Development, Baltimore, MD.

Wojcik, A.M., & Glenwick, D.S. (1987, November). *A developmental analysis of self, teacher, and peer competence perceptions of behaviorally disor-*

dered children. Paper presented at the meeting of the Association for Advancement of Behavior Therapy, Boston, MA.

Wood, M.E. (1978). Children's developing understanding of other people's motives for behavior. *Developmental Psychology, 14,* 561–562.

Wootten, J., Merkin, S., Hood, L., & Bloom, L. (1979, April). *Wh- questions: Linguistic evidence to explain the sequence of acquisition.* Paper presented at the meeting of the Society for Research in Child Development, New York, New York.

Yarrow, L.J., (1960). Interviewing children. In P.H. Mussen (Ed.), *Handbook of research methods in child development* (pp. 561–602). New York: Wiley.

Yarrow, M.R., & Campbell, J.D. (1963). Person perception in children. *Merrill-Palmer Quarterly, 9,* 57–72.

CHAPTER 3

Methodological and Psychometric Considerations in Child Reports

RANDALL C. FLANERY

INTRODUCTION

The growing interest in child report measures represents an exciting convergence of diverse trends originating in areas of psychology that developed relatively independently despite similarities of purposes, methods, or content. One trend is the increasingly broad recognition of the unique competencies of the child, an acknowledgment that children are not simply miniature adults. An interest in the quality of instruments that measure children's views of themselves and others unites researchers and clinicians. One finds similar questions about the methodology of child self-report measures raised by behaviorally oriented researchers and by psychometricians. And finally, developmental psychology has begun to articulate ways in which developmental processes—emotional, cognitive, and behavioral—impact upon the solicitation and interpretation of child self-report measures. It is a stimulating, mutually enriching mix of historical trends, theoretical perspectives, and methodological innovation.

CHILD SELF-REPORTS ARE ALSO
PSYCHOLOGICAL MEASURES

Before proceeding, it is necessary to identify two basic assumptions upon which the present chapter rests. The first assumption is that child self-reports are an integral component of any adequate child (child, in the present case, is a generic term for humans age 5 through 19 years) assessment. This may appear so obviously self-evident as to be unworthy of note, and yet it is not uncommon to read research about child behavior in which no information is obtained from the child. Similarly, clinical decisions regarding children depend heavily upon teacher and parent reports, almost to the exclusion of the child's own views and concerns. A fundamental tenet of this chapter is that children's thoughts and feelings about themselves and those around them are crucial to scientific and clinical understanding and are best obtained from the child.

Information provided by children is unique and cannot be reproduced by any other method. While parents and teachers can provide valuable and probably more accurate data than children, they are not synonymous with child reports. This is most true when the concern is a child's affective experience, such as anxiety or fears. Adult judgments are highly inferential and routinely underestimate the intensity and breadth of child experience, especially for negative emotional states (Kurdek & Berg, 1987). Even the accuracy of parental reports of more objective data such as school attendance (Schnelle, 1974) and specific aggressive behavior (Herjanic & Reich, 1982) may be problematic. A recent meta-analytic study has demonstrated low correlations between data provided by adult informants and children's own reports (Achenbach, McConaughy, & Howell, 1987), suggesting that child and adult reports are not interchangeable and that each provides information not available from the other.

A second assumption is that measures designed to obtain data that will be used to draw inferences or make decisions about children are subject to the same standards that apply to all "diagnostic, prognostic and evaluative devices" (American Psychological Association, 1985, p. 3). Any method which systematically collects data about a child from a child, i.e., a child report, is a psychological measure in the same way that an achievement test or a personality measure is a test, whether the child report conforms to conventional notions of what a test looks like. As psychological "tests," child reports are subject to the criteria for determining the adequacy of a test or its applications as described in the *Standards for Educational and Psychological Testing* (APA, 1985).

APA Standards and Child Reports

The Standards are a concise summary of guidelines that test-developers and consumers can use to judge how well a measure does what it is said to do. The guidelines are empirical and rely upon psychometric principles that are relatively independent of any single theory. Among other things, the Standards specify that: (1) the process of test construction be well described, (2) test administration, data collection, and decision making be standardized, (3) measures have demonstrated evidence of reliability and validity (see Table 3.1 for an outline of these criteria), and (4) tests be used ethically.

The most compelling consideration is that the specific inferences to be made by the testing procedures be valid; that is meaningful and useful. The many ways in which data may be accumulated to support a test's validity have been categorized traditionally into "content-related, criterion-related, and construct-related evidence of validity" (APA, 1985, p. 9). These are not mutually exclusive categories. For example, evidence of the validity of the content of items of a depression inventory also bears upon the validity of the construct of depression which is allegedly being measured.

The value of psychometric methods is not uniformly accepted. Many behaviorists have argued strenuously for empirical methods, but mistrust traditional psychometric concepts which seem to embody trait-like assumptions, contrary to beliefs in the situational specificity and temporal instability of behavior.

TABLE 3.1 Psychometric Criteria

Reliability
    Temporal Consistency
    Internal Consistency
    Interrater Reliability
Validity
    Content
    Criterion-related Validity
    Concurrent Validity
    Predictive Validity
    Construct Validity

Recently, a rapprochement appears to be developing between behaviorists and psychometricians. Ollendick and Hersen (1984) have argued that within the fundamental assumptions of a behavioral perspective, an empirical orientation (a basic tenet of behaviorism) would require some evidence of temporal consistency and consistency among items, if stimulus situations are similar and change due to treatment or development is absent. Consistent with an integration of psychometric procedures and behavioral theorizing, recent research suggests that cross-situational and cross-temporal consistency of behavior under appropriate conditions is to be expected (Gresham, 1982) and should be demonstrated in order to support the utility of the measure (e.g., Cone, 1977).

Difference Between Child Report Measures and Traditional Tests

For the purpose of discussion, child report measures have been divided into three types: child self-report measures, peer assessments, and child interviews. Child self-reports are structured measures for assessing a child's view of him- or herself. Peer assessments are children's structured evaluation of their peers. A third class of child reports is child interviews. Like child self-reports, child interviews provide information about the respondent but tend to be less structured and rely more upon the skill of the interviewer. Child interviews solicit information about a range of topics whereas self-reports and peer assessments focus on relatively unitary concepts such as depression or popularity. These three types of child report measures are discussed at length throughout this book.

Child Self-Report Measures

Child self-reports generally look like traditional tests. The Children's Depression Inventory (CDI; Kovacs, 1985) is a representative child self-report measure whose psychometric properties have been studied more comprehensively than most child measures. The CDI is derived from the Beck Depression Inventory (Beck, Rush, Shaw, & Emery, 1979) and consists of 27 sets of statements illustrating the severity of depressive symptoms. Its structure resembles a traditional test: multiple items each assessing a similar (although not identical) aspect of a relatively unitary construct like childhood depression; items selected, altered, or rejected to maximize internal consistency. It is easy to see how test *Standards* should apply to self-report measures like the CDI.

Some child self-report tests originating from behavioral orientations embody different assumptions and thus do not obviously lend themselves to psychometric evaluation. Investigations of social competence often utilize assessments consisting of a collection of problematic situations. The child's responses are evaluated for degree of competence. Because it is assumed that behavioral responses are strongly situational and are somewhat changeable over time, items (situations) are expected to be relatively independent. From this point of view, evidence of split-half reliability or high internal consistency would be not only nonsensical but perhaps indicative of a poor measure (Freedman, Rosenthal, Donahoe, Schlundt, & McFall, 1978).

Peer Rating

Peer ratings are widely used methods for determining a child's social status (see Chapter 9). A form of peer ratings, peer sociometrics, dates to the 1930s (Koch, 1933). While a variety of methods are used, including rating scales, pair-comparisons, and partial-ranking procedures, all involve child judgments regarding the characteristics of peers. Some peer ratings resemble self-reports (e.g., multiple items, a single construct being assessed) except that the informant reports about another child. Such measures can be evaluated like most child self-report measures. Peer sociometrics often ask each student in a class to select peers "whom you like best" or with whom they are "best friends." Such measures may not be easily evaluated with traditional psychometric techniques, but issues of reliability and validity must still be addressed.

Child Interviews

Child interviews look least like traditional tests but the same *Standards* apply as much to these assessment procedures as do more conventional looking measures. It is only recently that structured interviews of children, designed to assess the psychological status of children, have been published (e.g., Herjanic, Herjanic, Brown & Wheatt, 1975); Hodges, Kline, Stern, Cytryn & McKnew, 1982; Kovacs, 1978; Edelbrock, Costello, Dulcan, Kalas, & Conover, 1985). (See Chapters 5 and 6.) The advent of published (and thus replicable) child interviews has stimulated considerable interest in their methodological and psychometric qualities (Flanery, 1985).

While it may be argued that standards which have evolved from traditional psychometric theory may be applied to child interviews, that is not to say that structured interviews are tests in the conventional sense. Structured interviews do not assess unitary, trait-like constructs. Indeed, the opposite is true. Most diagnostic interviews are designed to assess a broad range of content in as parsimonious a fashion as possible and tend to be atheoretical. Items are selected for pragmatic or clinical reasons, making the items very heterogenous. Interview data rely upon the skill of the administrator and are necessarily less standardized. The unique characteristics of interviews introduce variability, which is construed as error variance. The amount of error variance can make it difficult to demonstrate reliability and validity using standard psychometric criteria. To date, investigations have focused on reliability, especially interrater reliability, and to a lesser extent upon validity concerns, primarily content and concurrent validity.

METHODOLOGICAL CONSIDERATIONS

Child report measures are subject to all of the methodological challenges that adult measures are, in addition to those that are engendered by the respondents being children. While issues such as those involving reactivity, social desirability, response bias, and item formats apply to all tests including child measures, it is the fact of developmental change, a defining feature of children, that will be the focus of the discussion of methodological considerations.

Developmental Processes

Any discussion of child measures must begin with the fact that children change quantitatively and qualitatively. Young children differ profoundly from latency age children, who are not like adolescents, none of whom are like adults. While the fact of change may be obvious, it is not that apparent in some descriptions of existing child measures. For example, many child measures are modified versions of instruments originally developed for use with adults. While the practice is understandable, it poses dangers. The most common danger is to conceptualize children as less accomplished, miniature adults. Such a view predominated earlier in the history of psychology, but the overwhelming thrust of developmental research has been that children differ in many qualitative and quantitative ways across the life span, which will impact upon the nature and quantity of information they can report and upon the procedures for collecting data. Indeed, it has been argued that efforts to extrapolate adult measures for use with children are useless (Edelbrock, 1984). It is encouraging to see attempts to integrate developmental perspectives with child behavioral assessment (Ollendick & Hersen, 1984) and clinical interviewing of children (Bierman, 1984).

Relevant developmental changes include basic intellectual functioning such as comprehension and processing of information, as well as social cognitive processes involving perceptions of self and others. To illustrate, one cognitive change is from concrete operations to formal operations. Children who are operating at an earlier cognitive level will not necessarily construe an inquiry in the same way as an adolescent or an adult; nor will a particular response carry the same meaning across the life span. Similarly, social cognitions undergo developmental changes. For example, preschool children assign meaning to events egocentrically and utilize rigid categories such as "good" and "bad," whereas by adolescence, a more complex construction of social processes is operative, one in which people are seen to have multiple, even contradictory, motives and show some predictability based on their social roles and history. Intellectual and social developmental processes can have a profound effect upon the nature of assessment data obtained and upon how it is to be interpreted. (See Chapter 2 for a further discussion of developmental issues.)

Before utilizing a measure, it will be necessary to determine that the task of taking the test is within the capabilities of the child. The wording of questions must be age-appropriate, the complexities of the test procedures need to match the child's abilities, and the questions cannot tap information that exceeds the child's memory capacity.

The phenomena of interest may itself manifest developmental transitions. For example, the existence of childhood depression has been much debated (e.g., Cantwell & Carlson, 1979; Kashani, Husain, Shekim, Hodges, Cytryn, & McKnew, 1981). While there clearly is a Depressed Syndrome, it seems likely that the specific behaviors that constitute depression vary with age. Factor analyses of the Child Behavior Checklist (CBC; Achenbach & Edelbrock, 1979) showed that behaviors constituting a Depressed Syndrome for children age 6 to 11 years is not evident for children age 12 to 16 years. Similarly, the number and intensity of children's fears may vary with age (Miller, 1983). In other words, psychological phenomena may be subject to developmental processes.

Normative Data

The developmental changes identified above are a strong argument for obtaining normative data for child report measures. Given that human beings change substantially over the life span, it is difficult to understand child reports in the absence of an appropriate reference group. Suppose a child reports having 10 fears. Is 10 a lot or a few? Is clinical intervention required? Does the age or gender of the child make a difference? These questions can be answered only by comparing the result to the data of a specific reference group.

Normative data may be obtained from reference groups defined by any number of characteristics, but the variables that seem to be of greatest importance for child reports are age, psychologically disturbed versus nondisturbed, gender, socioeconomic status (SES), and race. The effects of these variables can be determined only by surveying very large numbers of children. It is an expensive, time-consuming, and generally thankless task, which is why there are so little normative data about psychological phenomena among children.

The available information, much of which is not even child report data, suggests that age and clinical status (disturbed versus nondisturbed) are especially important normative variables and that gender, SES, and race have a smaller impact (Edelbrock, 1984). Achenbach and Edelbrock (1981) have reported linearly decreasing prevalence of behavior problems as children age, at least as reported by parents. Some behaviors such as alcohol use and truancy increased as children become adolescents. Normative data exist for a few, widely used self-report instruments. Age, sex, and race norms are available for the Revised Children's Manifest Anxiety Scale (RCMAS; Reynolds & Paget, 1982) and the State-Trait Anxiety Inventory for Children (STAIC; Spielberger, 1973), although the STAIC data apply to a limited age range. Age and sex norms are available for the Fear Survey Schedule for Children-Revised (FSSC-R; Ollendick, 1983; Ollendick, Matson, & Helsel, 1985), and The Children's Internal-External Control Scale (Nowicki & Strickland, 1973).

The existence of any normative data is encouraging but the number of measures for which large scale normative data are absent is discouraging. Normative data for many measures of child affect, peer reports, or child interviews are virtually nonexistent. It would be useful to know how responses to these measures vary with age, clinical status, gender, race, and SES.

An important normative issue involves selecting tests to use with adolescents. It is not uncommon to have to choose between a measure of a construct for which adult norms or child (e.g., under 12 years) norms exist but not for ages 12 through 19 years. Since a decision must be made, the test consumer is forced to extrapolate beyond the available data. An energetic individual might choose to collect the necessary information. If a choice must be made, use the test for which normative data are available for a group most similar to the individual or group to be tested while cautioning about the limited support for the current use of the test. Another suggestion is to collect a sample for generating local norms, for example, a series of individuals served at the same institution. While not especially rigorous nor generalizable to other settings, it does provide some basis by which to judge an individual case.

Variables such as age, clinical status, gender, SES, and race are also likely to impact upon the reliability and validity of a measure. Edelbrock et al., (1985) recently reported that the test-retest reliability of a structured child interview was higher for older children. Similarly, predictive relationships (i.e., validity) may be more or less strong for different ages, sex, or disturbed versus nondisturbed children. Confidence in the inferences made with a test must be tempered in the absence of evidence about developmental changes in reliability or validity of a measure.

RELIABILITIES

A basic consideration of the quality of a measurement instrument is the consistency with which the instrument measures what it is supposed to measure, or its reliability. In other words, how free are test scores from errors of measurement (APA, 1985, p. 19)? Since there are a number of ways to estimate consistency of measurement, it is necessary to specify precisely how reliability was determined, under what circumstances, and with what kinds of populations. Reliability estimates include: (1) temporal consistency or stability, (2) internal consistency, and (3) interrater reliability. Each estimate uses different procedures and is sensitive to some sources of error but not to others. The anticipated use of the test will dictate which form(s) of reliability a consumer must examine when choosing a test.

Temporal Consistency

Estimates of temporal consistency or stability are attempts to specify how well a measure assesses an enduring quality over time. The assumption is that the attribute will not change much over some time interval. Thus, a measure of the trait, anxiety, a presumably enduring characteristic, will produce similar results if administered to the same individual weeks apart. This is also called test-retest reliability. More transitory phenomena would show little similarity over the same period of time.

Temporal consistency is highly relevant to all child report measures and is probably the most widely reported form of psychometric data. Nearly all standard measures report stability coefficients of about .80 for short time intervals. It is not expected that even the most stable of characteristics would show perfect test-retest reliability. Many factors such as fatigue, memory, changes in testing conditions, and errors in administration can produce differences in responses, thus reducing reliability coefficients.

One factor that can greatly reduce stability estimates is developmental change. If a child is undergoing a period of rapid developmental change during the test-retest interval, stability estimates will be lowered. In such circumstances, lower coefficients would not necessarily mean the measure is unreliable. Furthermore, the magnitude of the coefficient is highly dependent upon the test-retest interval. The longer the interval, the lower the coefficient. The Fear Survey Schedule for Children-Revised (FSSC-R) administered one week apart had a test-retest coefficient of .82, but a coefficient of .55 when tested three months apart (Ollendick, 1983). Choosing the appropriate interval and a satisfactory degree of stability can be quite challenging. Note that if the contemplated use of the FSSC-R requires evidence of stability over a six-month period, the consumer must make several complex judgments. Is it reasonable to extrapolate from three-month interval data to six months? If so, is the reported coefficient of .55 sufficiently high? These are not simple questions, but are ones that only the test consumer can answer.

Internal Consistency

Internal consistency estimates of reliability are most appropriate when a test or subtest consists of a relatively homogeneous set of items, each item presumably measuring the same construct. A number of statistical procedures have been developed to determine the degree of consistency in responding to a number of similar but not identical items (Wiggins, 1973). The procedures calculate the correlations between halves of all items (e.g., split-half reliability) or obtain an average correlation of all possible splits of items (Kuder-Richardson 20 formula or coefficient alpha; Wiggins, 1973). It should be noted that a number of methods exist for assessing internal consistency, but not all will be appropriate in any single instance. For example, correlations between the odd- and even-numbered items will be artificially inflated for speeded tests, and thus should not be used. Some tests tap a unidimensional construct whereas others assess a multidimensional domain. In the latter case, a more heterogeneous measure is appropriate, but will result in a numerically lower alpha coefficient which would not necessarily imply unreliability.

Internal consistency is easily and appropriately demonstrated with any multiple item questionnaire measure assessing a unitary construct, which includes most child self-report and many peer assessment measures. A rule of thumb for judging adequate internal consistency is an estimate such as an alpha coefficient above .80. Most published instruments easily achieve this standard. Some behavioral reports and peer sociometrics may not lend themselves to calculating internal consistency. For example, the Adolescent Problem Inventory (Freedman et al., 1978) notes the competence of responses to 44 situations. The developers argue that competent responding to one situation implies little about competence in another situation and thus assessing internal consistency is inappropriate and possibly misleading. Some peer assessment measures, especially peer sociometrics, consist of a single or a few items assessing a construct such as popularity. Since estimates of internal consistency calculated on only a few items might be misleading, the consumer may need to rely upon test-retest or interrater reliability in evaluating the instrument.

The concept of internal consistency does not readily apply to child interviews, which sample a broad range of content using items that are maximally different. Unlike a measure of single construct, interview items which are correlated, that is, share similar content, would be eliminated. Interviews often include items demanded by diagnostic criteria but which may have poor response distributions, e.g., skewed distributions or low frequency of endorsement, which would reduce correlation coefficients. In summary, estimates of internal consistency may not be legitimate for structured child interviews. In circumstances where consistency might be estimated, the coefficients might be erroneously interpreted as demonstrating unreliability.

Interrater Reliability

When the data of a measure are provided by one observer about someone else, interrater reliability is especially important. The concern is that different raters of the same phenomena produce comparable data. Interrater reliability is especially important for peer ratings and child interviews, less so for self-reports. In the latter case, reports by others, such as parents or teachers, may be compared to the child's own, but self-reports are more appropriately viewed as a validity question than a reliability issue (Flanery, 1985). The adequacy of peer ratings may be judged by comparing ratings by different peers of the same individual, although this seems to be underutilized to date.

Interrater reliability can be estimated by: (1) having a test protocol scored by different raters, (2) having two examiners score simultaneously the child's responses from the same administration, or (3) having two interviewers evaluate the same child independently. The correlation between the two examiners' scores is a measure of interrater reliability.

The first two methods assess consistency of scoring but not consistency of administration. Independent evaluations provide a more adequate assessment, but interpretation is complicated by the effects of repeated testing. For example, children reported 25% fewer psychiatric symptoms when interviewed nine days after the initial testing (Edelbrock et al., 1985).

The data of child interviews, based upon what the child says, are generally provided by an interviewer who must judge which category a child's response falls into. The Child Assessment Schedule (CAS; Hodges, Kline, Stern, Cytryn, & McKnew, 1982) is a 128-item interview in which the interviewer must code the child's response as true (symptom present), false (symptom absent), ambiguous (not clearly present or absent), no response, or not applicable. Categorizing requires some sensitivity and inference. How well different interviewers consistently code a behavior is a crucial index of the adequacy of a measure.

Poor Reliability or True Instability?

Classical psychometric theory is based on trait assumptions which, in their crudest form, assume that behavior is relatively unchanging over time. Thus, a lack of demonstrated reliability (whatever its form) is construed as evidence of measurement error; in other words, a poor test. A belief in the stability of human behavior is highly controversial and has been strongly challenged (Mischel, 1968; Cone, 1981). To the extent that behavior is variable, it becomes difficult to determine whether the instability of a measure is due to poor test construction or accurately reflects true behavioral variation over time. An alternative explanation of unreliability may be that the behavior in question is inherently variable.

As one considers whether the construct being measured is stable or variable, one begins to investigate the nature of one's theoretical understanding of the phenomenon of interest. Validity issues begin to come to the fore, illustrating that distinctions among types of reliability and validity are for convenience of communication and are to some extent arbitrary. A design may answer reliability concerns or validity questions according to the question and the phenomena being investigated.

VALIDITY

Tests are used to make inferences and it is the value, or validity, of the references that determines the adequacy of a test. Although it is often said that a *test* has validity, it is really the quality of the *inferences* that is at issue. A measure of child depression is valid to the extent it helps the examiner make good inferences; that is, it can be used to accurately identify the presence, severity, and nature of a child's depression.

Validity has been traditionally classified into three categories: content validity, criterion-related validity, and construct validity. The nature of the inference to be made will dictate the type of validity evidence needed. While each type of validity will be discussed, it should be remembered that rigid distinctions should be avoided and that one type of evidence may also have relevance for another class of validity. For example, evidence of the content validity of a measure is of intrinsic value and may also have implications for the validity of the construct being measured.

Content Validity

Content validity is evidence that the test "items, tasks, or procedures are representative of a previously defined universe or domain of content" (APA, 1985, p. 10). Usually some form of expert judgment is required to determine the relationship between specific items and the universe of interest, but explicitly described rules or algorithms can enhance a determination of content validity. According to Cronbach (1971), content validity requires: (1) an unambiguous definition of the relevant universe of content, (2) that the measure's items adequately sample or represent the specified universe, and (3) that the method for classifying responses and combining them into scores can be stated clearly. The criteria emphasize that care should be given equally to the items and to the responses. An initial step in constructing a test might include making a Table of Specifications (Hopkins & Antes, 1978) which would detail the relevant skills or traits of interest and behaviors representing those skills or traits. Such a procedure can demonstrate content validity (Golden, Sawicki, & Franzen, 1984).

It is during actual construction of a measure, when items are selected and modified, that content validity is achieved. At present, there are few statistical tools for evaluating content validity. It has occasionally been suggested that a factor analysis indicating one general factor for an instrument is evidence of content validity. Such an analysis shows that all items may be measuring a similar skill or trait but it does not demonstrate that those items derive from the identified domain. Additional evidence such as expert judgment is necessary to indicate representativeness.

Most published child report measures provide some evidence of content validity, describing the source of items and procedures for eliminating or altering items. Rarely is a Table of Specifications drawn up.

Even when test construction is described, it may be difficult to judge content validity. The CDI is a downward extension of the Beck Depression Inventory (BDI; Beck et al., 1979). If one believes that the BDI is valid and that the same items apply to children, then the content validity of the CDI has been demonstrated. However, questioning either belief challenges the content validity of the CDI.

A diagnosis is often an expected outcome of administering a child interview. If so, data necessary to make a diagnosis must be elicited by the interview. To the extent that interview items correspond to diagnostic criteria, content validity can be presumed to exist. In this context, concerns about items are primarily criticisms of diagnostic criteria rather than evidence of a lack of content validity for the interview. One's judgment of the validity of the diagnostic criteria will determine if an interview is content valid.

In evaluating the content validity of a measure, the consumer must be persuaded that good procedures were utilized in constructing the test. The more detailed the description of the criteria for generating and selecting items, the more likely the test has content validity. Ultimately, test users must decide for themselves whether the domain as defined by test constructors is indeed sampled by the test items.

Criterion-Related Validities

Criterion-related evidence of validity attempts to demonstrate that a measure can predict an individual's status based on other outcome criteria, either currently (concurrent validity) or in the future (predictive validity). Outcome criteria may be another test score, success or failure at a particular task, membership in a particular group, or classification of those who benefit from an intervention. Predictive validity is assessed by the accuracy with which a measure can predict an individual's criterion status in the future.

Concurrent validity may be demonstrated in many ways, but one way is to correlate test scores with scores of another measure. The CAS produces a symptom complex score which corresponds to a diagnosis of depression (Hodges, McKnew et al., 1982). A significant correlation (.53, $P < .001$) was observed between CAS Depression Symptom Complex and the CDI, evidence of concurrent validity. Such evidence suggests both measures may be valid but not which is more valid. This procedure is widely used and is reported for all types of child report.

A related method is to compare the child's report to information provided by another informant. Child interviews are routinely evaluated by comparing the child's responses to a parent's report about the child using the same interview questions (e.g., Herjanic & Reich, 1982). Moderate-to-high agreement is found for overt behavior and low agreement for affective states. The procedure has been fruitfully applied for child reports and peer-ratings.

Concurrent validity may be demonstrated by using the measure to differentiate "known groups" which have been defined previously on some other basis. Scores on a measure of depression (CDI) should be higher in a sample of children diagnosed by their therapists as depressed than in a group of children with no psychiatric disorder (Kovacs, 1978). Child interviews have been used to distinguish among inpatients, outpatients, and nonpatients (Hodges, McKnew, et al., 1982). Demonstrating validity with known groups is valuable but it is not a particularly demanding test of the adequacy of a measure. Often the groups differ in a very general way (disturbed-nondisturbed), affecting many domains of functioning. To find a difference may not be very difficult.

Predictive validity has not been widely reported for child report measures. It is a major gap in the literature.

Concurrent validity is generally easier to determine than predictive validity and is the more likely evidence to be provided. While all evidence bears upon the adequacy of a measure, the intended uses of a test will lend greater weight to one line of evidence rather than another. For example, a test may be shown to discriminate between anxious and less anxious adolescents, evidence of concurrent validity. Another researcher may wish to anticipate who will become more anxious after taking college entrance exams, a predictive inference. In the latter case, the test must be used cautiously. The assumed relationship between the predictor (the test of anxiety in adolescents) and the criterion (anxiety after taking college entrance exams) is likely but has not yet been demonstrated.

Sometimes a measure is validated with one population but is now to be used with a different group. Suppose a measure of fearfulness has been developed by quantifying the fears of 2,000 grade school children and it has been shown that social avoidance is correlated with high fearfulness scores. A clinician working with groups of mentally retarded children observes that the children who avoid social contact do poorly in his groups. He would like to identify the highly fearful children so that he can help them be less socially avoidant. Such a use of the test would be problematic until it is demonstrated that the same predictive relationship found in a normal population also exists for the retarded children.

The Problem of a More Valid Criterion

One problem that plagues all efforts to validate any psychological instrument is identifying a criterion against which to measure the new test. Often, it is hard to determine what might actually be a more valid criterion. In regard to peer nominations or structured child report checklists, a variety of options are available. Sometimes a measure is available that has a track record (i.e., previously established validity), or some incontrovertible marker exists. For example, clinical measures of depression are often seen to be valid if the measure can discriminate groups known to differ in how depressed their members are, such as a psychiatric clinic group and a pediatric group. Note, however, that the criterion membership in a diagnostic group (depressed versus not depressed), is actually obtained by an interview, whose validity may not have been demonstrated. The *APA Standards* address this point, ". . . the logic of criterion-related validity assumes that the criterion possesses validity. All too often tests are validated against any available criterion with no corresponding investigation of the criterion itself. The merit of a criterion-validity study depends on the appropriateness and quality of the criterion measure chosen" (APA, 1985, p. 27). The test consumer must determine the quality of the criterion when judging the adequacy of the validity evidence.

Construct Validity

Demonstrating the construct validity of a measure is a process of building a set of inferences about the conceptual entity the test allegedly measures. It is the accumulation of evidence about the nature of the inferences that can be made by using the tests, how the construct is different from other constructs, and how the construct (and the inferences to be made with the test) are related to other variables. The process of accumulating evidence of construct validity is lengthy and encompasses other forms of validity and reliability within it. All of the following might be used to document the construct-related validity of the test of fearfulness mentioned above: naturalistic observation of children's distance from feared objects is highly correlated with fearfulness scores (also concurrent validity), all items on the test are moderately correlated (internal consistency), fearfulness scores are moderately related to measures of anxiety and are unrelated to measures of depression (concurrent validity), and the items of the test were selected by a panel of researchers who work with fearful children (content validity).

Demonstrating construct validity is theory-building. Much has been written about how to think about construct validity (e.g., Campbell & Fiske, 1959; Cronbach & Meehl, 1955; Jackson, 1969; Wiggins, 1973), and some suggestions have been made regarding methods to use. The fact is that construct validation is very hard work. A major obstacle is the absence of precise, well-articulated theories. All of the procedures ultimately rely upon a theory that states what the construct is and is not, how it will be manifested in observable phenomena, and how it is related to other constructs. We have few such theories.

Campbell and Fiske (1959) have proposed using a multitrait-multimethod (MTMM) matrix for evaluating construct validity. A number of traits, including the one of interest, are assessed via several methods, and all scores are intercorrelated. Assuming three traits and three distinct methods, a nine-by-nine correlation matrix is generated. The magnitude of the correlation coefficients of different portions of the matrix are examined. Convergent validity is shown by high correlations among different measures of the same trait. Low correlations should be observed between measures of different constructs; this is referred to as discriminant validity. Unrelated traits, each assessed by a different method should have the lowest correlations.

A MTMM approach is an attempt to systematically evaluate the relationships among traits and methods in order to identify variation due to methods and traits. The approach requires a lot of data using several methods and, consequently, many subjects. It relies primarily upon visual inspection, not specific statistical tests. It is difficult to judge how much bigger one correlation must be than another or how to interpret an inconsistent pattern of correlations.

A particularly sophisticated alternative approach is called confirmatory factor analysis (CFA; Cole, 1987). CFA examines different underlying models of the data using goodness-of-fit criteria. It is possible to investigate assumptions about trait and method variance and consider alternative factor models for the same data set. The procedures are not limited to MTMM data and can be used with data provided by the multiple assessment (same method, e.g., all self-report measures) of a single construct as well as other combinations (e.g., multitrait monomethod, including MTMM data). The procedure is for testing models, not exploration of data. A specific model needs to be specified prior to the analysis. Indiscriminant use of CFA will capitalize upon chance relationships and produce spurious conclusions.

MTMM, factor analysis, and CFA are sophisticated statistical techniques, which are yet to be exploited fully in the study of child report measures. Evidence of construct validity of most measures of child report is completely lacking or is shown by a review of a body of literature using a single measure. Peer sociometrics have been used for decades. As a result, a collection of consistent findings using measures such as the Pupil Evaluation Inventory is possible (Hops & Lewin, 1984) and can be seen as rudimentary evidence of construct validity. Child self-report methods like the CDI (Kovacs, 1985) and the STAIC (Spielberger, 1973) have been used repeatedly, which makes it possible to begin to gauge their construct validity. Since child interviews are so very new and were designed for pragmatic purposes, very little can be said regarding construct validity.

Generalizability Theory

Generalizability theory is an effort to incorporate the various forms of reliability and validity within a comprehensive framework. As articulated by Cronbach and his colleagues (Cronbach, Gleser, Nanda & Rajaratnum, 1972), its fundamental tenet is that all observations may be generalized across definable universes. Thus, reliability and validity estimates are different ways that data from a measure may be generalized. In this scheme, interrater reliability, the degree of similarity of data provided by different raters, is an effort to generalize across the universe of raters. Similarly, assessing the same phenomena using different methods—for example, comparing questionnaire data to naturalistic observations—is a demonstration of generalization across the universe of methods. It also demonstrates convergent validity (Campbell & Fiske, 1959) and is an example of concurrent validity. Any number of universes may be defined and will vary according to the nature and uses of the instrument. It is up to the consumer to determine which forms of generalization are pertinent.

Generalizability theory is an elegant intellectual tour-de-force, whose contribution to assessment has been primarily conceptual (Jones, 1977). It is extremely helpful as an integrated framework for evaluating the adequacy of a measure. Its emphasis on generalization of observations helps to blur artificial distinctions between reliability and validity, and especially among different forms of validity which tend to become reified. Generalizability theory's broad conceptual framework explicitly identifies dimensions over which data may be generalized and it helps guard against blind spots resulting from unacknowledged assumptions. For example, many child measures are downward extensions of adult tests. A fundamental question is how generalizable are the scores? That is, do procedures used with adults produce comparable results with other age groups?

MEASUREMENT ACCURACY: AN ALTERNATIVE TO PSYCHOMETRICS

A Natural Science View of Measurement

The previous discussion has reviewed the classic concepts of reliability and validity, deriving from psychometric theory. The concepts are ones that have served well and have resulted in well-constructed instruments that may be used with at least modest confidence. The psychometric tradition, however, is not without its critics especially from behaviorally oriented researchers (e.g., Cone & Hawkins, 1977; Mischel, 1968, 1973). While trait theories and methods have been challenged on several points, the emphasis here will be upon a methodological alternative to psychometric procedures.

The alternative, identified as a "natural science point of view," has been cogently articulated by Johnston and Pennypacker (1980) with specific application to behavioral assessment by Cone (1981). The argument is that psychometric procedures rely upon the variability of psychological phenomena, in which the basic units of measurement are defined by individual differences in the construct of interest as measured by the instrument. In other words, psychometric procedures are methods for analyzing the observed variation in test responses. Thus, once a measure is devised which shows variation among individuals, the scientific task is to ask and then attempt to answer questions about variability—for example, is it stable over time; is a variation in the measure related to variation in other measures; do similar items produce similar distributions of responses? From a psychometric perspective, the phenomena and the measure to be studied must manifest variability; otherwise, psychometric procedures cannot be applied.

The alternative paradigm or natural science point of view demands that units of measurement be absolute and standard, and do not rely upon the inherent variability of the phenomena of interest. The analogy is made to measuring matter in motion. That is, there are standard units for distance, mass, and time, which in turn can be combined to define units like velocity. Rather than defining phenomena in terms of variability, psychological assessment is to be concerned with characteristics similar to distance or velocity, such as frequency, duration, or intensity of behavior. In this viewpoint, accuracy becomes the sine qua non of measurement, rather than analysis of variation.

Accuracy of Requirements of a
Measurement Device

Cone (1981), in applying a natural science viewpoint, has argued that the basic questions are: (1) occurrence of behavior, (2) repeated occurrence, (3) occurrence in different settings, (4) measurement of occurrence by different methods, and (5) whether occurrence is related to the occurrence of other behaviors. The questions entail absolute units, namely occurrence or nonoccurrence of carefully defined phenomena. In this view, a good instrument accurately detects the presence or absence of specified qualities. In order for a device to measure accurately, it must have: "(a) clearly spelled out rules/ procedures for using the device, and (b) an incontrovertible index against which data from its use can be compared (Cone, 1981, p. 57)." This is essentially a calibration of a measurement instrument. The device is used to measure a known quantity. If it produces the same result, it is accurate (also reliable). If it differs from the standard, it is inaccurate (although possibly reliable) and thus inadequte. It is important to note that variability is not relevant to evaluating the instrument.

An hypothetical example may help illustrate the procedure. A researcher is interested in social negativity; that is, verbal exchanges among children that are negative. The essential characteristics are defined such as insults, arguing, etc. The researcher develops a child report measure of social negativity. The psychometric approach might be to administer the measure to a large number of children six weeks apart while also administering questionnaires about aggressiveness and psychopathology. Such a measure would manifest differences among the children, which would probably be correlated with aggressiveness and psychopathology and show test-retest reliability above .80.

The natural science alternative might be to ask if the measure can be used accurately. Thus, can the device be used to detect when a socially negative exchange has occurred? Can it detect occurrence of social negativity at school and at home? Is social negativity related to the occurrence of aggressive acts? The procedures for answering these questions have not yet been developed (Cone, 1981, p. 63) but the possibilities are provocative. For example, the child reports might be calibrated by asking each respondent to read a transcription of a conversation prepared with a specified number of negative exchanges. A child's accuracy can be verified by comparing the number of exchanges the child reports to the number known to be in the transcripts.

Measurement Accuracy and Psychometrics

While such procedures appear not to have yet been demonstrated with child reports, they provide an interesting contrast to psychometric concepts. There are some phenomena in which individual differences are of fundamental importance and to which psychometric procedures may be legitimately and effectively applied. There are also phenomena for which the pressing assessment concern is accuracy, namely frequency of occurrence in different settings and in conjunction with other behaviors.

The occurrence of specific behaviors is the focus of much of a child interview. An interview may include items such as, "Have you ever skipped school?" or "Have you ever hit someone because you were mad at them?" The child might answer "no," nonoccurrence, or "yes," in which case the frequency of occurrence is of primary interest. In such a case, it is accuracy, not reliability, that is needed. That two raters agree upon the response (interrater reliability) is of less importance than whether it is an accurate report of events.

The concepts of measurement accuracy, reliability, and validity, while based upon different assumptions about measurement, are related. An instrument may be said to be reliable, in a psychometric sense, if it measures consistently over time, across similar items, and among observers. While it may be reliable, it may not be necessarily accurate. For example, a measure of aggressive behavior may show consistency between raters, high reliability, but the raters may be rating something other than aggressiveness and thus be inaccurate. Conversely, two raters scoring objective features of an individual's behavior by the same criteria must agree.

The accuracy of a measure implies nothing about the validity of the measure, and vice versa. Validity is concerned with determining the meaningfulness of scores produced by different instruments. Thus, an accurate instrument may or may not predict concurrent or future performance of a relevant construct. By the same token, a consistent but inaccurate measure can be a "valid" predictor. Recall the example of the social negativity scale. Raters' scores are less negative for more physically attractive children, that is, the measure is systematically inaccurate. If children also experience comments from attractive peers less negatively than to the same comments from unattractive peers, an apparently valid relationship will be observed with an inaccurate measurement device.

The concept of measurement accuracy is an appealing idea, especially for more behaviorally minded researchers. It seems especially appropriate for questions about the actual existence of a behavioral event. The concept has been proposed only recently and it is not yet apparent how it might be used. It does provide a counterbalance to a preoccupation with variance, which should count for something.

GUIDELINES FOR EVALUATING THE ADEQUACY OF CHILD REPORTS

As the previous discussion has shown, evaluating the adequacy of any psychological measure is an ongoing process. Applying rigid standards, irrespective of the specific purposes and characteristics of the assessment questions, may result in choosing less optimal instruments or suggesting that conclusions are more valid than they actually are. A set of guidelines is included. The guidelines enumerated in Table 3.2 are consistent with the more detailed and comprehensive framework to be found in the *APA Standards*. The guidelines are formulated as questions. No attempt has been made to identify which questions are most necessary nor could any measure satisfactorily answer all of them. They are *not* to be seen as a checklist in which the instrument with the most checkmarks is to be considered the "better" instrument.

Few psychological tests have been sufficiently evaluated to be unequivocally judged as to their adequacy, especially regarding construct validity. The available data on child measures are particularly inadequate. Thus, we may know what questions to be asked about a test while fully knowing that the data are not available.

The following suggestion is offered very humbly and is probably not going to be satisfying to many people. Forget about the tests that might be used. Rather, specify as precisely as possible the question to be addressed. To say, "I want to know how a child sees him- or herself," is not specific. Specify relevant subject characteristics (age, sex, SES, clinic status, construct[s]) to be used, the nature of the inference, and any testing limitations that might exist. With a clear formulation of your purpose, the type of data required may become apparent. If screening a large group of children is the purpose, a short, reliable, but less valid instrument might be preferred. If the decision is concurrent and about placement to receive an expensive treatment, predictive validity will be crucial. Emphasis must always be placed upon the *inference* to be made, not upon the test. A full understanding of the inference to be made will generally point the consumer towards the kind of evidence of adequacy needed.

While reliability and validity are crucial to clinicians and researchers, the situations may differ. A clinician must often make a deci-

TABLE 3.2 Guidelines for Judging the Adequacy of a Measure

A. How was the test developed?
   1. Did the test developers use widely accepted procedures, i.e., is it consistent with *APA Standards*?
   2. Was the test sample(s) representative of the population you plan to use the test with?
   3. Was the test developed on large enough samples?
   4. Are the data for evaluating the test current?
   5. Has the test been evaluated (and results published) by researchers other than the test developers?
   6. Do test procedures reflect an appreciation for the unique characteristics of children (i.e., is the test age-appropriate)?
B. Is the test reliable?
   1. Is the evidence of reliability appropriate?
   2. Are indices of internal consistency high enough (coefficients above .80)?
   3. Are scores stable over time? Is the time span used to assess stability relevant to your purposes?
   4. When interscorer or interobserver consistency is reported, are the reporters appropriate?
   5. When more than one form of reliability is appropriate, are all relevant data reported?
C. Is the test valid?
   1. In your opinion, do the test items measure what they are said to measure?
   2. Is evidence of criterion-related validity reported?
   3. Is the nature of the validity data consistent with your uses? If your research or clinical question is predictive, is the predictive validity of the measure reported?
   4. When the test is designed to discriminate among groups, do test scores actually differ among group samples?
   5. Are normative data reported? Are they relevant to the population you will use the test with?
   6. Do test scores correlate with theoretically meaningful variables and are uncorrelated with theoretically irrelevant variables?
   7. Has validity evidence been replicated, especially by someone other than the test developer?
   8. Is evidence of construct validity reported? If so, is it persuasive?
D. How practical is the measure?
   1. Can the child understand the test items?
   2. Is the testing time within the attention span of the child?
   3. Is the information to be provided within the child's abilities or experience to report?
   4. Will the child cooperate with test procedures?
   5. Is the measure sensitive to change?
   6. How reactive is the instrument?
   7. Can responses be easily biased?
   8. Does the quality of the data match the amount of effort to collect it?

sion; not deciding is not an alternative. A clinician must simply choose among what is available. Corcoran and Fischer (1987) have written a highly recommended book to help clinicians pick adequate instruments. Researchers have more latitude and also somewhat higher standards. If an adequate instrument is not available, researchers may develop their own, of course, demonstrating its reliability, validity, and accuracy.

REFERENCES

Achenbach, T.M. & Edelbrock, C.S. (1979). The Child Behavior Profile: 2. Boys aged 12–16 and girls aged 6–11 and 12–16. *Journal of Consulting and Clinical Psychology, 47,* 223–233.

Achenbach, T.M. & Edelbrock, C. (1981). Behavioral problems and competencies reported by parents of normal and disturbed children aged 4–16. *Monographs of the Society for Research in Child Development,* No. 88, 46 (1).

Achenbach, T.M., McConaughy, S.H., & Howell, C.T. (1987). Child/adolescent behavioral and emotional problems: Implications of cross-informant correlations for situational specificity. *Psychological Bulletin, 101,* 213–232.

American Psychological Association. (1985). *Standards for educational and psychological testing.* Washington, D.C.: Author.

Beck, A.T., Rush, A.J., Shaw, B.F., & Emery, G. (1979). *Cognitive therapy of depression.* New York: Guilford Press.

Bierman, K.L. (1984). Cognitive development and clinical interviews with children. In B. Lahey & A.E. Kazdin (Eds.), *Advances in clinical child psychology* (vol. 6, pp. 217–250). New York: Plenum.

Campbell, D.T. & Fiske, D.W. (1959). Convergent and discriminant validation by the multitrait-multimethod matrix. *Psychological Bulletin, 56,* 81–105.

Cantwell, D.P. & Carlson, G. (1979). Problems and prospects in the study of childhood depression. *Journal of Nervous and Mental Disease, 167,* 522–529.

Cole, D.A. (1987). Utility of confirmatory factor analysis in test validation research. *Journal of Consulting and Clinical Psychology, 55,* 584–594.

Cone, J.D. (1977). The relevance of reliability and validity for behavioral assessment. *Behavior Therapy, 8,* 411–426.

Cone, J.D. (1981). Psychometric considerations. In M. Hersen & A.S. Bellak (Eds.), *Behavioral assessment: A practical handbook* (2nd ed.) (pp. 38–68). New York: Pergamon.

Cone, J.D. & Hawkins, R.P. (1977). *Behavioral assessment: new directions in clinical psychology.* New York: Brunner/Mazel.

Corcoran, K. & Fischer, J. (1987). *Measures for clinical practice: A sourcebook.* New York: Free Press.

Cronbach, L.J. (1971). Test validation. In R.L. Thorndike (Ed.), *Educational measurement.* Washington, D.C.: American Council on Education.

Cronbach, L.J., Gleser, G.C., Nanda, H., & Rajaratnum, W. (1972). *The dependability of behavioral measurements: Theory of generalizability for scores and profiles.* New York: Wiley.

Cronbach, L.J. & Meehl, P.E. (1955). Construct validity in psychological tests. *Psychological Bulletin, 52,* 281–302.

Edelbrock, C. (1984). Developmental considerations. In T.H. Ollendick & M. Hersen (Eds.), *Child behavioral assessment: Principles and procedures* (pp. 20–37). New York: Pergamon.

Edelbrock, C., Costello, A.J., Dulcan, M.K., Kalas, R., & Conover, N.C. (1985). Age differences in the reliability of the psychiatric interview of the child. *Child Development, 56,* 265–275.

Flanery, R.C. (1985). Psychometric issues: Is validity relevant to structured interviews? Madison, WI: University of Wisconsin Hospital. (ERIC Document Reproduction Service No. ED256-780).

Freedman, B.J., Rosenthal, L., Donahoe, C.P., Schlundt, D.G., & McFall, R.M. (1978). A social-behavioral analysis of skill deficits in delinquent and nondelinquent adolescent boys. *Journal of Consulting and Clinical Psychology, 46,* 1448–1462.

Golden, G.J., Sawicki, R.F., & Franzen, M.D. (1984). Test construction. In G. Goldstein & M. Herson (Eds.). *Handbook of psychological assessment* (pp. 12–37). New York: Pergamon.

Gresham, F.M. (1982). Social interactions as predictors of children's likability and friendship patterns: A multiple regression analysis. *Journal of Behavioral Assessment, 4,* 39–54.

Herjanic, B., Herjanic, M., Brown F., & Wheatt, T. (1975). Are children reliable reporters? *Journal of Abnormal Child Psychology, 3,* 41–48.

Herjanic, B. & Reich, W. (1982). Development of a structured psychiatric interview for children: Agreement between child and parent on individual symptoms. *Journal of Abnormal Child Psychology, 10,* 307–324.

Hodges, K., Kline, J., Stern, L., Cytryn, L., & McKnew, D. (1982). The development of the Child Assessment Schedule for research and clinical purposes. *Journal of Abnormal Child Psychology, 10,* 173–189.

Hodges, K., McKnew, D., Cytryn, L. Stern, L., & Kline, J. (1982). The Child Assessment Schedule (CAS) Diagnostic Interview: A report on reliability and validity. *Journal of the American Academy of Child Psychiatry, 21,* 468–473.

Hopkins, C.D. & Antes, R.C. (1978). *Classroom measurement and evaluation.* Itasca, IL: F.E. Peacock Publishers.

Hops, H. & Lewin, L. (1984). Peer sociometric forms. In T.H. Ollendick & M. Hersen (Eds.), *Child behavior assessment: Principals and procedures* (pp. 124–147).

Jackson, D.N. (1969). Multimethod factor analysis in the evaluation of convergent and discriminant validity. *Psychological Bulletin, 72,* 30–49.

Johnston, J.M. & Pennypacker, H.S. (1980). *Strategies and tactics of human behavioral research.* Hillsdale, NJ: Lawrence Erlbaum Associates.

Jones, R.R. (1977). Conceptual vs. analytic uses of generalizability theory in behavioral assessment. In J.D. Cone & R.P. Hawkins (Eds.), *Behavioral assess-*

ment: *New directions in clinical psychology* (pp. 330–343). New York: Brunner/Mazel.

Kashani, J.H., Husain, A., Shekim, W.O., Hodges, K., Cytryn, L., & McKnew, D.H. (1981). Current perspectives on childhood depression: An overview, *American Journal of Psychiatry, 138,* 143–153.

Koch, H.L. (1933). Popularity in preschool children: Some related factors and a technique for its measurement. *Child Development, 4,* 164–175.

Kovacs, M. (1978). *The Interview Schedule for Children (ISC).* Unpublished manuscript, Western Psychiatric Institute, Pittsburgh, PA.

Kovacs, M. (1985). The Children's Depression Inventory. *Psychopharmacology Bulletin, 21,* 995–998.

Kurdek, L.A. & Berg, B. (1987). Children's Beliefs About Parental Divorce Scale: Characteristics and concurrent validity. *Journal of Consulting and Clinical Psychology, 55,* 712–718.

Miller, L.C. (1983). Fears and anxieties in children. In G.E. Walker & M.C. Roberts (Eds.), *Handbook of clinical child psychology.* New York: Wiley.

Mischel, W. (1968). *Personality and Assessment.* New York: Wiley.

Mischel, W. (1973). Toward a cognitive social learning reconceptualization of personality. *Psychological Review, 80,* 252–283.

Nowicki, S., Jr., & Strickland, B.R. (1973). A locus of control scale for children. *Journal of Consulting and Clinical Psychology, 40,* 148–154.

Ollendick, T.H. (1983). Reliability and validity of the Revised Fear Survey Schedule for Children (FSSC-R). *Behavior Research and Therapy, 21,* 685–692.

Ollendick, T.H. & Hersen, M. (1984). An overview of child behavioral assessment. In T.H. Ollendick & M. Hersen (Eds.), *Child behavioral assessment: Principles and procedures* (pp. 3–19). New York: Pergamon.

Ollendick, T.H., Matson, J.L., & Helsel, W.J. (1985). Fears in children and adolescents: normative data. *Behavioral Research and Therapy, 23,* 465–467.

Reynolds, C.R. & Paget, K.D. (1982). National normative and reliability data for the Revised Children's Manifest Anxiety Scale. Paper presented at the annual meeting of the National Association of School Psychologists, Toronto.

Schnelle, J.F. (1974). A brief report on the invalidity of parent evaluations of behavior change. *Journal of Applied Behavior Analysis, 7,* 341–343.

Spielberger, C.D. (1973). *State-Trait Anxiety Inventory for Children.* Palo Alto, CA: Consulting Psychological Press.

Wiggins, J.S. (1973). *Personality and predictions: Principles of personality assessment.* Reading, MA: Addison-Wesley.

PART II

Interviews with Children and Adolescents

CHAPTER 4

Interview Techniques and Establishing Rapport

STEPHEN R. BOGGS
SHEILA EYBERG

"But he hasn't got anything on," a little child said.
—THE EMPEROR'S NEW CLOTHES
HANS CHRISTIAN ANDERSON

INTRODUCTION

What young children say is unlikely to be as socially controlled as the communication of adults. As Hans Christian Anderson so aptly illustrates, children very often describe events the way they see them, without censoring to conform to rules established by an adult community. Sometimes, however, children have been taught very specific censoring rules to which they may comply rigidly. And, of course, children may fail to describe accurately or completely the events in their environment due to a relatively limited verbal repertoire. Despite this complexity, it is both possible and important to make sense of a child's communication through careful consideration of their developmental capacities and their individual learning histories.

Psychologists consider the child interview an integral part of the psychological assessment process, regardless of theoretical orientation (Kanfer, Eyberg & Krahn, 1983). Although the validity of verbal report in assessment has been looked upon with most skepticism by behaviorally oriented psychologists, they in fact use the interview more than any other method of assessment (Swan & McDonald, 1978).

The primary goals of the initial child interview are: (1) to establish rapport, (2) to gather information about the child's perceptions of the reasons for referral, and (3) to observe the child's behavior directly. The child's behavior provides clues about physical, affective, and cognitive development that might need further systematic assessment (Greenspan, 1981). As Gross (1985) has pointed out, direct observation during the interview can also provide the opportunity to gather important information about the child's activity level and attention span as well as social skills (e.g., eye contact, cooperativeness, confidence). Observation of general characteristics of the child during the interview period provides hypotheses about the family as well. For example, observing hygiene tells you something about the parents' care and training of the child.

Parents can usually describe their child's behavior in great detail but they find it much more difficult to describe accurately their child's thoughts and feelings (Lapouse & Monk, 1958). Because what the child thinks and feels about current problems can sometimes illuminate major influences on his or her behavior, it is imperative for the psychologist to assess his or her perceptions of relevant issues. The child's report about current problems also contributes information about his or her motivation and desire for change. Finally, events outside the parents' supervision may also influence the child's behavior; in such cases, the child may be the only relevant informant.

Primary among our goals in interviewing children must be establishing rapport. Rapport refers to a positive relationship between interviewer and child that sets the tone for the entire assessment process and helps increase both the amount and accuracy of the information provided. For the child, characteristics of this relationship include feelings of warmth, trust, and safety during the assessment session. For the interviewer, they include feelings of positive regard, genuineness, and empathy toward the child. An important outcome of the relationship is that the child sees the interviewer as a potential helper, and the interviewer sees the child as someone needing and deserving of help.

The techniques used during the interview to accomplish these goals are generally referred to as process skills. Process in psychotherapy refers to all observable events that occur between a patient and therapist during their formal interaction (Orlinsky & Howard, 1986). For the purposes of our discussion of the child interview, we will focus primarily on those interviewer behaviors that seem to lead the interview most efficiently and effectively to a successful outcome. Unfortunately, empirical evidence has not emerged from the literature that defines what interviewer behaviors and strategies most readily elicit information from the child.

The present chapter describes interviewing techniques and strategies commonly used in clinical settings that have been found useful in facilitating communication with the child during the initial interview. Use of the general term "child" refers to all children from preschool age through adolescence. Where discussion focuses on more specific developmental levels, these will be indicated in the text. General communication skills will be discussed, strategies for conducting the child interview will be presented and suggestions for future research will be offered.

COMMUNICATION SKILLS

During the child interview obtaining rapport with the child and eliciting the child's cooperation are ongoing goals throughout the interaction. As pointed out by Kanfer et al. (1983), there are a number of identifiable communication skills that are helpful in achieving these goals. The use of these skills cannot be prescribed in a step-by-step format but rather must be sensitively intertwined within the context of information gathering. Similarly, timely application of these skills cannot be taught in the abstract but are ultimately learned through direct training and experience with a variety of children. Nevertheless a description of these techniques is prerequisite to this learning process. The application of these skills will be illustrated through examples in various clinical situations.

Acknowledgments

Acknowledgments are verbal or nonverbal behaviors of the interviewer that have little or no manifest content but are intended to recognize the child's efforts, express empathy, or provide feedback to the child that the interviewer is listening and understanding. These behaviors are most often provided while the child is talking about thoughts and feelings related to topics introduced by the interviewer.

Examples:

"Mm-hmm"
Looks of concern

Head nod
Smiles
"Oh"
"I see."

The style of delivery of such statements and gestures must be matched to the child's social development. Preschool-age children are unlikely to respond to subtle social cues such as raising eyebrows or slight nodding of the head, but instead will require more effusive responses from the interviewer.

Acknowledgments are often thought of as neutral, but they do tend to influence the child to continue talking. This is desirable if the topic is of importance to the interview, but the chance of inadvertent reinforcement of irrelevant content is great. Interviewers need to monitor the use of acknowledgment carefully and be aware of its potential effects on the child's conduct during the interview.

TABLE 4.1 Communication Skills

Skill	Definition	Example
Acknowledgment	A verbal or nonverbal behavior that has little or no manifest content.	"Mm-hmm," head nod.
Descriptive statement	A nonevaluative comment that describes the present situation.	"You look like you're thinking hard about that question."
Reflective statement	A statement that repeats what the child has said.	"You sound pretty happy that she kept her promise."
Praise statement	A statement that expresses explicit positive evaluation.	"You're doing a nice job of explaining this to me."
Question	An expression of inquiry made to elicit information.	"What chores do your parents want you to do?"
Command	An instruction in declarative form.	"Tell me more about that."
Summary statement	A condensed reiteration of preceding content.	"We've talked about everyone who lives at your house."
Critical statement (to be avoided)	A statement that expresses disapproval.	"That isn't very nice."

Descriptive Statements

A descriptive statement is a nonevaluative comment that simply describes the present situation. Most often it is a statement about what the child is doing, but may also include comments about the child's appearance and demeanor.

Examples:

"You look like you're thinking hard about that question."
"I notice you smiled when I asked about grandma."
"It looks like you're a little nervous about being here today."
"That little girl doll is playing by herself."

Describing serves several purposes: (1) it adds to the nonthreatening nature of the interaction by helping the child see that the interviewer is genuinely accepting of his or her behavior; (2) it tends to hold the child's attention on the current topic or activity of the interview; (3) it serves to encourage the child to elaborate further and helps to organize and clarify for the child; (4) it allows the young child in the play therapy interview to continue with current activity while making it clear to the child that the interviewer is paying attention.

Sometimes children's anxiety leads to silence in the interview. Allowing silence to continue often serves to increase anxiety for the child. A preschool-age child playing silently may be comforted by brief statements about the play activity, particularly if the silence has been preceded by a question. For the older child, a descriptive statement such as one that either expresses the acceptability of the silence (e.g., "That's kind of a hard question to think about right now") or that redirects the child's attention to a less threatening topic (e.g., "Maybe we can talk more about that later, because right now I'd like to talk about. . .") reduces this tension and keeps the interview flowing productively.

Descriptive statements of the interviewer must be carefully chosen so that the younger child understands the interviewer's comments and the older child does not interpret the statements as condescending. For example, the description, "Your new blue dress looks so 'grown-up'!" may help to establish rapport upon meeting a 6-year-old child, but would have the opposite effect if delivered to a 16-year-old.

The amount of information contained in each descriptive state-ment should be limited for the younger child. A good rule-of-thumb with preschool-age children is to convey only one concept in any sentence. Similarly, for the school-age child, the interviewer's descriptions should be fairly short and concise with careful choice of age-appropriate vocabulary. Adolescents, however, will be likely to understand more complex language and more varied content contained in a descriptive statement. One cue that the interviewer may use in "tailoring" descriptors to the individual child is the child's own vocabulary. It is important to remember though that some children have picked up phrases or clichés they do not really understand and which might prompt the interviewer to use descriptors that are beyond the child's comprehension. Techniques for checking children's understanding of the words they use will be discussed later.

Reflective Statements

Reflective statements essentially repeat what the child has just said. The interviewer may use exactly the same words or may say the same thing using synonymous words or phrases. Reflective statements may reflect only a portion of the child's statement or may elaborate the child's statement, but they do not change the basic content or emotion of the child's message.

Examples:

Preschool-age child: "The thunder is scary."
Interviewer: "The thunder *is* scary."

Older child: "It was real neat when she let me put up the poster."
Interviewer: "When your mom let you put it up you really liked that."
Interviewer: "You sound pretty happy that she kept her promise."

Perhaps more than other interviewer statements, effective reflection requires some practice. Especially with exact reflection, voice inflection slightly dissimilar to the child's is typically required to convey genuineness. Reflections that paraphrase a child's meaning become increasingly useful with older children.

Effective reflective statements demonstrate acceptance and interest in what the child says and convey understanding. They allow the child to agree or disagree with the interviewer's understanding and to elaborate with further detail.

Reflecting a child's statement is a technique that can be used when the interviewer is unsure of a child's usage of a term or phrase and the child's meaning remains unclear. This may occur either when the child uses youthful jargon or when the child uses words that the interviewer suspects are not understood by the child. By repeating the questioned phrase in the child's own words, the interviewer provides a prompt that may result in a clarifying statement from the child.

Reflection can also be used to guide the interview into areas of particular importance for the assessment. Kanfer et al. (1983) described this strategy as "selective reflection." Frequently a child will relate two or more distinct ideas in one statement. The interviewer is then provided with an opportunity to lead the child into further discussion of the most relevant aspect of the verbalization by reflecting the content of interest. For example, if a child were to state, "I get scared when the other kids call me those names, but I'm OK once the teacher makes them leave me alone and gives me something fun to do," the interviewer would have many options for the direction of the conversation. Reflection such as, "The other kids scare you sometimes," is likely to elicit comment on additional instances of fearful responses to peers; "Sometimes other children call you names," yields further description of the child's experience while being teased; "Your teacher is really watching out for you," leads to elaboration of the child's perception of the teacher; "There are fun things at school," guides the discussion toward the pleasurable events in the school environment.

Praise Statements

Praise is a statement that indicates approval of the child. While most of the clinician's behavior in the interview conveys acceptance and approval of the child, what distinguishes praise is the explicit positive evaluative component of the verbalization.

Examples:

"That's hard to remember, but I like how you keep trying."
"You're doing a nice job of explaining this to me."
"It's great that you've been sitting so quietly while we talk (play)."
"It sounds like you really thought about that and handled it the best way you could have."

Praise needs to be used judiciously in the initial stages of the interview. Particularly with adolescents, early praise can be perceived as insincere. Once the initial rapport has been established, "labeled praise," which specifies exactly what it is the interviewer is encouraging, can be powerful in strengthening the rapport and increasing the child's information-giving. Labeled praise encourages the child to continue topics of importance to the assessment. It reassures the child that what he or she is saying is acceptable. The specific praise statements that the interviewer uses as well as the interviewer's prosody will of course differ with the age of the child. For example, the praise statement, "That's so *polite* of you to say 'thank-you'!" to a preschool-age child, could be made less effusively to a school-age child but its content would probably be inappropriate for a teenager.

Questions

A question is one of the most direct ways of soliciting specific information. Unlike the previous interviewing techniques discussed, questions make an explicit demand upon the child.

Examples:

"When does Daddy come visit you?"
"What chores do your parents want you to do?"
"Where have you thought about going to college?"

Productive questions are ones which allow the child freedom to express spontaneous thoughts and feelings safely on the topics that are introduced. There are several different types of questions from which the interviewer may choose.

Questions may be open ended or closed ended. Open-ended questions are typically preferred because they yield more information per question. To illustrate with an obvious example, asking, "Are you five years old?" could get a "no" answer, requiring another question, whereas, "How old are you?" would result in the desired information immediately. Open-ended questions also greatly minimize the possibility that the interviewer will lead the child to state conclusions that are suggested by the question itself. Leading questions, such as, "Do you think you need to work harder in school," are likely to get a "yes" answer, but really provide little, if any, useful information. There are a few situations when a closed-ended question may be helpful for pinning down a specific fact. For example, a child victim of sexual abuse may have been instructed not to talk about abusive incidents. An interviewer could ask such a hesitant child a closed-ended question such as, "Have you been told not to talk to me about this?" permitting a less threatening answer through head nodding.

Questions may also be indirect. Indirect questions are ones presented as declarative statements delivered with tentative beginnings, such as, "I wonder . . ." (Tuma & Sobotka, 1983). These statements implicitly request a response from the child but are perceived as less demanding than direct questions. When dealing with potentially threatening content, this type of question helps to maintain rapport and reduce the child's defensiveness.

As with reflective statements, reflective questions are helpful in structuring the direction of the child's talk during the interview. Because they present more of a demand for the child's response, they more readily elicit specific information on the same topic than do reflective statements. If a child stated, "I don't like daddy and mommy anymore," a reflective question such as, "You don't like your daddy and mommy?" would result in further discussion of the child's feelings towards the parents. Reflective questions help to guide the course of the interview even more directly when selective reflection, described earlier, is used in phrasing the question. In the example above, the question, "You don't like daddy?" would focus the interview on the child's feelings toward the father specifically.

Reflective questions are also especially helpful in clarifying child statements that the interviewer actually does not understand. A child might comment, "I felt creepy when Mom acted so weird." Reflecting with the question, "You felt creepy?" would require the child to explain further his or her meaning of the term "creepy," while the question, "Your mom acted weird?" would influence the child to describe the parent's unusual behavior and would help the interviewer to assess and clarify the child's perception of that behavior.

One type of question that we believe is actually counterproductive is the question that begins with "why." A "why" question is perceived by children as requiring them to account for or justify behavior rather than to describe what led up to the behavior. These questions typically result in feelings of defensiveness and perhaps hostility toward the interviewer. For example, the question, "Why is it that you don't take your pills?" would be better rephrased as, "What things don't you like about taking pills?"

In formulating questions to ask a child, the interviewer must take care to use words that the child will understand. As with descriptions, the choice of words and the amount of information contained in a question must be matched to the child's verbal and cognitive development.

Questions about the child's past or present affective state are often difficult to deliver clearly. Young children typically are not able to discriminate the differences between the words and phrases that adults use to describe the many nuances of human emotion. Preschool-age children can rarely describe feelings beyond mad, sad, scared, or happy (Harter, 1983; also see Chapter 2). Asking a child to describe specific behaviors or the behaviors of others in specific situations sometimes yields this information more readily than asking the child to label moods. Similarly, it is much more difficult to interpret responses to feeling questions asked in a general rather than a specific context. For example, a question such as, "What did you do when Jimmy called you an alien?" might result in, "I got red and started crying," from which the interviewer might infer a state of hurt embarrassment. Asking, "How did you feel when Jimmy called you an alien?" would probably result in an unrevealing or misleading answer, such as "Upset" or "Mad." The generalized feeling question, "How do you feel when you get teased?" could lead to even less informative answers (e.g., "I don't know").

Qualifying phrases added to questions can confuse rather than clarify. Such phrases are an attempt to gain exact information quickly, but also require more sophisticated answers from the child. A question such as, "Which of your parents' rules are hardest to follow in the morning?" forces the child to consider at least four sets of information: rules, time, parent, and difficulty of compliance. A more productive strategy might be to ask, "What are some hard rules to follow?" and then ask additional questions regarding when each rule applies and who enforces the rule.

Commands

The most direct way of requesting information from the child is to give a command. A direct command in the interview is a statement which provides no other appropriate option to the child except to comply with the instruction.

Examples:

"Tell me your name."
"Describe that man to me."
"Tell me more about that."
"Look at this picture."
"Bring your drawing paper over here."

Direct commands such as these are seldom used during the interview except when very concrete information or activity is wanted. When commands are used, the command should call for a response that the child is developmentally able to produce. For example, directing a two-year-old child to "Tell me your address" would be inappropriate. In addition, the command should require only one answer or other behavior at a time. It is difficult for children to remember a string of instructions tied together in a single command. Finally, commands should be specific rather than general. By describing concisely the information or activity desired, the interviewer prevents confusion and misunderstanding.

After a child has complied with a direct command, it is very important to reward the child's efforts. Praise statements are an excellent way to let the child know that the behavior pleased the interviewer. Acknowledging compliance in this way also increases the likelihood that the child will respond appropriately the next time a specific request is made.

Summary Statements

Summary statements are used to review material covered during preceding segments of the interview. The interviewer concisely describes the information given by the child.

Examples:

"You've told me about how the doctors and nurses scare you and that your mom can make you feel better when they've left. I'd like to hear more about what your mom does to help you."

"We've talked about your grades and your teacher. What is one of your favorite things to do with your friends at school?"

Summary statements can be very useful for focusing on information of particular interest when the child has provided more than one content area during a communication to the clinician. As demonstrated in the first example above, the interviewer is able to guide the child's information-giving by summarizing the topics presented by the child and by placing the content to be further examined at the end of the summary. A statement focusing on the material of greater interest then prompts the child to continue in this area.

Summary statements can also be used to introduce entirely new topics. The second example above illustrates the use of this technique. The issues previously discussed are stated in order to provide closure and the new topic area is introduced with an open-ended question.

Critical Statements

Critical statements are verbalizations that communicate disapproval of the child or the child's behavior. Such statements are not productive in the context of the interview and should be carefully avoided.

Examples:

"Stop moving around in your chair and answer that question."
"That was pretty dumb of you, wasn't it?"
"You aren't describing that very clearly."
"I don't think you're trying hard enough right now."

Critical statements can take the form of commands that direct the child to cease current activity, insults to the child, and statements that imply that what the child is doing is inappropriate. These statements foster negative reactions such as frustration and anger, and lead to decreased cooperation. There is perhaps no more direct way to destroy rapport built during earlier parts of the interview than to introduce criticism into the interaction.

It is likely, however, that inappropriate child behavior will occur during interviews with some children. There are several alternatives to criticism that the interviewer can use both to prevent such behavior from occurring and to intervene when confronted with negative behavior. First, the interviewer can set rules at the beginning of the interview which the child can use to limit behavior. Such rules are especially useful when a playroom is used for interviewing younger children. If rules have been made clear to the child, the interviewer can remind the child of the rule rather than directly instructing the child to stop an activity. A second strategy for preventing unacceptable behavior is to praise frequently the child for his or her good behavior throughout the interview. Labeled praise for attending to the interviewer, sitting quietly, or playing nicely will help keep the child responding in ways conducive to information-gathering.

Once inappropriate behavior has occurred, the interviewer has several choices for intervention. Whenever possible, the behavior should be ignored. This strategy is useful when the child's behavior is not likely to result in injury to a person or destruction of property. It is important when ignoring is used that the interviewer note the first instances of appropriate behavior and praise the child accordingly. Most inappropriate behavior of the older child in the interview can be ignored. For example, aggressive talk or profane language used by the adolescent can simply be ignored. The interviewer could reflect the expressed feeling or content using more acceptable words, thus modeling for the child appropriate expression. A second strategy for intervening is to give an instruction for an incompatible behavior. The interviewer can then reward the child for engaging in the positive activity and continue with the interview. Fi-

Special problems arise in setting arrangement when the child is to be interviewed while hospitalized for medical treatment. In pediatric settings, private play areas or rooms set aside for lengthy interviews are very unusual. Frequently, the only space reliably available is the child's bed and the small area surrounding it. Using this space requires minimizing distractions and bringing all necessary toys, parent questionnaires, and writing materials to the room. Minimizing distractions is particularly difficult given that the child may have roommates, visitors, easy access to remote control television, etc. The way to deal with this potentially chaotic situation is to create the best setting possible after initial introductions are made (see next section). Pulling the bed curtain to create the illusion of a private area, instructing the child to turn off radios, televisions, and tapeplayers, and taping a "do not disturb" note on the outside of the bed curtain usually suffice. We suggest sitting or standing next to the bed rather than sitting on the bed during the initial interview with the ill child. This demonstrates respect for the child's personal space and may prevent the child from feeling too trapped or invaded. Any toys or drawing materials brought to the room may be placed on the bed or on the child's meal table so that comfortable access is possible.

Meeting the Child and Family

Usually the first contact with the child and family occurs in a clinic waiting area or hospital room. Initial observation of the child in these settings provides valuable input regarding possible child or family problems. Although this period of observation is necessarily brief, the child's general physical condition, conduct and response to parents and other children in the room can suggest topics for discussion in the subsequent interview.

Introductions can be crucial for establishing rapport with the child and family. The clinician must present as a confident and concerned individual who is competent to conduct the upcoming interview. It is suggested that the interviewer introduce him- or herself using a formal title and address the parents similarly. This approach to the family clearly establishes that the relationship is to be a professional rather than a casual one (Kanfer et al., 1983; Reisman, 1973). After addressing the parents, introduction to the child follows immediately so that it is apparent to the child that he or she is an important participant in the interaction. The interviewer should at this time make a particular effort to communicate warmth and friendliness to the child. Regardless of the child's age, he or she will likely be suspicious of the psychologist. Preschool-age children, in particular, may associate this "visit with the doctor" with

nally, if the behavior is such that it must be immediately stopped, the interviewer can physically intervene by restraining the child or physically guiding the child to a safer activity. If restraint is necessary or the child must be repeatedly guided, it is recommended that the interview be terminated and the parents notified of the difficulty.

STAGES OF THE INTERVIEW

The process of conducting an interview can be divided into five distinct stages: preparing for the interview, meeting the child and family, beginning the interview, obtaining the child's report, and closing the interview. Within each stage, there are special strategies available for obtaining and maintaining rapport with the child and for assuring that desired information is gained.

TABLE 4.2   Stages of the Child Interview

Preparing for the interview
    Gather initial information about child and reasons for referral.
    Review relevant literature about presenting problem.
    Arrange conducive interview setting.
Meeting the child and family
    Observe child and family prior to introduction.
    Formally introduce self.
    Describe structure of the interview.
Beginning the interview
    Explain purpose of interview to the child.
    Ask child for his or her concerns.
    Discuss confidentiality, if appropriate.
    Discuss playroom rules, if appropriate.
Obtaining the child's report
    Move from least to most distressing topics.
    Deal sensitively with child resistance.
    Minimize parent interruption.
Closing the interview
    Express appreciation for cooperation.
    Summarize major topics discussed.
    Solicit additional concerns.
    Inform child of follow-up plans.

Preparing for the Interview

There are several preparatory steps that contribute significantly to the success of an assessment interview. These include gathering initial information regarding the child and reasons for referral, reviewing the literature concerning the child's presenting problem or medical condition, and arranging a setting that will be conducive to planned activities. Being well-prepared for the interview will increase feelings of confidence in the clinician and will contribute significantly to the task of establishing rapport.

The first preparatory step occurs when the child's parent calls to schedule the interview. The individual receiving this call should be trained to obtain from the parent general information related to the referral. The problem prompting the professional consultation, chronic medical conditions of the child, and prior psychological services can be briefly described by the parent at this time. Should the referral be received from an individual other than the child's parents, contact is made with the family as soon as possible so that this information can be gathered.

Once the interview is scheduled, the child's parents can be sent a packet of pre-interview materials. This packet often includes an introductory letter, forms for gathering general information on the child's developmental, educational, and medical history, and standardized behavior checklists which will provide information on behavioral characteristics of the child. The introductory letter is valuable for giving the family realistic expectations for the assessment. It usually includes information regarding time and location of the interview, discussion of fees and payment procedures, a general format of the assessment process with an estimated time of completion and a brief explanation of the questionnaires and measures enclosed. The general information questionnaires are designed to provide the clinician with information typically needed for assessment purposes. Having a parent record such standard information at home saves the family time and expense. We have found that useful content areas to include in a general questionnaire are: the age, sex, and employment of all family members; reasons for requesting the upcoming assessment; educational history of each family member and developmental and medical information regarding the child. The standardized measures useful for the pre-interview packet are short behavior checklists of home and school behavior problems which the parent can complete without instructions beyond those included on the measure. Examples include the Eyberg Child Behavior Inventory (Robinson, Eyberg, & Ross, 1980) and the Achenbach Child Behavior Checklist

(Achenbach, 1979) for the parents to fill in, and the Teacher Rating Scale (Edelbrock & Achenbach, 1985) and the Sutter-Eyberg School Behavior Inventory (Funderburk & Eyberg, 1989), which the parent can have completed by the child's teacher. Such measures are easily scored after the family's arrival at the clinic or hospital but before initial contact with the interviewer. The entire pre-interview packet can be either brought by the family to the scheduled session or mailed back well ahead of the family's arrival.

The next preparation procedure is the interviewer's review of professional literature relevant to the child's problem as described during the referral contact. If there appear to be areas of concern outside the interviewer's expertise, such as limitations imposed by unusual neurological conditions or psychological adjustment to physical illnesses, it will be important to obtain a general overview of the problem, its physical effects, and its treatment. For example, if the child has cystic fibrosis it will be helpful to have knowledge regarding the illness so that the child's compliance to medical regimens and the child's concerns about the future course of the disease can be assessed. Obviously, if the clinician is working primarily in a medical setting, such information is crucial for the upcoming interview.

The previous steps generate important information that must be remembered during the interview itself. Making a brief list of general topic areas relevant to understanding the life events important to most children (favorite activities, family compositions, favorite friends, school activities, etc.) as well as of selected topic areas determined through review of the child's hospital chart or pre-interview packet will assist in maintaining both organization and smooth transitions between content domains.

Finally, the interviewer must arrange a setting conducive to the child interview. Here developmental considerations become quite important. For the preschool-age child, it is helpful to conduct the interview in a playroom where toys can be placed that are likely to suggest areas of discussion. A dollhouse with figures representing family members may prompt play that can lead to questioning about the child's perception of the roles and behavior of other members of his or her family. Similarly, "doctor kits" can provide a context for understanding how the child reacts to medical personnel and procedures. The playroom may be appropriate for the school-age child as well, but the contents of the room would be varied to correspond with the child's more mature interests (drawing materials, constructional activities, etc.). A teenager may be uncomfortable if taken to a playroom even if no toys are displayed. A more traditional interview setting, such as an office or consultation room, is most appropriate for this age group.

previous unpleasant medical experiences and older children may feel that they are going to be interrogated concerning their misbehavior or faults. The interviewer can help to counter initial fears by brief comments that compliment the child's appearance or dress, or that express interest in the child's current activity or any personal object the child may have brought. Of course, nonverbal behaviors, such as smiling and shaking hands, are important as well for communicating positive feelings toward the child.

In pediatric settings, the psychologist is asked by the child's medical team to conduct an assessment or to provide treatment. Sometimes the child and family may not be aware that a psychological consultation was ordered resulting in the interviewer introducing him- or herself and being met with looks of surprise or distress. This awkward situation is best prevented rather than allowed to occur and then "smoothed over" by explanation. The appropriate procedure for all medical settings is to contact the child's attending physician or resident prior to meeting the child and to inquire about the family's knowledge of the visit. If the family has not been informed, then a request should be made that the reasons for psychological consultation be explained by a physician well ahead of the planned interview. It is wise to recontact the physician just prior to meeting the child and parents to assure that this was accomplished and that the family has agreed to the consult.

After the introduction, providing the parents and child with expectations about the structure of the session will help alleviate concerns about the interview. Children should be told that the interviewer wants to just talk (play) with them for a while and where their parents will be during the interview.

In clinical practice, it is very common for the parents to be asked to complete additional assessment instruments while the child is with the interviewer. Presenting such measures to the parents creates an opportunity to instruct the child to come with the interviewer to the office or playroom while the parents work on the material they were given. Alternatively, in the hospital room, the materials provide a rationale for asking the parents to go to the family room where they can complete the forms without distraction while the interviewer talks with the child. If the assessment is to include a family interview or standardized direct observation of parent-child interactions (e.g., Eyberg & Robinson, 1983), the child can also be informed that the parents will join him or her a bit later.

The major problem that may be encountered at this stage of the interview is the child's refusal to separate from parents. For children below age three and one-half years, separation fears are quite common. If at all possible, children in this age group should be interviewed with the parent(s) or other trusted adult present. For older children, separation problems are minimized if the interviewer has been successful in establishing expectancies and communicating friendliness and warmth during the greeting process. In addition, such difficulties are less likely to occur if the interviewer directs the child with instructions rather than questions. "Would you like to come with me now?" implies that the child may appropriately refuse, while, "Come with me to the playroom (office), Pam," directs the child to comply. If a child does refuse to separate from the parents, alternative strategies for conducting the assessment should be considered. The entire family can initially be seen together and after a period of nonthreatening, positive interaction the parents can be asked to leave while the interviewer and the child "get to know one another better." Allowing the parents to sit just outside the door and assuring the parents that "things will be just fine" will increase both the child's and parent's comfort with the separation. If the child continues to express significant distress, it is recommended that further attempts at separation be abandoned and that the family be interviewed together.

Beginning the Interview

The assessment interview is likely to be an entirely new experience for the child. Because children are almost always apprehensive about the interview, it is essential that the early part of the session be spent in activity or conversation that calms the child and allows for opportunity to continue building rapport.

Explaining the purpose of the interview is a good way to begin. We believe that even very young children should be involved as informed participants in the interview to the greatest extent possible; children should be told in a way they can understand what the interview is for and how it will benefit them. The interview might be started by saying, "We're going to be talking (and playing) together today so that I can learn as much as possible about you and any problems you or your family may be having. I'm going to think of things that you or your parents might do to help with any problems I learn about." An alternative beginning is for the interviewer to determine what ideas the child has about the interview and then provide clarification for any misconceptions. An open-ended question, such as, "What did your mom or dad tell you about the reasons you were coming here today," or "What did your doctor tell you about the reasons I was coming here today," leads to this information.

After describing the purpose of the interview, asking children what questions they may have to ask you will often provide additional opportunities to alleviate the child's concerns. For some children it is helpful to explain what a psychologist is (e.g., "A psychologist is a doctor you can talk to about what's going on and how you're feeling. Sometimes by talking we can figure out together some ways to make things better").

Before the child begins to answer any of the interviewer's questions, discussing confidentiality openly and honestly with the adolescent or school-age child acknowledges the clinician's respect for the child's autonomy and does a great deal to enhance rapport. The issue of confidentiality in relation to children and their parents is both an ethical and legal one and is discussed in detail elsewhere (e.g., APA Task Force on Legal Issues, 1982; Ehrenreich & Melton, 1983; Eisenstadt & Bodiford, 1987; Keith-Spiegel & Koocher, 1985).

Whether any interview information is confidential depends largely on the purpose of the interview. For the assessment-only interview, the interviewer should describe very clearly what the referral question is and who the information is for. In cases where the purpose of the interview is for treatment intake and the information is for the interviewer-therapist, a brief meeting with the entire family to establish "ground rules" before interviewing the child individually is advisable. In this meeting, the interviewer can request that the child and parents agree that information given by family members privately will not be revealed to others without permission of the individual concerned. It is important to add to the agreement that the interviewer will break confidentiality only if it is necessary to protect someone from harm or if a court orders the interviewer to do so. In most cases, the family will agree to these rules. If they do not, at least the interviewer has made explicit the limits of his or her ability to keep information confidential and has clearly communicated to the child that the interview is not an attempt to trick or coerce.

In the play interview with a preschool-age child, discussion of confidentiality is not necessary. Instead the interviewer moves from an age appropriate description of the purpose of the interview to providing structure for the child by briefly explaining the playroom rules (if indicated) and suggesting that the child choose a toy from those present. After the child has initiated play, the interviewer can begin describing the child's activity. Joining the play if invited or imitating the child's activities through parallel play assists in demonstrating to the child that the interviewer is someone who is interested and accepting. Reflective statements during these early moments of the interview will communicate to the child that the interviewer is also someone who understands and listens.

Obtaining the Child's Report

After a positive relationship between the interviewer and the child has begun to emerge, the process of systematic information gathering can begin. It is important to keep in mind that the interview is not the only assessment tool of the child psychologist and that standardized measures, interviews with parents and teachers, and structured direct observations can be used to answer many specific questions. The interview content focuses primarily on the child's perceptions, thoughts, and feelings that relate to the purpose of the interview.

As a general rule, topics are introduced in an order that moves gradually from least threatening to those that relate most directly to the presenting problems. This allows time for the child to become comfortable with the interviewer and to develop some degree of trust that his or her comments or opinions will be respected. In addition, the interviewer will be more likely to understand the child's perception of problematic events after the child has described his or her understanding of the context in which the problems occur.

When threatening topics are presented to the child, the child may become evasive or refuse to continue speaking. This resistance can block the interviewer from learning important information. If the situation is not handled sensitively, rapport can be seriously damaged.

Resistance in the interview can represent either avoidance of anxiety-producing thoughts and feelings related to the current topic or avoidance of real or imagined consequences for revealing the requested information. If the source of the resistance appears to be the former, the interviewer can redirect the child's attention away from the topic momentarily and then approach the issue more gradually. With a preschool-age child, descriptions of the child's concurrent play activity eases the tension and gives the interviewer time to plan his or her strategy for guiding the child back to the topic. With an older child, the interviewer can describe the child's uneasiness and suggest that the topic might be discussed further at a later time. For example, a statement such as, "I see you're upset and not wanting to talk about this right now. I think it's important though and we may come back to it later," results in the interviewer relieving tension and leaving open the possibility of returning to the topic.

Sometimes the child's resistance appears to be a response to possible consequences for revealing information. If a trusting and safe environment has been established in the interview prior to this point, then the possibility should be considered that the child has been instructed not to discuss a particular matter. If this seems to be the case, the interviewer may acknowledge that children are sometimes warned to avoid talking about certain things and then directly ask if this is the problem. An earlier example of the appropriate use of closed-ended questions illustrates this situation. We believe it is important to convey clearly to the child that withholding information is his or her choice and that the interviewer will not think less of the child for refusing to talk about a specific issue.

Under certain circumstances, it is necessary or desirable to interview a child and one or both parents together. If this is due to necessity, as when the child refuses to separate, then the parent can be asked to assume an unobtrusive position in the interviewing area and the interview process can proceed as planned. Unfortunately, in this situation the parent often becomes an uninvited participant when the child chooses not to answer a question or gives an answer that the parent perceives as incorrect. The parent is most likely trying to be helpful, but such interruptions will slow rapport-building and inhibit expression of the child's own ideas and feelings. Unwanted contributions of this sort can usually be stopped by turning to the parent and saying calmly and pleasantly, "I appreciate your help, but right now I'd like to hear what Trevor thinks about things. I'll be asking you similar questions later."

If the family interview is desirable, as when the clinician wishes to observe the interactions between child and parents while family problems are discussed, then care must be taken to include all family members equally. Recently we observed an interview with a mother and an 11-year-old boy during which the interviewer and the mother quickly began discussing important issues regarding the child's fights with his siblings and essentially ignored the child. The boy fidgeted in his chair, looked around the room, tried to make a few comments, and eventually settled back to listen intently to the adult conversation about him. Clearly, no rapport was established with this child! Frequent open-ended questions directed toward the child such as, "What do you think about that, Drew?" and responses to the child's spontaneous comments on the subject would easily engage the child in the interview process and give him the message that his opinion was a valued and respected contribution.

Closing the Interview

Once the interviewer has covered all major areas of interest for the assessment, it is important to let the child know that the interviewer appreciated his or her help. Closure for the interview should also summarize the major topic areas discussed, paying special attention to the issues or problems expressed by the child. A final effort should be made to demonstrate the importance of the child's input and participation by asking a question that provides opportunity for additional child comments, such as, "What else do you think I might need to know about you or the problem(s) that I haven't asked about yet?". Next, the child should be informed about further assessment that may take place and reminded again what the interviewer plans to do with the information given during the interview. Finally, if recommendations are to be made for treatment of identified problems, and the clinician has begun to formulate such plans, the child should be informed of these ideas.

DIRECTIONS FOR FUTURE RESEARCH

Although process in the adult interview has been examined (e.g., Matarazzo & Wiens, 1972) and many process studies of adult psychotherapy have been reported (see Orlinsky and Howard, 1986, for a review), process analyses of the child interview have not kept pace. Given that a distinguishing characteristic of the discipline of child psychology is emphasis on an empirical approach to assessment and intervention, it is imperative that researchers begin to examine the process variables considered so important in the child interview.

Descriptive analyses of interviewer and child interactions would provide valuable information for the development of further research efforts. Direct observation of interviewer and child behaviors during child interviews would generate data that could then be studied to determine the probability of occurrence of specific classes of child behavior (e.g., "talk") given the prior occurrence of specific classes of interviewer behavior (e.g., "reflect"). If significant sequential relationships were identified, interviewer behavior could be systematically manipulated in subsequent studies to test for significant functional relationships. Patterson and Forgatch (1985) provide an example of the use of this methodology to examine the effect of therapist behavior on behavior of adult clients during parent behavior management training. These investigators were able to demonstrate that increases in therapist's teaching and confronting produced increases in client noncompliance.

Alternatively, interviewer behaviors thought to be influential in the interview could be studied through examination of differential child response when a specific interviewer behavior is present versus absent or when one interviewing technique is compared to another. To illustrate, one group of children could be interviewed using only closed-ended questions and one group interviewed using only open-ended questions.

Dependent measures of "talk time" or "content relevant talk" would reveal which interviewing strategy produced the most desirable result.

Relating process to outcome in the context of an assessment interview is another area for future research. Operationally defining the appropriate outcome variables of a child interview involved in: (1) obtaining specific, accurate information and (2) establishing a positive relationship would provide possibilities for developing measures to assess the effectiveness of different interviewing techniques and strategies.

SUMMARY AND CONCLUSIONS

Successfully engaging a child in the interview process for the purposes of establishing rapport, gathering information, and observing the child's behavior requires the clinician to be skilled in communication techniques and interviewing strategies with children. Specific process skills and their application during the child interview are discussed in the first section of this chapter. These skills include: acknowledging, describing, reflecting, praising, questioning, summarizing, and avoiding critical statements. The second section offers a format for conducting each stage of the interview with a focus on techniques appropriate to the child's level of development and on the setting in which the interview is conducted. The lack of empirical research regarding process variables in child interviewing is noted, and a final section offers suggestions for future research.

REFERENCES

Achenbach, T.M. (1979). The child behavior profile: An empirically based system for assessing children's behavioral problems and competencies. *International Journal of Mental Health, 7*, 24–42.

American Psychological Association, Task Force on Legal Issues, Division of Child, Youth, and Family Services. (1982). *Position statement: Standards regarding consent for treatment and research involving children.*

Edelbrock, C., & Achenbach, T.M. (1985). *Manual for the Teacher's Report Form and Teacher Version of the Child Behavior Profile.* Burlington: University of Vermont.

Ehrenreich, N.S., & Melton, G.B. (1983). Ethical and legal issues in the treatment of children. In C.E. Walker & M.C. Roberts (Eds.), *Handbook of clinical child psychology* (pp. 1285–1305). New York: Wiley.

Eisenstadt, T.H., & Bodiford, C.A. (1987, June). A review of children's rights in psychological treatment. Paper presented at the meeting of the Florida Psychological Association, Orlando, FL.

Eyberg, S., & Robinson, E. (1983). Dyadic parent-child interaction coding system: A manual. *Psychological Documents, 13*, 24. (Ms. No. 2582).

Funderburk, B., & Eyberg, S. (1989). Psychometric characteristics of the Sutter-Eyberg Student Behavior Inventory: A school behavior rating scale for use with preschool. *Behavioral Assessment, 11*, pp. 297–313.

Greenspan, S.I. (1981). *The clinical interview of the child.* New York: McGraw-Hill.

Gross, A.M. (1985). Children. In M. Hersen & S.M. Turner (Eds.), *Diagnostic Interviewing* (pp. 309–335). New York: Plenum.

Harter, S. (1983). Cognitive-developmental considerations in the conduct of play therapy. In C.E. Schaefer & K.J. O'Conner (Eds.), *Handbook of play therapy* (pp. 95–127). New York: Wiley.

Kanfer, R., Eyberg, S.M., & Krahn, G.L. (1983). Interviewing strategies in child assessment. In C.E. Walker & M.C. Roberts (Eds.), *Handbook of clinical child psychology* (pp. 95–108). New York: Wiley.

Keith-Spiegel, P., & Koocher, G.P. (1985). *Ethics in psychology: Professional standards and cases.* New York: Random House.

Lapouse, R., & Monk, M.A. (1958). An epidemiologic study of behavior characteristics in children. *American Journal of Public Health, 48*, 1134–1144.

Matarazzo, J.D., & Wiens, A.N. (1972). *The interview: Research on its anatomy and structure.* Chicago: Aldine-Atherton.

Orlinsky, D.E., & Howard, K.I. (1986). Process and outcome in psychotherapy. In S.L. Garfield & A.E. Bergin (Eds.), *Handbook of Psychotherapy and Behavior Change* (3rd ed.) (pp. 311–381). New York: Wiley.

Patterson, G.R., & Forgatch, M.S. (1985). Therapist behavior as a determinant for client noncompliance: A paradox for the behavior modifier. *Journal of Consulting and Clinical Psychology, 53*, 846–851.

Reisman, J.M. (1973). *Principles of psychotherapy with children.* New York: Wiley.

Robinson, E.A., Eyberg, S., & Ross, A.W. (1980). The standardization of an inventory of child conduct problem behavior. *Journal of Clinical Child Psychology, 9*, 22–28.

Swan, G.E., & McDonald, M.C. (1978). Behavior therapy in practice: A national survey of behavior therapists. *Behavior Therapy, 9*, 799–807.

Tuma, J.M., & Sobotka, K.R. (1983). Traditional therapies with children. In T.H. Ollendick & M. Hersen (Eds.), *Handbook of child psychopathology* (pp. 391–426). New York: Plenum.

CHAPTER 5

Structured Diagnostic Interviews

KAY HODGES
JAN NEAL COOLS

INTRODUCTION

The successful use of structured interviews with adults led to the development of similar instrumentation for use with children. Disenchantment with the lack of reliability of psychiatric diagnoses, which was problematic for conducting rigorous research, provided an impetus for developing structured assessment interviews and more operationalized definitions of psychiatric diagnoses (Matarazzo, 1983). The purpose of this chapter is to provide an overview of issues relevant to structured interviews for children as well as to present in considerable detail several of these interviews. First, an overview of the development of structured interviews and a discussion of ethical issues relevant to clinical and research application will be presented.

HISTORICAL OVERVIEW

Semistructured versus Structured Interviews

Structured interviews* represent an approach quite divergent from the traditional play interview. In a play interview, the examiner typ-

---

*The studies described in this chapter have primarily utilized DSM-III diagnoses. However, the structured interviews described herein have recently been modified to reflect changes that appear in DSM-III-R.

109

ically asks the children about themselves and/or why their parents brought them to a clinic. Observations about the child's nonverbal actions and spontaneous discussion are made. However, the assumption that a child cannot respond to direct questions about symptomatology and subjective experience appears to have been largely abandoned. In fact, diagnostic play interviews sometimes took the form of semistructured interviewing, in which the clinician would loosely inquire about a set of basic topics (Greenspan, 1981; Lourie & Rieger, 1974; Simmons, 1974). Of the available interviews, the Mental Health Assessment Form (Kestenbaum & Bird, 1978) as well as the original (1978) version of the Child Assessment Schedule (CAS) (Hodges, Kline, Fitch, McKnew, & Cytryn, 1981; Hodges, Kline, Stern, Cytryn, & McKnew, 1982; and Hodges, McKnew, Cytryn, Stern, & Kline, 1982) represent more semistructured interviews. Such semistructured interviews have a number of common characteristics, including: (1) a set of suggested topics and/or set of tentative questions that can be used, (2) an understanding that there can be considerable variation in the presentation of these questions, depending on the characteristics of the specific child, (3) response items which are structured, (i.e., the items which the clinician rates or judges to be present or absent), and (4) information relevant to diagnosis is intentionally obtained, but making a differential diagnosis based solely on the child's responses is usually not possible given the body of information generated.

A semistructured approach has certain advantages, compared to highly structured formats, especially in working with younger, preadolescent children. It permits matching the task demands of the interview to the child's developmental level. Techniques known to be useful with younger or more cognitively and/or emotionally immature children can be used, such as: encouraging the child to draw representations of their family or feelings; employing therapeutic toys; and utilizing visual representations, for instance, constructing a "calendar" with the child to help in reporting on time spans. With the semistructured interview, it is assumed that other sources of information will be incorporated to augment what the child can provide, especially the parent report. However, this is not essentially different from the assumptions that are made about most structured interviews.

In contrast, structured diagnostic interviews tend to have the following characteristics: (1) the interview questions are specified; (2) the information generated should permit making a diagnosis; and (3) the administration of the interview should be standardized across interviewees. As with the semistructured interviews, the response items are of course standardized. In addition, users expect that psychometric data should be provided, such as information relevant to reliability and validity. The users of the interviews anticipate that in their application of the instrument, it will be as reliable and valid as presented in the previous psychometric studies. This is similar to the assumptions made about traditional psychological tests. This expectation is of course based on the assumption that several conditions are met including, at minimum, that: (1) the interview is administered in its standardized or recommended format; (2) interrater reliability is established for inexperienced raters; and (3) the population being studied is sufficiently similar to the validity samples to permit the assumption of generalizability.

Of the various interviews, the Diagnostic Interview Schedule for Children (DISC) (Costello, Edelbrock, Dulcan, Kalas, & Klaric, 1984) could be considered the most structured, since absolutely no variation in the interview is advised. The reason for this lack of variation is that the DISC was designed for epidemiological research and thus would be administered by lay interviewers. At the other end of the continuum, the CAS has three versions which vary from semistructured to highly structured.

For research purposes, the structured interviews tend to be preferred. However, a case can be made for using more semistructured approaches, which have often been used in developmental research. From this perspective, the interviewer is seen as needing the flexibility to vary the administration to meet the needs of the particular subject. The goal is to obtain valid information from the child, utilizing reasonable adaptations as needed. In contrast, the rigor is applied to the method of interpreting or coding the information provided by the child (e.g., clear guidelines as to how to identify a symptom such as obsessions).

In clinical practice, both the semistructured and structured interviews can be helpful in comprehensively and systematically obtaining information. Especially for clinicians working in outpatient settings, this can be somewhat reassuring in regard to professional liability issues, since the clinician would have inquired about topics thought to be critical to a thorough diagnostic examination. Also, use of these interviews can lead to a somewhat more efficient recording of the interviewer's notes and report-writing. When utilizing the more structured interviews, it is typically necessary to supplement the structured diagnostic interview with more traditional clinical inquiry since one does not necessarily substitute for the other (Carlson, 1983). The interviews differ in the degree to which they inquire about various areas of functioning which are typically incorporated in a traditional interview (e.g., family relations).

To the extent that these interviews are useful clinically, they can be helpful tools in training clinicians. Their use insures that trainees learn how to do a "review of systems" of psychological issues. The interviews often provide clear definitions of critical terminology (e.g., terms for characterizing verbalizations and thought processes, such as "circumstantiality"). In any case, in training clinicians, it seems wise to insure that they have knowledge of semistructured or structured interviews as well as develop the traditional clinical skills which have come to be valued by the profession (e.g., as described in Lourie & Rieger, 1974).

Development of Structured Interviews

Since approximately 1975, a number of child clinicians and researchers in the United States began experimenting with a more structured approach to interviewing children and/or their parents about the child's symptomatology. The major child researchers who led these early efforts included Rutter in England (Rutter & Graham, 1968), Herjanic (Herjanic, Herjanic, Brown, & Wheatt, 1975), Kestenbaum (Kestenbaum & Bird, 1978), Hodges (Hodges & Fitch, 1979), as well as Puig-Antich and his colleagues (Puig-Antich & Chambers, 1978).

Rutter's use of a more structured and systematic psychiatric assessment in the Isle of Wight epidemiological study demonstrated the usefulness of such procedures (Rutter, Tizard, Yule, Graham, & Whitmore, 1976). However, it is noteworthy that the psychiatric interview about the child's symptoms administered to the parent was lengthier and more elaborate than the direct interview with the child. This was in keeping with the practices at the time—the parent was interviewed about the child's development and symptoms, while the child typically was engaged in a play therapy interview in which his or her symptoms might or might not be directly inquired about (Lourie & Rieger, 1974). In contrast to existing practices, a systematic, direct interview procedure for the child was incorporated in this early work by Rutter.

Kestenbaum and Bird's (1978) efforts resulted in the Mental Health Assessment Form. This is a semistructured procedure for use in rating the behavior and responses of children during an interview. It provided a very general suggested line of questioning to aid the examiner, and there was no attempt to standardize the presentation of the interview. In contrast, The Diagnostic Interview for Children and Adolescents (DICA), developed by Herjanic (Herjanic et al., 1975), represented an attempt to standardize both the presentation of questions to the child as well as the response items to be rated by the interviewer. The DICA was modeled after the predecessors of the Diagnostic Interview Schedule (Robins, Helzer, Croughan, & Ratcliff, 1981) developed by a group of researchers in St. Louis, at the Washington University School of Medicine. Robins et al.

were concerned with the arduous task of developing explicit clinical criteria for psychiatric disorders and a standardized method for eliciting the data about these criteria (i.e., a structured interview) (Matarazzo, 1983). Likewise, the Schedule for Affective Disorders and Schizophrenia for School Age Children (K-SADS), developed by Puig-Antich and his colleagues (Puig-Antich & Chambers, 1978), was directly modeled from an adult interview developed by researchers at Columbia University, the Schedule of Affective Disorders (SADS) (Endicott & Spitzer, 1978).

The Child Assessment Schedule (CAS), (Hodges et al., 1981) was developed from a traditional child clinical interview, with the intent of obtaining information relevent to diagnosis, treatment planning, as well as assessment of coping skills. It also provides for standardized questions and corresponding response items. Subsequently, the Interview Schedule for Children (ISC) was developed as a result of the work of Kovacs and her colleagues (Kovacs, 1983) in their efforts to develop an assessment procedure for their longitudinal study of children with depression. An additional interview, the Diagnostic Interview Schedule for Children (DISC) emerged as a result of interest shown by the epidemiological branch of the National Institute of Mental Health (NIMH) in developing a child interview parallel to the Diagnostic Interview Schedule (DIS) (Costello et al., 1984).

These efforts at developing structured interviews for children have been productive in terms of facilitating research in child psychopathology. The CAS (Kashani, Orvaschel, Rosenberg, & Reid, 1987; Verhulst, Berden, & Sanders-Woudstra, 1985), the DICA (Kashani et al., 1987), the DISC (Costello et al., 1984), and the K-SADS (Kashani et al., 1983) have all been employed in epidemiological studies. These interviews have also been used to study children who are at risk for psychiatric illnesses. This literature includes children who are at risk because they have psychiatrically disturbed parents, have experienced stressful life events, or have physical illnesses. The use of a structured interview approach, combined with the utilization of operational diagnostic criteria, hopefully results in more reliable diagnostic decisions or quantification of symptoms and more homogeneous study samples. Even when different diagnostic interviews are used across studies, the results are hopefully more comparable, resulting in a more efficient accumulation of the relevant knowledge base.

ETHICAL ISSUES RELATED TO STRUCTURED INTERVIEWS

Structured interviews have been utilized for both clinical and research purposes. As such, the ethical principles that apply in the areas of research (American Psychological Association, 1982; Society for Research in Child Development, 1973) as well as clinical practice (American Psychological Association, 1981) need to be heeded.

There are a number of ethical issues to be considered with the use of structured interviews for research purposes. The major questions center around the potentially harmful nature of the questions, such as suicidal ideation and the researcher's role if children identify themselves at some risk (i.e., having suicidal ideation). Two research studies have shown none or minimal psychological risk to children who were administered structured interviews (Herjanic, Hudson, & Kotloff, 1976; Lewis, Gorsky, Cohen, & Hartmark, 1985). No parents reported any subsequent harmful behavior or events. Also, while suicide in latency-aged children is very rare, studies with psychiatric and community samples indicate that it is not rare for children to have transient thoughts of killing themselves (Hodges & Siegel, 1985). A second ethical issue involves deciding in advance who will be notified if the child is seen as potentially at risk and addressing this issue in the consent form (Burbach, Farha, & Thorpe, 1986).

PSYCHOMETRIC REVIEW OF THREE STRUCTURED INTERVIEWS

In the discussion that follows, three interviews will be extensively reviewed, specifically: the Child Assessment Schedule (CAS), the Diagnostic Interview for Children and Adolescents (DICA), and the Diagnostic Interview Schedule for Children (DISC). Since the Mental Health Assessment Form has only reliability data available (Kestenbaum & Bird, 1978), no detailed review is warranted. Two of the structured interviews, the K-SADS and the ISC, are not included in this review of general interviews for children. They were primarily developed for selecting subjects in research on child and adolescent depression. Moreover, data on these interviews, as administered to the child, have not been reported by their authors. Additional information on the ISC and the K-SADS is available in a variety of reviews (Costello, 1986; Hodges & Siegel, 1985; Kovacs, 1986; Puig-Antich, Chambers, & Tabrizi, 1983; Ryan et al., 1987).

For each interview, the instrument will be described, along with its administration, scoring, and interpretation. This will be followed by a review of the data reflecting on reliability and validity. Each of the interviews to be reviewed has a parallel version to be administered to the parent. However, for the purposes of this review, which focuses on the child's ability to self-report, only data relevant to the interview when administered to the child will be included. Even if separate interview data from various informants are to be clinically interpreted, from a scientific perspective, it is important to be informed about the psychometric properties of interviews when children are the reporters, as opposed to adults. Table 5.1 provides summary information about the basic characteristics and types of psychometric data available for each of the three interviews.

Before proceeding, it may be helpful to comment about the kappa statistic, which has increasingly come to be a preferred reliability statistic for dichotomous data because it corrects for chance agreement. There is no clear agreement in the literature regarding the clinical interpretation of the kappa (Bartko & Carpenter, 1976). In this review, a kappa of .50 or greater will be used as a general guideline suggesting an acceptable value and .70 or greater as good (Costello et al., 1984; Spitzer, Fleiss, & Endicott, 1978). Also, it is important to be mindful that kappa is sensitive to the base rates of disorders, with a drop in kappa with low prevalence (Robins, 1985). Thus, caution should be exercised in comparing kappa values across studies.

THE CHILD ASSESSMENT SCHEDULE

Description

The CAS was developed from a traditional child clinical interview. Many questions are open-ended so the child is free to make spontaneous comments about complaints or problems (e.g., feelings about parental figures). There are three sections to the interview: content area questions, onset and duration questions, and interviewer observational judgments. In the first part, the interviewer asks the child a set of questions pertaining to school, friends, activities and hobbies, family, fears, worries, self-image, mood (especially sadness), somatic concerns, expression of anger, and thought disorder symptomatology. In the second section, symptoms identified in the first part of the CAS are evaluated for onset and duration. These questions are presented at the end of the interview because interjecting them in the interview, after clusters of diagnostically-related symptoms, appears to reduce reliability (i.e., the children learn to respond negatively because to do otherwise results in repeatedly being asked numerous questions about onset and duration, which are cognitively difficult for children).

After the interview is completed, the examiner records his/her observations of the child for 53 behaviors. Each answer is scored as

TABLE 5.1　Characteristics of Child/Adolescent Interviews

	CAS	DICA	DISC
Description			
Degree of structure	Semistructured to structured	Highly structured	Highly structured
Number of questions	Approx. 150	266	264
Response options	Yes/no/ambiguous	Yes/no	Yes/no/sometimes
Time for completion	45–70 min.	60–90 min.	60 min. or more
Parental version available	P-CAS	DICA-P	DISC-P
Interviewer	Clinician recommended	Lay or clinician	Lay or clinician
Scoring manual available	Yes	No	No
Information Generated			
Scales	Total score 9 symptom scales 11 content area scales	None	Total score 27 symptom scales
Diagnoses	Computer algorithms DSM-III & DSM-III-R	Computer algorithms DSM-III & DSM-III-R	Computer algorithms DSM-III[a]

Psychometric Data Reported on Child Version of Interviews[b]

	CAS	DICA	DISC
Reliability: Interrater			
For diagnostic agreement	Yes[c]	No	Yes[c]
For item-by-item agreement	Yes	Yes	Yes
For total interview score	Yes	No	Yes
For scale scores related to diagnoses	Yes	No	No
For scale scores related to spheres of functioning	Yes	No	No

(Continued)

TABLE 5.1 *(Continued)*

	CAS	DICA	DISC
Reliability: Test-Retest			
For diagnostic agreement	Yes	Yes	Yes
For item-by-item agreement	Yes	No	No
For total interview score	Yes	No	Yes
For scale scores related to diagnoses	Yes	No	Yes
For scale scores related to spheres of functioning	Yes	No	No
Validity: Contrast Group			
Comparing psychiatric versus nonpsychiatric samples	Yes	No	Yes
Comparing psychiatric patients differing in severity of illness level	Yes	No	No
Comparing disturbed versus nondisturbed children from community samples	Yes	No	No
Validity: Parent–Child Concordance			
Between a parent and child interview:			
for diagnostic agreement	No	Yes	Yes
for total interview score	Yes	No	Yes
for scale scores related to diagnoses	Yes	No	Yes
for scale scores related to spheres of functioning	Yes	No	No
Between parent questionnaire and child interview	Yes	No	Yes

[a] DSM-III-R version only available for parent version of DISC.

[b] Yes/no category in chart reflects on the existence of relevant psychometric data, not whether the actual results support the interview's reliability or validity. See text for relevant comments.

[c] These were not primarily psychometric studies; the results were not reported separately for various diagnoses, limiting the yield of information.

"Yes/True," "No/False," "Ambiguous," or "Not Scorable." The response items are phrased such that an affirmative response always indicates the presence of symptomatology. The CAS takes approximately 45 to 70 minutes to administer, depending on the child's age, symptomatology, and style of relating. Table 5.2 contains example items for the CAS.

The CAS was designed to be used primarily with children aged 7 to 12 years old. However, it has also been successfully used with younger children with above average cognitive and language abilities and with

TABLE 5.2 Example Items from CAS[a]

Examples from Part I—Questions Asked of the Child

Sample from Worries and Concerns Section[b]		*No*	*NS*	*Amb*	*Yes*[c]
Many children worry about different things, do you have worries? Tell me about them. Anything else?	Denies any worries	____	____	____	____97
(If desired, ask about response items as follows:)					
Now I am going to tell you some worries that some children have. You tell me if these are worries for you.					
• Do you worry about bad things like storms, fire?	Excessive worry about natural disaster (e.g., fire, flood, storms, dark) or external concerns (i.e., lose job).	____	____	____	____98
• Do you worry about your parents or other people in your family?					
• becoming sick?	Worries that a family member is or will become sick.	____	____	____	____99 SA
• dying or getting hurt?	Worries that a family member will die or be harmed.	____	____	____	____100 SA

118

(continued)

TABLE 5.2 *(Continued)*

Examples from Part I—Questions Asked of the Child

Sample from Worries and Concerns Section[b]		No	NS	Amb	Yes[c]
• arguing?	Worries that parents will argue (verbal).	____	____	____	____101
• physically fighting or getting hurt?	Worries that parents will fight (physical).	____	____	____	____102
• getting a divorce or leaving?	Worries about marital separation, divorce, or that a family member will leave.	____	____	____	____103

Examples from Part II—Onset and Duration Questions

Separation Anxiety (SA)

How long have you had this problem? (e.g., felt upset when you were away from your parents?; worried a lot about your parents?)	*Minimum duration:* Last 2 weeks (should be current or recent)	____	____	____	____251
Has anything happened that made you start worrying about your mom or dad (or that you might get lost or kidnapped)?	*Unrealistic:* Worry about harm befalling major attachment figures or worry about being separated from them is unrealistic.	____	____	____	____252

[a] From Hodges (1985).

[b] Additional diagnostic items for Separation Anxiety (SA) appear in sections thematically related to the content of the item (e.g., school refusal in the section about school).

[c] NS = Not Scorable; Amb = Ambiguous.

adolescents. For the latter, Runyan and his colleagues (Runyan, Everson, Edelsohn, Hunter, & Coulter, 1988) supplemented the CAS with questions about substance use and sexually related experiences. There are three versions available for the CAS, which roughly correspond to the task demands appropriate for very young children (i.e., 5- to 7-year-olds) (the original version dated 1978), preadolescent children (the second revision dated 1983/85), and adolescents (the third revision dated 1986). In the most recent version of the CAS, items relevant to the Research Diagnostic Criteria (Spitzer, Endicott, & Robins, 1978) for endogenous depression have been added. For all three versions, the content of the core items and the general format is retained, with the latter versions primarily adding elaborations.

The CAS was originally developed with the intent that it would be administered by persons who are very familiar with the instrument and who have had experience in interviewing and assessing children. This usually requires a minimum of a master's degree in a mental health field, with expertise in the area of childhood diagnosis and psychopathology. However, the more structured versions of the interview have been used by trained laymen (Hodges, McKnew, Burbach, & Roebuck, 1987). A parent form of the CAS (P-CAS), which parallels the child interview, yields the same diagnoses and scores as the CAS. For research applications, it is generally recommended that the information from the CAS and the P-CAS be generated separately and retained. In addition, an integrated clinical diagnosis(es) can be made which is based on consideration of both interviews as well as information from other significant sources. The same approach is also helpful in clinical applications, but with the parent(s) and child preferably being interviewed by the same interviewer.

Detailed guidelines for administering, scoring, and interpreting the interview are contained in two manuscripts, the "Manual for the Child Assessment Schedule" (Hodges, 1985) and the "Guidelines to Aid in Establishing Interrater Reliability with the Child Assessment Schedule" (Hodges, 1983).

The information generated by the CAS can be interpreted in three formats: (1) clinical interpretation; (2) diagnoses generated either from the child's or parent's responses; and (3) quantitative scores. The following diagnoses can be made with the CAS: attention deficit disorders, conduct disorders, anxiety disorders of childhood or adolescence (separation anxiety and overanxious), schizoid disorder, oppositional disorder, enuresis, encopresis, major depressive episode, dysthymia disorder, obsessive compulsive disorder, and phobic disorders. In addition, screening questions are asked for numerous other diagnoses to identify whether there is sufficient symptomatology to warrant further inquiry. All the diagnostic criteria are not included for these rare diagnoses, because to do so would make the interview clinically impractical by burdening it with questions not needed for most psychiatrically referred children. The manual maps CAS items to the specific DSM-III (American Psychiatric Association, 1980) criteria for each disorder. The manual has been updated also to provide for the DSM-III-R (American Psychiatric Association, 1987) criteria.

In addition to generating diagnoses, several quantitative scores can be derived from the CAS which can be useful in making group comparisons. The CAS is scored for total pathology, content areas, and symptom complexes. The total pathology score, which is the sum of the total number of items endorsed by the child, is an indication of the child's overall level of symptomatology. Scores can be calculated for the content areas of school, friends, activities and hobbies, family, etc., in the same manner as the total pathology score. Scores can also be generated for the "symptom complex scales," which are composed of the items contributing to the various diagnostic categories (e.g., for attention deficit disorder, conduct disorder, etc.).

Reliability Studies

Four studies, conducted at independent research settings, have evaluated the interrater reliability of the CAS. In the studies in which correlation coefficients were determined, the total CAS score correlations were consistently above .90, with the individual content and symptom complex scale scores having moderate to high reliability (Hodges, McKnew et al., 1982; Turner, Beidel, & Costello, 1987; Verhulst et al., 1985). Two studies have utilized the kappa statistic, one to examine item by item correspondence between raters (Edelsohn, 1985; Hodges, Kline et al., 1982) and another to determine diagnostic concordance (Turner, Beidel, & Costello, 1987). In the Edelsohn (1985) study, kappa values reflected high concordance when calculated for either unweighted or weighted kappas as well as when calculated for each item of the CAS per child or per rater pair. High diagnostic concordance (K=.82) was observed in Turner et al (1987).

A test-retest study (Hodges, Cools, & McKnew, 1986, in press) demonstrated satisfactory to good test-retest reliability for the following diagnostic categories: conduct disorders, oppositional disorder, major depressive episode, dysthymia, and separation anxiety. DSM-III diagnoses were based solely on the interview with the child and were computer generated. Test-retest reliability was also determined for summed symptom scores for the total interview, the diagnostic categories, and the content areas. All the correlations were significant ($p < .01$), indicating good reliability for the total CAS score and the various scale scores.

Validity Studies

The validity of the CAS has been addressed by studies conducted across several independent research sites (Hodges, 1987). Several methods have been used, including contrast group, correspondence with self-report, correspondence with parental report, correspondence with clinical judgment, and response to interventions. The evidence for each of these will be briefly discussed.

Evidence of contrast group validity has been generated by three studies (Hodges, Kline et al., 1982; Hodges, Kline, Barbero, & Flanery, 1985; Hodges, Kline, Barbero, & Woodruff, 1985; Verhulst, Althaus, & Berden, 1987). Psychiatric inpatients, outpatients, and nonclinic controls were compared in Hodges, Kline et al. (1982). The total pathology score on the CAS, and most of the content area scale scores, differentiated between normal controls and psychiatric patients, as well as between psychiatric inpatients and outpatients, who differed on severity of symptomatology. The CAS correctly classified two-thirds of the subjects into the three groups (i.e., controls, outpatients, inpatients). Using inpatient or outpatient status as a criterion for psychiatric illness, the total CAS score had a sensitivity of 78% and a specificity of 84%. Additional studies by Hodges and her colleagues (Hodges, Kline, Barbero, & Flanery, 1985; Hodges, Kline, Barbero, & Woodruff, 1985) compared pediatric patients with psychosomatic recurrent abdominal pain to behaviorally disordered and healthy controls. There were significant differences between the three groups in the expected direction on the CAS total score and the symptom complex (diagnostic) scales.

A third study by Verhulst and his colleagues (Verhulst et al., 1987, Verhulst et al., 1985) demonstrated contrast group validity between disturbed and nondisturbed children. The independent morbidity criterion used was psychiatric judgment of a child's functioning based solely on another interview administered to the parents. In this study with 116 children, selected from a larger epidemiological study of Dutch children, the CAS was administered to the children and a semistructured interview, developed by Graham and Rutter (1968) and modified by Richman, Stevenson, and Graham (1982), was administered to the parents. Analysis of covariance revealed significant differences between the two morbidity groups on the CAS total score, 8 out of 10 content areas, and the observational judgment section. In addition, a stepwise discriminant analysis was conducted. The CAS correctly classified 76% of the cases as either disturbed versus nondisturbed.

Evidence of validity has also been provided by findings demonstrating correspondence between the CAS and reports from the children, the parents, and clinicians. The CAS depression symptom complex score correlated significantly (r=.53) with self-report on the Children's Depression Inventory (Kovacs, 1978), as did the CAS anxiety complex scale score (r=.54) with the State Trait Anxiety Inventory for Children (Spielberger, 1973), (Hodges, Kline et al., 1982). In addition, significant relationships have been observed between the CAS and maternal report on the Child Behavior Checklist (CBCL; Achenbach & Edelbrock, 1983) on their respective total pathology scores, as well as on their comparable hyperactivity scales, aggression-conduct disorder scales, and depression scales (Edelsohn, 1985; Hodges, Kline et al., 1982; Verhulst et al., 1985).

In the study by Verhulst et al. (1987), parent-child concordance was examined, comparing the CAS to the Graham-Rutter parent interview on content areas which were reasonably similar. There were significant correlations between the total scores for the two interviews (r=.58, p<.001), as well as for 8 out of 10 comparable content areas. These studies by Verhulst and his colleagues (Verhulst et al., 1985; Verhulst et al., 1987) also demonstrated correspondence between the CAS total score and a clinician's rating on a five-point severity scale (r=.61). The rating psychiatrist had access to both child and parent interviews (Verhulst et al., 1987).

Additional evidence of validity is offered by two studies which have utilized the CAS to evaluate response to intervention. In the Runyan et al. (1988) study with sexually abused children, the intervention was psychosocial, and in a study by Bousha (1985) with acting-out children, response to psychotherapy was evaluated. Runyan and his colleagues determined the reduction in symptoms from initial evaluation compared to follow-up five months later. (Data from their 18-month follow-up are not yet available.) They were interested in the effects of two social/legal interventions: efforts to criminally prosecute the perpetrator and court testimony by the child. The symptoms for the children uninvolved in criminal prosecution, compared to the children who were involved in prosecution of the abuser, were significantly more reduced at follow-up on the CAS total score as were the depression, anxiety, and conduct disorder scale scores. However, if criminal prosecution was pursued, it was additionally found that those children who had an opportunity to testify in court experienced significant reduction in their symptomatology, as reflected on the CAS total score, anxiety scale, and conduct disorder scale. These results suggest that waiting for criminal prosecution of the perpetrator has a negative impact on the mental health of these sexually abused children. However, allowing the child to testify in juvenile court may speed resolution of the child's distress.

In the study by Bousha (1985), the CAS was successfully used in evaluating the effectiveness of treatment of children referred for acting-out problems. Treatment was associated with a significant reduction on the total CAS score and conduct disorder scale score, compared to being in a wait-list control condition. In addition, these results paralleled the pre-post treatment effects observed for the other evaluation measures, including the CBCL.

An offspring study by Turner et al. (1987) compared a group of healthy school children to the offspring of parents with: an anxiety disorder, dysthymia, or no psychiatric disorder. These four groups were compared on the CAS total score and the various content areas as well as on presence or absence of a DSM-III diagnosis, based on the CAS computer algorithm. The multivariate analysis of variance revealed significant differences between the four groups on the CAS total score and on 9 out of 11 content areas. The offspring of nondisturbed parents and the normal school children scored significantly lower on the CAS total score as well as on a number of content areas, compared to the offspring of dysthymic and anxiety-disordered parents. In regard to diagnosis, children of anxiety-disordered parents were nine times as likely to have any disorder, compared to children of normal parents, and were seven times as likely to have an anxiety disorder. In addition, the children of anxiety patients were at least twice as likely to have a diagnosis than offspring of dysthymic patients.

Generalizability

The CAS has been used with numerous target populations ranging in type and severity of symptomatology. In general, there is evidence for reliability and validity when used with the following populations: healthy normals, psychiatric outpatients, psychiatric inpatients, and children at risk whose range of pathology and distress level varies from adequately adjusted to severely disturbed. The strength of the CAS appears to be that it differentiates well between disturbed and nondisturbed children and can also make distinctions in types of symptomatology (e.g., anxiety, depression, and conduct disorder symptoms). Both the quantitative scores and the generation of DSM-III diagnoses have been successfully applied. There was no evidence of sex or age differences in concordance between parent and child report (Verhulst et al., 1987).

THE DIAGNOSTIC INTERVIEW FOR CHILDREN AND ADOLESCENTS

Description

The Diagnostic Interview for Children and Adolescents (DICA) is a highly structured interview developed for epidemiological and clinical research. It was developed at Washington University by Herjanic, Welner, and their colleagues (Herjanic et al., 1975). The original version of the DICA was patterned after the Renard Diagnostic Interview (Helzer, Robins, Croughan, & Welner, 1981). This version was designed to assess symptomatology according to the modified International Classification Criteria and the Feighner criteria (Feighner et al., 1972). When the DICA was revised in 1981, it was patterned after the Diagnostic Interview Schedule (DIS) (Robins et al., 1981) and was designed to assess symptomatology according to DSM-III criteria (Welner, Reich, Herjanic, Jung, & Amado, 1987). Like the DIS, the DICA is intended to be administered by lay interviewers and not to require the interviewer to make clinical judgments. The interview takes approximately one and one-half hours to administer. It is stated that it is appropriate for children ages 6 to 17 years. There is a parent interview, the DICA-P, in which the parents are asked in third person the same questions to which the children respond. Table 5.3 shows example items from the DICA.

The initial part of the DICA and DICA-P is a joint interview. The first 19 questions make inquiries about demographics, special school assignments, and pediatric and psychiatric history. The answers are coded yes/no and many "gate" questions are asked (i.e., sets of subsequent questions are not asked if interviewee responds negatively to initial inquiry). The DICA contains 266 questions, with an additional 10 items completed by the examiner based on observations. The DICA-P differs from the DICA in that developmental and medical histories are included as are questions regarding symptoms about a few diagnoses that cannot be made from the child's report (i.e., infantile autism, stereotypic movement disorder).

The interview questions are grouped according to diagnosis. Following each section, a criterion page assists in counting symptoms and assessing whether DSM-III criteria for the diagnosis are met. Both the child and the parent are asked about duration and onset for major symptoms for each diagnostic category. The following diagnoses can be made using the DICA: attention deficit disorder, oppositional disorder, conduct disorder, alcohol abuse, drug abuse, depression, mania, separation anxiety, overanxious disorder, phobias, obsessive compulsive disorder, enure-

TABLE 5.3   Example Items from DICA[a]

Sample from Anxiety Disorders (Separation Anxiety) Section

CODE

1 = No
2 = Yes

Some children (adolescents) worry a great deal about being away
from their parents or from home.
(Use past tense with children age 13 or over, when appropriate.)

158. When you are not with your parents do you worry a lot about
something bad happening to them (like they might get sick or hurt
or die)?

_____
(67)

159. Do you worry a great deal that something bad might happen to
you (like getting kidnapped or killed), so that you couldn't see your
parent(s) (or loved ones) again?

_____
(68)

160. Do you ever refuse to go to school (or try to stay home), because
you are afraid that something bad (like sickness, accident, or death)
might happen to your parent(s) (or loved person)?

_____
(69)

If No to Q. 158 + 159 + 160, skip to Q. 174.
If yes to any, ask:

161. Do you ever have to have your mother or dad (or another adult)
stay close to you in order to go to sleep at night? (If child is
uncertain, ask) Does _____ (mother, father, grandparent – insert
appropriate word) lie down on the bed with you when it's time to
go to bed?

_____
(70)

162. Does it upset you to be left in a room by yourself at home?

_____
(71)

163. Have you ever had a chance to go away to camp or to visit
someone and refused to go, because you were afraid to leave
home?

_____
(72)

164. Have you ever gone away from home for a few days, like going to
camp, and been so upset and worried that you went back home
right away?

_____
(73)

[a] Reprinted with permission of Wendy Reich. From *Diagnostic Interview for Children
and Adolescents*, Washington University School of Medicine. Obtained by personal
communication, Wendy Reich (1988).

sis, encopresis, gender identity disorder, possible psychosis, anorexia, and bulimia.

For scoring purposes, the DICA provides an index which matches items to DSM-III criteria for the diagnoses. Also, computer algorithms are available (e.g., Earls, Reich, Jung, & Cloninger, 1988).

Reliability Studies

Efforts to establish interrater reliability for the DICA have not been well described in the literature. The methodology is described as 10 interviewers independently scoring one of two taped child interviews (Herjanic et al., 1975; Herjanic & Reich, 1982). The statistical analysis yielded percent agreements of 84% and 85%. Test-retest reliability has been reported for the latest version (1981) of the DICA (Welner et al., 1987). The sample consisted of 27 psychiatric inpatients with a mean age of 12.5 years. Kappa values ranged from .76 to 1.00 for six major diagnostic categories, reflecting high test-retest reliability. For both depression and anxiety, the values provided were for the presence of any disorder. The degree to which clinical judgment was incorporated in assigning diagnoses is not clear. The interviewers themselves were lay. The coding of the interviews was checked by two psychiatrists who made diagnoses using the guidelines prepared for the interview according to DSM-III criteria. It is not known whether the same reliability values would be obtained if the diagnoses were determined by other clinicians or computer generated.

Validity Studies

To assess the validity of the DICA, several types of studies have been conducted, including contrast group, parent/child concordance, and correspondence with clinical judgment. This work has been conducted by colleagues at Washington University in St. Louis.

One contrast group study was conducted comparing psychiatric and pediatric outpatients (Herjanic & Campbell, 1977). However, since the data analyzed in the study were a composite of the child and parent responses, it does not shed much light on the child version of the DICA. Three-fourths of the responses were taken from the parent DICA. The authors did note that the sections which used the child responses were the poorest discriminators between the two groups (i.e., neurotic and somatic symptoms).

Four studies have yielded information relevant to parent-child agreement. On a sample of pediatric and psychiatric patients, Herjanic et al. (1975) calculated percent agreement on individual questions between the parent and child responses. Ambiguous answers or failures to respond resulted in deletion of the question from the analysis, which may have increased the agreement. There was an average agreement of 80%.

Subsequent studies have examined parent-child concordance utilizing a new sample and the kappa statistic. In Herjanic and Reich (1982), agreement between parent and child on individual symptoms was addressed, while in Reich, Herjanic, Welner, and Gandhy (1982), agreement on diagnosis, comparing the child and parent interviews, was investigated. The sample for both studies was 307 children between the ages of 6 and 16. The authors reported the kappa for each of the symptom items on the interview. Using their criterion of a kappa of .50 as indicative of reliable agreement, only 10% of the 168 items met this criterion. The authors noted that the most reliable questions inquired about symptoms that were concrete, observable, severe, and/or unambiguous (e.g., "appeared in juvenile court," "has been in hospital," "has monthly periods"). When there was disagreement, the children tended to report more symptoms of a subjective nature, while mothers reported significantly more behavioral symptoms. There was least agreement on items related to affects and cognitions, such as anxiety, depression, homicidal thoughts and psychotic symptoms.

The same data were used to assess concordance between diagnoses generated from parent and child reports (Reich et al., 1982). Diagnoses were computer generated. The set of diagnoses examined included: normal variation, conduct disorder, enuresis, encopresis, antisocial personality, possible depression, behavior disorder, neurotic disorders, and mixed behavior-neurotic disorder. Only two diagnoses obtained kappas of .50 or higher: antisocial personality (.58) and enuresis (.54). The authors concluded that even though the values were disappointing, the child-parent agreement seemed to fall within the same range as does adult-adult agreement in comparable circumstances. They cite diagnostic agreement studies in which the responses of adult patients were compared to first degree relatives.

In the most recent parent-child diagnostic agreement study on the DICA (Welner et al., 1987), the 1981 revised DICA was utilized. Diagnoses were determined by psychiatrists, using the coding guide prepared in the interview according to DSM-III criteria. As mentioned previously, it is not clear whether subjective judgment was involved. Both "definite" diagnoses (i.e., all DSM-III criteria were met) and "probable" diagnoses (i.e., one symptom was lacking or the duration was uncertain) were considered concordant. Kappa values of .50 or higher were obtained for the following diagnoses: attention deficit disorder, conduct disorder, affective disorder, and oppositional disorder. The results for conduct disorder (K=.80) reflected particularly high agreement. These are good indicators of parent-child agreement, keeping in mind that some latitude was permitted in determining concordance and, possibly, diagnosis. In any case, it would appear that the new version of the DICA results in higher kappas for parent-child agreement.

In a study on the offspring of alcoholics by Earls et al. (1988) the degree of parent-child agreement for individual diagnoses was determined. Computerized algorithms were used to generate the diagnoses. Only one diagnosis, conduct disorder, had a kappa of .50 or greater. Disappointingly low kappas were found for attention deficit disorder, oppositional disorder, depression, and anxiety. When the authors examined the patterns of agreement and disagreement between the parent and child, they found that children appeared to report more conduct disorders and parents reported more depressive disorders. This is noteworthy given that generally the opposite pattern has been observed. Perhaps for these alcoholic parents, it is difficult for them to give recognition to the conduct disordered behavior of their children and easier for them to explain their problems in terms of more neurotic-like symptoms.

Data on diagnostic concordance between the DICA and DICA-P was generated by another offspring study (Sylvester, Hyde, & Reichler, 1987) with children of anxiety and affectively disordered parents. The internal scoring system for the interview was used. Kappas were calculated for overanxious disorder, major depression, attention deficit disorder (ADD), and behavior disorder (mostly consisting of oppositional disorder). None of the kappas were greater than .50. In fact, all the values were slight except for ADD, which had a kappa value of .42.

Correspondence between the DICA and clinical judgment was examined in the recent study by Welner et al. (1987). The criterion for clinical judgment was discharge summary diagnoses. These diagnoses were compared to diagnoses based on the DICA, which were determined by two psychiatrists using the DSM-III as a guide. The kappa values were greater than .50 for two of the diagnoses, affective disorder and attention deficit disorder.

An offspring study conducted by Earls et al. (1988) compared children of alcoholics, of antisocial parents, and of medical controls. Subjects ranged in age from 6 to 17. Analysis of variance on the mean number of symptoms appeared to be nonsignificant. However, chi-square analyses conducted on type of diagnosis differentiated the three groups. Parental alcoholism was associated with more attention deficit disorders, oppositional disorders, and anxiety disorders in the children.

An offspring study conducted at the University of Washington (Sylvester et al., 1987) compared children of controls, parents with a panic disorder, and parents with depression. Chi-square analyses were significant, with the percentages of child disorders differing across the parent groups for presence of anxiety disorder, depressive disorder, and attention deficit disorder (ADD). There were no significant differences between the offspring of panic and depressed proband groups for percentage of various psychiatric disorders.

Generalizability

The DICA was designed to be suited for epidemiological work and thus is highly structured and can be administered by lay interviewers. The subject samples for the DICA validity studies have included psychiatric and pediatric patients. Nonreferred adolescents and at-risk offspring have also been studied. It would be reasonable to assume that the results of those studies could be generalized to other samples of psychiatric patients. With the new DICA version (1981), good parent-child concordance may be achieved, provided that the same procedure for determining diagnoses are used. However, given the relative lack of contrast validity group studies on the child version of the DICA, the instrument's ability to distinguish disturbed from nondisturbed children or adolescents could not be assumed. With nonreferred samples, over-diagnosis has been reported as a problem. However, procedures such as employed by Kashani et al. (1987) may help offset this tendency.

As for age and sex effects, two studies (Herjanic et al., 1975 and Reich et al., 1982) have examined differences in parent-child concordance. No age effects were found in the former study, but significant effects for parent-child concordances were observed in the latter. For children 6 to 9, no diagnoses were concordant; for 10- to 11-year-olds, only enuresis; and for 12- to 16-year-olds, both enuresis and antisocial personality. In addition, the concordance for antisocial personality was observed only for boys. In the Herjanic et al. (1975) study, better concordance was present for girls on items related to behavior and mental status. Sex differences in parent versus child report may be expected, but from the results, it is not clear whether better agreement would be expected for boys or girls.

THE DIAGNOSTIC INTERVIEW SCHEDULE FOR CHILDREN

Description

The Diagnostic Interview Schedule for Children (DISC) is a highly structured interview for children designed for use in epidemiologic studies. The interview itself was commissioned by the National Institutes of Mental Health (NIMH) in the hope of developing a suitable instrument for use in community and epidemiologic studies. It is modeled after the DIS for adults and incorporates features of other structured and semistructured interviews for children and adolescents. It is intended for use with children aged 6 to 17 and to be able to be given by lay interviewers. The interview is designed with the intent that it requires no clinical judgment to administer. It takes approximately one hour to administer, but depending upon the number of symptoms endorsed, may take longer.

The questions are organized by diagnosis. The child version contains 264 items and the parent version contains 302 items. The interview contains many "gate" questions, so that if the child does not endorse certain symptoms, detailed questions regarding that symptom are not asked. Table 5.4 lists example items from the DISC.

It is recommended that practice interviews be done with videotapes in order to become familiar enough with the interview to read it fluently. The interview itself contains no variations, and therefore any variation would be interviewer-specific and would be avoided by the careful structuring of the interview.

The interview generates current diagnoses. The questions inquire about events of the past year, since questions regarding recent history are necessary in order to make certain diagnoses. Answers are scored 0, 1, or 2; referring to "No," "Sometimes," and "Yes," respectively. Duration is coded in weeks or months and answers to questions regarding severity are recorded verbatim.

The DISC-P is a parallel interview for parents that was designed to elicit similar information about the child from the parent. The parent form of the DISC asks some additional questions of the parent to permit making diagnoses that cannot be made from child report alone. The DISC-P takes approximately 70 minutes to administer.

The diagnoses made by the DISC include attention deficit disorders, conduct disorders, separation anxiety, avoidance disorder, overanxious disorder, oppositional disorder, anorexia nervosa, bulimia, enuresis, encopresis, alcohol abuse/dependence, substance abuse, cannabis dependence/abuse, tobacco dependence, schizophrenia, major affective disorder, cyclothymic disorder, dysthymic disorder, phobias, panic disorder, obsessive/compulsive disorder, gender identity disorder, and transsexualism.

Additional diagnoses made by the DISC-P include infantile autism, elective mutism, psychogenic fugue, hypochondriasis, Tourette's disorder, pervasive developmental disorder, psychogenic amnesia, conversion disorder, tic disorder, and pica.

TABLE 5.4   Example Items From DISC[a,b]

Sample from Separation Anxiety Disorder Items

101	Some children worry a great deal about their (parents) being away. Do you worry that something bad might happen to your parents (like they might get sick, or be hurt, or die)?	0 GO TO 104 1 GO TO 102 2 GO TO 102	101
102	What do you worry about? Tell me more about that.		
103	How long have you been worried about that?	(Months)⬚⬚	103
104	Do you worry that your (parents) might go away and not come back?	0 GO TO 106 1 GO TO 105 2 GO TO 105	104
105	How long have you been worried about that?	(Months)⬚⬚	105
106	Do you worry that something bad might happen to you, so you couldn't see your (parents) again (like getting kidnapped or killed)?	0 GO TO 110 1 GO TO 107 2 GO TO 107	106
107	What do you worry about?		
108	Tell me more about that.		
109	How long have you been worried about that?	(Months)⬚⬚	109
110	Do you try to stay home in order to be with your (parents)?	0 GO TO 112 1 GO TO 111 2 GO TO 111	110
111	How long have you been doing that?	(Months)⬚⬚	111
112	When you have to go to school, do you often feel sick, or have stomach aches, or headaches, or feel sick to your stomach, or want to throw up?	0 GO TO 115 1 GO TO 113 2 GO TO 113	112
113	Tell me more about that.		
114	How long has that been happening?	(Months)⬚⬚	114

[a] Reprinted with permission from *DISC-Diagnostic Interview Schedule for Children,* May, 1985, written by Anthony Costello, M.D., and Mina Dulcan, M.D.

[b] 0 = No, Never, Not at all; 1 = Maybe, Sometimes, Perhaps a little; 2 = Yes, Always, Definitely.

The DISC and DISC-P are interpreted with the use of computer algorithms that were developed as literal translations of the DSM-III criteria. Most studies with the DISC have analyzed data in terms of presence or absence of disorder, but the capability also exists to generate symptom scores using the computer algorithms. The parent and child data are collected and scored separately.

Reliability Studies

Interrater reliability was initially addressed by Costello et al. (1984) in the original NIMH report. Each child was interviewed by both a lay and a clinical interviewer. Concordance was based on the presence or absence of DSM-III diagnoses, using computer algorithms. The kappa was greater than .50 for: oppositional disorder, enuresis, substance abuse, and one subtype of conduct disorder—nonaggressive, socialized. In the same study, interrater reliability was tested using three lay interviewers who scored 10 videotaped interviews. Agreement on the average symptom scores for rater pairs was studied, yielding correlation means of .97 to .98.

In a study by Anderson, Williams, McGee, & Silva (1987), interrater reliability was evaluated on 60 audiotaped interviews. Kappa statistic was computed for all questions with a prevalence greater than 5%. It was found that approximately two-thirds of the items had a kappa value of .50 or above, with the remaining one-third having lower kappa values. Interrater reliability for diagnoses was also calculated. However, it appears that subjective judgment was utilized in assigning diagnoses, with a child psychiatrist considering the match with DSM-III criteria and the severity of the items. The kappa values reported were in the acceptable range of greater than .50.

Edelbrock, Costello, Dulcan, Kalas, & Conover (1985) used the data from the original NIMH study, cited above, to examine the test-retest reliability as a function of the child's age. They determined the reliability for average symptom score, collapsing across symptom areas, for children classified into three age groups. The intra-class correlations for the three groups were as follows: ages 6 to 9, .43; ages 10 to 13, .60; and ages 14 to 18, .71. As was expected, there was better test-retest agreement for older children. The change in total symptom scores from the first to second interviews was significant for all age groups, with lower scores at time two. The DISC was included in a test-retest reliability design in a study by Bird et al. (1987). However, information from the DISC, DISC-P, and other sources or consultants were utilized in making diagnoses. Thus, the data for the DISC alone could not be examined.

Validity Studies

Numerous types of validity studies have been conducted using the DISC, including contrast group, parent-child diagnostic concordance, correspondence with parental report and correspondence with teacher report.

Contrast group validity was studied by Costello, Edelbrock, and Costello (1985) in a sample of 40 children who had been referred to a psychiatric clinic for evaluation and 40 matched children visiting their pediatricians. The psychiatrically referred patients reported significantly more symptoms than their pediatric controls on 12 nonoverlapping scales and for total symptom score. In addition, diagnoses were generated, using the DISC computer algorithm scoring, based on the DSM-III. For the presence of any diagnosis, the sensitivity (i.e., percentage of ill cases correctly identified) was 95%, and specificity (i.e., percentage of well cases correctly identified) was 25%. Due to the over-diagnosis in the nonreferred pediatric group, an alternate set of criteria was employed to define psychiatric illness. The original criteria were referred to as reflecting "mild to moderate" disorders, while the alternate set was to reflect "severe" disorders. With the "severe" criteria, the sensitivity was 45%, and specificity was 80%. When apparently very stringent criteria were used to identify severe pathology, so as to not over-diagnose well children, less than half of the psychiatric children were identified as ill. The pediatric sample in this study was also examined from the perspective of their pediatrician's view of whether the child had a psychiatric problem (Costello & Edelbrock, 1985). The correspondence was poor between the identification of a psychiatric illness as judged by the pediatrician and as determined from the DISC. In another nonreferred sample studied by Breslau (1987), marked overestimation of some psychiatric symptoms was observed.

Parent-child concordance was examined for the original NIMH study sample (Costello et al., 1984) of 303 children selected from referrals to a triage unit, to inpatient care, and to group homes. In Costello et al. (1984) agreement on diagnoses, comparing parent and child interviews, was reported, while agreement between parent and child on individual symptoms was addressed by Edelbrock, Costello, Dulcan, Conover, & Kalas (1986). Diagnoses were determined by the original DISC computer algorithms. The kappa statistic was greater than .50 for conduct disorder, with all other diagnoses falling below that level.

Parent-child agreement on the DISC symptoms for the same sample was low to moderate (Edelbrock et al., 1986). The Pearson correlations for the total symptom score and for the average across all symptoms was as follows for three age groupings: for 6- to 9-year-olds, .09 and .10; for 10- to 13-year-olds, .10 and .27; and for 14- to 18-year-olds, .29 and .35. Thus, moderate levels were only achieved for adolescents. It is noteworthy that the direction of parent-child differences was similar across the three age groups. Children reported more affective/neurotic symptoms and substance abuse. Parents reported more behavior and conduct problems. Moreover, the parent-child agreement was very poor ($r=.17$ for total sample) for the symptoms relevant to diagnoses of anxiety, depression, and phobias, whereas the agreement was moderate ($r=.51$ for the total sample) for symptoms relevant to diagnoses of conduct disorder, oppositional disorder, ADD, and substance abuse.

Correspondence with parental report has been addressed in two studies. In Costello, Edelbrock, and Costello (1985), the total symptom score on the DISC was compared with the total CBCL behavior problem score. The correlation was .14 for the psychiatric group and .29 for the pediatric group. A chi-square analysis comparing CBCL cases above and below the 90th percentile with the presence or absence of "severe" disorder on the DISC was also nonsignificant.

The relationship between the DISC and: (1) parent report on the CBCL, as well as (2) the teacher's report on the Teacher's Report Form (TRF) (Achenbach & Edelbrock, 1986) and the Revised Behavior Problem Checklist (RBPC) (Quay & Peterson, 1983) were examined in a study by Brandenburg et al. (1988). The sample consisted entirely of children and adolescents who were seriously emotionally disturbed, half of whom were being served in school-based programs and the other half of whom were located in residential programs. The results of the CBCL indicated that there were significant, although modest, correlations between the externalizing scale on the CBCL and a number of the DISC symptom scales measuring behavior disturbances (i.e., conduct disorder, oppositional disorder, ADD). These ranged from .18 to .24. As for the correspondence with teachers, the highest correlation was between the diagnosis of attention deficit disorder and the externalizing scale on the TRF ($r=.20$). The internalizing disorders derived from the DISC did not correlate more consistently with the internalizing scale of the CBCL or TRF, compared to their externalizing scales. Correspondence between the DISC and the RBPC was somewhat stronger. Moderate-sized positive correlations were obtained between the RBPC socialized aggressive factor scale and similar symptom scales on the DISC (aggressive conduct disorder [$r=.32$], nonaggressive conduct disorder [$r=.46$], oppositional disorder [$r=.22$], and alcohol/drug use [$r=.40$]).

Generalizability

The DISC is a highly structured interview designed for use in epidemiologic studies and for administration by lay interviewers. It has been used with psychiatric and pediatric samples of children from 6 to 18 years old. However, based on the reliability studies, it could be assumed to be valuable only for adolescents or older children and for behavioral disorders. Similarly, parent-child concordance was poor except for older adolescents and for the diagnosis of conduct disorder. In research applications, the DISC quantitative scores (i.e., total score and other symptom scores) could be useful in differentiating disturbed and nonreferred samples. Based on the existing psychometric studies, DISC generated diagnostic information (i.e., presence of a disorder; type of disorder) could not be assumed to distinguish ill from nonreferred children. Thus, the DISC probably has limited clinical utility. Research applications appear to be most appropriate for older children and adolescents who have conduct disorders, and for research designs in which total and symptom scores are used, rather than diagnoses.

COMPARISONS AMONG THE INTERVIEWS

Three studies have addressed the issue of comparability of the structured child interviews. One compared the diagnostic concordance separately for the child and parent versions for the CAS and the K-SADS (Hodges et al., 1987). Another (Carlson, Kashani, Thomas, Vaidya, & Daniel, 1987) compared the DICA and the K-SADS, on correspondence between interview-yielded diagnoses and clinical diagnoses from the chart discharge summary. A third study by Cohen, O'Conner, Lewis, Velez, and Malachowski (1987) compares the DISC and the K-SADS, based on diagnoses generated from combining the information from the parent and child interviews.

The results of these three studies, in which comparisons were made with the K-SADS, can be briefly summarized. There was no evidence of concordance for the DISC. For the comparisons to the CAS and DICA, there was good concordance for the child's report of conduct disorder. Secondly, there was good agreement for affective disorders between the K-SADS and both the CAS and DICA when parent information is included, which is how the K-SADS is utilized. Furthermore, for the CAS, there was good concordance with the K-SADS for affective disorders for the child interview alone. Thus, the empirical data suggests that researchers and clinicians should feel that they have a choice in selecting an instrument, including when the focus is on depression; in this regard the K-SADS, CAS, and DICA may be useful. Thirdly, it appears that the most problematic diagnoses from the perspective of concordance and reliability are ADD and the anxiety disorders. Furthermore, of the anxiety disorders, separation anxiety appears to fare somewhat better than the other anxiety disorders, as observed across numerous studies (see Hodges et al., 1987). A major obstacle in achieving better psychometric results lies with the diagnostic criteria for the disorders.

CURRENT STATE OF AFFAIRS: SUMMARY AND CRITIQUE

The empirical data reviewed in this chapter is very encouraging, especially given that the discussion has been restricted to interviews as administered to the child. Interrater and test-retest reliability can be established, even for latency-aged children, although the findings differ across the interviews. Interrater reliability based on an item-by-item comparison has been established for all three interviews. Test-retest reliability for presence or absence of a diagnosis has been established for most diagnoses for the CAS and the DICA. Only oppositional disorders and the nonaggressive subtype of conduct disorders were reliable for the DISC. The reliability of summed symptom scores has not been reported for the DICA. For the CAS, good test-retest reliability was found for total score for the entire interview and for all of the diagnosis-related scales. However, for the DISC, there was unacceptable reliability for children under 10 years, acceptable reliability for behavioral disorder clusters for the 10- to 13-year-olds, and acceptable reliability for the interview total and diagnostic clusters for 14 years and older. Thus, the CAS has generally good reliability for symptom scores and diagnoses; the DICA for diagnoses; and the DISC, for symptom scores for adolescents.

The absence of external validity indicators for the most frequently used childhood diagnostic categories renders validation of psychiatric interviews a very difficult task. The two main approaches have been contrast group and concurrent validity, with the latter typically assessing correspondence with an approximation to a "gold standard," such as clinician opinion or parental report. There is evidence of contrast group validity for the CAS, and to a lesser extent, for the DISC, but none for the DICA.

Despite the known history of unreliability of psychiatric diagnoses (Matarazzo, 1983; Robins, 1985), there have been efforts to validate the interviews with clinician's judgments. For the DICA, there was correspondence between interview-generated diagnoses and the discharge summary for two diagnoses (i.e., attention deficit disorder, affective disorder). For the CAS, the total score was found to be significantly correlated with severity rating by psychiatrists. No studies have been done with the DISC, except for a comparison to pediatricians' judgments which produced nonsignificant results.

An attempt has also been made to utilize parent report as the "gold standard." However, there is an increasing awareness that only moderate correlations between parent and child should be expected (Achenbach, McConaughy, & Howell, 1987). Correspondence with the CBCL parent questionnaire was good for the CAS and nonsignificant for the DISC for psychiatric patients; with no comparison having been made for the DICA. Correspondence between a parent and child interview on summed symptom scores for the entire interview and subscales was good for the CAS; good primarily for behavior disorders for adolescents for the DISC; and not studied in the DICA. Item-by-item agreement was studied only in the DICA, and the results were discouraging. Diagnostic concordance between parent and child interviews has not been reported for the CAS; has been studied in the DISC with poor results; and in the DICA with mixed results. Three of four studies with the DICA have yielded disappointing results, with the most recent study on the 1981 version suggesting good correspondence. However, it is noteworthy that these studies were not comparable since the DICA study used clinican determined, not computer generated, diagnoses.

These findings on structured interviews are encouraging although more psychometric studies are certainly needed. In terms of practical use, these findings suggest that for children between 7 and 12 years of age, the CAS is probably the interview of choice. Reliability and validity have been demonstrated for the CAS with preadolescent and early adolescent children. The studies on the DICA have been done with samples with a wide age range (7 to 17), with the mean age being in early adolescence (e.g., 12.4). No separate analyses were conducted for preadolescents. Although separate analyses were completed on the DISC, the results were particularly disappointing for the younger children. All three interviews have been used with adolescents, including the CAS (see Kashani et al., 1989; Kashani, Rosenberg, & Reid, in press; Runyan et al., in press). The DICA or DISC would appear preferable if detailed information on substance use/abuse is needed from the interview itself or if the sample consists of seriously disturbed patients who have disorders more typically seen in adults than children (i.e., psychosis, mania).

If making diagnoses is important, conduct disorder can be made reliably with all three interviews. Determining the presence of any anxiety disorder or any depressive disorder can be made with the DICA and CAS. If quantitative analyses on some symptom scores are planned, then only the CAS and the DISC would appear appropriate since the DICA lacks reliability or validity data on symptom scores.

SUGGESTIONS FOR USING STRUCTURED INTERVIEWS AND IMPLICATIONS FOR FUTURE RESEARCH

In future research efforts aimed at improving the reliability and validity of structured interviews, several issues need to be addressed. These include, but are certainly not restricted to, consideration of: (1) degree of structure in the interview, (2) procedure for generating diagnoses, (3) level of training for interviewers, (4) modifications to improve sensitivity to developmentally related processes, (5) the current inadequacies in childhood taxonomy, and (6) the need to integrate information from multiple informants.

Degree of Structure in the Interview

There is still controversy in the literature over the degree of structure that is desirable for research interviews. Determining the optimal degree of structure in a child interview is ultimately an empirical question that needs to be addressed further. However, the generally disappointing results with the DISC have led numerous researchers to conclude that less highly structured interviews may yield more clinically valid data. In fact, in the adult literature, dissatisfaction with the DIS has led to the development of less structured, more clinically oriented interviews (Spitzer, 1983). Also, it appears particularly problematic to base the scoring of response items on the verbatim response of the interviewee (a "yes" or "no"). For example, Breslau (1987) observed that this was the apparent problem which resulted in overestimation of obsessions, compulsions, and psychotic symptoms on the DISC. It is preferable to have the interviewer focus on the intent of the question or diagnostic criteria being inquired about in scoring the response. With the CAS, it was observed that detailed guidelines for scoring were desirable so that the interviewer can score the item according to the information provided by the interviewee, but within the context of understanding the criteria which should be applied (Hodges, 1983). For example, these guidelines clarify that normal bedtime routines reported by the children would not qualify as a compulsion; likewise, ruminations about actual traumatic events would not qualify as an obsession.

Procedure for Generating Diagnoses

Diagnoses have typically been generated via computer algorithm or a clinician making a decision. Either represents a defendable approach. However, there is a recent trend to use clinicians to make diagnoses even when the interview is administered by lay interviewers. This has been the case for both the DICA (Kashani et al., 1987; Welner et al., 1987) and the DISC (Shekim et al., 1985). Clinicians have been utilized to make diagnoses primarily because of the anticipated overestimation of disorders, that is, false positives. Overestimation of disorders has been a consistent problem, for example, with the original DSM-III based computer algorithm used for the DISC (see Cohen, Velez, Kohn, Schwab-Stone, & Johnson, 1987). In their study with the DICA, Kashani et al. (1987) concluded that even if lay interviewers were used, at least judgments about severity as well as about degree of impaired functioning and/or need for treatment should be made by a trained professional. However, clinician-determined diagnoses are not satisfactory unless the formal or informal "rules" utilized in generating diagnoses are specified. It may not be that computers over-diagnose, but that clinicians fail to make a diagnosis even when the DSM-III criteria are met. This may be because some informal criteria for "caseness" has not been met (e.g., a school-aged child must have some difficulty in attending school to be classified as having separation anxiety, even though DSM-III does not require it). Likewise, the clinician may fail to make a diagnosis because of the context in which it co-occurs with other diagnoses or known facts, even though such hierarchical exclusions may not be specified in DSM-III. Without specifying the "rules" clinicians follow, results may not be replicable or generalizable. Samples of subjects identified as having the same diagnosis across various studies may differ greatly. For example, in the DIS research, the prevalence of disorders across study sites was quite similar for the lay interviewers using the DIS. However, prevalence figures differed considerably for some disorders for the clinical interviewers, suggesting that they were interpreting diagnostic criteria differently (Robins, 1985).

Level of Training for Interviewers

The level of professional training needed for interviewers is also an empirical question open to further study. The findings to date suggest that interviewers who are professionally trained in mental health are preferable. However, the empirical studies needed to address this issue have not been conducted. Typically, level of training has been confounded with degree of structure in the interview and procedure for generating diagnoses.

Modifications to Improve Sensitivity to Developmentally Related Processes

Psychometric studies on the specific interviews should reveal specific items or typical areas in need of improvement. In trying to address these, it seems wise to first determine if lack of sensitivity to developmentally related processes could be contributing to the poor performance of items. The questions asked of the child draw on the child's: knowledge of emotions, knowledge about the self, ability to make comparisons between his and others' functioning; and understanding of time and sequence. The research in some of these areas (e.g., self-concept) is quite applicable to the kinds of questions included in structured interviews. However, in some areas, the existing research is not sufficiently similar to serve as a guide in modifying interview items, such as an understanding of time concepts relevant to onset and duration. In addition, this developmental research will likely need to study both well and disturbed children, with varying levels of severity, to comment on the developmental course in acquiring these cognitive and affective skills. For example, research has shown that disturbed children demonstrate significant deficits and/or developmental lags in processing social information (Dodge & Frame, 1982; Selman, 1980).

Coping with the Current Inadequacies in Childhood Taxonomy

The research on structured interviews has highlighted some of the problematic areas that exist within the nosology of childhood disorders. Compared to other diagnoses, anxiety disorders, and to a lesser extent affective disorders, appear to be more unreliable, especially if subtypes of the diagnoses are considered (Hodges et al., 1987; Hodges & Siegel, 1985). However, this appears to reflect more on problems with diagnostic classification than on structured interviews. As Spitzer (1983) has emphasized, the validity issue with structured interviews is concerned with the procedure itself, not with diagnostic categories. In terms of practical use of the interviews, a conservative approach would be to use summed symptom scores for clusters of anxiety-related items, and for determining diagnoses, to do so for the presence or absence of any anxiety disorder.

Until these issues can be more fully addressed, the authors and users of interviews will have to continue to struggle with them. There appear to be at least four areas, which are somewhat overlapping, that need to be addressed. They include: (1) the criteria defining a disorder, including whether differential weights will be given to criteria, (2) impairment criteria needed to differentiate cases from noncases, (3) the definition of hierarchical relationships among disorders in order to deal with the high level of co-occurrence among disorders, and (4) the integration of information from various sources other than the patient. Until advances are made in these areas for the various diagnoses, the task of trying to develop reliable and valid assessment procedures will be problematic. It appears that the overestimation of disorders observed with structured interviews using computer scoring may be due in part to inadequacies in DSM-III in capturing the clinician's decision-making criteria and process, along the dimensions mentioned above. Given the variability among clinicians and the lack of external validity data, obviously this represents a painstaking task.

Inevitably, users of structured interviews will help to resolve or address some of these problematic issues. Cross-sectional and longitudinal studies which include an item pool larger than the DSM-III criteria will help define the clustering of criteria at different developmental stages. In fact, the work of Kashani and his colleagues with the CAS revealed age-related differences in the manifestations of anxiety and depressive symptoms in 8-, 12-, and 17-year-olds (Kashani et al., 1989; Kashani et al., in press). In addition, useful guidelines may evolve as a result of users of the structured interviews trying to manage these problems. Kashani et al., (1987) found that the degree of apparent overestimation of diagnoses with the DICA necessitated establishing a method for "caseness" which involved rating the child's severity of impairment and need for treatment. While such global ratings can be made as an addendum to the current interviews, considerable work will still remain in order to develop reliable and valid impairment criteria. This would extend beyond the scope of structured interviews. Empirical studies which identify disorders that typically co-occur may help establish guidelines in regard to the problem of multiple diagnoses. For example, Achenbach and his colleagues (Achenbach & Edelbrock, 1983) have used the CBCL to develop "typologies" which characterize patterns of coexisting syndromes.

Collecting and Integrating Information from Multiple Informants

Obtaining both parent and child reports of symptoms appears desirable. This can be done with parallel interviews or by administering the interview to the child and a symptom questionnaire to the parents. The reason is not because children are necessarily less reliable. Rather, they represent a perspective in their own right. Numerous researchers have noted that a significant number of children would have gone undiagnosed if the child report had not been obtained (Gershon et al., 1985; Reich & Earls, 1987).

The generally disappointing results found in the parent-child concordance studies do not appear to reflect on inherent difficulties with structured interviews. In a meta-analysis conducted by Achenbach, McConaughy & Howell (1987) on 120 studies, a mean correlation of .25 was found between the child/adolescent and parent across a variety of measurement techniques. Parents have a special relationship with their child which may render them particularly poor observers or reporters, for either unconsciously or consciously motivated reasons. For example, depressed parents have been noted to be inaccurate reporters (Kashani, Orvaschel, Burk, & Reid, 1985; Moretti, Fine, Haley, & Marriage, 1985) as well as parents of abused children (Everson, Hunter, Runyan, Edelsohn, & Coulter, 1989).

If both parent and child can be interviewed, it seems preferable to retain and analyze the separate reports as well as to integrate the information for the purposes of "summary diagnoses." Additionally, it is preferable if the guidelines for integrating information can be made explicit and specified in detail. Given the lack of guidelines for integrating information and the absence of any consensus, this issue is usually resolved in case conferences typically held in clinical research settings. However, as Poznanski and her colleagues (Mokros, Poznanski, Grossman, & Freeman, 1987; Poznanski, Mokros, Grossman, & Freeman, 1985) have commented on, this is commonly a "battle of the wills" rather than a "meeting of the minds." They too emphasize the need for developing guidelines for making these decisions.

CONCLUSION

Structured interviews for children have now become an integral, if not critical, part of research in child psychopathology. They have helped to identify shortcomings in our knowledge base as well as to enhance it. The task incumbent on researchers is to continue to study the psychometric properties of these instruments. The ultimate goal is to provide ways for children of various ages to report meaningful information relevant to their mental health needs.

REFERENCES

Achenbach, T.M., & Edelbrock, C. (1983). *Manual for the Child Behavior Checklist and Revised Child Behavior Profile*. Burlington, VT: Queen City Printers.

Achenbach, T., & Edelbrock, C. (1986). *Manual for the Teacher's Report Form and Teacher Version of the Child Behavior Profile*. Burlington, VT: University of Vermont, Department of Psychiatry.

Achenbach, T.M., McConaughy, S., & Howell, C. (1987). Child/adolescent behavioral and emotional problems: Implications of cross informant correlations for situational specificity. *Psychological Bulletin, 101*, 213–232.

American Psychiatric Association. (1st ed. 1952; 2nd ed. 1968; 3rd ed. 1980; 3rd rev. ed. 1987). *Diagnostic and statistical manual of mental disorders*. Washington, DC: Author.

American Psychological Association. (1981). Ethical principles of psychologists. *American Psychologist, 36*, 633–638.

American Psychological Association. (1982). *Ethical principles in the conduct of research with human participants*. Washington, DC: Author.

Anderson, J., Williams, S., McGee, R., & Silva, P. (1987). DSM-III disorders in preadolescent children: Prevalence in a large sample from the general population. *Archives of General Psychiatry, 44*, 69–76.

Bartko, J.J., & Carpenter, W.T., Jr. (1976). On the methods and theory of reliability. *Journal of Nervous and Mental Disease, 163*, 307–317.

Bird, H., Canino, G., Gould, M., Ribera, J., Rubio-Stipec, M., Woodbury, M., Huertas-Goldman, S., & Seeman, M. (1987). Use of the Child Behavior Checklist as a screening instrument for epidemiological research in child psychiatry: Results of a pilot study. *Journal of the American Academy of Child and Adolescent Psychiatry, 26*, 207–213.

Bousha, D.M. (1985). *A controlled investigation of therapeutic focus in limit-setting insight-oriented psychotherapy with acting-out children*. Unpublished doctoral dissertation, University of Rochester, Rochester, NY.

Brandenburg, N.A., Quay, H.C., Friedman, R.M., Silver, S., Duchowski, A.J., Kutash, K., & Prange, M. (1988). *Concordance between categorical and dimensional measures of childhood and adolescent psychopathology*. Manuscript submitted for publication.

Breslau, N. (1987). Inquiring about the bizarre: False positives in Diagnostic Interview Schedule for Children (DISC) ascertainment of obsessions, compulsions, and psychotic symptoms. *Journal of the American Academy of Child and Adolescent Psychiatry, 26,* 639–644.

Burbach, D.J., Farha, J.G., & Thorpe, J.S. (1986). Assessing depression in community samples of children using self-report inventories: Ethical considerations. *Journal of Abnormal Child Psychology, 14,* 579–589.

Carlson, G.A. (1983). *Structured diagnostic interviews: A clinician's perspective.* Paper presented at the meeting of the American Academy of Child Psychiatry, San Francisco, CA.

Carlson, G., Kashani, J., Thomas, M., Vaidya, A., & Daniel, A. (1987). Comparison of two structured interviews on a psychiatrically hospitalized population of children. *Journal of the American Academy of Child and Adolescent Psychiatry, 26,* 645–648.

Cohen, P., O'Connor, P., Lewis, S., Velez, C., & Malachowski, B. (1987). Comparison of DISC and K-SADS-P interviews of an epidemiological sample of children. *Journal of the American Academy of Child and Adolescent Psychiatry, 26,* 662–667.

Cohen, P., Velez, N., Kohn, M., Schwab-Stone, M., & Johnson, J. (1987). Child psychiatric diagnoses by computer algorithm: Theoretical issues and empirical tests. *Journal of the American Academy of Child and Adolescent Psychiatry, 26,* 631–638.

Costello, A.J. (1986). Assessment and diagnosis of affective disorders in children. *Journal of Child Psychology and Psychiatry, 27,* 565–574.

Costello, A.J., Edelbrock, L.S., Dulcan, M.K., Kalas, R., & Klaric, S.H. (1984). *Report on the NIMH Diagnostic Interview Schedule for Children (DIS-C).* Washington, DC: National Institute of Mental Health.

Costello, E.J., & Edelbrock, C. (1985). Detection of psychiatric disorders in pediatric primary care: A preliminary report. *Journal of the American Academy of Child Psychiatry, 24,* 771–774.

Costello, E.J., Edelbrock, C.S., Costello, A.J. (1985). Validity of the NIMH diagnostic interview schedule for children: A comparison between psychiatric and pediatric referrals. *Journal of Abnormal Child Psychology, 13,* 579–595.

Dodge, K.A., & Frame, C.L. (1982). Social cognitive biases and deficits in aggressive boys. *Child Development, 53,* 620–635.

Earls, F., Reich, W., Jung, K.G., & Cloninger, C.R. (1988). Psychopathology in children of alcoholic and antisocial parents. *Alcoholism: Clinical and Experimental Research, 12,* 481–487.

Edelbrock, C., Costello, A.J., Dulcan, M.K., Conover, N.C., & Kalas, R. (1986). Parent-child agreement on child psychiatric symptoms assessed via structured interview. *Journal of Child Psychology and Psychiatry, 27,* 181–190.

Edelbrock, C., Costello, A.J., Dulcan, M., Kalas, R., & Conover, N.C. (1985). Age differences in the reliability of the psychiatric interview of the child. *Child Development, 56,* 265–275.

Edelsohn, G. (1985). *Reliability and validity of two mental health assessment instruments in a sample of sexually abused girls.* Manuscript submitted for publication.

Endicott, J., & Spitzer, R.L. (1978). A diagnostic interview: The Schedule for Affective Disorders and Schizophrenia. *Archives of General Psychiatry, 35,* 837–844.

Everson, M., Hunter, W., Runyan, D., Edelsohn, G., & Coulter, M. (1989). Maternal support following disclosure of incest. *American Journal of Orthopsychiatry, 59,* 197–207.

Feighner, J., Robins, E., Guze, S., Woodruff, R., Winokur, G., & Munoz, R. (1972). Diagnostic criteria for use in psychiatric research. *Archives of General Psychiatry, 26,* 57–63.

Gershon, E.S., McKnew, D., Cytryn, L., Hamovit, J., Schreiber, J., Hibbs, E., & Pellegrini, D. (1985). Diagnoses in school-aged children of bipolar affective disorder patients and normal controls. *Journal of Affective Disorders, 8,* 283–291.

Graham, P., & Rutter, M. (1968). The reliability and validity of psychiatric assessment of the child: II. Interview with the parent. *British Journal of Psychiatry, 114,* 581–591.

Greenspan, S.I. (1981). *The Clinical Interview of the Child.* New York: McGraw Hill.

Helzer, J., Robins, L., Croughan, J., & Welner, A. (1981). Renard diagnostic interview. Its reliability and procedural validity with physicians and lay interviewers. *Archives of General Psychiatry, 38,* 393–398.

Herjanic, B., & Campbell, W. (1977). Differentiating psychiatrically disturbed children on the basis of a structured interview. *Journal of Abnormal Child Psychology, 5,* 127–133.

Herjanic, B., Herjanic, M., Brown, F., & Wheatt, T. (1975). Are children reliable reporters? *Journal of Abnormal Child Psychology, 3,* 41–48.

Herjanic, B., Hudson, R., & Kotloff, K. (1976). Does interviewing harm children? *Research Communications in Psychology, Psychiatry, and Behavior, 1,* 523–531.

Herjanic, B., & Reich, W. (1982). Development of a structured psychiatric interview for children: Agreement between child and parent on individual symptoms. *Journal of Abnormal Child Psychology, 10,* 307–324.

Hodges, K. (1983). *Guidelines to aid in establishing interrater reliability with the Child Assessment Schedule.* Unpublished manuscript.

Hodges, K. (1985). *Manual for the Child Assessment Schedule.* Unpublished manuscript.

Hodges, K. (1987). Assessing children with a clinical research interview: The child assessment schedule. In R.J. Prinz (Ed.), *Advances in Behavioral Assessment of Children and Families,* (Vol. 3, pp. 203–233). Greenwich, CT: JAI Press.

Hodges, K., Cools, J., & McKnew, D. (1986). Child Assessment Schedule: Test-retest reliability. Paper presented at the meeting of the American Academy of Child Psychiatry, Los Angeles.

Hodges, K., Cools, J., & McKnew, D. (in press). Test-retest reliability of a clinical research interview for children: The Child Assessment Schedule (CAS). *Psychological Assessment: A Journal of Consulting and Clinical Psychology.*

Hodges, V.K., & Fitch, P. (1979). *Development of a mental status examination interview for children*. Paper presented at the meeting of the Missouri Psychological Association, Kansas City, MO.

Hodges, K., Kline, J., Barbero, G., & Flanery, R. (1985). Depressive symptoms in children with recurrent abdominal pain and in their families. *Journal of Pediatrics, 107,* 622–626.

Hodges, K., Kline, J., Barbero, G., & Woodruff, C. (1985). Anxiety in children with recurrent abdominal pain and their parents. *Psychosomatics, 26,* 859–866.

Hodges, K., Kline, J., Fitch, P., McKnew, D., & Cytryn, L. (1981). The Child Assessment Schedule: A diagnostic interview for research and clinical use. *Catalog of Selected Documents in Psychology, 11,* 56.

Hodges, K., Kline, J., Stern, L., Cytryn, L., & McKnew, D. (1982). The development of a child assessment schedule for research and clinical use. *Journal of Abnormal Child Psychology, 10,* 173–189.

Hodges, K., McKnew, D., Burbach, D.J., & Roebuck, L. (1987). Diagnostic concordance between the Child Assessment Schedule (CAS) and the Schedule for Affective Disorders and Schizophrenia for School-Age Children (K-SADS) in an outpatient sample using lay interviewers. *Journal of the American Academy of Child and Adolescent Psychiatry, 26,* 654–661.

Hodges, K., McKnew, D., Cytryn, L., Stern, L., & Kline, J. (1982). The Child Assessment Schedule (CAS) diagnostic interview: A report on reliability and validity. *Journal of the American Academy of Child Psychiatry, 21,* 468–473.

Hodges, K., & Siegel, L.J. (1985). Depression in children in adolescents. In E.E. Beckam & W.R. Leber (Eds.), *Depression: Treatment, assessment, and research* (pp. 517–555). Homewood, IL: Dow-Jones-Irwin.

Kashani, J.H., Beck, N.C., Hoeper, E.W., Fullahi, C., Corcoran, C.M., McAllister, J.A., Rosenberg, T.K., & Reid, J.C. (1987). Psychiatric disorders in a community sample of adolescents. *American Journal of Psychiatry, 144,* 584–589.

Kashani, J.H., McGee, R.D., Clarkson, S.E., Anderson, J.C., Walton, L.E., Williams, S., Silva, P.A., Robins, A.J., Cytryn, L., & McKnew, D.H. (1983). Depression in a sample of nine year old children: Prevalence and associated characteristics. *Archives of General Psychiatry, 40,* 1217–1227.

Kashani, J., Orvaschel, H., Burk, J., & Reid, J. (1985). Informant variance: The issue of parent-child disagreement. *Journal of the American Academy of Child Psychiatry, 24,* 437–441.

Kashani, J., Orvaschel, H., Rosenberg, T., & Reid, J. (1989). *Psychopathology among a community sample of children and adolescents: A developmental perspective. Journal of the American Academy of Child and Adolescent Psychiatry, 28,* 701–706.

Kashani, J., Rosenberg, T., & Reid, J. (in press). An investigation of developmental perspectives in child and adolescent depressive symptomatology. *American Journal of Psychiatry.*

Kestenbaum, C.J., & Bird, H.R. (1978). A reliability study of the mental health assessment form for school-age children. *Journal of the American Academy of Child Psychiatry, 17,* 338–347.

Kovacs, M. (1978). *Children's Depression Inventory (CDI)*. Unpublished manuscript.

Kovacs, M. (1983). *The interview schedule for children.* Manuscript submitted for publication.

Kovacs, M. (1986). A developmental perspective on methods and measures in the assessment of depressive disorders: The clinical interview. In M. Rutter, C.E. Tizard, & P.B. Read (Eds.), *Depression in young people: Clinical and developmental perspectives* (pp. 435–465). New York: The Guilford Press.

Lewis, S.A., Gorsky, A., Cohen, P., & Hartmark, C. (1985). The reactions of youth to diagnostic interviews. *Journal of the American Academy of Child Psychiatry, 24,* 750–755.

Lourie, R., & Rieger, R.E. (1974). Psychiatric and psychological examination of children. In S. Arieti (Ed.), *American handbook of psychiatry* (Vol. 2, pp. 3–36). New York: Basic Books.

Matarazzo, J.D. (1983). The reliability of psychiatric and psychological diagnosis. *Clinical Psychology Review, 3,* 103–145.

Mokros, H., Poznanski, E., Grossman, J., & Freeman, L. (1987). A comparison of child and parent ratings of depression for normal and clinically referred children. *Journal of Child Psychology and Psychiatry, 28,* 613–627.

Moretti, M., Fine, S., Haley, G., & Marriage, K. (1985). Childhood adolescent depression: Child-report versus parent-report information. *Journal of the American Academy of Child Psychiatry, 24,* 298–302.

Poznanski, E., Mokros, H., Grossman, J., & Freeman, L. (1985). Diagnostic criteria in childhood depression. *American Journal of Psychiatry, 142,* 1168–1173.

Puig-Antich, J., & Chambers, W. (1978). *The Schedule for Affective Disorders and Schizophrenia for School-Age Children (Kiddie-SADS).* New York: New York State Psychiatric Institute.

Puig-Antich, J., Chambers, W.J., & Tabrizi, M. (1983). The clinical assessment of current depressive episodes in children and adolescents: Interviews with parents and children. In D.P. Cantwell & G.A. Carlson (Eds.), *Affective disorders in childhood and adolescence: An update.* New York: Spectrum Publications.

Quay, H., & Peterson, D. (1987). *Manual for the Revised Behavior Problem Checklist.* Coral Gables, FL: Author.

Reich, W., & Earls, F. (1987). Rules for making psychiatric diagnoses in children based on multiple sources of information: Preliminary strategies. *Journal of Abnormal Child Psychology, 15,* 601–616.

Reich, W., Herjanic, B., Welner, Z., & Gandhy, P.R. (1982). Development of a structured psychiatric interview for children: Agreement in diagnosis comparing child and parent interviews. *Journal of Abnormal Child Psychology, 10,* 325–336.

Richman, N., Stevenson, J., & Graham, P. J. (1982). *Pre-school to school: A behavioral study.* London: Academic Press.

Robins, L. (1985). Epidemiology: Reflections on testing the validity of psychiatric interviews. *Archives of General Psychiatry, 42,* 918–924.

Robins, L., Helzer, J., Croughan, J., & Ratcliff, K. (1981). National Institute of Mental Health diagnostic interview schedule: Its history, characteristics, and validity. *Archives of General Psychiatry, 38,* 381–389.

Runyan, D.K., Everson, M., Edelsohn, G.A., Hunter, W., & Coulter, M. (1988). Impact of legal intervention on sexually abused children. *Journal of Pediatrics,* 113, 647–653.

Rutter, M., & Graham, P. (1968). The reliability and validity of the psychiatric assessment of the child: I. Interview with the child. *British Journal of Psychiatry, 114,* 563–579.

Rutter, M., Tizard, J., Yule, W., Graham, P., & Whitmore, K. (1976). Isle of Wight Studies 1964–1974. *Psychological Medicine, 6,* 313–332.

Ryan, N.P., Puig-Antich, J., Ambrosini, P., Rabinovich, H., Robinson, D., Nelson, B., Iyengar, S., & Twomey, J. (1987). The clinical picture of major depression in children and adolescents. *Archives of General Psychiatry, 44,* 854–861.

Selman, R.L. (1980). *The growth of interpersonal understanding: Developmental and clinical analyses.* New York: Academic Press.

Shekim, W.A., Kashani, J., Beck, N., Cantwell, D., Martin, J., Rosenberg, J., & Costello, A.J. (1985). The prevalence of attention deficit disorders in a rural midwestern community sample of nine-year-old children. *Journal of the American Academy of Child Psychiatry, 24,* 765–770.

Simmons, J.E. (1974). *Psychiatric examination of children.* Philadelphia: Lea and Febiger.

Society for research in child development (1973). *Ethical standards for research with children.* Chicago: Author.

Spielberger, C.D. (1973). *Preliminary manual for the state-trait anxiety inventory for children.* Palo Alto, CA: Consulting Psychologists Press.

Spitzer, R. (1983). Psychiatric diagnosis: Are clinicians still necessary? *Comprehensive Psychiatry, 24,* 399–411.

Spitzer, R.L., Endicott, J., & Robins, E. (1978). Research diagnostic criteria: Rationale and reliability. *Archives of General Psychiatry, 35,* 773–782.

Spitzer, R.L., Fleiss, J.L., & Endicott, J. (1978). Problems of classification: Reliability and validity. In M.A. Lipton, A. DiMascio, & K.F. Killam (Eds.), *Pharmacology: A Generation of Progress.* (pp. 857–869). New York: Raven Press.

Sylvester, C., Hyde, T., Reichler, R. (1987). The Diagnostic Interview for Children and Personality Inventory for Children in studies of children at risk for anxiety disorders or depression. *Journal of the American Academy of Child and Adolescent Psychiatry, 26,* 668–675.

Turner, S.M., Beidel, D.C., & Costello, A. (1987). Psychopathology in the offspring of anxiety disorders patients. *Journal of Consulting and Clinical Psychology, 55,* 229–235.

Verhulst, F.C., Althaus, M., & Berden, G. (1987). The Child Assessment Schedule: Parent-child agreement and validity measures. *Journal of Child Psychology and Psychiatry, 28,* 455–466.

Verhulst, F.C., Berden, G.F., & Sanders-Woudstra, J.A.R. (1985). Mental health in Dutch children: II. The prevalence of psychiatric disorder and relationship between measures. *Acta Psychiatrica Scandinavica, 72,* (Suppl. 324), 1–44.

Welner, Z., Reich, W., Herjanic, B., Jung, K.G., & Amado, H. (1987). Reliability, validity, and parent-child agreement studies of the Diagnostic Interview for Children and Adolescents (DICA). *Journal of the American Academy of Child and Adolescent Psychiatry, 26,* 649–653.

CHAPTER 6

Specialized Structured Interviews: Type A Interviews for Children and Adolescents

JOHN C. SMITH
TERENCE A. GERACE

INTRODUCTION

The Type A behavior pattern in adults, characterized by competitiveness, impatience, and hostility, has been related prospectively to coronary heart disease (CHD) (Rosenman, Friedman, Straus, Wurm, Kositchek, Hahn, & Werthessen, 1964; Friedman, Rosenman, Straus, Wurm, & Kositchek, 1968; and Blumenthal, Williams, Kong, Schanberg, & Thompson, 1978), the number one cause of death in the United States (National Cancer for Health Statistics, 1986). Three lines of reasoning encourage the

150

study of Type A behavior in children. First, atherosclerosis, the underlying process behind CHD, starts in childhood (Strong & McGill, 1969). Second, Type A behavior most likely develops during childhood (Matthews, 1978). And third, Type A behavior is difficult to modify in adults (Suinn, 1978). This chapter examines the psychometric properties and usefulness of the structured interviews used to assess Type A behavior in preadolescents and adolescents.

Because the concept of Type A behavior was developed to describe the behavior of adults, this chapter begins by summarizing the conceptual origins of the Type A construct in adults. The main body of the chapter first reviews the development of structured interviews to assess Type A behavior both for adults and for children and then examines the reliability and validity of structured interviews for children. The conclusion section aims to integrate the findings from studies of the structured interviews to assess Type A in children, evaluate the utility of these structured interviews, and suggest directions for future research on assessing Type A behavior in children using the structured interview method.

ORIGINS OF THE TYPE A CONSTRUCT

Efforts to reduce the incidence of CHD have led to the discovery of characteristics, risk factors, that increase one's likelihood of developing CHD. The "major" modifiable risk factors are cigarette smoking, elevated blood cholesterol, and high blood pressure (Truett, Cornfield, & Kannel, 1967). Yet even with knowledge of the status of these risk factors, longitudinal studies have been able to predict fewer than half of the deaths from CHD (Keys, Aravanis, Blackburn, van Buchem, Buzino, Djordjevic, Fidonza, Karvonen, Menotti, Puddu, & Taylor, 1972). Thus, the search continues for other causes of CHD.

In the 1950s, two cardiologists, Drs. Meyer Friedman and Ray H. Rosenman proposed a new risk factor—the Type A behavior pattern (Friedman and Rosenman, 1959). They defined the Type A behavior pattern as "an action-emotion complex that can be observed in any person who is *aggressively* involved in a chronic, incessant struggle to achieve more and more in less and less time, and if required to do so, against the opposing efforts of other things or other persons" (Friedman & Rosenman, 1974, p 67). Behaviors that characterize the Type A behavior pattern are chronic time urgency, enhanced aggressiveness, and a strong sense of competitiveness. The behavior pattern usually evolves to include a free-floating but well-rationalized hostility. Individuals who exhibit the Type A behavior pattern are referred to as Type As, whereas those who do not are referred to as Type Bs. Only a small proportion of adults cannot be distinguished as Type A or Type B.

Three factors are relevant to exhibiting the Type A behavior pattern. First, the environmental milieu must contain challenges and demands for rapid and dominating behavior. Second, the individual must be susceptible to these challenges and demands. That is, the person must value the outcomes of responding to environmental challenges. And third, the individual must perceive rapid and dominating behavior as appropriate in a given situation. Thus, the Type A behavior pattern is a multi-caused and recurrent style of behavior that an individual displays in response to life situations. For example, an administrator at a medical school can be seen rushing from one meeting to another, trying to get more and more done in less and less time. He bolts into his front office where his secretaries work and grabs one of their phones to use before reaching his inner office. He curses out loud because the party he is calling is not available. In this scenario the environment places many demands on the administrator. The person perceives that rapid and authoritative responses are appropriate for many of the environmental demands. The results are rapid and impulsive behavior accompanied by frustration and displaced aggression when momentary goals are blocked by other people or things in the environment—the Type A behavior pattern.

CORONARY PRONENESS OF TYPE A

The initial studies linking Type A behavior and CHD were retrospective (e.g., Friedman and Rosenman, 1959; Rosenman and Friedman, 1961). In 1960 the Western Collaborative Group Study (Rosenman, et al., 1964) was initiated to prospectively determine the relationship between the Type A behavior pattern and the incidence of CHD. The study found the relative risk for CHD was 2.2 times greater for Type As than for Type Bs (Rosenman, Brand, Jenkins, Friedman, Straus, & Wurm, 1975).

Since the initiation of the Western Collaborative Group Study, Type A has also been related to coronary atherosclerosis at autopsy (Friedman, et al., 1968), and in angiographic studies (Blumenthal, et al., 1978; Frank, Heller, Kornfeld, Sporn, & Weiss, 1978; Zyzanski, Jenkins, Ryan, Flessas, & Everist, 1976). In a unique study, intervention to reduce Type A in coronary patients resulted in a significantly lower rate of recurrent myocardial infarctions compared to traditional cardiac rehabilitation (Friedman, Thoresen, Gill, Ulmer, Thompson, Powell, Price, Elek, Rabin, Breall, Piaget, Dixon, Bourg, Levy, & Tasto, 1982).

Not all studies of Type A and CHD, however, have yielded positive associations (e.g., Shekelle, Hulley, Neaton, Billings, Borhani, Gerace, Jacobs, Lasser, Mittlemark, & Stamler, 1985; MacDougall, Dembroski, Dimsdale, & Hackett, 1985). For a thorough discussion of the relationship between Type A and CHD see the review by Matthews and Haynes (1986).

To improve the specificity of detecting adults at increased risk for CHD, other researchers have focused their efforts on identifying factors that influence the assessment of Type A using the structured interview and exploring the links between individual behavioral components of Type A and CHD. A brief review of their findings provides useful direction for the study of Type A behavior in children.

Components of Type A Behavior and CHD

Components of the Type A behavior pattern have been studied in order to reduce the proportion of people predicted to be at increased risk for CHD. For example, Matthews, Glass, Rosenman, and Bortner (1977) identified two factors that distinguished men who developed CHD from those who did not. The first factor, labeled "competitive drive," included enjoyable competition at work, "explosive voice modulation," and hostility. The second factor, labeled "impatience," consisted of self-reports of time urgency.

Dembroski and his colleagues have pursued the notion that hostility may be the coronary-prone component of the Type A behavior pattern. For example, they found that ratings of hostility derived from the structured interview were significantly related to the severity of coronary artery disease at the time of catheterization (Dembroski, MacDougall, Williams, Haney, & Blumenthal, 1985; MacDougall, Dembroski, Dimsdale, & Hackett, 1985). But how is hostility characterized?

Hostility appears to be a multidimensional construct. For example, factor analyses of the Buss-Durkee Hostility Inventory yield two factors (Buss and Durkee, 1957). One factor primarily reflects the Suspicion and Resentment subscales. The other factor reflects the Assault and Verbal Hostility subscales. One examination of these components of hostility and degree of coronary artery disease revealed a positive association for the Assault and Verbal Hostility factor but not for the Suspicion and Resentment factor or the global hostility score composed of both factors (Siegman, Dembroski, & Ringel, 1987). Perhaps only a specific type of hostility plays a role in the development of CHD.

These studies of the coronary proneness of Type A behavior in adults suggest that research of Type A in children should include assessment methods modeled after techniques used to assess adults and examine separate components of the Type A pattern. The study of individual components of Type A in children may be especially important because the components may differ in their antecedents and developmental processes.

THE TYPE A STRUCTURED INTERVIEW FOR ADULTS

The Type A behavior pattern was first measured using a structured interview (Friedman & Rosenman, 1959; Rosenman et al., 1964). The structured interview today contains questions about drive and ambition, past and present competitive, aggressive, and hostile feelings, and sense of time urgency. Assessment of the interview is based on overt behaviors, such as voice emphasis, voice loudness, speed of speech, latency of response to questions, interruptions, and the content of responses to the interview questions. Interviews were originally scored on the following five-point scale (Chesney, Eagleston, & Rosenman, 1980):

> A-1=Fully developed pattern.
> A-2=Many Type A characteristics present,
>   but not the complete pattern.
> X=An even mix of Type A and Type B characteristics.
> B-3=Many Type B characteristics,
>   but with some Type A characteristics.
> B-4=Relative absence of Type A characteristics.

Studies of which behavioral characteristics best predict interview assessments generally indicate that voice emphasis is the major cue, with speed of speaking and latency of response to questions also accounting for significant amounts of variance (see review by Jacobs & Schucker, 1981). Content of responses usually accounts for a significant, but much smaller amount of variance in structured interview scores. Thus, the structured interview is assessed primarily by observing the voice stylistics displayed during the interview. In the words of Rosenman et al. (1964, appendix), "the correct classification of a subject depended far more upon the motor and emotional qualities accompanying his response to specific questions than the actual content of his answers. To minimize or to misunderstand this last differential is to fail in the correct behavioral assessment of a subject."

A model of the process for assessing Type A in adults via a structured interview will help organize our understanding of the development of structured interviews to assess Type A in children. The process of assessment using the structured interview method can be described within a general model. The model presumes that Type A behavior results when a susceptible individual reacts to an appropriate environment. Thus, the display of Type A behavior depends on variables associated with the person and variables associated with the environment. The measurement of Type A behavior further requires an observer to document the occurrence of Type A behavior and a scale of possible values to quantify the measurement.

Applying this model yields five areas to examine when assessing Type A in children. The first area includes variables related to the person. For example, which age ranges can be tested and how do boys differ from girls? Second, what interview environment is appropriate for children? That is, what should be the content of the questions and in what manner should the questions be asked? Third, which behaviors are considered Type A behaviors in children? Is the content of children's speech less affected than adults' by what they think they should say? Fourth, what scale of measurement will be sensitive to developmental changes yet also be reliable? Fifth, are the scores valid?

To address the five areas, issues common to each structured interview for children are discussed first. Then, specific findings for each structured interview are reviewed. Finally, all the findings will be considered together and conclusions will be presented.

GENERAL ASPECTS OF STRUCTURED INTERVIEWS FOR CHILDREN

Before researchers can describe the nature of Type A behavior in youngsters, they must develop and adequately test procedures for assessing Type A. Thus, the *sine qua non* of studying Type A in children is the availability of an instrument that reliably and validly measures Type A behavior. Since a structured interview is the method of choice to assess Type A behavior in adults (Byrne, Rosenman, Schiller, & Chesney, 1985), several researchers have used the structured interview method to assess Type A behavior in children.

At least four groups of investigators have developed interviews to measure Type A behavior in youths. The first group described their interview in 1976 (Butensky, Faralli, Heebner, & Waldron, 1976). This interview was scored almost exclusively on the content of the answers and was essentially a self-report of Type A behaviors. Since there are no reported data on the reliability or validity of this early instrument and since the other interviews are much more similar to the adult structured interview (Rosenman, et al., 1964), no more will be said regarding this pioneering effort. The other three interviews are: the Adolescent Structured Interview (Siegel & Leitch, 1981; Siegel, Matthews, & Leitch, 1981), the Miami Structured Interview (Gerace & Smith, 1985; Smith, Gerace, Christakis, & Kafatos, 1985; Smith & Gerace, 1987), and the Student Structured Interview (Kirmil-Gray, Eagleston, Thoresen, Heft, Arnow, & Bracke, 1987).

Content of Interview Questions

Like the adult structured interview, the interviews for children contain questions on impatience, competitiveness, and aggressiveness. In contrast to the adult interview, the interviews for children cover situations relevant to youngsters, such as activities at school instead of activities at work. Table 6.1 shows example questions from three of the structured interviews for children.

Administration of the Interviews

Similar to the adult interview, the children's interviews are administered in a standardized manner and the questions are asked moderately fast. Certain words are emphasized so the interview sounds engaging. Some questions are drawn out to test whether the child will interrupt the interviewer. For example, "Most kids who go to school get up fairly early in the morning. In your particular case uh-what-uh-wha, wha, what-uh-time-uh-do-uh-do you-uh usually get up in the morning?" (Gerace & Smith, 1985).

Interviewers require training to achieve the prescribed manner of interviewing. Training to administer the adult structured interview may familiarize trainees with the level of standardization needed to interview children. Separate training, however, using one of the structured interviews for children, is necessary to achieve an appropriate interviewing style. It is noteworthy that researchers working with each of the three children's interviews have noted that children must be interviewed in a less confrontational and forceful style than called for with adults. When questioned harshly by an adult, children will become overly submissive or withdrawn.

Scoring of the Interviews

Structured interviews for youngsters have been scored using three strategies. First, global Type A scores modeled after the original proce-

TABLE 6.1 Sample Items from Structured Interviews to Assess Type A Behavior in Children

---

Adolescent Structured Interview[a]

Would you say that you work harder to accomplish things than most of your friends?

Would you consider yourself to be an ambitious and hard-driving sort of person or more relaxed and easy-going?

What irritates you most about your school or the people at your school?

If you saw a friend doing something rather slowly, and you know that you could do it faster and better yourself, would it make you restless to watch him or her?

Do you hurry in doing most things?

Miami Structured Interview[b]

Do you like to do better than other kids?

Do you like competitive games where you can try to beat other kids?

Tell me something you don't like about school.

What if you are in a rush, and you are walking with someone who is walking much slower than you are and is slowing you down, how would you feel?

Do you ever feel in a hurry to get things done?

Student Structured Interview[c]

Do you think you work harder than most of the people in your class?

Would other people say you are calm and easy-going or that you are hard-driving?

What bothers you most about school or your classmates?

If you agree to meet someone at, say, 3 o'clock in the afternoon and they are late, would it bother you?

How often do you feel in a hurry to get things done?

---

[a]Adapted from Siegel and Leitch (1981). Permission granted from J. Siegel.

[b]Developed by J. Smith and T. Gerace, Miami. Permission granted by J. Smith.

[c]Adapted from Kirmil-Gray, et al., 1987. Permission of authors granted.

dure for adults can be assigned. The global score indicates the intensity or completeness of the Type A behavior pattern. Ratings are made on ordinal scales, such as strong A (A-1), mild A (A-2), even mix of A and B (X), mild B (B-3), and extreme B (B-4). One advantage of using this method with children is that longitudinal studies could test the stability of Type A behavior by using a similar scoring system in children and adults.

The global Type A score is based on observations of several behaviors. Assessments rely heavily on the voice stylistics of interviewees (e.g., word emphasis, latency of response, and speed of speech). The content of responses is much less important (Rosenman, et al., 1964). The score is a subjective rating and is usually assigned after auditing audio recordings of interviews. The ability to rate children's interviews requires training to achieve agreement with scores of experienced raters.

A second method of scoring children's interviews calls for rating each voice stylistic separately. This procedure is similar to the global Type A rating approach since both focus on voice stylistics. The most frequently studied voice stylistics are those that best predict the global Type A score, such as word emphasis, speed of speech, and response latency. Rating individual voice stylistics may have the advantages of more objectivity, higher reliability of ratings, and the potential to investigate if particular voice stylistics are good predictors of the global Type A score or other behavioral endpoints.

The third approach to scoring interviews is to rate whether the content of the answers indicates the child's behavior is Type A. Responses to individual questions on the interview can be scored on a dichotomous scale and a total score produced by summing the number of Type A-like responses. For example, answering "Yes" to the question, "Do you hurry in doing most things?" would be scored as a Type A answer. This method of scoring is based entirely on self-reports. Thus, the structured interview method can produce scores based on both direct observations of behavior during the interview and self-reports of behaviors outside the interview.

INDIVIDUAL STRUCTURED INTERVIEWS FOR CHILDREN

Before generalizing further across the interviews, the research on each interview is presented separately. In order to give an historical perspective, the interviews are presented chronologically by publication date.

Adolescent Structured Interview

The Adolescent Structured Interview (ASI) was developed initially to explore whether the structured interview method could be used with boys and girls ages 13 to 18 years (Siegel & Leitch, 1981). The ASI contains 22 questions about situations that should elicit Type A behavior in the susceptible adolescent. The ASI takes about 10 minutes to administer. Table 6.1 shows example items from the ASI.

The administration of the ASI is structured in that questions are asked in a similar manner for each adolescent. The style of administration is less challenging and confrontational than that of the adult structured interview. Specialized training to administer the ASI is needed in order to keep the interviewing style consistent across interviewers or studies. The amount of training would vary with the talent and skills of the potential interviewer.

The ASI has been scored using global Type A scores, individual speech stylistics, and the content of the responses. The global Type A score is rated on a scale of strong A (A-1), weak A (A-2), a mixture of A and B (X), and the absence of Type A (B). The ASI has also been scored separately for the following six speech dimensions: interruptions by the respondent, loud and explosive speech, rapid and accelerated speech, quickness of response, passive hostility, and competition for control of the interview (Siegel, Matthews, & Leitch, 1981). Except for interruptions, the stylistics were rated on five-point scales. Scoring the ASI for content involves determining whether the response to each question is characteristic of the Type A behavior pattern. For example, a "Yes" response to the question, "Do you always feel anxious to get going and finish whatever it is you have to do?" would be scored as a Type A response. The Type A score based on content is the sum of the questions answered in a manner characteristic of the Type A behavior pattern.

Factor analysis of the speech dimensions and the content ratings yielded three subscales (Siegel, Matthews, & Leitch, 1981). The first subscale, labeled the "Interview Behaviors," comprises the overt voice stylistics observed during the interview. The second subscale, labeled "Impatience," consists of self-reports of rapid and time urgent behavior (e.g., "hurries in doing most things," "always feels anxious to get going"). The third subscale, labeled "Hard-driving," includes self-reports of working hard (e.g., "works harder than friends," self-description of hard-driving).

The interrater reliability of the ASI has only been reported for the global Type A scores. Table 6.2 summarizes the interrater reliability findings for the ASI and two other structured interviews for children. The initial report of interrater reliability showed agreement on 75% of 40 interviews scored either Type A or Type B (Siegel & Leitch, 1981). In another study interrater agreement reached 93% on a scale of A, X, and B for 15 boys aged 9 and 10 years (Matthews & Jennings, 1984). These levels of interrater reliability are similar to what has been reported with other structured interviews for children (Gerace & Smith, 1985; Kirmil-Gray, et al., 1987).

The validity of the ASI global Type A score and the factor analytically derived subscales of the ASI have been examined. The criteria used to test the validity of the ASI scores include instruments intended to assess global Type A, individual items from self-report scales intended to

TABLE 6.2   Interrater Reliability of Three Type A Interviews for Children: Percentages of Interviews on Which Two Raters Agreed

Scale	Adolescent Structured Interview (ASI)	Miami Structured Interview (MSI)			Student Structured Interview (SSI)
A verus B	75[a]	81	83	96[c]	—
sample size	40	88	69	65	
A, X, B	93[b]	—	—	—	—
sample size	15				
A-1, A-2, B-3, B-4	—	57	51	56[c]	—
sample size		88	69	65	
Median split of voice stylistics		—			79[d]
sample size					65
Median split of content		—			71[d]
sample size					65

[a]Siegel & Leitch, 1981.

[b]Matthew & Jennings, 1984.

[c]Gerace & Smith, 1985, Type Xs excluded prior to calculations.

[d]Kirmil-Gray, et al., 1987.

assess the global Type A pattern, and self-report scales of components of Type A.

Validity of the Global Type A Score

Evidence that the ASI global Type A score has some cross-situational validity comes from finding significant associations between the ASI global Type A score and the Matthews Youth Test for Health (MYTH) (Matthews & Jennings, 1984), the Tacoma Type A cluster, and the Tacoma Social Insecurity cluster (Siegel & Leitch, 1981). No associations, however, resulted with scores from the Bortner Adjective Rating Scale, a seven-item self-report instrument for assessing Type A behavior in adults (Bortner, 1969). Table 6.3 summarizes the findings on the validity of the ASI.

The MYTH is a 17-item rating scale that is completed by school teachers (Matthews & Angulo, 1980). It is designed to measure Type A behavior in elementary school students and has been empirically related to aggressive, competitive, and impatient behaviors (Matthews & Angulo, 1980). The Tacoma Type A cluster is a 12-item, true-false, self-report instrument constructed to test the validity of the ASI. Items in the Tacoma Type A cluster refer to competitiveness, impatience, hostility, and efforts to control the environment. The Tacoma Social Insecurity cluster includes four "true-false" items that refer to bashfulness, self-confidence, ease of conversing in group settings, and emotional reactions to criticism. Information is currently unavailabile on the reliability and validity of the Tacoma Type A cluster or the Social Insecurity cluster.

It is also important to examine whether specific components of Type A are related to the ASI global scores since the global score may measure only some components of the Type A pattern. The ASI global Type A scores showed significant associations with only 5 of the 23 measures of Type A characteristics that were examined (Siegel & Leitch, 1981; Siegel, Mathews, & Leitch, 1981). Global Type A scores associated in a positive direction with the "Active" and "Angry" scales from the Edwards Personality Inventory (see Table 6.3), and the items "Often thinks about other things when people are talking to him/her," and

TABLE 6.3 Associations Between Adolescent Structured Interview (ASI) Ratings and Validation Measures of Type A Behavior[a]

Validation Measure	ASI Rating			
	Global Type A	Interview Behaviors	Impatience Content	Hard-driving Content
Tacoma Type A cluster	$p<.05$	$p<.05$	$p<.05$	$p<.05$
Tacoma Social Insecurity cluster	$p<.05$*	—	—	—
Bortner Adjective Rating Scale	NS	NS	$p<.05$	$p<.05$
MYTH Type A	$r=.42$	—	—	—
ASI Global Type A	N/A	$r=.81$	$r=.15$	$r=.13$
Edwards Personality Inventory Scale				
Active	$p<.05$	$p<.05$	$p<.05$	$p<.05$
Angry	$p<.05$	$p<.05$	$p<.05$	NS
Impressed by status	NS	NS	$p<.05$	NS
Desires recognition	NS	NS	$p<.05$	$p<.05$
Is a hard worker	NS	NS	NS	$p<.05$
Competitive	NS	NS	NS	$p<.05$
Persistence	NS	NS	NS	NS

(continued)

TABLE 6.3   (*Continued*)

Validation Measure	ASI Rating			
	Global Type A	Interview Behaviors	Impatience Content	Hard-driving Content
Items from the Tacoma Type A cluster:				
Often thinks about other things when people are talking to him/her	p<.05	p<.05	NS	NS
Rarely stays in bed when ill	p<.05	p<.05	NS	NS
Has frequent feelings of anger	NS	p<.05	NS	NS
Often cries when frustrated	NS	p<.05	NS	NS
Prefers to work alone	NS	p<.05	NS	NS
Needs to feel in control of a situation	NS	p<.05	NS	p<.05
Gets impatient waiting in line	NS	NS	p<.05	NS
Does most things in a hurry	NS	NS	p<.05	NS
Tries not to depend on others	NS	NS	p<.05	NS
Responds to frustration with irritation	NS	NS	NS	NS
Tries to hold in emotions	NS	NS	NS	NS
More likely to encourage someone who is failing than to praise someone succeeding	NS	NS	NS	NS
Tacoma Social Insecurity Items				
Has trouble thinking of the right things to talk about when in a group of people	p<.05	—	—	—
Frequently has to fight against showing bashfulness	NS	—	—	—
Certainly lacking in self-confidence	NS	—	—	—

(continued)

TABLE 6.3 *(Continued)*

Validation Measure	ASI Rating			
	Global Type A	Interview Behaviors	Impatience Content	Hard-driving Content
Is hurt terribly by scolding or criticism	NS	—	—	—
Bortner Adjective Rating Scale Items				
Never late/casual about appointments	—	NS	p<.05	NS
Tries to do many things at once	—	NS	p<.05	NS
Rushed/never rushed	—	NS	p<.05	NS
Fast (eating, walking, etc.)/slow	—	NS	p<.05	p<.05
Competitive/not competitive	—	NS	NS	p<.05
Few interests outside work or school	—	NS	NS	p<.05
Expresses feelings/sits on feelings	—	NS	NS	NS

p<.05 designates that the mean ratings for Type As were significantly higher than the mean for Type Bs (alpha=.05).

r=designates a statistically significant Pearson correlation (alpha=.05) for the interview four-point scale.

NS designates no significant relationship with Type A (alpha=.05).

— designates that association was not tested.

N/A designates that an analysis is not applicable.

*Type Bs scored higher than Type As.

[a] Adapted from Siegel & Leitch (1981) and Seigel et al., (1981).

"Rarely stays in bed when ill" from the Tacoma Type A cluster (see Table 6.3). A negative association resulted with the Tacoma Social Insecurity cluster item "Has trouble thinking of the right things to talk about when in a group of people," (see Table 6.3). As expected, a strong correlation (r=.81) resulted with the "Interview Behaviors" factor, composed of ratings of voice stylistics which are also the primary basis for determining the ASI global Type A rating. Although these positive results support the validity of the global Type A score for measuring some characteristics related to the Type A pattern, there is no consistency among these criteria to indicate that the global Type A rating measures "classic" components of the Type A pattern, i.e., competitiveness, impatience, and hostility.

Among the characteristics that showed less than "moderate" relationships to the global Type A ratings were items indicative of all the "classic" components of the Type A behavior pattern. For example, small correlations (rs<.16) occurred with the "Impatience" and "Hard-driving" factors based on the content of interview responses and the competitive scale from the Edwards Personality Inventory. Global Type A scores also did not relate to 10 items from the Tacoma Type A cluster that refer to impatience, anger, and striving to control the environment and three of the four items on the Tacoma Social Insecurity cluster. Global Type A scores did not relate to the following scales: "Is a hard worker," "Persistence," "Desires recognition," and "Impressed by status."

Taken together, these findings suggest that the ASI global Type A score can predict global Type A scores on some instruments. Examination of the relationships between global Type A scores and individual components of Type A, however, revealed no theoretically meaningful pattern of significant associations.

Validity of Component Scores from the ASI

An "Interview Behaviors" rating was the first subscale derived from factor analysis of voice stylistics and content of responses during the ASI (Siegel, Matthews, & Leitch, 1981). The "Interview Behaviors" scale consisted entirely of ratings of voice stylistics. The examination of the validity of the "Interview Behaviors" scale utilized many of the same criteria from the examination of the ASI global Type A score. As shown in Table 6.3, the "Interview Behaviors" scale correlated strongly with the ASI global Type A score (r=.81). This finding is not surprising since the global score is based primarily on the same voice stylistics that contribute to the "Interview Behaviors" scale.

The "Interview Behaviors" and global Type A scores also showed significant associations with the Tacoma Type A cluster and the Active and Angry scales from the Edwards Personality Inventory. These results suggest that the relationships observed between the global Type A scores and these validity criteria resulted partially because of the predictive power of voice stylistics, and not the content of the responses during the structured interview.

Surprising, however, is the finding that the "Interview Behaviors" scale showed significant associations with four self-report items not associated with the global Type A score. For instance, "Has frequent feelings of anger" and "Needs to feel in control of a situation" (see Table 6.3). This disparity between the "Interview Behaviors" and global Type

A scores may suggest, first, that the "Interview Behaviors" scores can be more reliably scored than the global Type A score. Unfortunately, no data on the reliability of the "Interview Behaviors" scores are available. Second, the "Interview Behaviors" score, with its equal weighting for each voice stylistic, is perhaps a more valid indicator of some Type A behaviors than the subjective judgments that comprise the global Type A score.

The items on the Tacoma Type A cluster that related to the "Interview Behaviors" score suggest that voice stylistics may reflect a desire to be in control of situations and a propensity to show frustration and anger. Interestingly, the "Interview Behaviors" scores did not relate to speed and impatience as measured by items on the Tacoma Type A cluster and the Bortner Adjective Rating Scale. Thus, children's voice stylistics may reflect anger and striving to control, but not the impatience component of the Type A behavior pattern.

"Impatience" was the second factor analytically derived scale from the ASI content and stylistic ratings. The "Impatience" score is based on the content of responses to nine questions in the ASI such as "Gets restless when watching a slow worker," "Walks rapidly," and "Hurries in doing most things." The "Impatience" scores showed almost no association to the ASI global Type A score ($r=.15$). Several self-report measures, however, showed significant association with the "Impatience" scores, including the Tacoma Type A cluster, the Bortner Adjective Rating Scale, and the "Active," "Angry," "Desires recognition," and "Impressed by status" scales from the Edwards Personality Inventory (see Table 6.3). Analysis of individual items from the Tacoma Type A cluster and the Bortner Adjective Rating Scale revealed that the "Impatience" scale related almost exclusively to items referring to time or speed. Thus, the "Impatience" scale from the ASI appears to be a good indicator of self-perceived time urgency.

The final scale obtained from the ASI is "Hard-driving." This scale is composed of three items from the content analysis of ASI questions. The items are "Believes friends would describe subject as hard-driving," "Self-description of Hard-driving," and "Works harder than friends" (Siegel, Matthews, & Leitch, 1981). The "Hard-driving" scale showed a weak association with the ASI global Type A score ($r=.13$), but significant association with the Tacoma Type A cluster and the Bortner Adjective Rating Scale. The "Hard-driving" scale also showed agreement with The Edwards Personality Inventory scales of "Hard worker," "Desires recognition," "Competitive," and "Active." Analysis of items from the Tacoma Type A cluster and the Bortner Adjective Rating Scale showed "Hard-driving" was related to "Need to feel in control," "Few interests outside school," "Acts fast," and "Competitive." These associations suggest that the "Hard-driving" scale from the ASI is a reliable indicator of self-descriptions of working hard.

Conclusions on the Validity of the ASI

Four general comments can summarize the findings on the validity of the ASI Type A scores. First, ASI global scores are related to scores from criteria based on direct observation of behaviors, such as the MYTH, and the "Interview Behaviors" factor. Second, the ASI global Type A score is primarily a measure of voice stylistics. Third, the "Interview Behaviors," and probably the ASI global Type A, scores may be indicators of efforts to control and frustration or anger in response to the environment, but probably not impatience. Fourth, scores for "Impatience" and "Hard-driving" can be derived from self-reports during the ASI. The scales derived from the content of self-reports provide information independent of voice stylistics during the ASI.

The findings of independent sources of information from behavior observations and self-reports for adolescents are similar to findings with adults. For instance, low to moderate agreement between scores from the adult structured interview and the Jenkins Activity Survey has been observed (e.g., Byrne et al., 1985). This pattern of findings for adults has led to the hypothesis that the structured interview assesses a behavioral hyperactivity to provocative situations whereas self-reports of Type A indicate a "cognitive preference" for a rapid, achievement-oriented life style (Matthews, 1982). A similar interpretation for youths may be appropriate. That is, the global Type A score from the ASI may reflect a propensity toward more intense behavioral reactions to the environment. This enhanced behavioral propensity does not appear to be highly conscious as suggested by the low or absent association between the global Type A ratings and ratings of content from the ASI and the majority of self-report criteria.

Assets and Limitations of the ASI

In summary, an asset of the ASI is that a scoring system has been developed for the content based scales of "Impatience" and "Hard-driving." Information from these component scales may improve our understanding of the interplay between different dimensions within the Type A pattern. The ASI is most applicable to English-speaking adolescents. The wording of some ASI questions is probably too difficult for preadolescents. Issues regarding the ASI that have yet to be resolved include documentation of its validity separately for boys and girls and further examination of the validity of the "Impatience" and "Hard-driving" scales using behavioral observations for criteria.

Miami Structured Interview

The Miami Structured Interview (MSI) was developed at the University of Miami School of Medicine as part of a cross-cultural study of risk factors for CHD in preadolescent and adolescent males in the United States, a country of high CHD incidence, and Greece, a country of low CHD incidence (Christakis, Kafatos, Fordyce, Kurtz, Gerace, Smith, Duncan, Cassady, & Doxiadis, 1981). The instrument was designed to assess Type A behavior for: (1) a wider range of ages (7 to 18 years) than tested with previous interviews, (2) large-scale epidemiological studies that require brief, economical testing procedures, and (3) cross-cultural studies conducted in different languages (e.g., English and Greek).

The Miami Structured Interview contains 11 main questions with follow-up probes that refer to situations that might elicit competitiveness, impatience, or hostility in a susceptible child. All of the questions refer to situations that may be experienced by children of a broad age range and cultural background.

Administration of the MSI

The MSI is administered in a standardized and engaging fashion. Standardization of the presentation is necessary in order to compare responses among children and across different samples. Training is required to achieve an interviewing style consistent with that developed by the originators. A training program involving audiotaped and written materials has been used by other researchers to learn to appropriately administer the MSI.

Each administration of the interview includes all the questions delivered with a consistent pace and pattern of word emphasis. Engagement of the participants, or maintenance of attention and interest, is maximized by starting with "warm-up" questions to reduce anxiety (e.g., "What is your name?" "What do you like to be called?" and "How old are you?"), using the prescribed pace and pattern of word emphasis, telling the student the interviewer is interested in what the student has to say rather than what other people say about students, and assuring confidentiality. Although the MSI takes about 10 minutes to completely administer, it produces about five to six minutes of audiotaped material to score.

Scoring the MSI

Interviews have been rated on the five-point scale (A-1, A-2, X, B-3, B-4) originally used with the adult structured interview. Interview ratings have also been combined to yield more general scales such as A (A-1 and A-2 combined) versus not A (X, B-3, and B-4 combined). The MSI has been rated on the basis of voice stylistics. Voice stylistics indicative of Type A include emphatic speech, rapid word production, and short latency between the end of questions and the answers. Content of responses, which contributes little to assessments using the adult structured interview (Jacobs & Shucker, 1981), has not been used in rating the MSI so the interview could be used in multi-language studies.

Reliability of the MSI

Of the Type A structured interviews for children, the MSI has been the most extensively studied with regards to reliability. Interrater reliability, test-retest reliability, and the "interviewer effect" have been examined. Findings from these studies of the MSI are useful for developing a general understanding of the process of assessing Type A in children with the structured interview.

Interrater reliability. Gerace and Smith (1985) examined interrater reliability in three samples of males ages 7 to 18 who volunteered for the American-Hellenic Heart Study, a longitudinal, cross-cultural study of CHD risk factors (Christakis et al., 1981). The first sample, 44 Greek-American males, was interviewed twice. The second sample, called Mixed Americans, consisted of 69 Greek-American and non-Greek American males. The third sample contained 65 native Greek boys for whom interviews were conducted in Greek. As shown in Table 6.2, interrater agreements on the scale of A (A-1 and A-2 combined) versus B (B-3 and B-4 combined, Xs omitted) were 81%, 83%, and 96%, respectively. These levels of agreement indicate that the interrater reliability of the MSI is similar to those of the adult structured interview (e.g., 79% to 89%; Friedman et al., 1968; MacDougall, Dembroski, & Musante, 1979) and the Adolescent Structured Interview (75%, Siegel & Leitch, 1981). Interrater agreement for the MSI on the four-point scale A-1, A-2, B-3, and B-4 ranged from 51% to 57%, which is lower than levels of 64% to 72% reported for the adult structured interview (Friedman et al., 1968 and MacDougall et al., 1979). The lower levels of agreement on the four-point scale of the MSI relative to the adult structured interview may be due to the shorter length of the MSI.

Gerace and Smith (1985) also investigated interrater reliability on the five-point rating scale by examining the nature of the disagreements between raters. They detected bias indicated by one rater consistently rating in the "more A" direction or, conversely, the other rater consistently rating in the "more B" direction. This type of bias probably arises from complexities in the attentional and decision-making process involved in rating the interviews. Attentional processes include suppressing awareness of the content of responses while recognizing and remembering voice stylistics such as response latency, emphasis, speed of speech, acceleration of speech, loudness, length of responses, interruptions, sighs, clicks, and repeated words. Differences in how raters interpreted the voice stylistics may also have contributed to the systematic pattern in interrater disagreements. That is, the raters may have attended to the same stylistics, but differentially weighed them in determining ratings. The susceptibility of the structured interview process to this type of bias is emphasized by two other findings. First, Gerace and Smith (1985) found that data reported by Jenkins, Rosenman & Friedman (1968) also showed a statistically significant pattern in the disagreements between raters of the adult structured interview. Second, Scherwitz, Graham, Grandits, & Billings (1987) reported significant differences across raters in how voice stylistics were used to arrive at structured interview ratings for adults.

Another method of examining interrater reliability is to compare the prevalences of Type A assigned by two raters. If two raters produce different prevalences of Type A from the same or similar samples of interviews, then there is evidence for systematic bias between the raters. Gerace and Smith (1985) conducted such an analysis for the three samples of interviews from the American-Hellenic Heart Study described above. They found that one rater assigned a prevalence of 60 per 100 to the Greek-American sample while the other rater assigned 35 per 100. This finding illustrates that rater bias can exist even when two raters agree on an acceptable percentage of interviews (81%).

Bias introduced by raters can be reduced by frequently recalibrating the raters. One method to accomplish this was illustrated by Gerace and Smith (1985). The procedure evolved from a need to assess over 2,000 Type A interviews conducted during the American-Hellenic Heart Study (Christakis et al., 1981). First, the interviews were randomly divided between two raters. Second, both raters independently assessed the same 20 interviews following every 60 interviews they rated. Then, the raters jointly reviewed, discussed, and rerated interviews on which they initially disagreed by two categories on the five-point scale.

After implementing the periodic review and discussion of disagreements, Smith and Gerace (1983) compared the prevalence of ratings from auditors within each of the seven samples in the American-Hellenic Heart Study. This test of interrater reliability was indirect because the raters listened to different samples of interviews. The interviews were randomly distributed between raters so there is no reason to expect different prevalences of Type A ratings from the two raters. Using the A versus not A scale, no significant biases were detected. Thus, feedback from reviewing and discussing disagreements may help raters to assess interviews similarly.

Taken together the findings on the interrater reliability of the MSI lead to three conclusions. First, levels of interrater agreement are comparable to those obtained with the adult structured interview, especially for the Type A versus Type B scale. Second, the structured interview assessment process is a complex, multi-dimensional scaling process that is susceptible to rater biases. Third, rater bias can be minimized by recalibration of raters through their review and discussion of disagreements.

Test-retest reliability. To study the development of Type A behavior in children requires an instrument that successfully measures Type A in the same youngsters over time. Ideally, an assessment from a structured interview should not be affected by previous exposure to the instrument, that is, it should have good test-retest reliability. The instrument should not be "reactive" so that repeated use with the same persons affects its sensitivity or specificity. For instance, reduced sensitivity can arise if "carryover effects" from prior administrations decrease the challenging nature of the questions. Reduced specificity can occur if the level of impatience increases because participants recall being asked the same questions.

To assess the test-retest reliability of the MSI, Gerace and Smith (1985) administered the MSI twice to 44 males ages 7 to 18 years. Each youngster received the MSI from one interviewer (test), then immediately from the second interviewer (retest). The researchers reasoned that a short test-retest interval would maximize any carryover effects and minimize developmental changes in behavior pattern. To avoid confounding test or retest and interviewer, 23 participants went from interviewer one to interviewer two while 21 went from interviewer two to interviewer one. High test-retest reliability was evidenced by 91% of participants (40 out of 44) being assigned to the same major category (A versus not A) for the test and retest. Using the five-point rating scale, 66% of the participants were rated identically on the test and retest.

The 91% major category agreement between the test and retest strongly suggests the MSI can be used more than once with the same person without losing sensitivity. Only 1 out of 21 test As was not rated Type A at the retest. The participants' voice stylistics and content of responses during the test and retest interviews were remarkably similar. These findings suggest that the MSI situation upon retest will not lose its ability to set the occasion to type male youngsters using the A versus not A scale. Since 34% of the participants were not rated identically on the five-point scale, care must be taken in interpreting data from longitudinal studies when this scale is used.

Interviewer effect. Do interviewers differentially affect the behavior of youngsters during the MSI? The comparability of the behaviors elicited by different interviewers is another important aspect of the reliability of the structured interview. Comparability across interviewers within a study is necessary in order to justify combining ratings from different interviewers. Standardization of interview presentation is also essential in order to compare findings across studies that use different interviewers.

The interviewer effect was studied using the same participants and procedures described above for assessing the MSI's test-retest reliability (Gerace & Smith, 1985). No interviewer effect was detected using the A versus not A scale. However, when the five-point rating scale was analyzed as interval data (A-1=1, A-2=2, X=3, B-3=4, B-4=5), the two interviewers differed significantly on their average Type A scores. Perhaps the verbal or nonverbal behavior of the interviewers differentially affected the voice stylistics of some participants and consequently the behavioral ratings they received. In another examination of the interviewer effect Gerace and Smith (1983) compared the distributions of behavior types between two English-speaking interviewers and between two Greek-speaking interviewers. No significant associations occurred between interviewers and prevalence of behavior pattern types on the A versus not A scale or the five-point rating scale.

These studies of the interviewer effect suggest that similarly trained interviewers can generate comparable distributions of behavior types using the MSI. An interviewer effect, however, may be detectable under highly controlled conditions. The fact that interviewer differences can affect ratings supports the importance of training aimed at having the structured interview presented in a standardized fashion.

Validity of the MSI

The validity of the MSI was initially studied for American and Greek male preadolescents (ages 7 to 11 years old) and adolescents (ages 12 to 16 years old) in the American-Hellenic Heart Study (Smith, Gerace, Christakis, & Kafatos, 1985). Classroom behavior was selected as the criterion for testing validity and was measured with the MYTH, a rating scale completed by teachers (Matthews & Angulo, 1980). The MYTH was selected as the validation criterion because: (1) it provides observations of overt behaviors rather than self-reports of behavior, (2) it showed some validity for measuring Type A characteristics in American preadolescents (Matthews & Angulo, 1980), and (3) it measures behaviors exhibited by children in the classroom which are likely to be similar in cross-cultural settings. MYTH questionnaires for preadolescents were completed by teachers who taught the student more than two subjects. For adolescents, each student's mathematics and language teachers (English teachers in the U.S.A. and Greek teachers in Greece) both completed the MYTH.

Validity of the MSI scores was studied by comparing MYTH scores of MSI determined Type As and not Type As (Smith et al., 1985). As shown on Table 6.4, some evidence for the validity of the A versus not A scale of the MSI resulted for American adolescents and Greek preadolescents and adolescents. The American preadolescents were the only group for which the validity of the MSI was not supported, even though the MYTH was developed primarily for this population!

A second study of the validity of the MSI ratings for American boys examined correlations between MSI ratings on the five-point scale and the MYTH Type A scores (Smith & Gerace, 1987). The validity of the MSI ratings for American preadolescents was supported by a significant

TABLE 6.4   Association Between Miami Structured Interview (MSI) Ratings and Matthews Youth Test for Health (MYTH) Scores[a]

MYTH Score	Subject taught by MYTH rater		
	More than two	Mathematics	Language
Type A			
Preadolescents			
USA	NS	NS	r=.34
Greece	p<.05	—	—
Adolescents			
USA	—	p<.05, r=.39	r=.36
Greece	—	p<.05	NS
Competitiveness-Leadership			
Preadolescents (USA)	NS	r=.32	r=.40
Adolescents (USA)	—	r=.42	r=.35
Impatience-Aggression			
Preadolescents (USA)	NS	NS	NS
Adolescents (USA)	—	NS	NS

p<.05 designates that the mean ratings for Type As were significantly higher than the mean for not Type As (alpha=.05).

r= designates a significant (alpha=.05) Pearson correlation with MSI five-point scale.

NS designates a not significant t-test or correlation (alpha=.05)

— designates that association was not tested.

[a] Adapted from Smith & Gerace (1987) and Smith et al., (1985).

association of interview ratings and MYTH scores from English teachers (r=.34), but not for mathematics teachers or teachers of more than two subjects. For American adolescents, the validity of the MSI ratings was supported by significant associations with MYTH scores from both English (r=.36) and mathematics teachers (r=.39). (See Table 6.4).

Further investigation of the validity of MSI ratings asked whether interview assessments were related to individual components of the Type A pattern such as competitiveness and impatience (Smith & Gerace, 1987). First, factor analysis of data from the MYTH yielded components labeled "competitiveness-leadership" and "impatience-aggression." A similar factor structure of the MYTH had been reported earlier by Matthews and Angulo (1980). MSI ratings showed reliable correlations with the "competitiveness-leadership" component, but not with the "impatience-aggression" component for American preadolescents and adolescents. Thus, the MSI appears to assess a socially desirable component of Type A, "competitiveness-leadership," but perhaps not the less desirable component, "impatience-aggression."

At least three issues may be relevant to why the MSI ratings did not relate to the "impatience-aggression" scores. First, to assess hostility with the MSI may require attention to the content of responses (Dembroski, 1978). Recall that the MSI was scored solely on voice stylistics so it could be used in multi-language studies (e.g., Smith et al., 1985). Second, the "impatience-aggression" component of the MYTH may be multidimensional and only some aspects may relate to Type A scores from the MSI. In support of this, investigators have found that some items on the MYTH impatience-aggression component relate to measures of conduct-disorder or hyperactivity (Hunter et al., 1983; Whalen & Henker, 1986; and Robinson, Frame, DeVincentis, & Zeichner, 1987). In addition, findings of Siegman et al. (1987) support the idea that hostility is multidimensional in adults. Third, children may not display hostility during the structured interview because either the adult/child dyad is not conducive for children to show hostility, or the kind of hostility that adults may show in the structured interview has not yet developed in children. Future research will be necessary to test these hypotheses.

In summary, studies of the reliability and validity of the MSI lead to the following conclusions. Interrater reliability is comparable to other Type A structured interviews and other assessment techniques requiring clinical judgments such as radiography. Periodic recalibration of raters can help minimize rater bias. The test-retest data suggest that for longitudinal studies the dichotomous scoring system of the MSI is less susceptible to error than the five-point scale. Study of the interviewer effect shows that careful training of interviewers is necessary to prevent bias.

The MSI has some validity for measuring Type A behaviors that are displayed in the school settings of preadolescent and adolescent boys from diverse cultural backgrounds. Among the components of Type A, the MSI reflects at least the "competitive-leadership" dimension. Further study is warranted to determine whether other components of the Type A pattern, particularly "hostility," can be assessed with the MSI. The study of hostility in children is particularly important because hostility may be a coronary-prone ingredient of the Type A pattern. An important issue to address is whether hostility in adulthood is preceded by a qualitatively similar hostility in childhood or other precursors. Therefore, since the traditional components of the Type A pattern may be multidimensional or have different precursors in children, multiple criteria are needed to delineate which components of the Type A pattern contribute to MSI ratings.

Assets and Limitations of the MSI

The major strengths of the MSI compared to the other interviews discussed in this chapter are its applicability to a broader age range and demonstrated cross-cultural validity. The MSI functions well with youngsters ages 8 to 18 years and has shown validity in two diverse cultural settings, the U.S.A. and Greece. Extensive reliability studies, including test-retest reliability and interviewer effect studies, also support its use in longitudinal studies involving repeated administrations.

Two important questions yet to be answered regarding the MSI are whether the instrument will prove reliable and be supported in validation studies with female youngsters. Although some researchers have used the MSI with young females, the results have not been published.

Student Structured Interview

The Student Structured Interview (SSI) was developed as part of the Stanford Health in Youth Project which examined the relationships between Type A and physical health, social behavior, and academic performance (Kirmil-Gray et al., 1987). Similar to the MSI, the SSI is intended for both preadolescents as young as nine years old and adolescents. The 24 questions in the SSI are similar to those in the adult structured interview (Rosenman et al., 1964) except the wording is simplified and situations that are described are appropriate to youngsters. The SSI, however, contains more items regarding anger and hostility than the adult structured interview. The SSI takes approximately 10 minutes to administer.

Administration

The SSI is presented similarly to all children. The interviewer models Type A behavior by speaking quickly and periodically interrupting the child's speech. A confrontational style is avoided, however, to prevent children from withdrawing. As with the other interviews for children, the interview situation is intended to set the occasion for the display of Type A behavior by the susceptible individual. Training of interviewers is required to achieve and maintain the appropriate style of presentation.

Scoring

The SSI has been scored separately for Type A Behavior and Content. The Behavior score combines ratings of intensity, competitiveness, and arousal by the interviewer, with ratings of nine voice stylistics made from audio recordings of the interview. The nine voice stylistics include the following: explosive words, clipped words, uneven speech, repeated words, interruptions, sighs, response latency, volume, and speed. The final Behavior score is the sum of the interviewer ratings and the voice stylistics ratings.

The Content score is based on an assessment of responses to 19 of the main questions. The content of each response is rated on a three-point scale of low, medium, and high degree of Type A behavior. The Content score is the sum of the 19 item ratings.

Reliability

As shown in Table 6.2, interrater reliability has been examined for the Behavior and Content scores of the SSI (Kirmil-Gray et al., 1987). Using median splits Kirmil-Gray and colleagues observed 79% interrater agreement for the Behavior score and 71% for the Content score. Thus, interrater reliability for the SSI dichotomous scales approaches the levels observed for the Type A versus Type B scale of the ASI (75% agreement) and the MSI (81% to 96% agreement).

Validity

The convergent validity of the Behavior and Content scores was examined in two samples of children using the MYTH, the Student Type A Behavior Scale (STABS) which is a self-administered questionnaire, and a Parent Observation Checklist (Kirmil-Gray et al., 1987). Discriminant validity was also evaluated using self-report scales for State-Trait Anxiety (Spielberger, 1973) and Depression. Table 6.5 shows the correlations between the SSI Behavior score, the Content score and the three convergent validity criteria and three discriminant validity scales.

TABLE 6.5   Associations of Behavior and Content Scores from the Student Structured Interview (SSI) with Convergent and Discriminant Validity Criteria*

| Criteria | Student Structured Interview Scores | | | |
| | Behavior | | Content | |
	Sample 1	Sample 2	Sample 1	Sample 2
Convergent Validity				
MYTH Type A score	r=.40	r=.24	NS	r=.13
Student Type A Behavior				
Scale	NS	r=.12	r=.48	r=.49
Parent Observation				
Checklist	NS	NS	NS	r=.14
Discriminant Validity				
State anxiety	r=.18	NS	r=.34	r=.22
Trait anxiety	r=.20	r=.09	r=.27	r=.35
Depression	NS	NS	r=.35	r=.25

Sample 1, n=120.
Sample 2, n=652.
r= designates a significant Pearson correlation (alpha=.05).
NS designates a not significant correlation (alpha=.05).
*Adapted from Kirmil-Gray.

For the Behavior score, a modest association was observed with the MYTH (rs=.40 and .24). There was little or no association with the self-report Student Type A Behavior Scale (rs<.13). The pattern of results is similar to that with the ASI and MSI which suggests there may be separate behavioral and self-perceived dimensions of Type A behaviors. The notion of separate behavioral and self-perceived dimensions of Type A behavior is further supported by the findings that the SSI Content scores were more related to the self-report Student Type A Behavior Scale scores than to the MYTH scores, which rely on observations of behavior by classroom teachers.

Unexpectedly, neither the Behavior or Content scores showed even a modest association with the Parent Observation Checklist (rs<.15). The investigators suggested that this finding may have been due to inadequate scale construction for the Parent Observation Checklist (Kirmil-Gray et al., 1987). Nevertheless, the question remains whether structured interview scores are predictive of behaviors in the home setting.

Examination of the discriminant validity of the SSI (see Table 6.5) revealed that the Behavior scores showed small or no associations with State or Trait anxiety (r<.21) and no associations with the Depression Scale. In contrast, the Content scores showed consistent associations with State anxiety, Trait anxiety, and the Depression Scale (rs=.22 to .35). Additionally, the self-report Student Type A Behavior Scale showed a correlation of r=.56 with the Trait Anxiety scale in a sample of 652 children (Kirmil-Gray, et al., 1987). Thus, scores based on observations of behaviors during the SSI were relatively "clean" of factors related to anxiety or depression, whereas self-report measures of Type A appear to reflect something in common with anxiety or depression.

Assets and Limitations of the SSI

A strength of the SSI is its applicability to a broad age range of children. The SSI also contains more questions about hostility than the adult structured interview or the ASI. The SSI has used a unique scoring system that captures the information in voice stylistics but does not require training on the global assessment of Type A structured interviews. This scoring system, which involves rating individual voice stylistics, is substantially more cumbersome to implement than the global scoring used with the ASI and MSI. Also unique about the SSI is that the content score is a global Type A score. Thus, the scoring system could be viewed as a disadvantage because it is the most labor intensive, yet it does not provide scores for any components of the Type A pattern. The global content score should be used cautiously because of its association with scores on both anxiety and depression. Whether this relationship will prove to be reliable and useful has yet to be determined.

INTEGRATION OF FINDINGS ON STRUCTURED INTERVIEWS

Reliability

Interrater reliability has been evaluated with each of the structured interviews. All have shown 70% or greater interrater agreement with the Type A versus Type B scale or median splits. Levels greater than 80% appear obtainable when systematic programs of recalibrating the raters are used. Periodic retraining of raters is warranted because of the subjective nature of scoring individual voice stylistics and making the global Type A assessment.

The potential for rater bias exists even when interrater agreement appears satisfactory. Thus, comparisons of the prevalence of Type A behavior should be made with caution. Examining interrater disagreements can indicate when bias is a particular problem.

The use of four or five category interview scales (e.g., A-1, A-2, X, B) may be desirable for investigating the association of Type A behavior with other characteristics in large samples. Interrater agreement rates of less than 60%, however, prohibit making judgments about individual children using such rating scales.

The examination of test-retest reliability over a short time interval suggests that the structured interview procedure does not cause changes in subsequent assessments with the same procedure. Thus, the method can be useful for longitudinal studies where participants are remeasured.

Examinations of the interviewer effect show that the manner in which the interview is administered can affect the ratings for individuals. Thus, it is important to train interviewers to maintain a consistent manner of conducting Type A structured interviews. The potential interviewer effect also means special caution must be taken when one is considering combining data from different interviewers or comparing prevalence estimates across interviewers. Studies using multiple interviewers would be strengthened if the potential interview effect was systematically evaluated.

Taken as a whole, the indicators of reliability of the structured interviews for children strongly suggest that each of the structured interviews can achieve acceptable levels of reliability. Stringent training and systematic monitoring of reliability, however, are necessary if consistently high levels of reliability are to be achieved.

Validity

The Type A behavior pattern is defined as involving a variety of behaviors, including competitiveness, time urgency, and hostility. The main theme running through the present review is that the structured interview method can measure multiple aspects of the Type A pattern in children. But questions remain about the organization of the behavior pattern in children.

Perhaps the best place to start to sort out what can be measured with the structured interview method for children is to differentiate between a "behavioral" dimension and a "self-perceived" dimension. The structured interview method offers an opportunity to assess both the "behavioral" and "self-perceived" dimensions of the Type A behavior pattern. The "behavioral" dimension can be measured by the behaviors observed during the structured interview and is predictive of overt behaviors displayed in the classroom. The "self-perceived" dimension can be measured with the content of answers to questions in a structured interview and reflects cognitive attributes of Type As. The similarity of this interpretation to findings with adults (Matthews, 1982) suggests that the behavior pattern known as Type A in adults also exists in children.

The "behavioral" and "self-perceived" dimensions can be broken down further to reveal more specific components of the Type A behavior pattern. Observations of Type A behaviors during the structured interview can predict a behavioral reactivity in the forms of competitiveness, leadership, need for control, displays of frustration, and showing anger. The "self-perceived" information appears more strongly related to components of impatience, and hard-driving. Thus, the structured interview method provides multiple indices of Type A characteristics. The issue here is not so much which structured interview one should use, but how it can be applied to particular needs.

CLINICAL AND RESEARCH UTILITY

The utility of structured interviews to assess Type A behavior in children can first be considered in comparison to other methods of measuring Type A in children. Perhaps the most widely used instrument to assess Type A in children has been the MYTH (Matthews & Angulo, 1980), which is a rating scale completed by school teachers. Some of the strengths of the MYTH are that it involves direct observations of behavior based on repeated experience with the child in a natural setting. It can also be scored for two Type A-component scores, and it is a relatively easy and economical method to use. Compared to the MYTH, the structured interview method is superior in some regards and shares some limitations. Structured interviews are superior in that they provide a more standardized setting in which to observe behaviors, the observers are better trained to detect the specific behaviors of interest, and the interview method is not limited to children in school. Structured interviews can also provide self-reported information. In common with the MYTH, structured interviews do not have component scoring systems that have been well validated using behavioral observations as criteria, and discriminant validity is an issue of uncertain magnitude. That is, the MYTH has items that are also sensitive to characteristics of attention deficit syndrome, or hyperactivity (Hunter et al., 1983; Whalen & Henker, 1986), and structured interview scores based on content may be related to anxiety or depression (Kirmil-Gray et al., 1987). Thus, the MYTH may be adequate for studies of preadolescents when ease and economy are important. Otherwise, a structured interview may be more informative.

Another broad class of instruments to consider is self-report questionnaires. One such measure is the Hunter-Wolf Type A scale for children (Wolf, Sklov, Wenzl, Hunter, & Berenson, 1982). The Hunter-Wolf Type A scale contains 24 items which describe a broad spectrum of attributes characteristic of Type A. Each item is posed as a seven-step continuum to convey opposite ends of a behavioral dimension. The child indicates on each item how he or she would describe himself or herself. This type of scale provides self-report information in much the same way that structured interviews can be scored for content. Interestingly, test-retest reliability has been low for children younger than 13 years of age (Amos, Hunter, Zinkgraf, Miner, and Berenson, 1987). Advantages of such an instrument over structured interviews are the ease and economy of using self-report questionnaires. The disadvantage is that self-reports do not capture the overt behavioral Type A characteristics.

Evaluation of the utility of structured interviews to measure Type A behavior in children also requires consideration of the clinical usefulness of information obtained for an individual. The clinical relevance of Type A measures for children is, at best, unclear. The health correlates and consequences of Type A behavior in children are not well understood. In fact, the coronary proneness of the Type A pattern for adults has been questioned (e.g., Shekelle et al., 1985). As the clinical relevance of Type A for adults becomes clearer, the potential clinical utility of assessing Type A in children will become more certain.

At present, the utility of the Type A construct for children is best viewed as a research tool. The Type A construct and the structured interview method of assessment are of interest to researchers from a variety of behavioral sciences. First, behavioral scientists interested in methodological issues can find fascinating and complex issues that require attention. Questions of multidimensional scaling, for example, are central to understanding the validity of the Type A construct in children. Researchers interested in the development of behavior can study maturational changes as well as the antecedent and consequent variables related to Type A in children. Researchers interested in thought processes may want to study reasons for the independence of Type A scores based on self-reports and behavior observations. The construct of Type A behavior in children also offers the potential to study the socialization of behaviors such as aggressiveness, hostility, and competitiveness. Clearly, the Type A behavior pattern and its assessment offer a variety of opportunities for the behavioral scientist. Of the instruments for measuring Type A in children, structured interviews offer the richest source of information.

CONCLUSIONS

Taken as a whole, the studies of the structured interview for children allow several conclusions. First, the reliability of the procedure is sufficient to continue its use in the study of Type A behavior in preadolescents and adolescents. Potential biases due to raters or interviewers necessitate careful training and monitoring of both raters and interviewers.

Second, it is clear that the Type A pattern and its components are multidimensional. The careful use of the structured interview method yields a global Type A assessment that is both standardized and related to overt competitiveness, leadership, need for control, displays of frustration, and showing anger, which are part of the Type A behavior pattern.

Third, the structured interview method can also provide self-report data on impatience and hard-driving, similar to that obtained using paper and pencil questionnaires. Thus, the structured interview method can yield measures of varied components of the Type A behavior pattern.

Important questions remain about whether: (1) the components measurable with the structured interview method can be further subdivided in meaningful ways, (2) hostility and its potential components can be assessed using the structured interview method, (3) the components observable in children predict the same components later in life, (4) children possess as yet unrecognized precursors of adult Type A behaviors, and (5) Type A or its precursors develop in a noncontinuous manner?

One approach to improve our understanding of Type A behavior in children is to cross-classify youngsters on multiple characteristics of Type A pattern. For example, Robinson et al. (1987) cross-classified fourth- and fifth-graders as high or low on competitiveness and aggression. The high competitive/low aggressive group scored highest on socially desirable characteristics such as academic performance, leadership, and self-esteem. The high aggressive/low competitive boys scored highest on conduct disorder and anxiety. Thus, clinically relevant subgroups may be better identified as measurement strategies become more sophisticated.

Of course, the characteristics of the greatest interest to health professionals are those associated with disease endpoints. Today our understanding of why Type A is related to CHD in adults is unclear. Thus, further research on adults is needed to guide the research on children aimed at identifying the development of "coronary-prone" behaviors.

In closing, the structured interview method can be viewed as a "slice of life" assessment technique because it relies on how people behave as well as how they say they behave. The issues of how to conduct the structured interview method with children and the dimensions which can be assessed are just beginning to be understood. Still, the structured interview appears to be a viable method for assessing Type A behavior in children and is worthy of continued study.

REFERENCES

Amos, C.I., Hunter, S. MacD., Zinkgraf, S.A. Miner, M.H., & Berenson, G.S. (1987). Characterization of a comprehensive Type A measure for children in a biracial community: The Bogalusa Heart Study. *Journal of Behavioral Medicine, 10,* 425–439.

Blumenthal, J.A., Williams, R., Kong, Y., Schanberg, S.M., & Thompson, L.W. (1978). Type A behavior and angiographically documented coronary disease. *Circulation, 58,* 634–639.

Bortner, R.W. (1969). A short rating scale as a potential measure of pattern A behavior. *Journal of Chronic Diseases, 22,* 87–91.

Buss, A.H., & Durkee, A. (1957). An inventory for assessing different kinds of hostility. *Journal of Consulting Psychiatry, 20,* 343–348.

Butensky, A., Faralli, V., Heebner, D., & Waldron, I. (1976). Elements of the coronary-prone behavior pattern in children and teenagers. *Journal of Psychosomatic Research, 1976, 20,* 439–444.

Byrne, D.G., Rosenman, R.H., Schiller, E., & Chesney, M.A. (1985). Consistency and variation among instruments purporting to measure the Type A behavior pattern. *Psychosomatic Medicine, 47* (3)

Chesney, M.A., Eagleston, J.R., & Rosenman, R.H. (1980). The Type A structured interview: A behavioral assessment in the rough. *Journal of Behavioral Assessment, 2,* 255–272.

Christakis, G., Kafatos, A., Fordyce, M., Kurtz, C., Gerace, T., Smith, J., Duncan, R., Cassady, J., and Doxiadis, S. (1981). Cultural and nutritional determinants of coronary heart disease risk factors in adolescents: A USA–Greece cross-cultural study, preliminary results. *Progress in Clinical Biological Research, 77,* 799–810.

Dembroski, T.M. (1978). Reliability and validity of methods used to assess coronary-prone behavior. In *Coronary-Prone Behavior.* T.M. Dembroski, S.M. Weiss, J.L. Shields, S.G. Haynes, and M. Feinleib (Eds.), Springer-Verlag: New York, 95–106.

Dembroski, T.M., MacDougall, J.M., Williams, R.B., Haney, T.L. & Blumenthal, J. (1985). Components of Type A, hostility, and anger-in: Relationship to angiographic findings. *Psychosomatic Medicine, 47,* 219–233.

Frank, K.A., Heller, S.S., Kornfeld, D.S., Sporn, A.A., & Weiss, M.B. (1978). Type A behavior pattern and coronary angiographic findings. *Journal of the American Medical Association, 240,* 761–763.

Friedman, M., & Rosenman, R.H. (1959). Association of specific overt behavior pattern with blood and cardiovascular findings. *Journal of the American Medical Association, 169,* (12), 1286–1296.

Friedman, M., & Rosenman, R.H. (1974). *Type A behavior and your heart.* Knopf: New York.

Friedman, M., Rosenman, R.H., Straus, R., Wurm, M., & Kositchek, R. (1968). The relationship of behavior pattern A to the state of the coronary vasculature— A study of fifty-one autopsy subjects. *American Journal of Medicine,* 44, 525–537.

Friedman, M., Thoresen, C.E., Gill, J.J., Ulmer, D., Thompson, L., Powell, L., Price, V., Elek, S.R., Rabin, D.D., Breall, W.S., Piaget, G., Dixon, T., Bourg, E., Levy, R.A., & Tasto, D. (1982). Feasibility of altering Type A behavior pattern after myocardial infarction. *Circulation,* 66(1), 83–92.

Gerace, T.A., & Smith, J.C. (1983). Miami Type A interview for Preadolescents and Adolescents: A Third Examination of the Interviewer Effect. In *CVD Epidemiology Newsletter,* American Heart Association Council on Epidemiology, R.B. Shekelle (Ed), (33), 16.

Gerace, T.A., & Smith, J.C. (1985). Children's type A interview: Interrater, test-retest reliability, and interviewer effect. *Journal of Chronic Diseases,* 38, (9), 781–791.

Hunter, S., Parker, F., Williamson, D., Webber, L., & Berenson, G. (1983). Type A behavior pattern and observed hyperactivity in children—Bogalusa heart study. In *CVD Epidemiology Newsletter,* American Heart Association Council on Epidemiology, R.B. Shekelle (Ed), 42.

Jacobs, D.R., & Schucker, B. (1981). Type A behavior pattern, speech, and coronary heart disease. In *Speech evaluation in medicine.* H.K. Darby (Ed). Grune & Stratton, Inc., 363–383.

Jenkins, C.D., Rosenman, R.H., & Friedman, M. (1968). Replicability of rating the coronary-prone behaviour pattern. *British Journal of Preventive Social Medicine,* 22, 16–22.

Keys, A., Aravanis, C., Blackburn, H., van Buchem, F.S.P., Buzino, R., Djordjevic, B.S., Fidonza, F., Karvonen, M.J., Menotti, A., Puddu, V., & Taylor, H.L. (1972). Probability of middle-aged men developing coronary heart disease in five years. *Circulation,* 45, 815–828.

Kirmil-Gray, K., Eagleston, J.R., Thoresen, C.E., Heft, L., Arnow, B., & Bracke, P. (1987). Developing measures of Type A behavior in children and adolescents. *Journal of Human Stress,* 13(1), 5–15.

MacDougall, J.M., Dembroski, T.M., Dimsdale, J.E., & Hackett, T.P. (1985). Components of Type A, hostility, and anger-in: Further relationships to angiographic findings. *Health Psychology,* 4, 137–152.

MacDougall, J.M., Dembroski, T.M., & Musante, L. (1979). The structured interview and questionnaire methods of assessing coronary-prone behavior in male and female college students. *Journal of Behavioral Medicine,* 2, 71–83.

Matthews, K.A. (1978). Assessment of developmental antecedents of the coronary-prone behavior pattern in children. In *Coronary-prone behavior.* T.M. Dembroski, S.M. Weiss, J.L. Shields, S.G. Haynes, and M. Feinleib (Eds.), Springer-Verlag: New York, 207–217.

Matthews, K.A. (1982). Psychological perspectives on the Type A behavior pattern. *Psychological Bulletin,* 91, 293–323.

Matthews, K.A., & Angulo, J. (1980). Measurement of the Type A behavior pattern in children: Assessment of children's competitiveness, impatience-anger, and aggression. *Child Development, 51,* 466–475.

Matthews, K.A., Glass, D.C., Rosenman, R.H., & Bortner, R.W. (1977). Competitive drive, pattern A, and coronary heart disease: A further analysis of some data from the Western Collaborative Group Study. *Journal of Chronic Diseases, 30,* 489–498.

Matthews, K.A., & Haynes, S.G. (1986). Type A behavior pattern and coronary disease risk. *American Journal of Epidemiology, 123,* 923–960.

Matthews, K.A., & Jennings, J.R. (1984). Cardiovascular responses of boys exhibiting the Type A behavior pattern. *Psychosomatic Medicine, 46, 960,* 484–497.

National Center for Health Statistics: *Vital Statistics of the United States, 1981.* Vol II, Mortality, Part A. DHHS Pub No. (PHS) 86-1101. Public Health Service, Washington. U.S. Government Printing Office, 1986.

Robinson, S.L., Frame, C.L., DeVincentis, C., & Zeichner, A. (1987). Psychological components of the Type A behavior pattern in fourth and fifth grade boys. Presented at the *Annual Convention of the American Psychological Association.* August, New York, NY.

Rosenman, R.H., Brand, R.J., Jenkins, D., Friedman, M., Straus, R., & Wurm, M. (1975). Coronary heart disease in the Western Collaborative Group Study: Final follow-up experience of 8 1/2 years. *Journal of the American Medical Association, 233,* 872–877.

Rosenman, R.H., & Friedman, M. (1961). Association of specific behavior pattern in women with blood and cardiovascular findings. *Circulation, 24,* 1173–1184.

Rosenman, R.H., Friedman, M., Straus, R., Wurm, M., Kositchek, R., Hahn, W., & Werthessen, N.T. (1964). A predictive study of coronary heart disease—The Western Collaborative Group Study. *Journal of the American Medical Association, 189* (1), 103–110.

Scherwitz, L., Graham, L.E., Grandits, G., & Billings, J. (1987). Speech characteristics and behavior-type assessment in the Multiple Risk Factor Intervention Trial (MRFIT) structured interviews. *Journal of Behavioral Medicine, 10* (2), 173–195.

Shekelle, R.B., Hulley, S.B., Neaton, J.D., Billings, J., Borhani, N.O., Gerace, T.A., Jacobs, D., Lasser, N., Mittlemark, M., & Stamler, J. (1985). The MRFIT behavior pattern study II. Type A behavior and incidence of coronary heart disease. *American Journal of Epidemiology, 122,* 559–570.

Siegel, J.M., & Leitch, C. (1981). Assessment of Type A behavior pattern in adolescents. *Psychosomatic Medicine, 43,* 45–56.

Siegel, J.M., Matthews, K.A., & Leitch, C. (1981). Validation of the Type A interview assessment of adolescents: A multidimensional approach. *Psychosomatic Medicine, 43,* (4), 311–321.

Siegman, A.W., Dembroski, T.M., & Ringel, N. (1987). Components of hostility and the severity of coronary artery disease. *Psychosomatic Medicine, 49*(2), 127–135.

Smith, J.C., & Gerace, T.A. (1983). Miami Type A interview for preadolescents and adolescents: Measures of interrater reliability. In *CVD Epidemiology*

Newsletter, American Heart Association Council on Epidemiology, R.B. Shekelle (Ed), (33), 15.

Smith, J.C., & Gerace, T.A. (1987). Validity of the Miami Structured Interview-1 for assessing Type A behavior, competitiveness, and aggression in children. *Journal of Psychopathology and Behavioral Assessment, 9,* (4). 369–382.

Smith, J.C., Gerace, T.A., Christakis, G., & Kafatos, A. (1985). Cross-cultural validity of the Miami Structured Interview-1 for Type A in children: The American Hellenic Heart Study. *Journal of Chronic Diseases, 38* (9), 793–799.

Spielberger, C.D., Manual for the State-Trait Anxiety Inventory for children. Palo Alto, CA Consulting Psychologists Press.

Strong, J.P., & McGill, H.C. (1969). The pediatric aspects of atherosclerosis. *Journal of Atherosclerosis Research, 9,* 251–265.

Suinn, R.M. (1978). The coronary-prone behavior pattern: A behavioral approach to intervention. In *Coronary-prone behavior.* T.M. Dembroski, S.M. Weiss, J.L. Shields, S.G. Haynes, and M. Feinleib (Eds.), Springer-Verlag: New York, 231–236.

Truett, J., Cornfield, J., & Kannel, W. (1967). A multivariate analysis of the risk of coronary heart disease in Framingham. *Journal of Chronic Diseases, 20,* 511–524.

Whalen, C.K., & Henker, B. (1986). Type A behavior in normal and hyperactive children: Multisource evidence of overlapping constructs. *Child Development, 57,* 688–699.

Wolf, T.M., Sklov, M.C., Wenzl, P.A., Hunter, S. MacD., & Berenson, G.S. (1982). Validation of a measure of Type A behavior pattern in children: Bogalusa Heart Study. *Child Development, 53,* 126–135.

Zyzanski, S.J., Jenkins, C.D., Ryan, T.J., Flessas, A., & Everist, M. (1976). Psychological correlates of coronary angiographic findings. *Archives of Internal Medicine, 136,* 1234–1237.

PART III

Applications of Self-Report Measures with Children and Adolescents

CHAPTER 7

Assessment of Childhood Depression

ALAN E. KAZDIN

INTRODUCTION

Childhood depression has been an area of tremendous research activity within the last 15 years. The development of research can be traced to several significant advances. To begin with, alternative conceptualizations had for many years discouraged results on childhood depression. For example, until recently, psychoanalytic views have dominated child clinical work. Variations of psychoanalytic theory had asserted that depression as a clinical disorder does not exist in children as it does in adults (e.g., Mahler, 1961; Rie, 1966). The passing of this view provided a climate more sympathetic to discussion and research on childhood depression (Anthony, 1975; Bemporad & Wilson, 1978).

Another conceptual position acknowledged that depression could exist in children, but that its manifestations differed significantly from adult depression. This view proposed that depression is manifest in several other symptoms than dysphoric mood and loss of interest. Depression was said to be "masked" or expressed in "depressive equivalents" (Cytryn & McKnew, 1974; Glaser, 1968; Malmquist, 1977). The symptoms that putatively mask depression have included the full gamut of prob-

Completion of this chapter was supported by a Research Scientist Development Award (MH00353) and by a grant (MH35408) from the National Institute of Mental Health.

lem behaviors evident in childhood. Without clear and specific criteria for identifying depression, conducting research on the disorder was obviously difficult (Kovacs & Beck, 1977).

An important influence that promoted research on childhood depression was the emergence of the third edition of the *Diagnostic and Statistical Manual of Mental Disorders* (DSM-III; American Psychiatric Association, [APA] 1980). DSM-III more clearly specified the criteria for diagnosing alternative disorders in general compared to previous editions of the system. Specification of a relatively clear set of diagnostic criteria raised the question of whether children could meet criteria for major depression and other affective disorders. Studies utilizing standardized and semistructured interviews or more informal means consistently showed that depression could be reliably diagnosed in children and adolescents (Carlson & Cantwell, 1979; Kashani, Barbero, & Bolander, 1981; Puig-Antich, Blau, Marx, Greenhill, & Chambers, 1978).

The investigation of adult depression provided many important leads that have helped the explosive development of research in childhood depression. First, diagnosis of affective disorders has made important advances in research with adults. Depression has been one of the disorders where subtypes and variations have been carefully specified and validated through family studies and differential response to treatment (see Paykel, 1982). The importance of maintaining distinctions among subtypes has been suggested in response to medication among depressed children (Puig-Antich et al., 1987).

Second, alternative models of depression and their supportive research also proliferated in studies of adults. Diverse conceptual models including intrapsychic, cognitive, behavior, genetic, biochemical, and others have emerged, each with its own variations. The models, specific research paradigms, and treatments derived from them pointed to obvious directions for the study of children. Third, the study of depression in adults generated a variety of laboratory assessment techniques. Various biological methods (e.g., blood assays, sleep evaluation, drug challenges) have been directly transplanted from adults to children.

In addition to the diverse influences already noted, the development of alternative assessment methods has contributed greatly to research on childhood depression. Questionnaires, inventories, and interviews developed with adults have been revised to be applicable to children. Multiple assessment devices have emerged and with them a number of studies designed to chart the course and correlates of depression. Although work on childhood depression is relatively new, already a considerable amount of knowledge has accumulated. In the process, a number of salient issues have been identified. The purpose of the present chapter is to discuss the assessment of childhood depression, particularly those measures based on child report. In addition, major issues and limitations of current assessment practices and the implications for future research are addressed.

CHARACTERISTICS OF CHILDHOOD DEPRESSION: AN OVERVIEW

Diagnosis of Depressive Disorders

Evaluation of alternative assessment methods requires delineation of depression as a specific type of dysfunction. It is important to distinguish depression as a *symptom* from depression as a *syndrome* or *disorder*. As a symptom, depression refers to sad affects and as such is a common experience of everyday life. As a syndrome or disorder, depression refers to a group of symptoms that go together. Sadness may be part of a larger set of problems that include the loss of interest in activities, feelings of worthlessness, sleep disturbances, changes in appetite, and others.

There are many alternative diagnostic systems and different types of depressive syndromes or disorders that they cover (Carlson & Garber, 1986; McConville & Bruce, 1985). Alternative diagnostic systems include: Research Diagnostic Criteria (Spitzer, Endicott, & Robins, 1978), International Classification of Diseases (World Health Organization, 1987), and a system proposed by the Group for the Advancement of Psychiatry (1966). The major diagnostic system in use in the United States is the *Diagnostic and Statistical Manual of Mental Disorders* (DSM). In the third edition (DSM-III; APA, 1980), a major advance was made in specifying diagnostic criteria for delineating alternative disorders. The general model of DSM-III was to specify a core or essential set of symptoms to delineate a particular disorder. Some number of symptoms from this set is required for a particular disorder to be diagnosed. Other diagnostic criteria often include a particular duration of the symptoms and the absence of another condition (e.g., organic disorder) that might explain the presence of symptoms.

Beginning in 1983, the diagnostic categories were reevaluated to incorporate research findings on alternative disorders and experience in applying the specific diagnostic categories. A revision of the DSM-III criteria has emerged and is referred to as DSM-III-R (APA, 1987). In DSM-III-R several changes were made in various disorders in terms of clarifying the criteria, changing subtypes, and deleting and adding alternative disorders. For affective disorders, the changes were relatively minor.

Depression is part of a larger category referred to as Mood (rather than Affective) Disorders. The criteria for major depression in DSM-III-R are illustrated in Table 7.1. As in DSM-III, depressive symptoms may be included in other types of disorders as well. Table 7.2 enumerates several other categories of depressive disorders. In each of the disorders, there may be sad affect, loss of interest in the usual activities, and other symptoms. The severity, duration, and precipitants of the symptoms are major determinants of the type of depressive disorder that is defined.

Assessment to Reach a Diagnosis

Until recently, there have been no standardized assessment procedures in widespread use to obtain a DSM-III diagnosis. A number of interviews have emerged and assess a variety of symptoms so that DSM-III diagnoses can be reached. Major diagnostic instruments available for children and adolescents include the *Schedule for Affective Disorders and Schizophrenia for School-Age Children* (Chambers et al., 1985), the *Interview Schedule for Children* (Kovacs, 1978), the *Child Assessment Schedule* (Hodges, McKnew, Cytryn, Stern, & Kline, 1982), the *Diagnostic Interview for Children and Adolescents* (Herjanic & Reich, 1982), and the *Diagnostic Interview Schedule for Children* (Costello, Edelbrock, & Costello, 1985). From these interviews, DSM-III diagnoses can be derived.

TABLE 7.1   DSM-III-R Symptoms of Major Depression

At least five of the following symptoms have been present during the same two-week period; at least one of the symptoms was either (1) depressed mood, or (2) loss of interest or pleasure.

(1) Depressed mood,
(2) Loss of interest or pleasure in all or almost all activities,
(3) Significant weight loss or weight gain,
(4) Insomnia or hypersomnia,
(5) Psychomotor agitation or retardation,
(6) Fatigue or loss of energy,
(7) Feelings of worthlessness or excessive or inappropriate guilt,
(8) Diminished ability to think or concentrate, and
(9) Thoughts that he or she would be better off dead or suicidal ideation.

Adapted from DSM-III-R (APA, 1987).

TABLE 7.2   DSM-III-R Diagnostic Categories that Include Depressive Symptoms Other than Major Depressive Disorder

Disorder or Condition and Key Characteristics

Dysthymia
   Essentially a mood disorder in which the symptoms of major depression are
   evident in less severe form. The symptoms may be chronic, lasting for at
   least two years (one year for children and adolescents) during which there
   has been depressed mood most of the day more days than not.

Separation Anxiety Disorder
   Many of the symptoms of depression such as sadness, excessive worrying,
   sleep dysfunction, somatic complaints, apathy, and social withdrawal may
   emerge as part of fear of separation from those to whom the child is
   attached. In such cases, the symptoms may be clearly associated with the
   theme of separation. For example, worrying may have a specific focus on
   worry about being away from the parent. Similarly, somatic complaints
   may occur to remain at home or to foster increased attention to the child.

Adjustment Disorder with Depressed Mood
   Depressive symptoms may emerge as a reaction to an identifiable
   psychosocial stressor such as divorce of the parents, leaving friends during
   a move away from home, or serious illness of a parent. In such cases, the
   symptoms are in temporal proximity (within three months) of the stressor.
   The reaction is viewed as a maladaptive reaction because the person's
   functioning in everyday life is disrupted or because the symptoms are in
   excess of a "normal" or usually expected reaction. The symptoms are likely
   to remit after a period of adjustment with the new circumstances.

Uncomplicated Bereavement
   Within DSM-III-R, bereavement resembles an Adjustment Disorder in terms of
   its association with a particular event. However, it is not listed as a
   disorder because it is considered as a normal reaction to the loss of a
   loved one. Bereavement is often associated with several depressive
   symptoms or a full depressive syndrome and temporary impairment in
   school and social functioning. Yet, the reaction is not regarded as clinically
   significant unless the symptoms remain well beyond a "reasonable" period
   of adjustment or begin to recur with repeated episodes long after the loss.

(Presumably, each will be revised to address the changes required to
use DSM-III-R. See Chapter 5 for a discussion of structured interviews in
child assessment.)

   As an example, consider the Schedule for Affective Disorders and
Schizophrenia for School-Age Children (K-SADS or Kiddie-SADS; Cham-

bers et al., 1985). The interview begins with the unstructured portion in which general questions are asked about the child's functioning, what the basis is for coming to the clinic, and how well the child is performing at home and at school. The structured portion of the interview that follows consists of a large number of questions about specific symptoms across a wide range of disorders. The full interview is provided to the parent(s) and then is repeated separately with the child. Based on information from the parent and child, the interviewer provides a summary evaluation of each symptom. When the parent and child agree in their responses to the questions for a symptom, the interviewer's ratings usually reflect that same answer (or score). When there is a discrepancy, the interviewer makes a judgment based on all the available information. This may include information obtained from external sources as available from clinical intake practices.

As noted earlier, several studies have shown that depression can be reliably diagnosed. Most of these studies have used diagnostic interviews such as the K-SADS. This does not necessarily mean that depression is always detected or perfectly assessed by the various interviews. However, for clinical and research purposes, the diagnosis can be made with some consistency.

Prevalence

A question of major interest obviously is the extent to which children experience depressive symptoms and mood disorder. Depression has been studied among nonreferred ("normal") children and adolescents as well as among various clinic samples. Most research has addressed the prevalence of severe depressive symptoms by identifying subsamples of youths whose scores on various inventories reflect relatively (i.e., statistically) extreme levels of depression.

For example, using a peer-based measure, Lefkowitz and Tesiny (1985) found severe depression (extreme scores exceeding two standard deviations above the mean) in 5.2% of a sample of over 3,000 normal third-, fourth-, and fifth-grade children. In another study, 7.3% and 1.3% of high school students showed moderate and severe levels of depression, respectively, using cutoff criteria developed with adults (Kaplan, Hong, & Weinhold, 1984). These and other studies utilize different methods of assessing depression and different criteria for defining extreme scores. In addition, even when extreme or optimal cutoff scores are used for various self- and parent-report measures, the children who are identified do not necessarily meet diagnostic criteria for depressive disorders (Kazdin,

Colbus, & Rodgers, 1986). Thus, information on the prevalence of depression as a disorder has been difficult to cull from many of the assessment studies.

Other studies have utilized specific diagnostic criteria to evaluate depression as a disorder. In the general population, approximately 2% have been identified as depressed in randomly selected child populations ages 7 to 12 using DSM-III criteria (Kashani et al., 1983; Kashani & Simonds, 1979). In clinical populations, typical estimates of those with a diagnosable disorder fall between 10% and 20% (Puig-Antich & Gittelman, 1982).

As for the overall prevalence rates for children and adolescents, there remain rather large discrepancies in the currently available studies. The large discrepancies may result in part from the different ages that are studied. For example, using DSM-III diagnostic criteria, evidence suggests that young children (ages 1 to 6 years) referred for treatment may have markedly lower rates (1%) of major depression than children ages 9 to 12 (13%) (Kashani, Cantwell, Shekim, & Reid, 1982; Kashani, Ray, & Carlson, 1984). Also, differences in prevalence rates are likely to be due to the use of different measures, the difficulty in administering similar measures to children of different ages, and the use of different diagnostic criteria. The clarity of prevalence data for depressive disorders among children is likely to improve with the increased use of standardized descriptive criteria for diagnostic purposes, the development of standard diagnostic interviews, and continued evidence that diagnoses can be invoked with acceptable reliability (e.g., Chambers et al., 1985; Orvaschel, Puig-Antich, Chambers, Tabrizi, & Johnson, 1982).

Sex Differences

In adulthood, depression generally is more prevalent among women than among men. To date, research has typically found no sex differences in prevalence of depressive disorders in clinic and nonclinic samples of children (ages 6 to 12) (e.g., Kashani et al., 1983; Lefkowitz & Tesiny, 1985; Lobovits & Handal, 1985). On the other hand, research has suggested that among adolescents, the prevalence is greater in females than in males (e.g., Mezzich & Mezzich, 1979; Reynolds, 1985). Differences in severity of depression between males and females appear to begin in early adolescence and to increase over the next several years (Kandel & Davies, 1982). Yet differences in prevalence rates between adolescent males and females are not always found (Kaplan et al., 1984). Consequently, further work and large-scale epidemiological studies are still needed.

Developmental Differences

The criteria to diagnose depression in children have been developed from investigation of adults. There is always the risk that extensions to children will miss the mark because of the failure to take into account developmental considerations. Developmental changes in affective, cognitive, biochemical, motoric, and other systems are likely to be important in the manifestations of symptoms in children. For these reasons, the need to adopt a developmental perspective is invariably recommended in studying childhood depression (e.g., Cicchetti & Schneider-Rosen, 1984; Dignon & Gotlib, 1985; Sroufe & Rutter, 1984).

Multivariate studies of child symptoms suggest that there may well be developmental differences. For example, Achenbach and Edelbrock (1983) studied parent checklist ratings of boys and girls in different age groups (4- to 5-, 6- to 11-, 12- to 16-year-olds). A depression factor emerged in analyses of Child Behavior Checklist ratings of all groups except boys and girls ages 12 to 16. For boys, no depression factor emerged; for girls in this age range, the depression factor clustered with items specifically related to withdrawal, being secretive, shy and timid, and liking to be alone. For the groups where a depression factor did emerge, the specific symptoms that clustered on this factor varied as a function of sex and age. For example, for boys ages 6 to 11, suicidal talk was associated with other symptoms of depression, although this was not the case at ages 4 to 5. For girls ages 6 to 11, anxiety and feelings of being persecuted were associated with other depressive symptoms; at ages 4 to 5, these symptoms were not part of the depression factor. The results suggest that depressive symptoms may be organized quite differently as a function of age and gender.

To date, research has shown many similarities in the manifestations of depression among children and adults. For example, studies have shown that many cognitive attributes (e.g., attributional style, locus of control, hopelessness, cognitive distortion), biological correlates (e.g., in response to drug challenges, measures of endocrine functioning), and overt behaviors are similar among depressed children and adults (e.g., Haley, Fine, Marriage, Moretti, & Freeman, 1985; Kaslow, Rehm, & Siegel, 1984; Kazdin, Esveldt-Dawson, Sherick, & Colbus, 1985; Kazdin, Rodgers, & Colbus, 1986; Moyal, 1977; Puig-Antich, 1986). In these studies, the search for developmental differences has encompassed a relatively broad age range (e.g., 6 to 14 years of age). Similarities in cognitive processes, symptoms of depression, and the correlates of depression among different age groups at this point have been the rule rather than the exception.

There are differences that have been found between depression in children, adolescents, and adults. First, data for adults indicate that depression is more prevalent in women than in men, at least in Western cultures, with a female-to-male ratio of approximately 2:1 (Whybrow, Akiskal, & McKinney, 1984). As mentioned already, studies of children have not revealed consistent sex differences in prevalence of major depression (Carlson & Cantwell, 1979; Kashani, Cantwell, Shekim, & Reid, 1982). On the other hand, some differences have been found between depressed boys and girls that have not been evident with adults. For example, associations between depression and other chacteristics (e.g., nonverbal behavior, unpopularity, somatic complaints) appear to be higher and more consistent among girls than boys (Jacobsen, Lahey, & Strauss, 1983; Kazdin, Sherick, Esveldt-Dawson, & Rancurello, 1985).

Second, some of the serious concomitants of depression are clearly less evident in children than in adults. As a major case in point, suicide in children below the age of 12 is extremely rare (Hawton, 1986), and as a result of the low base rate, suicide is less likely to be manifest in childhood depression. On the other hand, suicidal ideation, threats, and attempts are not that rare and are often evident in both child and adolescent patient samples, especially those with depressive disorder (Carlson & Cantwell, 1982; Pfeffer, Conte, Plutchik, & Jerrett, 1979). Third, biological correlates of depression are not identical for children and adults. For example, EEG sleep patterns characteristic of depressed adults have not been evident among depressed children (e.g., Young, Knowles, MacLean, Boag, & McConville, 1982). In general, several developmental differences have been found. However, the weight of the evidence points to more similarities than differences at the present time.

ASSESSMENT METHODS

Over the last several years, major advances have been made in the development of assessment techniques for children and adolescents (Cantwell & Carlson, 1983; Kazdin, 1988). The range of measures has increased and data have become available on the psychometric properties of several measures. In the discussion that follows, measures are evaluated in which the children are the source of information either in evaluating their own depression or that of their peers.

Self- and Peer-Report Measures

Among the alternative assessment methods, self-report scales have dominated. Self-report is particularly important in assessing depression, given that key symptoms, such as sadness, feelings of worthlessness, and loss of interest in activities reflect subjective feelings and self-perceptions. Many of the more commonly used measures of depression among children and adolescents are enumerated in Table 7.3. The range of measures currently available can be illustrated by highlighting selected measures, their methods of administration, characteristics, strengths, and limitations.

Children's Depression Inventory (CDI). The most widely used measure is the CDI (Kovacs, 1981). The measure, adapted originally from the Beck Depression Inventory, includes 27 items regarding the cognitive, affective, and behavioral signs of depression. Each item presents three alternative statements. The children read the items themselves or have the items read to them. Children select one of the three alternatives that characterize them within the last two weeks. For example, for one of the items, children are asked to select one of each set of these alternatives: (a) I am sad once in a while; (b) I am sad many times; or (c) I am sad all of the time. For each item, the child's score (0, 1, or 2) is based on the more extreme statement that is endorsed (in the direction of depression). Although the most frequent use of the CDI is as a self-report measure, items are occasionally rephrased for completion by parents who rate the depression of their children.

The CDI has been shown to provide high internal consistency (e.g., Cronbach's alpha > .80) and moderate test-retest reliability (from one week up to six months), to distinguish clinic from nonclinic groups of children, and to correlate in the expected directions with measures of related constructs such as self-esteem, perceived personal competence, negative cognitive attributions, hopelessness, and others (e.g., Kazdin, French, Unis, Esveldt-Dawson, & Sherick, 1983; Kovacs, 1981; Saylor, Finch, Baskin, Furey, & Kelly, 1984; Saylor, Finch, Spirito, & Bennett, 1984; Seligman et al., 1984; Weisz, Weiss, Wasserman, & Rintoul, 1987). Normative data have appeared in these and other studies to facilitate evaluation of the level of dysfunction of children relative to their same-age and gender peers (Finch, Saylor, & Edwards, 1985; Nelson, Politano, Finch, Wendel, & Mayhall, 1987; Smucker, Craighead, Craighead, & Green, 1986). In general, the CDI is one of the more well-researched measures to date. The measure has been used for youth ages 6–17 (e.g., Kazdin, Rodgers, & Colbus, 1986; Kovacs, 1981).

The findings have also raised ambiguities regarding the CDI. For example, selected findings in the above studies have indicated that the CDI does not necessarily predict depression scores from other measures and does not invariably discriminate depression from other diagnoses or from maladjustment. Complexities have also emerged in the test-retest data. For brief intervals, such as one week, low and high test-retest

TABLE 7.3 Selected Self-Report Measures, Interviews, and Clinical Rating Scales for Childhood and Adolescent Depression

Measure	Response Format	Age* Range	Special Features
Self-Report Inventories			
Children's Depression Inventory (Kovacs & Beck, 1977)	27 items, each rated on 0- to 2-point scale	6–17	Derivatives of Beck Depression Inventory. Items reflect affective, cognitive, and behavioral symptoms.
Short Children's Depression Inventory (Carlson & Cantwell, 1979)	13 items, rated on 0- to 4-point scale	7–17	Derivative of Short Beck Depression Inventory. Departs slightly from CDI in duration required for symptoms to be endorsed and in response alternative format.
Children's Depression Scale (Lang & Tisher, 1978)	66 items, each item on a card; cards sorted into boxes reflecting 1- to 5-point scale	9–16	Depression subscales reflect affective symptoms, social problems, preoccupation with sickness and death, and guilt. Also positive subscale measuring pleasure and enjoyment.
Self-Rating Scale (Birleson, 1981)	18 items, scored on a 3-point scale	7–13	Items reflect range of affective, cognitive, behavioral symptoms. Sample item, "I like to have fun."
Modified Zung (Lefkowitz & Tesiny, 1980)	16 items; yes/no format for presence or absence	4th–5th grade	Derived from adult scale; modifications include reduced number of items, rewording and different response format. Sample item, "Do you often feel like crying?"

(continued)

TABLE 7.3 *(Continued)*

Measure	Response Format	Age* Range	Special Features
Self-Report Inventories			
Face Valid Depression Scale for Adolescents (Mezzich & Mezzich, 1979)	35 items, scored 0 to 1 (true/false) as characteristic of respondent	12–18	Derived from MMPI items from which clinicians selected. Includes items specific to adolescents as well as items common to both adolescents and adults. Sample item, "Do you want to leave home?"
Center for Epidemiological Studies-Depression Scale (modified for Children) (Weissman et al, 1980)	20 items, each on 0- to 4-point scale	6–17	Derivative of adult scales of same name. Many items dealing with friends and parents. Sample item, "Have you wanted to do something opposite of what your parents wanted?"
Beck Depression Inventory (modified for adolescents) (Chiles et al., 1980)	33 items, each on a scale varying from 0 to 2, 3, or 4 points	13–15	Derivative of Beck Depression Inventory. Change in language rather than content.
Reynolds Adolescent Depression Scale (Reynolds & Coats, 1986)	30 items, each on a 4-point scale	High school students	Items derived from symptoms included in major, minor, and unipolar depression.
Child Depression Scale (Reynolds, Anderson, & Bartell, 1985)	30 items rated on a 4-point scale	8–13	Items selected to measure depression in school rather than clinic settings. Thus, clinically severe characteristics (e.g., suicide) are replaced by less severe behavior (e.g., hurting oneself).

(continued)

TABLE 7.3 (*Continued*)

Measure	Response Format	Age* Range	Special Features
Self-Report Inventories			
Multiscore Depression Inventory (Berndt, Petzel, & Berndt, 1980)	118 true-false items	≥ 13	Overall total score plus scores for 10 sub-scales (e.g., low self-esteem, pessimism, learned helplessness, guilt) are provided. Recommended especially for "normal" individuals.
Children's Depression Checklists (Eddy & Lubin, 1988)	34 adjectives which are checked if they describe how the person feels.	Adolescents	Adapted from adjective checklists used with adults. Child version has two separate forms.
Interviews			
Bellevue Index of Depression (Petti, 1978)	40 items, each rated on 4-point scale of severity and 3-point scale for duration	6–12	Items devised on the basis of the Weinberg criteria; interview can be given separately to child, parents and others; recommendation is to combine scores from different sources.
Bellevue Index of Depression-Modified (Kazdin, French, Unis, & Esveldt-Dawson, 1983)	26 items, each rated on a 5-point scale for severity and 3-point scale for duration	6–13	Similar to BID; few items, scores not combined from different scores.

(continued)

TABLE 7.3 (*Continued*)

Measure	Response Format	Age* Range	Special Features
Self-Report Inventories			
Behavior Inventory for Depressed Adolescents (Chiles et al., 1980)	27 items rated by clinicians on varying Likert-format based on multiple sources of information	< 13	Approximately two-thirds of items derived from Hamilton Depression Scale for adults— others derived especially for this scale. Sample item, "The adolescent cries frequently while alone."
Children's Depression Rating Scale (Poznanski et al., 1979)	16 items scored after interview; symptoms rated on 6-point scale for severity	6–12	Devised from format of Hamilton Depression Scale for adults. Administered also to parents and others to combine different sources.
Children's Affective Rating Scale (McKnew et al., 1979)	3 items (mood, verbal behavior and fantasy) each rated on 10-point scale for severity following interview	5–15	Global clinical ratings rather than self-report of problems by child.
Interview Schedule for Children (Form C) (Kovacs, 1978)	Multiple items and subitems covering symptoms of depression, conduct disorders and other symptom constella-tions; rated for severity on 10-point scale for most items	8–13	Current phenomen-ology of child; duration varies to reflect current conditions, specific symptoms queried with varying durations. Parent and child are administered interview.

(continued)

TABLE 7.3   (*Continued*)

Measure	Response Format	Age* Range	Special Features
Self-Report Inventories			
Schedule for Affective Disorders for School-Age Children (Chambers et al., 1985)	Multiple items covering several disorders based on RDC criteria; depression symptom areas rated for degree of severity for scales varying in point values	6–16	Modeled after adult SADS; provides several diagnoses based on RDC criteria. Parent and child are interviewed.
Peer Report			
Peer Nomination Inventory of Depression (Lefkowitz & Tesiny, 1980)	20 items; persons list names of persons to whom item applies	2nd–7th grades	Subscales measuring depression, happiness, and popularity. Requires a group of persons (e.g., in a classroom) who know and can nominate each other.

*The age ranges need to be viewed as tentative guidelines. They reflect recommended uses or actual uses. However, insufficient data are available to evaluate the extent to which measures are valid or differentially valid within the range provided or could be extended beyond the range without sacrifice.

correlations have been found (rs=.38, vs. .87) for nonreferred ("normal") and emotionally disturbed children, respectively (Saylor, Finch, Spirito, & Bennett, 1984). More typically, moderate test-retest correlations have been found spanning periods of several weeks (Kazdin, French, Unis, & Esveldt-Dawson, 1983; Kovacs, 1981). There may be important differences in the stability of CDI severity scores as a function of age, sex, and clinic versus nonclinic samples.

Children's Depression Scale (CDS). A somewhat broader measure than the CDI is the CDS (Lang & Tisher, 1978). The measure includes 66 items that comprise two broad scales, *depression* (48 items) and *positive affective experience* (18 items). The depression scale includes subscales measuring *affective responses* (e.g., "I feel like crying often when I am at school."), *social problems* (e.g., "Often I feel lonely."), *self-esteem* (e.g., "I hate the way I look or the way I act."), *preoccupation with sickness and death* (e.g., "I feel more tired than most children I know."), *guilt* (e.g., "Often I feel as if I'm letting my mother/father down."), and *miscellaneous depression items* (e.g., "Often I am upset about my mother's health.") that do not cluster on the other dimensions. The positive experience scale includes a *pleasure and enjoyment* scale (e.g., "I'm always looking forward to the next day.") and *miscellaneous positive items* (e.g., "Many people care about me a lot.").

Each item is printed on a separate card which is read to the child. The card is placed by the respondent in one of five pre-marked boxes that reflect a Likert-type scale (1=very wrong [unlike me], 5=very right [like me]). The card sort format was adopted to reduce stereotypic responding by requiring separate thought and effort in selecting individual response alternatives. Scores for the subscales are based on the sum of the ratings for the constituent items (7 to 10 items per subscale). The measure yields total depression and total positive scores. Higher scores on a scale reflect a greater degree of that characteristic, whether depressive symptoms or positive affective experience. As with several other self-report measures, items have been rephrased so that parents can evaluate depression of their children.

Although the CDS has been translated and adopted in research and clinical settings in several countries (see Tisher & Lang, 1983), few reports of its use have been published (e.g., Kazdin, 1987; Rotundo & Hensley, 1985). These studies have shown that the overall measure and the depression and positive affective experience scales have a high degree of internal consistency (Cronbach's alpha > .85). The scores for the two major scales as well as the subscales correlate significantly and in the expected direction with other measures of childhood depression or related constructs such as self-esteem and hopelessness. In addition, the scale discriminates children who are diagnosed as clinically depressed from nonreferred samples and from clinic samples with other diagnoses.

A strength of the measure is the inclusion of several subscales. These scales have been derived on an a priori basis. Initial evidence from one factor analysis has not supported the structure of the scale as originally proposed (Rotundo & Hensley, 1985). A single overall general factor appears to account for the majority of the items. However, this needs to be studied further and may well depend on the factoring method and rotation decisions in the analysis of the scale. The initial analysis has supported depression and positive experience scales of the measure. The inclusion of these two scales alone may be an important and novel addition to the assessment of childhood depression, given that depression and pleasure are only moderately correlated (rs= −.36 and −.53 for child and parent CDS scores) (Kazdin, 1987). Thus, positive affective experience is not simply the inverse of depression.

Peer Nomination Inventory of Depression (PNID). Peer ratings have been utilized to evaluate diverse facets of psychopathology including depression. The advantage of peers is that they observe each other in a wide range of settings and for extended periods and consequently have a reasonably good basis for their evaluations. Peer measures occasionally have been constructed by altering items from self-report inventories (e.g., Malouff, 1984).

For childhood depression, the primary peer-based measure is the PNID (Lefkowitz & Tesiny, 1980). The measure depends upon the group context because peers within the group (e.g., the same classroom at school) are asked about characteristics of different children. The measure consists of 20 items in which children are asked several specific questions. The 20 items comprise three subscales: depression (e.g., "Who often looks sad?"), happiness (e.g., "Who often smiles?"), and popularity ("Who would you like to sit next to in class?"). In response to each question, the child identifies the peer(s) to whom the characteristic applies. A child's own score is the sum (or proportion) of nominations he or she receives on each of the subscales.

The measure has been evaluated in studies that have provided evidence for internal consistency (Cronbach's alpha > .85), test-retest stability (from two to over six months), and interrater agreement. Also, normative data have been gathered for over 3,000 third-, fourth-, and fifth-grade children. Validation studies have shown only weak relations between PNID scores and self-report or teacher ratings of depression. Yet, PNID scores correlate with school performance, self-concept, teacher ratings of work skills and social behavior, and peer ratings of happiness and popularity (Lefkowitz & Tesiny, 1985; Lefkowitz, Tesiny, & Gordon, 1980; Tesiny & Lefkowitz, 1982).

General comments. The three measures discussed previously illustrate assessment work and a few of the child-report strategies in use. The full range of validation studies are not easily represented given the extensive work that is underway.[1] A variety of measures are available. The self-report measures, such as the CDI, are relatively easy to adminis-

---

[1]For an examination of the characteristics of individual assessment techniques and their advantages and limitations, the reader is referred elsewhere (Kazdin, 1988).

ter and consume relatively little time to complete and score. Although peer reports represent a novel assessment method format and peers bring special knowledge to bear on child behavior, measures such as the PNID raise other issues. Administration is not feasible in most clinical contexts where a peer group with knowledge of the child is unavailable. When there is interest in diagnosing or assessing depression clinically, involvement of peers may not be feasible.

Other Assessment Modalities: Briefly Noted

Although self-report plays a central role in the assessment of childhood depression, it would be misleading not to mention the range of other measures and their significance for elaborating clinical dysfunction.

Ratings by significant others. Measures completed by significant others are often used to evaluate childhood depression. In fact, almost all of the self-report measures have also been rephrased so that parents can report on their child's depression. Ratings by parents are important because they are likely to identify symptoms different from those identified by the child. For example, behavioral correlates of depression (e.g., irritability) and changes in eating and sleep patterns are readily evident to the parent and probably less clearly reported by children. Although parent-report measures have been utilized in several studies (Kazdin, 1988), no single measure has emerged with clearly superior reliability or validity data.

Clinicians, teachers, and peers also may provide important information about the child. Clinician ratings can be completed with the *Children's Depression Rating Scale* (Poznanski et al., 1989, 1984), a measure adapted from the frequently used Hamilton Rating Scale for Depression for adults (Hamilton, 1967). The clinician rates symptoms of depression based on the child's verbal report and nonverbal behavior (e.g., appearance of sad affect). Ratings by teachers also have been used to assess child depression. Here too, self-report child depression measures are often used by changing the language of the items for teachers.

Measures of overt behavior. Many characteristics of depression refer to overt behaviors or observable characteristics such as diminished social and motor activity, sad facial expression, and slowed speech. With adult populations, overt behaviors have been observed directly. Several studies have measured nonverbal behavior. Research has shown that depressed adults, when compared to normal controls or other patient groups, often show reduced eye contact with others, slower speech, and fewer hand, head, and body movements during conversation (e.g., Jones

& Pasna, 1979; Waxer, 1976). Moreover, selected nonverbal behaviors change in response to treatment (e.g., Fisch, Frey, & Hirsbrunner, 1983; Miller, Ranelli, & Levine, 1977).

Although nonverbal behavior has been rather extensively studied with depressed adults, few direct extensions have been reported with children. In one investigation with child psychiatric patients (ages 7 to 12), nonverbal behaviors were assessed during interviews and evaluated in relation to self- and parent-report measures of child depression and psychiatric diagnosis (Kazdin, Sherick, Esveldt-Dawson, & Rancurello, 1985). Nonverbal behaviors were assessed as the child answered questions about everyday life (e.g., "What have you been doing in school?") or told stories in response to Thematic Apperception Test cards. Nonverbal behaviors included eye contact, facial expressiveness, response latency, bodily movements, gestures, frowning, and others. The results revealed low negative correlations for child and parent reports of depression and nonverbal behaviors such as facial expressiveness, body movements, gestures, and a positive correlation with tearfulness. There were, however, important gender differences with girls showing more consistent relations between nonverbal behaviors and measures of depression.

Nonverbal behavior during interviews does not exhaust the range of options for direct observation. Research with adults has suggested the utility of observing behavior during daily functioning. For example, Williams, Barlow, and Agras (1972) observed talking, smiling, and several motor behaviors of depressed patients. They found moderate to high negative correlations of a total sum of these behaviors with clinician and self-report ratings of depression. Overt behaviors observed on the ward have also reflected improvements in treatment and predict posthospital adjustment better than clinician and self-report ratings (Fossi, Faravelli, & Paoli, 1984; Williams et al., 1972).

Direct observational codes have been developed to assess depression in children. For example, in one study, inpatient children (ages 8 to 13 years old) were observed during free-time periods over the course of a week (Kazdin, Esveldt-Dawson, Sherick, & Colbus, 1985). Behaviors were observed to comprise three categories: social activity, solitary behavior, and affect-related expression. Children high in depression, as defined by a parent interview measure (BID-R), engaged in significantly less social behavior and showed less affect-related expression than children low in depression. These results are consistent with studies of depressed adults that have found deficiencies in social interaction and expressions of affect (e.g., Lewinsohn & Shaffer, 1971; Linden, Hautzinger, & Hoffmann, 1983).

The above codes do not, of course, exhaust the range of options for direct observations. Other studies have reported use of direct observation of playing alone, initiating and participating in social interaction, engaging in on-task and disruptive classroom behavior, completing activities of daily living, and role-play performance where specific features of depression are operationalized and evaluated (Altmann & Gotlib, 1988; Frame, Matson, Sonis, Fialkov, & Kazdin, 1982; Michelson, DiLorenzo, & Petti, 1981). These studies suggest that several overt behaviors are related to depressive symptoms. A limitation is the fact that each program has developed idiosyncratic observational codes so that there is no accumulation of knowledge, psychometric information, or validity in relation to a particular observational system or set of behaviors. On the other hand, the consistency of findings for social behavior, as defined and measured differently among studies, may attest to the robust relation between depression and overt behavior.

Biological and psychophysiological measures. Advances have emerged already in the area of biological assessments. These methods encompass a number of laboratory-based measures that have been carefully developed over several years in research with adults. The specific measures are not only useful in validating other methods of assessment such as ratings by significant others but also have implications for testing etiological views and biological correlates of affective disorders.

Assessment of neuroendocrine functioning has been evaluated more extensively among children than other biological strategies. The research has followed rather extensive exemplars from the literature on adults. Adult depressed patients (endogenous depressives) have been shown to secrete excess cortisol during depressive episodes, a characteristic which returns to normal during recovery (see Depue & Kleiman, 1979). Cortisol hypersecretion is assessed by drawing blood repeatedly (e.g., over a 24-hour period). Plasma concentrations of cortisol show more frequent periods of secretion, higher peak values, and greater amounts of secretion. Research has also shown that endogenous depressed adults hyposecrete growth hormone in response to insulin-induced hypoglycemia. This research has been extended to children showing similar findings with depressed patients (see Puig-Antich, 1986).

Electrophysiological recordings have been used extensively to evaluate sleep of depressed adults. Sleep characteristics such as decreased total sleep time, decreased delta wave sleep, shortened rapid eye movement latency, and early morning and intermittent awakenings, are some of the many characteristics shown to distinguish depressed adults (see Kupfer et al., 1983). Evaluations of sleep architecture among depressed children have not shown consistent differences parallel to those obtained with adults (Young et al., 1982). The discrepancy of findings between adult and child populations may prove significant given the continuity of many other biological correlates over the developmental spectrum.

The above measures do not exhaust the biological correlates that have been studied in children. The primary focus has been the assessment of biological markers that have emerged in research on adult depressives. Biological assessments make a major contribution in understanding depression and its possible biological substrates. The measures reflect a different level of assessment from symptoms experienced by the child or dysfunction evident to parents and teachers. The relationship between the presence of specific symptoms and results from biological assessments of the sort highlighted here remain to be explored in children.

The use of biological assessment raises a number of issues that warrant mention. Because many of the procedures are invasive, concerns emerge about subjecting youths to discomfort and risk. Some techniques currently in use (e.g., insulin-induced hypoglycemia) are risky and simply not feasible for clinical use. Other techniques evaluated with adults (e.g., lumbar puncture) are useful for obtaining information about neurochemistry but have understandably been avoided with children. Although some of the biological measures do corroborate diagnoses, they do not invariably provide confirming evidence. For example, in a recent study, a biological measure (growth hormone secretion during sleep) accurately identified one-half of the depressed children (Puig-Antich et al., 1984). While this finding is highly significant on conceptual grounds, the measure would not be sufficient for screening or diagnostic purposes until higher levels of identification were obtained. Biological measures nevertheless are likely to be refined and serve multiple functions apart from validation of other assessment techniques. Such measures will help to identify mechanisms underlying depressed symptoms and markers for diagnosis, treatment prescriptions, and prognosis.

Other modalities. Apart from behavioral and biological measures, projective techniques have received attention in a few investigations. These techniques, of course, are designed to present ambiguous stimuli and response opportunities to the child. Investigations have evaluated different facets of the Rorschach test, the Thematic Apperception Test, the Children's Apperception Test, and the Draw-A-Person Test (see Kazdin, 1988). In general, measures derived from these instruments have not yielded consistent differences between depressed and nondepressed youths. When differences have emerged, molecular responses have been identified (e.g., number of color responses on the Rorschach) with unclear theoretical or applied significance.

Self-Report Measures of Related Constructs

There are a number of measures that may be of interest or use because they address specific characteristics of depressive symptoms in greater depth or because they address key areas that are likely to be influenced by depressive symptoms. Table 7.4 lists a number of measures that assess areas central to current conceptual views of depression. The measures convey areas that reflect specific theoretical models about salient characteristics that are presumed to correlate with, if not contribute directly to, depression (e.g., learned helplessness, hopelessness, pleasant activities, social skills deficits, stressful events). Research has indicated that these areas of functioning are related to depression both in children and adults (see Kazdin, 1988). It is important to underscore the relevance of a broad range of methods beyond self-report and domains beyond those encompassed by measures in Table 7.4. Depression entails changes in affect, cognitions, behaviors, and responses from others. Diverse measures of other characteristics (e.g., family environment, parent child interaction) may be of interest as well (e.g., Hops et al., 1987).

TABLE 7.4 Selected Measures of Constructs Related to Depression

Measure	Response Format	Age[a] Range	Special Features
Cognitive and Attributional Processes[b]			
Self-Perception Profile (Harter, 1982)	36 forced-choice questions, true-false and like me-unlike me	3rd–8th grades	Children are asked to describe themselves ("What I am like"). The scale is designed to measure several domains of self-perception, in six subscales including scholastic competence, social acceptance, athletic competence, physical appearance, behavioral conduct, and global self-worth.

(continued)

TABLE 7.4 *(Continued)*

Measure	Response Format	Age[a] Range	Special Features
Cognitive and Attributional Processes[b]			
Children' Negative Cognitive Error Questionnaire (Leitenberg et al., 1986)	24 items; children rate degree of similarity to their own thoughts	4th–8th grades	The items present hypothetical situations or events followed by a statement about the event that reflects cognitive errors (catastrophizing, overgeneralizing, personalizing, and selective abstraction). These cognitive processes are based on Beck's cognitive therapy of depression.
Multidimensional Measure of Children's Perceptions of Control (Connell, 1985)	24 items children rate for degree to which event is true of them	8–17	Evaluates how children perceive sources of control and includes external, internal, and uncertain sources.
Children's Attributional Style Questionnaire (Seligman & Peterson, 1986)	48 items in a forced choice format	3rd–6th grades	The questions permit assessment of alternative combinations of three attributional dimensions (internal-external cause; global-specific characteristics, stable-unstable characteristics) and perceived valence of the outcome (good-bad). These characteristics pertain to processes considered important in a learned helplessness model of depression.

(continued)

TABLE 7.4   *(Continued)*

Measure	Response Format	Age[a] Range	Special Features
Cognitive and Attributional Processes[b]			
Hopelessness Scale for Children (Kazdin et al., 1986)	17 true-false items	6–13	The items focus on children's expectations toward the future. Developed as a measure to parallel the scale developed by Beck.
Social and Interpersonal Processes			
Matson Evaluation of Social Skills with Children (Matson et al., 1983)	62 and 64 items (child-report, teacher-report forms) rated on a 5-point scale	4–18	Items pertain to social skills assertiveness, jealousy, and impulsiveness all in relation to inter-personal interaction. Items reflect degree to which character-istic is true of the child.
Loneliness Quetionnaire (Asher & Wheeler, 1985)	20 items rated on a 5-point scale	3rd–6th grades	The measure focuses on loneliness at school and related characteristics at school. Sixteen items measure loneliness; 8 additional filler items focus on hobbies and preferred activities and are not part of the scoring.
Reinforcers and Activities			
Children's Reinforcement Schedules (Cautela et al., 1983)	3 separate forms based on child's age; child rates prefer-ences for activities on a 3-point scale	K–6th grade	Object is to identify events that can be used as reinforcers but also might be construed as method to assess pleasure children report in response to a variety of events.

(continued)

TABLE 7.4 (*Continued*)

Measure	Response Format	Age[a] Range	Special Features
Cognitive and Attributional Processes[b]			
Adolescent Reinforcement Survey Schedule (Holmes et al., 1987)	89 items rated on a 5-point scale for the degree person likes the event	17–26	This is similar in purpose to the Children's Reinforcement Schedules noted previously.
Adolescent Activities Checklist (Carey et al., 1986)	100 activities; youths rate frequency of occurrence within the last 2 weeks and degree to which experience was pleasant	8th–12th grades	Includes two subscales for pleasant and unpleasant activities. The measure parallels similar measures on pleasant and unpleasant events, parallels work with adults by Lewinsohn and colleagues on pleasant events and activities.
Stressful and Life Events			
Life Events Checklist (Johnson & McCutcheon, 1980)	46 items that list stressful events	12–17	The respondents indicate whether the event occurred in the past year, whether it was bad or good, and degree of impact (4-point scale) on their lives. The measure permits separation of several different facets of stressful events. Items include many generic events but focus particularly on adolescents (e.g., "getting one's own car").

(*continued*)

TABLE 7.4   *(Continued)*

Measure	Response Format	Age[a] Range	Special Features
Cognitive and Attributional Processes[b]			
Life Events Record (Coddington, 1972)	30–42 stressful events varying as a function of age group	Preschool– high school	The events are rated as occurred and then summed according to their life change units, i.e., separate weighted scores based on the presumed readjustment that would usually be required for such event. These units were developed separately in research obtained from multiple adult samples (e.g., mental health workers, teachers). For young children, parents complete the measures; older children complete the scale themselves. Parallel to the Holmes-Rahe scale for adults.

[a] The age ranges are provided as guidelines for reasons similar to those specified in Table 7.3.

[b] The categories in which the measures are grouped are provided as a guide. Some of the measures could be placed in other categories.

CURRENT ISSUES AND CONSIDERATIONS

The previous discussion outlines many types of measures of depression, as well as measures of related areas. However, the availability of several different measures should not inadvertently imply that the assessment strategies are well developed. Actually, several fundamental questions can be raised about current measures, how they are to be used and interpreted, and their relevance for research and practice.

Children as a Source of Information

The major issue in the use of self-report measures is the extent to which children are capable of or willing to report on their depressive symptoms. This concern does not merely derive from the fact that children might deny symptoms. Rather, measures often ask subtle questions about the presence of specific symptoms, whether children could identify the basis for the symptom, the duration and intensity, and so on. Research has clearly established that both clinic and nonclinic samples can report on their depressive symptoms (Cantwell & Carlson, 1983). However, children often report fewer symptoms than do parents and clinicians (Kazdin, Colbus, & Rodgers, 1986; Kazdin, French, Unis, & Esveldt-Dawson, 1983; Orvaschel et al., 1982; Tisher & Lang, 1983).

Research has suggested that children are likely to be better reporters of symptoms related to private or internal experience, whereas significant others, such as parents and teachers, are better informants in relation to the children's overt behaviors (see Edelbrock, Costello, Dulcan, Conover, & Kalas, 1986). Depression as a clinical syndrome includes subjective states, such as feelings of worthlessness and low self-esteem, as well as overt behavioral signs such as changes in sleep and eating. It is not clear whether utilizing different informants for different symptoms offers advantages.

Parents are frequently used as the source of information to assess their children's depression. In general, parents are a primary source of information because they are readily available as informants, are knowledgeable about the child's behavior across time and situations, and usually play a central role in the referral of children for treatment (Achenbach & Edelbrock, 1983). However, the information parents provide about their child's functioning raises its own interpretive problems. Several studies have shown that maternal perceptions of child adjustment and functioning are related to maternal psychopathology (especially anxiety and depression), marital discord, stressors, and social support outside of the home (e.g., Forehand, Lautenschlager, Faust, & Graziano, 1986; Griest, Wells, & Forehand, 1979; Mash & Johnston, 1983; Moretti, Fine, Haley, & Marriage, 1985). Thus, parent reports cannot be assumed to be based solely on the child's subjective states or behaviors.

Convergence of Assessments

An issue that has frequently emerged is the extent to which measures of depression correspond with each other. There are separate issues here, two of which are the extent to which measures of depression correlate among themselves and to which information from different sources converge.

Relations among measures. The extent to which measures of childhood depression correlate with each other has been frequently studied. Several studies have shown that alternative measures of depression correlate with each other (e.g., Kazdin, French, Unis, & Esveldt-Dawson, 1983; Reynolds, Anderson & Bartell, 1985; Rotundo & Hensley, 1985). The demonstrations show these relations most consistently when multiple measures are administered to the same rater (e.g., child). Between-rater measures often do not correlate well, as discussed in the next section. Similarly, measures of depression and related constructs correlate consistently when the same rater completes the measures. Thus, measures of self-esteem, hopelessness, negative cognitive attributes, and others, highlighted previously, relate to measures of depression. As an initial validation step, the convergence of related measures is an important step. However, it is appreciably less hazardous in the path toward validation than other steps, such as demonstration of discriminant validity.

Correspondence of sources. Common rater variance can account for the convergence of measures in several validational studies. A major issue for the assessment of childhood depression is the relation of reports from different sources, such as parents, teachers, and peers. Considerable research has examined the extent to which alternative sources of information agree on the behavioral and emotional problems of children (see Achenbach, McConaughy, & Howell, 1987). Comparisons have included studies evaluating the agreement among children, parents, teachers, and mental health workers. Across a variety of studies, Achenbach et al. (1987) found that children and parent evaluations of child behavior showed reliable but relatively low agreement (mean r=.25). Correspondence between child and teacher and child and mental health worker evaluations was also low (rs=.20 and .27, respectively). The low levels of correspondence are not just due to the fact that children are included in the comparisons. Agreement between parent and mental health worker evaluations of children was within the same range (mean r=.24).

For present purposes, the low child-parent agreement is noteworthy given the heavy, if not exclusive, reliance on information from these two sources in attaining psychiatric diagnoses. The low agreement challenges the current model and procedures for identifying disorders. The model allows for disagreement between sources but assumes that there is a uniform set of symptoms that different methods will reveal. When discrepancies emerge between sources of information, the implicit assumption is that one source of information is likely to be correct, i.e., identify the true set of symptoms. The situational specificity of behavior and the low correlations between alternative measures of a characteristic, well studied in personality research, are insufficiently considered in the diagnostic process.

It is reasonable to assume that the child actually behaves in a particular way that can be described "objectively." Yet the reports of children and parents as well as others reflect important differences; different raters can be accurate yet vary in the symptoms they identify. Different perspectives and performance across different situations can account for the seemingly discrepant conclusions that are reached about a child's dysfunction. (Also, see Chapters 3 and 10 for further discussions of accuracy versus validity.)

The issue is one of validity or the extent to which reports from different informants (child, parent, teacher, peers, clinicians, or others) relate to and predict other criteria. Evidence points to the validity of information about the child from self- and parent-reports. For example, child self-report measures of depression correlate with suicidal attempt and ideation, hopelessness, low self-esteem, negative attributional style, and child-rearing practices of the parent, such as abuse (e.g., Haley et al., 1985; Kazdin, French, Unis, & Esveldt-Dawson, 1983; Kazdin, French, Unis, Esveldt-Dawson, & Sherick, 1983; Kazdin, Moser, Colbus, & Bell, 1985; Sacco & Graves, 1984). Parental report of their children's depression correlate with diminished social interaction patterns on the part of the child and overt signs of expressive affect (Kazdin, Esveldt-Dawson, Sherick, & Colbus, 1985). Thus, both child and parent reports are valid measures of childhood depression. Yet, child and parent reports usually correlates poorly or not at all with each other. A similar conclusion might be reached involving other sources of information. For example, teacher and peer reports of childhood depression have been validated with their own correlates, as reflected in academic performance and popularity (e.g., Tesiny & Lefkowitz, 1982; Tesiny, Lefkowitz, & Gordon, 1980).

The major difficulty in validating alternative rater reports has been the absence of independent criteria that are free from the bias or input of one of the raters. For example, psychiatric diagnosis or clinical ratings occasionally are used to validate other measures such as self- or parent-report measures. Yet, diagnosis or clinical ratings often rely upon child or parent reports and do not provide an independent source of information. There is a strong method factor already known to operate in studies of convergent and discriminant validity of measures of depression (Kazdin, Esveldt-Dawson, Unis, & Rancurello, 1983; Reynolds et al., 1985; Saylor, Finch, Baskin, Furey, & Kelly, 1984). Thus, validation requires criteria that rely upon different assessment methods and sources of information.

Because ratings of children's depression from alternative sources correlate with important facets of dysfunction or child behavior, they all may reflect potentially useful information. Yet, for purposes of understanding the relative utility of alternative measures, it will be important to identify alternative sources and measures that predict severity of dysfunction, onset and course of mood disorders, and response to treatment. Such research remains to be completed.

Problems of Discriminant Validity

Convergence of measures of depression and related constructs has been repeatedly demonstrated. A more difficult validational task has been to show that measures of depression are different from and do not correlate highly with measures of other unrelated constructs. Discriminant validity refers to the finding that a measure correlates more highly with other measures of the same or related constructs than with measures of unrelated constructs. Current evidence has revealed mixed results for the discriminant validity of measures of childhood depression. (See Chapter 3 for a detailed discussion of this issue.)

Perhaps a relevant discrimination one might require of a measure of depression is the separation of clinically depressed from nondepressed patients. Several studies have shown that depressed children score significantly more highly than nondepressed peers on depression measures (e.g., Asarnow & Carlson, 1986; Kazdin, 1987; Rotundo & Hensley, 1985), although the differences are not always clinically or statistically significant (e.g., Faulstich, Carey, Ruggiero, Enyart, & Gresham, 1986; Kazdin, French, Unis, & Esveldt-Dawson, 1983). In some cases, measures such as the CDI separate disturbed from nondisturbed youth, rather than make a finer discrimination among patients in clinical samples (Carey et al., 1987; Saylor, Finch, Spirito, & Bennett, 1984).

Discriminant validity has been studied in a number of investigations designed to provide multitrait-multimethod assessment evaluations. The evidence has been mixed for convergent and discriminant validity that such studies are designed to address (Kazdin, Esveldt-Dawson, Unis, & Rancurello, 1983; Reynolds et al., 1985; Wolfe et al., 1987). Relatively consistent findings have been found to indicate that measures converge (correlate) as predicted. However, evidence for discriminant validity is usually weak. A consistent finding, related to points discussed previously, is that there is a strong method component which in this case refers to high correlations between measures completed by the same rater (e.g., child or parent).

Part of the difficulty in discussing discriminant validity in relation to depression is that the impact of depressive symptoms may be broad and spill into several areas of functioning. Thus, it is conceivable on a priori grounds that depression might well be related to overall dysfunction or several symptom areas. Perhaps the most difficult area to illustrate issues of discriminant validity is in the relation of anxiety and depression. This relation reflects both diagnostic and assessment dilemmas.

Depression and anxiety are often related. Diagnostic studies of clinical samples have shown that children with one of these disorders often meet criteria for the other as well (Bernstein & Garfinkel, 1986; Strauss, Last, Hersen, & Kazdin, 1988). Even in cases where children with a diagnosis of depression or anxiety do not meet criteria for the other disorder, they are likely to show symptoms of that disorder (Hershberg, Carlson, Cantwell, & Strober, 1982). Assessment studies examining child self-report have shown that measures of childhood depression correlate in the moderate range (e.g., rs range from approximately .35 to .60) (Reynolds et al., 1985; Wolfe et al., 1987). The moderate correlations have suggested to some researchers that it may be more meaningful to conceive of a broader classification of internalizing symptoms, rather than the more specific symptom patterns which are not easily distinguished (Wolfe et al., 1987). The benefits of conceptualizing dysfunction into relatively broad categories (e.g., internalizing) or narrow categories (e.g., depression, anxiety) may depend on the purposes to which assessment is directed (e.g., family studies, treatment).

Categorical versus Dimensional Assessment

Alternative assessment devices have been used for clinical and research purposes to identify children who are "depressed." However, depression can refer to different facets of the individual including a single symptom such as sadness, a state- or trait-like characteristic as reflected in severity of affect across multiple symptoms, or a clinical syndrome, such as major depressive disorder. In many studies, particularly in nonclinical settings (e.g., schools), children are identified on the basis of state- or trait-like characteristics. Performance on a measure of severity of symptoms is examined and alternative cutoff scores are used to define a subsample as depressed. With various inventories, such as the CDI, departures from "normal" can be delineated based on standard deviation units that define a particular percentile or on criteria that distinguish children with and without a formal psychiatric diagnosis of major depression.

Children with severe levels of performance on various inventories such as the CDI may not necessarily meet diagnostic criteria for major depression, and vice versa. Research has identified specific cutoff scores for alternative inventories and the extent to which scores correctly identify children with a diagnosis of major depression (Kazdin, Colbus, & Rodgers, 1986). Even so, empirically derived cutoff scores that maximize sensitivity and specificity yield a high percentage of false positives and false negatives.[2]

The purpose in noting the discrepancy between assessment of severity of depressive symptoms and diagnosis of depressive disorder is not to imply that one is necessarily a criterion for the other. Yet for assessment purposes, it is critical to note that scores on alternative inventories are not tantamount to results obtained from interviews designed to diagnose affective disorder. The utility of dimensional versus categorical assessment of depression may vary according to the purposes of the investigator. The use of self-report scales that describe severity of dysfunction is not likely to yield samples with depressive disorders as defined by contemporary diagnostic criteria. If the goal is to obtain diagnostic groups or to study subtypes, assessment procedures specifically directed to these objectives are obviously essential.

The differences in categorical and dimensional assessment are familiar but need to be considered in planning and interpreting research. Findings obtained from studies in which depression is defined by diagnostic criteria are likely to vary from those obtained from studies using various cutoff scores to identify extreme groups. It is of course possible, and no doubt desirable, within a given study to have information pertaining both to the diagnosis and severity of depression.

RESEARCH DIRECTIONS FOR ASSESSMENT

Selection of Measures

No single measure has been shown to assess the multiple facets of dysfunction that depression can reflect nor to evaluate the diverse conceptual models that are currently posed. For the clinician and researcher, it is obvious that assessment of depression needs to include multiple measures that encompass different methods of assessment (e.g., interviews, direct observations), perspectives (e.g., child, parent, teacher), and domains (e.g., affect, cognitions, behavior). Apart from the advisabil-

---

[2]In this context, sensitivity refers to the percentage of children who receive a diagnosis and who are positively identified as depressed on the measure (questionnaire, inventory) as well (true positives); specificity is the percentage of children who do not receive the diagnosis and who are not identified as depressed by the measure (true negatives).

ity of multichannel assessment strategies in general, specific findings within the area of childhood depression lobby for a broad assessment battery.

Findings have shown that there may be significant method variance in the assessment of depression, that different methods of assessment may not intercorrelate highly, and that measures that do not correlate highly with each other may still reliably predict different external criteria (e.g., social behavior, suicidal risk) (see Kazdin, Esveldt-Dawson, Sherick, & Colbus, 1985; Kazdin, Esveldt-Dawson, Unis, & Rancurello, 1983; Saylor, Finch, Baskin, Furey, & Kelly, 1984; Saylor, Finch, Spirito, & Bennett, 1984). Based on these considerations, an assessment battery minimally should sample: (1) different sources of information (e.g., the child and a significant other), (2) performance in different settings (e.g., performance at home and at school), (3) multiple domains of depressive symptoms (e.g., affect, cognitions, and behavior), and (4) overall adjustment (e.g., as in measures of adjustment or psychopathology).

Other considerations may dictate more specifically the domains of assessment, specific constructs, and concrete assessment strategies. The *conceptual model* adhered to in clinical work or research obviously can dictate the measures that are used. Specific behavioral and cognitive models have led clinical researchers to select measures that focus on social skills, activities and reinforcing consequences, and negative attributions. Similarly, biological models have dictated the search for neurohumors and metabolites of endocrine function. Adoption of a particular model may not invariably lead one to specific measures. For example, psychodynamic models of childhood depression have yet to establish assessment techniques shown to reliably identify more dynamic facets of depression in children. Certainly greater research activity is warranted here.

Interest in *specific symptoms* may also dictate the measures that are selected. Salient symptoms or correlates may point to the need for specific measurement strategies. For example, in adults anhedonia, or reduced and diminished experience of pleasure, has been the focus of considerable research. Anhedonia is a central symptom of depression and has important implications for the prediction of recovery from symptoms and the delineation of alternative subtypes (Clark, Fawcett, Salazar-Grueso, & Fawcett, 1984; Young, Scheftner, Klerman, Andreasen, & Hirschfeld, 1986). Anhedonia may be critical for evaluating other aspects of functioning. Similarly, the presence of hopelessness may be of interest in part because of the relation to suicidal ideation or attempt (e.g., Kazdin, Rodgers, & Colbus, 1986). In the child arena, interest in specific symptom domains may require improvisation of measures and development of new measures.

Overall, several measures of childhood depression have emerged. Although research is needed on individual scales, the field might profit from investigations to help direct informed selection among alternative measures. Research on the relation and redundancies among alternative measures and their relative strengths and weaknesses for different purposes would be helpful as well. Different measures may fare differently when used for such diverse purposes as initial screening, diagnosis, and evaluation of treatment outcome. Different facets of depression, their relation to each other, and possible diagnostic significance also warrant study. The focus on depression and positive affective experience as assessed by one scale discussed previously reflects a direction along these lines by looking more at areas obviously relevant to depression but beyond depressive symptoms alone.

Extrapolations from Adult Depression

The rapid progress in the investigation of childhood depression is due in large part to the extrapolation of conceptual views, assessment approaches, and laboratory techniques from the study of adult to the study of childhood depression. An obvious first step is to examine and explore models and assessment and treatment strategies that have proven to be useful in the context of adult dysfunction. Extrapolation of concepts and methods from the adult to the child disorder is important for many obvious reasons, not the least of which is identifying the boundaries of the continuity of dysfunction across the developmental spectrum.

Much of the work with children has been based largely on examining the literature with adults and extending the investigations to children. Although the value of such extensions has been demonstrated, it is important for research not to be too heavily wedded to the work on adult depression. It is useful to consider some of the obvious unique characteristics of children that do not derive from extrapolations of the adult literature (see Dignon & Gotlib, 1985; Rutter, Izard, & Read, 1986). For purposes of assessment as well as of treatment, there may be domains that warrant special attention because of the unique characteristics of children. For example, a distinguishing feature of children is their living situation and the role of their parents in their daily lives. Because of the potential influence that parents can exert over their children, the assessment of family and parent child interaction may be particularly relevant in understanding child symptom patterns.

Several avenues of work support the focus on the family (Burbach & Borduin, 1986). To begin, depressed children are more likely to come from homes with a depressed parent than children without such a diagnosis.

Focus on the depression of the parent may have impact on the child's symptoms as well. The impact may be through different parent-child interaction patterns. For example, in relation to the children, depressed parents display less affection and happy affect and show more problems in communicating, more dysphoric affect, and greater ambivalence toward their families (Hops et al., 1987; Weissman, Paykel, & Klerman, 1972). Families with a depressed parent are also characterized by less cohesion and expressiveness, more conflict, and less emphasis on the development of independence, moral and religious values, and participation in joint recreational activities (Billings & Moos, 1983). These characteristics may contribute to or exacerbate the symptoms that may subsequently emerge in the child. From the standpoint of assessment, it may be quite useful to incorporate measures related to family functioning in addition to those that reflect specific symptoms.

School represents another unique situation for children that may be incorporated into assessment. Interactions in relation to peers may be especially important to assess because of the special role peers play in development. Here too the data may reveal information relevant to prognosis and treatment, beyond the delineation of specific depressive symptoms. In general, new or varied models of assessment and treatment might be developed based on scrutiny of unique features of child development. Research that extends beyond extrapolation of adult models may identify important features that might help prevent the unfolding of depression over the course of childhood and adulthood.

SUMMARY AND CONCLUSIONS

Childhood depression is an area of tremendous activity. The proliferation of work in the area can be attested to in part by the number of recent books devoted to the topic (e.g., Cantwell & Carlson, 1983; Petti, 1983; Rutter et al., 1986; Trad, 1987). Diagnosis and assessment are major domains of work. Delineation of diagnostic criteria for children and adolescents within the last decade is a broader influence that has greatly facilitated research on childhood disorders in general. Developments in depression research have accelerated in large part because of the advances in the study of adult depression. Biological, environmental, and psychosocial theories of depression have been extrapolated to children and adolescents. In addition, assessment techniques developed with adults have served as a model for developing parallel measures for children. The most prominent example perhaps is the development of the Children's Depression Inventory, a descendant of the very widely used

Beck Depression Inventory. Many other self-report scales of depression and constructs related to depression (e.g., cognitive style, hopelessness) have developed, often following the lead of parallel work with adults. Self-report measures are by no means the only assessment methods. Psychophysiological and biochemical measures, peer ratings, and direct observations, also have contributed to the understanding of childhood depression (Kazdin, 1988).

Notwithstanding the development of several measures, basic issues remain to be elaborated. The often poor correspondence among alternative methods of assessment and perspectives (e.g., child, parent, and teacher) raise multiple issues. The utility of information from alternative sources and how to integrate these warrants further research. Also, differences obtained when depression is defined through extreme scores of dimensional (e.g., self-report) scales or diagnostic criteria need to be clarified. The multiplicity of measures has led to a large number of criteria in use to refer to youth as depressed. The emerging body of knowledge no doubt will raise seemingly contradictory findings in part because the different criteria and measures identify different populations.

The extension of diagnostic criteria, conceptual models, laboratory techniques, and assessment methods for adults to children and adolescents has clearly led to major advances. The benefits of these latter extensions can be attested to by the large number of findings showing developmental continuities. Perhaps few disorders have been as thoroughly studied as depression in such a parallel fashion. Although the models and approaches developed with adults have been remarkably heuristic, they would bear a heavy cost if they inadvertently constrained the pursuit of novel approaches based on understanding child development and the role of special influences during childhood.

REFERENCES

Achenbach, T.M., & Edelbrock, C.S. (1983). Manual for the Child Behavior Checklist and Revised Child Behavior Profile. Burlington, VT: University Associates in Psychiatry.

Achenbach, T.M., McConaughy, S.H., & Howell, C.T. (1987). Child/adolescent behavioral and emotional problems: Implications of cross-informant correlations for situational specificity. Psychological Bulletin, 101, 213–232.

Altmann, E.O., & Gotlib, I.H. (1988). The social behavior of depressed children: An observational study. Journal of Abnormal Child Psychology, 16, 29–44.

American Psychiatric Association. (1980). Diagnostic and statistical manual of mental disorders (3rd ed.). Washington, DC: Author.

American Psychiatric Association. (1987). *Diagnostic and statistical manual of mental disorders-Revised.* Washington, DC: Author.

Anthony, E.J. (1975). Childhood depression. In E.J. Anthony & T. Benedek (Eds.), *Depression and human existence* (pp. 231–277). Boston: Little, Brown.

Asarnow, J.R., & Carlson, G.A. (1986). Depression Self-Rating Scale: Utility with child psychiatric inpatients. *Journal of Consulting and Clinical Psychology, 53,* 491–499.

Asher, S.R., & Wheeler, V.A. (1985). Children's loneliness: A comparison of rejected and neglected peer status. *Journal of Consulting and Clinical Psychology, 53,* 500–505.

Bemporad, J.R., & Wilson, A. (1978). A developmental approach to depression in childhood and adolescence. *Journal of the American Academy of Psychoanalysis, 6,* 325–352.

Berndt, D.J., Petzel, T., & Berndt, S.M. (1980). Development and initial evaluation of a multiscore depression inventory. *Journal of Personality Assessment, 44,* 396–404.

Bernstein, G.A., & Garfinkel, D.B. (1986). School phobia: The overlap of affective and anxiety disorders. *Journal of the American Academy of Child Psychiatry, 25,* 235–241.

Billings, A.G., & Moos, R.H. (1983). Comparisons of children of depressed and nondepressed parents: A social-environmental perspective. *Journal of Abnormal Child Psychology, 11,* 463–486.

Birleson, P. (1981). The validity of depressive disorder in childhood and the development of a self-rating scale: A research project. *Journal of Child Psychology and Psychiatry, 22,* 73–88.

Burbach, D.J., & Borduin, C.M. (1986). Parent-child relations and the etiology of depression: A review of methods and findings. *Clinical Psychology Review, 6,* 133–153.

Cantwell, D.P., & Carlson, G.A. (Eds.). (1983). *Affective disorders in childhood and adolescence: An update.* New York: Spectrum.

Carey, M.P., Faulstich, M.E., Gresham, F.M., Ruggiero, L., & Enyart, P. (1987). Children's Depression Inventory: Construct and discriminant validity across clinical and nonreferred (control) populations. *Journal of Consulting and Clinical Psychology, 55,* 755–761.

Carey, M.P., Kelley, M.L., Buss, R.R., & Scott, W.O.N. (1986). Relationship of activity to depression in adolescents: Development of the adolescent activities checklist. *Journal of Consulting and Clinical Psychology, 54,* 320–322.

Carlson, G.A., & Cantwell, D.P. (1979). A survey of depressive symptoms in a child and adolescent psychiatric population. *Journal of the American Academy of Child Psychiatry, 18,* 587–599.

Carlson, G.A., & Cantwell, D.P. (1982). Suicidal behavior and depression in children and adolescents. *Journal of the American Academy of Child Psychiatry, 21,* 361–368.

Carlson, G.A., & Garber, J. (1986). Developmental issues in the classification of depression in children. In M. Rutter, C.E. Izard, & P.B. Read (Eds.), *Depression* in young people: Developmental and clinical perspectives (pp. 399–434). New York: Guilford.

Cautela, J.R., Cautela, J., & Esonis, S. (1983). Forms for behavior analysis with children. Champaign, IL: Research Press.

Chambers, W.J., Puig-Antich, J., Hirsch, M., Paez, P., Ambrosini, P.J., Tabrizi, M.A., & Davies, M. (1985). The assessment of affective disorders in children and adolescents by semistructured interview: Test-retest reliability. Archives of General Psychiatry, 42, 696–702.

Chiles, J.A., Miller, M.L., & Cox, G.B. (1980). Depression in an adolescent delinquent population. Archives of General Psychiatry, 37, 1179–1184.

Cicchetti, D., & Schneider-Rosen, K. (1984). Toward a transactional model of childhood depression. In D. Cicchetti & K. Schneider-Rosen (Eds.), Childhood depression: New directions for child development (pp. 5–27). San Francisco: Jossey-Bass.

Clark, D.C., Fawcett, J., Salazar-Grueso, E., & Fawcett, E. (1984). Seven-month clinical outcome of anhedonic and normally hedonic depressed inpatients. American Journal of Psychiatry, 141, 1216–1220.

Coddington, R.D. (1972). The significance of life events as etiological factors in the diseases of children: A study of normal population. Journal of Psychosomatic Research, 16, 205–213.

Connell, J.P. (1985). A new multidimensional measure of children's perceptions of control. Child Development, 56, 1018–1041.

Costello, E.J., Edelbrock, C.S., & Costello, A.J. (1985). Validity of the NIMH Diagnostic Interview Schedule for Children: A comparison between psychiatric and pediatric referrals. Journal of Abnormal Child Psychology, 13, 579–595.

Cytryn, L., & McKnew, D.H. (1974). Factors influencing the changing clinical expression of the depressive process in children. American Journal of Psychiatry, 131, 879–881.

Depue, R.A., & Kleiman, R.M. (1979). Free cortisol as a peripheral index of central vulnerability to major forms of polar depressive disorders: Examining stress-biology interactions in subsyndromal high-risk persons. In R.A. Depue (Ed.), The psychobiology of the depressive disorders (pp. 177–204). New York: Academic Press.

Dignon, N., & Gotlib, I.H. (1985). Developmental considerations in the study of childhood depression. Developmental Review, 5, 162–199.

Eddy, B.A., & Lubin, B. (1988). The Children's Depression Adjective Check Lists (C-DACL) with emotionally disturbed adolescent boys. Journal of Abnormal Child Psychology, 16, 83–88.

Edelbrock, C.S., Costello, A.J., Dulcan, M.K., Conover, N.C., & Kalas, R. (1986). Parent-child agreement on child psychiatric symptoms assessed via structured interview. Journal of Child Psychology and Psychiatry, 27, 181–190.

Faulstich, M.E., Carey, M.P., Ruggiero, M.A., Enyart, P., & Gresham, F. (1986). Assessment of depression in childhood and adolescence: An evaluation of the Center for Epidemiological Studies Depression Scale for Children (CES-DC). American Journal of Psychiatry, 143, 1024–1027.

Finch, A.J., Jr., Saylor, C.F., & Edwards, G.L. (1985). Children's Depression Inventory: Sex and grade norms for normal children. *Journal of Consulting and Clinical Psychology, 53,* 424–425.

Fisch, H.U., Frey, S., & Hirsbrunner, H.P. (1983). Analyzing nonverbal behavior in depression. *Journal of Abnormal Psychology, 92,* 307–318.

Forehand, R., Lautenschlager, G.J., Faust, J., & Graziano, W.G. (1986). Parent perceptions and parent-child interactions in clinic-referred children: A preliminary investigation of the effects of maternal depressive moods. *Behaviour Research and Therapy, 24,* 73–75.

Fossi, L., Faravelli, C., & Paoli, M. (1984). The ethological approach to the assessment of depressive disorders. *Journal of Nervous and Mental Disease, 172,* 332–341.

Frame, C., Matson, J.L., Sonis, W.A., Fialkov, M.J., & Kazdin, A.E. (1982). Behavioral treatment of depression in a prepubertal child. *Journal of Behavior Therapy and Experimental Psychiatry, 3,* 239–243.

Glaser, K. (1968). Masked depression in children and adolescents. In S. Chess & A. Thomas (Eds.), *Annual progress in child psychiatry and child development* (Vol. 1, pp. 345–355). New York: Brunner/Mazel.

Griest, D., Wells, K.C., & Forehand, R. (1979). An examination of predictors of maternal perceptions of maladjustment in clinic-referred children. *Journal of Abnormal Psychology, 88,* 277–281.

Group for the Advancement of Psychiatry, Committee on Child Psychiatry. (1966). *Psychopathological disorders in childhood: Theoretical considerations and a proposed classification* (Vol. 6). New York: Author.

Haley, G., Fine, S., Marriage, K., Moretti, M., & Freeman, R. (1985). Cognitive bias and depression in psychiatrically disturbed children and adolescents. *Journal of Consulting and Clinical Psychology, 53,* 535–537.

Hamilton, M.A. (1967). Development of a rating scale for primary depressive illness. *British Journal of Social and Clinical Psychology, 6,* 278–296.

Harter, S. (1982). The Perceived Competence Scale for Children. *Child Development, 53,* 87–97.

Hawton, K. (1986). *Suicide and attempted suicide among children and adolescents.* Beverly Hills, CA: Sage.

Herjanic, B., & Reich, W. (1982). Development of a structured psychiatric interview for children: Agreement between child and parent on individual symptoms. *Journal of Abnormal Child Psychology, 10,* 307–324.

Hershberg, S.G., Carlson, G.A., Cantwell, D.P., & Strober, M. (1982). Anxiety and depressive disorders in psychiatrically disturbed children. *Journal of Clinical Psychiatry, 43,* 358–361.

Hodges, K., McKnew, D., Cytryn, L., Stern, L., & Kline, J. (1982). The Child Assessment Schedule (CAS) diagnostic interview: A report on reliability and validity. *Journal of the American Academy of Child Psychiatry, 21,* 468–473.

Holmes, G.R., Heckel, R.V., Chestnut, E., Harris, N., & Cautela, J. (1987). Factor analysis of the Adolescent Reinforcement Survey Schedule (ARSS) with college freshman. *Journal of Clinical Psychology, 43,* 386–390.

Hops, H., Biglan, A., Sherman, L., Arthur, J., Friedman, L., & Osteen, V. (1987). Home observations of family interactions of depressed women. *Journal of Consulting and Clinical Psychology, 55,* 341–346.

Jacobsen, R.H., Lahey, B.B., & Strauss, C.C. (1983). Correlates of depressed mood in normal children. *Journal of Abnormal Child Psychology, 11,* 29–40.

Johnson, J.H., & McCutcheon, S.M. (1980). Assessing life stress in older children and adolescents: Preliminary findings with the Life Events Checklist. In I.G. Sarason & C.D. Spielberger (Eds.), *Stress and anxiety* (Vol. 7, pp. 111–125). Washington, D.C.: Hemisphere.

Jones, I.M., & Pasna, M. (1979). Some nonverbal aspects of depression and schizophrenia occurring during the interview. *Journal of Nervous and Mental Disease, 167,* 402–409.

Kandel, D.B., & Davies, M. (1982). Epidemiology of depressive mood in adolescents: An empirical study. *Archives of General Psychiatry, 39,* 1205–1212.

Kaplan, S.L., Hong, G.K., & Weinhold, C. (1984). Epidemiology of depressive symptomatology in adolescents. *Journal of the American Academy of Child Psychiatry, 23,* 91–98.

Kashani, J.H., Barbero, G.J., & Bolander, F.D. (1981). Depression in hospitalized pediatric patients. *Journal of the American Academy of Child Psychiatry, 20,* 123–134.

Kashani, J.H., Cantwell, D.P., Shekim, W.O., & Reid, J.C. (1982). Major depressive disorder in children admitted to an inpatient community mental health center. *American Journal of Psychiatry, 139,* 671–672.

Kashani, J.H., McGee, R.O., Clarkson, S.E., Anderson, J.C., Walton, L.A., Williams, S., Silva, P.A., Robins, A.J., Cytryn, L., & McKnew, D.H. (1983). Depression in a sample of 9-year-old children. *Archives of General Psychiatry, 40,* 1217–1223.

Kashani, J.H., Ray, J.S., & Carlson, G.A. (1984). Depression and depression-like states in preschool-age children in a child development unit. *American Journal of Psychiatry, 141,* 1397–1402.

Kashani, J., & Simonds, J.F. (1979). The incidence of depression in children. *American Journal of Psychiatry, 136,* 1203–1205.

Kaslow, N.J., Rehm, L.P., & Siegel, A.W. (1984). Social-cognitive and cognitive correlates of depression in children. *Journal of Abnormal Child Psychology, 12,* 605–620.

Kazdin, A.E. (1987). Children's Depression Scale: Validation with child psychiatric inpatients. *Journal of Child Psychology and Psychiatry, 28,* 29–41.

Kazdin, A.E. (1988). Childhood depression. In E.J. Mash & L.G. Terdal (Eds.), *Behavioral assessment of childhood disorders* (2nd ed., pp. 157–195). New York: Guilford

Kazdin, A.E., Colbus, D., & Rodgers, A. (1986). Assessment of depression and diagnosis of depressive disorder among psychiatrically disturbed children. *Journal of Abnormal Child Psychology, 14,* 499–515.

Kazdin, A.E., Esveldt-Dawson, K., Sherick, R.B., & Colbus, D. (1985). Assessment of overt behavior and childhood depression among psychiatrically disturbed children. *Journal of Consulting and Clinical Psychology, 53,* 201–210.

Kazdin, A.E., Esveldt-Dawson, K., Unis, A.S., & Rancurello, M.D. (1983). Child and parent evaluations of depression and aggression in psychiatric inpatient children. *Journal of Abnormal Child Psychology, 11*, 401–413.

Kazdin, A.E., French, N.H., Unis, A.S., & Esveldt-Dawson, K. (1983). Assessment of childhood depression: Correspondence of child and parent ratings. *Journal of the American Academy of Child Psychiatry, 22*, 157–164.

Kazdin, A.E., French, N.H., Unis, A.S., Esveldt-Dawson, K., & Sherick, R.B. (1983). Hopelessness, depression and suicidal intent among psychiatrically disturbed inpatient children. *Journal of Consulting and Clinical Psychology, 51*, 504–510.

Kazdin, A.E., Moser, J., Colbus, D., & Bell, R. (1985). Depressive symptoms among physically abused and psychiatrically disturbed children. *Journal of Abnormal Psychology, 94*, 298–307.

Kazdin, A.E., Rodgers, A., & Colbus, D. (1986). The Hopelessness Scale for Children: Psychometric characteristics and concurrent validity. *Journal of Consulting and Clinical Psychology, 54*, 241–245.

Kazdin, A.E., Sherick, R.B., Esveldt-Dawson, K., & Rancurello, M.D. (1985) Nonverbal behavior and childhood depression. *Journal of the American Academy of Child Psychiatry, 24*, 303–309.

Kovacs, M. (1978). *Interview Schedule for Children (ISC)* (10th revision). Pittsburgh, PA: University of Pittsburgh School of Medicine.

Kovacs, M. (1981). Rating scales to assess depression in school aged children. *Acta Paedopsychiatrica, 46*, 305–315.

Kovacs, M., & Beck, A.T. (1977). An empirical clinical approach towards a definition of childhood depression. In J.G. Schulterbrandt & A. Raskin (Eds.), *Depression in children: Diagnosis, treatment, and conceptual models* (pp. 1–25). New York: Raven Press.

Kupfer, D.J., Spiker, D.G., Rossi, A., Coble, P.A., Ulrich, R., & Shaw, D. (1983). Recent diagnostic and treatment advances in REM sleep and depression. In P.J. Clayton & J.E. Barrett (Eds.), *Treatment of depression* (pp. 31–52). New York: Raven Press.

Lang, M., & Tisher, M. (1978). *Children's Depression Scale.* Victoria, Australia: Australian Council for Educational Research.

Lefkowitz, M.M., & Tesiny, E.P. (1980). Assessment of childhood depression. *Journal of Consulting and Clinical Psychology, 48*, 43–50.

Lefkowitz, M.M., & Tesiny, E.P. (1985). Depression in children: Prevalence and correlates. *Journal of Consulting and Clinical Psychology, 53*, 647–656.

Lefkowitz, M.M., Tesiny, E.P., & Gordon, N.H. (1980). Childhood depression, family income, and locus of control. *Journal of Nervous and Mental Disease, 168*, 732–735.

Leitenberg, H., Yost, L.W., & Carroll-Wilson, M. (1986). Negative cognitive errors in children: Questionnaire development, normative data, and comparisons between children with and without self-reported symptoms of depression, low self-esteem, and evaluation anxiety. *Journal of Consulting and Clinical Psychology, 54*, 528–536.

Lewinsohn, P.M., & Shaffer, M. (1971). The use of home observations as an integral part of the treatment of depression: Preliminary report and case studies. *Journal of Consulting and Clinical Psychology, 37,* 87–94.

Linden, M., Hautzinger, M., & Hoffmann, N. (1983). Discriminant analysis of depressive interactions. *Behavior Modification, 7,* 403–422.

Lobovits, D.A., & Handal, P.J. (1985). Childhood depression: Prevalence using DSM-III criteria and validity of parent and child depression scales. *Journal of Pediatric Psychology, 10,* 45–54.

Mahler, M. (1961). On sadness and grief in infancy and childhood. *Psychoanalytic Study of the Child, 16,* 332.

Malmquist, C.P. (1977). Childhood depression: A clinical and behavioral perspective. In J.G. Schulterbrandt & A. Raskin (Eds.), *Depression in children: Diagnosis, treatment and conceptual models* (pp. 33–59). New York: Raven Press.

Malouff, J. (1984). Development and validation of a behavioral peer-rating measure of depression. *Journal of Consulting and Clinical Psychology, 52,* 1108–1109.

Mash, E.J., & Johnston, C. (1983). Parental perceptions of child behavior problems, parenting self-esteem, and mothers' reported stress in younger and older hyperactive and normal children. *Journal of Consulting and Clinical Psychology, 51,* 86–99.

Matson, J.L., Rotatori, A.F., & Helsel, W.J. (1983). Development of a rating scale to measure social skills in children: The Matson Evaluation of Social Skills with Youngsters (MESSY). *Behaviour Research and Therapy, 21,* 335–340.

McConville, B.J., & Bruce, R.T. (1985). Depressive illnesses in children and adolescents: A review of current concepts. *Canadian Journal of Psychiatry, 30,* 119–129.

McKnew, D.H., Jr., Cytryn, L., Efron, A.M., Gershon, E.S., & Bunney, W.E., Jr. (1979). Offspring of patients with affective disorders. *British Journal of Psychiatry, 134,* 148–152.

Mezzich, A.C., & Mezzich, J.E. (1979). Symptomatology of depression in adolescence. *Journal of Personality Assessment, 43,* 267–275.

Michelson, L., DiLorenzo, T., & Petti. (1981). Behavioral assessment of imipramine effects in a depressed child. *Journal of Behavioral Assessment, 3,* 253–262.

Miller, R.E., Ranelli, C., & Levine, J.M. (1977). Nonverbal communication as an index of depression. In I. Hanin & E. Usdin (Eds.), *Animal models in psychiatry and neurology* (pp. 171–180). New York: Pergamon Press.

Moretti, M.M., Fine, S., Haley, G., & Marriage, K. (1985). Child and adolescent depression: Child-report versus parent-report information. *Journal of the American Academy of Child Psychiatry, 24,* 298–302.

Moyal, B.R. (1977). Locus of control, self-esteem, stimulus appraisal, and depressive symptoms in children. *Journal of Consulting and Clinical Psychology, 45,* 951–952.

Nelson, W.M., III., Politano, P.M., Finch, A.J., Jr., Wendel, N., & Mayhall, C. (1987). Children's Depression Inventory: Normative data and utility with emotionally disturbed children. *Journal of the American Academy of Child and Adolescent Psychiatry, 26,* 43–48.

Orvaschel, H., Puig-Antich, J., Chambers W., Tabrizi, M.A., & Johnson, R. (1982). Retrospective assesment of prepubertal major depression with the Kiddle-SADS-E. *Journal of the American Academy of Child Psychiatry, 21,* 392–397.

Paykel, E.S. (1982). *Handbook of affective disorders.* New York: Guilford.

Petti, T.A. (1978). Depression in hospitalized child psychiatry patients: Approaches to measuring depression. *Journal of the American Academy of Child Psychiatry, 22,* 11–21.

Petti, T.A. (Ed.) (1983). *Childhood depression.* New York: Haworth Press.

Pfeffer, C.R., Conte, H.R., Plutchik, R., & Jerrett, I. (1979). Suicidal behavior in latency age children. *Journal of the American Academy of Child Psychiatry, 18,* 679–692.

Poznanski, E.O., Cook, S.C., & Carroll, B.J. (1979). A depression rating scale for children. *Pediatrics, 64,* 442–450.

Poznanski, E.O., Grossman, J.A., Buchsbaum, Y., Banegas, M., Freeman, L., & Gibbons, R. (1984). Preliminary studies of the reliability and validity of the Children's Depression Rating Scale. *Journal of the American Academy of Child Psychiatry, 23,* 191–197.

Puig-Antich, J. (1986). Psychobiological markers: Effects of age and puberty. In M. Rutter, C.E. Izard, & P.B. Read (Eds.), *Depression in young people: Developmental and clinical perspectives* (pp. 341–381). New York: Guilford.

Puig-Antich, J., Blau, S., Marx, N., Greenhill, L.L., & Chambers, W. (1978). Prepubertal major depressive disorders: A pilot study. *Journal of the American Academy of Child Psychiatry, 17,* 695–707.

Puig-Antich, J., & Gittelman, R. (1982). Depression in childhood and adolescence. In E.S. Paykel (Ed.), *Handbook of affective disorders* (pp. 379–392). New York: Guilford.

Puig-Antich, J., Goetz, R., Davies, M., Fein, M., Hanlon, C., Chambers, W.J., Tabrizi, M.A., Sachar, E.J., & Weitzman, E.D. (1984). Growth hormone secretion in prepubertal children with major depression. II. Sleep-related plasma concentrations during a depressive epidode. *Archives of General Psychiatry, 41,* 463–466.

Puig-Antich, J., Perel, J., Lupatkin, W., Chambers, W.J., Tabrizi, M.A., King, J., Davies, M., Johnson, R., & Stiller, R. (1987). Imipramine in prepubertal major depressive disorders. *Archives of General Psychiatry, 44,* 81–89.

Reynolds, W.M. (1985). Depression in childhood and adolescence: Diagnosis, assessment, intervention strategies, and research. In T.R. Kratochwill (Ed.), *Advances in school psychology* (Vol. 4, pp. 133–189). Hillsdale, NJ: Lawrence Erlbaum.

Reynolds, W.M., Anderson, G., & Bartell, N. (1985). Measuring depression in children: A multi-method assessment investigation. *Journal of Abnormal Child Psychology, 13,* 513–526.

Reynolds, W.M., & Coats, K.I. (1986). A comparison of cognitive-behavioral therapy and relaxation training for the treatment of depression in adolescents. *Journal of Consulting and Clinical Psychology, 54,* 653–660.

Rie, H.E. (1966). Depression in childhood: A survey of some pertinent contributions. *Journal of the American Academy of Child Psychiatry, 5,* 653–685.

Rotundo, N., & Hensley, V.R. (1985). The Children's Depression Scale: A study of its validity. *Journal of Child Psychology and Psychiatry, 26,* 917–927.

Rutter, M., Izard, C.E., & Read, P.B. (Eds.). (1986). *Depression in young people: Developmental and clinical perspectives.* New York: Guilford.

Sacco, W.P., & Graves, D.J. (1984). Childhood depression, interpersonal problem-solving, and self-ratings of performance. *Journal of Clinical Child Psychology, 13,* 10–15.

Saylor, C.F., Finch, A.J., Jr., Baskin, C.H., Furey, W., & Kelly, M.M. (1984). Construct validity for measures of childhood depression: Application of multitrait-multimethod methodology. *Journal of Consulting and Clinical Psychology, 52,* 977–985.

Saylor, C.F., Finch, A.J., Jr., Spirito, A., & Bennett, B. (1984). The Children's Depression Inventory: A systematic evaluation of psychometric properties. *Journal of Consulting and Clinical Psychology, 52,* 955–967.

Seligman, M.E.P., & Peterson, C. (1986). A learned helplessness perspective on childhood depression: Theory and research. In M. Rutter, C.E. Izard, & P.B. Read (Eds.), *Depression in young people: Developmental and clinical perspectives* (pp. 223–249). New York: Guilford.

Seligman, M.E.P., Peterson, C., Kaslow, N.J., Tanenbaum, R.L., Alloy, L.B., Abramson, L.Y. (1984). Attributional style and depressive symptoms among children. *Journal of Abnormal Psychology, 93,* 235–238.

Smucker, M.R., Craighead, W.E., Craighead, L.W., & Green, B.J. (1986). Normative and reliability data for the Children's Depression Inventory. *Journal of Abnormal Child Psychology, 14,* 25–39.

Spitzer, R.L., Endicott, J., & Robins, E. (1978). Research Diagnostic Criteria: Rationale and reliability. *Archives of General Psychiatry, 35,* 773–782.

Sroufe, L.A., & Rutter, M. (1984). The domain of developmental psychopathology. *Child Development, 55,* 17–29.

Strauss, C.C., Last, C.G., Hersen, M., & Kazdin, A.E. (1988). Association between anxiety and depression in children and adolescents. *Journal of Abnormal Child Psychology, 16,* 57–68.

Tesiny, E.P., & Lefkowitz, M.M. (1982). Childhood depression: A 6-month follow-up study. *Journal of Consulting and Clinical Psychology, 50,* 778–780.

Tesiny, E.P., Lefkowitz, M.M., & Gordon, N.H. (1980). Childhood depression, locus of control, and school achievement. *Journal of Educational Psychology, 72,* 506–510.

Tisher, M., & Lang, M. (1983). The Children's Depression Scale: Review and further developments. In D.P. Cantwell & G.A. Carlson (Eds.), *Childhood depression* (pp. 181–203). New York: Spectrum.

Trad, P.V. (1987). *Infant and childhood depression: Developmental factors.* New York: Wiley.

Waxer, P. (1976). Nonverbal cues for depth of depression: Set versus no set. *Journal of Consulting and Clinical Psychology, 44,* 493.

Weissman, M.M. Orvaschel, H., & Padian, N. (1980). Children's symptom and social functioning self-report scales: Comparison of mother's and children's reports. *Journal of Nervous and Mental Disease, 168,* 736–740.

Weissman, M.M., Paykel, E.S., & Klerman, G.L. (1972). The depressed woman as a mother. *Social Psychiatry, 7,* 98–108.

Weisz, J.R., Weiss, B., Wasserman, A.A., & Rintoul, B. (1987). Control-related beliefs and depression among clinic-referred children and adolescents. *Journal of Abnormal Psychology, 96,* 58–63.

Whybrow, P.C., Akiskal, H.S., & McKinney, W.T. (1984). *Mood disorders: Toward a new psychobiology.* New York: Plenum.

Williams, J.G., Barlow, D.H., & Agras, W.S. (1972). Behavioral measurement of severe depression. *Archives of General Psychiatry, 27,* 330–333.

Wolfe, V.V., Finch, A.J., Jr., Saylor, C.F., Blount, R.L., Pallmeyer, T.P., & Carek, D.J. (1987). Negative affectivity in children: A multitrait-multimethod investigation. *Journal of Consulting and Clinical Psychology, 55,* 245–250.

World Health Organization. (1987). *International classification of diseases, injuries, and causes of death* (10th ed., draft). Geneva: World Health Organization.

Young, W., Knowles, J.B., MacLean, A.W., Boag, L., & McConville, B.J. (1982). The sleep of childhood depressives. *Biological Psychiatry, 17,* 1163–1168.

Young, M.A., Scheftner, W.A., Klerman, G.L. Andreasen, N.C., & Hirschfeld, R.M. (1986). The endogenous sub-type of depression: A study of its internal construct validity. *British Journal of Psychiatry, 148,* 257–267.

CHAPTER **8**

Assessment of Anxieties and Fears in Children

A.J. FINCH, JR.
JULIA A. McINTOSH

INTRODUCTION

Fear and anxiety are universally experienced emotional reactions that are described as unpleasant subjective feelings of distress accompanied by cognitive (e.g., rumination), behavioral (e.g., flight) and physiological (e.g., rapid heart rate) responses. While research in the area of childhood and adolescent fears has been sporadic at times, the study of anxiety has been more continuous and less interrupted. The present chapter will review the relationship between these two emotional responses and will discuss their measurement. Although the chapter is meant to provide a comprehensive overview, it is not intended to be an exhaustive review of the research in the area.

DISTINCTION OF TERMS

Anxiety and fear are hypothetical constructs which represent emotional responses. Considerable confusion exists in this area due to the fact that

234

these two terms are used interchangeably, as synonyms or as byproducts of one another. Since the assessment of either construct is closely related to questions regarding how anxiety and fear are defined, a clarification of these terms is essential in order to discuss the assessment of anxiety and fears in children and adolescents.

Croake and Knox (1973) stated that while the response of fear is readily associated with a clearly delineated stimulus, anxiety describes a reaction that has no identifiable stimulus which elicits the response. Similarly, Greer (1965) stated that the difference between anxiety and fear was in the specificity of the eliciting stimuli. In other words, with fear the individual is aware of the feared object and can clearly identify it. However, with anxiety there is a generalized sense of dread and subjective distress and the individual has limited awareness of the specific stimulus which elicits these feelings.

Similarly, it is not uncommon to find the terms fear and phobia used interchangeably (Poznanski, 1973). Here again are two terms which are sometimes not defined distinctively. It is evident that some fears are adaptive, and normal, responses such as the fear of a vicious dog. Consequently, many fears serve as normal and adaptive responses to real threats. Therefore, being fearful is not necessarily indicative of emotional problems. Furthermore, as Graziano, DeGiovanni, and Garcia (1979) pointed out, the fears of the young child may not only be adaptive in nature but also constitute an important part of a child's experiences in learning to successfully cope with problems. In contrast to fears, phobias generally denote an excessive and unreasonable response to a stimulus. Consequently, it is generally assumed that phobias reflect a more pathological condition than do fears.

Numerous researchers have noted that fears and generalized anxiety appear to be highly related. Evidence of this relationship comes from a volume of psychometric studies which have found that measures of generalized anxiety and measures of fears appear to be significantly related. This relationship has been demonstrated in children, adolescents, and adults (Greer, 1965; Grossberg & Wilson, 1965; Swinn, 1969). The correlations between anxiety and fear are moderate in magnitude suggesting that while anxiety and fear share some common variance, they are not identical.

Additional similarities in the two constructs arise from the fact that some of the factors influencing the development and maintenance of anxiety and fear are analogous. Johnson and Melamed (1979) list five elements which are considered to be influential in the development and evolution of these two emotional responses: (1) trauma, such as being injured by the feared object, (2) modeling another individual who is anxious or fearful, (3) individual differences such as temperament or excitability, (4) environment, such as unsafe conditions, and (5) reinforcement, such as comfort or removal from an anxiety/fear-producing environment. Once again it is obvious that these two constructs, anxiety and fear, are related in many ways and that the main distinction between them may be only whether the precipitating event or stimulus can be identified.

In fact, from reviewing the literature, it is obvious to the authors that most authors use the two terms interchangeably. In attempting to discuss the theoretical factors related to anxiety and fear, it is frequently impossible to determine about which emotion the various authors are writing. From the authors' reading in the area it would appear that the distinction between anxiety and fear arises when the issue of assessment and treatment are being discussed. In addition, it appears to us that those authors who are more behavioral in orientation have tended to talk about fears more than anxieties. Similarly, those individuals who have approached the issue from a "trait" or "personality" perspective have tended to discuss anxiety rather than fear. For most of our discussion in this chapter, such differences are probably not important. Consequently, for purposes of this chapter we will make the distinction between anxiety and fear when discussing their assessment but not when discussing their development. Although this decision may be arbitrary and confusing, it would seem to reflect the condition of the field.

ISSUES INVOLVING THE ASSESSMENT OF FEARS AND ANXIETY

As Graziano et al. (1979) pointed out, there generally are considered to be three components of the fear (anxiety) response: a cognitive channel—the thoughts and images that the individual has; a behavioral channel—what the individual actually does such as fight/flight; and a physiological channel—such as increased heart rate, the galvanic skin response, etc. During a fear response these different channels can vary inversely, covary, or be independent of one another. Therefore, it is impossible to specifically describe the fear or anxiety response by describing any one of these channels. Rather, in evaluating a fear (anxiety) response all three response channels must be considered. To emphasize one particular response mode as being the most important in illustrating a fear response is to ignore the other two and would result in an incomplete understanding. Self-report measures (whether interview or inventory) can be designed to assess the youngster's own perception of one or all of these channels and are the only method through which we can learn about the cognitive channel. Consequently, self-report would appear to be a vital component of any evaluation of fear (anxiety).

While several theories have been proposed to explain the development and continuation of fears and anxiety, they vary in the degree to which they emphasize the role of the individual's subjective experience. Strict operant models negate or deny the importance of the cognitive or physiological elements that are often found to be associated with the emotional response of anxiety and fear. Instead they focus on the observable behaviors and the environmental consequences that maintain them. In addition, the operant models have even avoided the traditional terminology in the area by focusing on avoidance and approach behaviors (Kratochwill & Morris, 1985). Consequently, the utility of self-report measures is not an issue in operant models since they focus exclusively on direct behavioral observations (Lick & Katkin, 1976).

The Stimulus-Response (S-R) model of fear (anxiety) argues that these emotional responses are developed through classical conditioning (Graziano, et al., 1979). In this model, awareness of the association between stimulus and response is not assumed. In addition, knowledge of the pairing of the original unconditioned stimulus with the conditioned stimulus is not necessary. Consequently, self-report would play a limited role in this position since the cognitive mode is ignored.

The theoretical model which appears the most comprehensive in its explanation of the role of the various response modes in fear/anxiety is the cognitive-mediational model (Meichenbaum, 1977). In the cognitive-mediational model, the individual's cognition or internal dialogue play an important role in the development of fear/anxieties. In this particular model intervening variables or hypothetical constructs perform an important role in the derivation and continuation of the experience or perception of fear(s) (Kratochwill & Morris, 1985). Self-report plays a major role within this theoretical framework, as self-report measures allow or permit the assessment of the child's or adolescent's subjective experience.

DEVELOPMENTAL DIFFERENCES IN CHILD AND ADOLESCENT FEARS (ANXIETY)

Several researchers have attempted to determine what factors influence the perception, experience, and reporting of fears in children and adolescents. Most of the research has demonstrated that both developmental and cultural factors contribute to the variation in reported fears (anxi-

ety). Within the developmental domain, cognitive and physical maturation both appear to result in some fairly consistent differences in reporting patterns. For example content, frequency, and intensity of reported
fears/anxiety have all been shown to vary according to age. In addition
certain cultural considerations appear to be closely related to the developmental patterns seen. Table 8.1 summarizes some of the developmental
and cultural differences discussed in this section.

In an early work examining children's fears, Valentine (1930) discussed the innate bases of fears (anxieties) in children. Since infants
demonstrated fearful behavior almost immediately after birth, it had
been proposed that there is an innate basis of fear (anxiety). The innate nature of fears (anxieties) was inferred by watching infants and
observing that they displayed fear (anxiety) responses that were similar
to those observed in adults. Separating what is innate and what is due
to learning and environmental influences is always a difficult, if not impossible, task and the study of an innate foundation for fears (anxieties)
is no exception. Furthermore, inferring an innate cause for a widely exhibited early behavior pattern is not in and of itself conclusive evidence.
However, Valentine's (1930) work does appear to support the notion of

TABLE 8.1   Developmental Information on Children's Fears

	Content of Fears	Frequency
Age groups:		
Infants	Most common fears are of loud sounds.	Number of fears decreases with increasing age.
Preschoolers	Most common fears are of formless imaginary entities.	
Grade School	Specific & real objects	
Adolescents	More global issues	
Gender:		
Males	Animals, heights	Males tend to report less fears than females at all ages.
Females	Being alone, physical punishment	
Socioeconomic Status:		
Low	Supernatural events, punishment, parental discord	Lower SES children report a greater number of fears than do higher SES children.
High	Fear of failure	

an innate basis for some fear (anxiety) responses. She observed that loud sounds were probably the earliest cause of fear in infants and that the fear (anxiety) responses varied only slightly from infant to infant. In addition, she noted that fears (anxiety) of the dark or permanent objects did not occur until a child was at least 25 months old. It might be concluded that becoming attentive to one's surroundings and not being able to fully grasp or understand one's milieu produces an adaptive response of fear (anxiety) in infants.

To comprehend the developmental sequence of children's fears (anxiety), it is necessary to study the responses of very young children. Jersild and Holmes (1933) researched the issue of fears (anxiety) in early childhood by having the parents of children six months to four years old keep daily diaries of their children's fear responses. In addition to the information gathered via the diaries, the parents and the teachers of the older preschoolers were interviewed. As might be expected, these children were most fearful (anxious) of the unknown and these fears tended to dissipate with increasing age. The tendency for the number of fears and the degree of reported anxiety to decrease with increasing age has been found in other research (Croake, 1969; Croake & Knox, 1973; Reynolds & Paget, 1983). Apparently many fears and anxieties are overcome or disappear as the child matures—which is not surprising given that with maturation comes a better understanding of one's environment. However, the decrease in reported fears and anxieties with age may be associated with an increased reluctance of children and adolescents to report them.

The content of reported fears (anxieties) is another example of the influence of developmental and cultural factors. Preschool children's fears and anxieties appear to be more formless and the content is usually an imaginary entity. For instance, the child may be fearful or anxious of a bogeyman monster that lurks in his or her closet at night and waits for the lights to be extinguished before he attacks. As children enter school and begin to mature cognitively, their reported fears and anxieties become more specific and realistic (Bauer, 1976). Older school-aged children tend to base their fears in reality, in that they fear things like bad grades or the disapproval of their parents. Bauer hypothesized that language development was related to the developmental experience of fear (anxiety) in that it allowed for a more refined and/or realistic scheme to identify and/or express the basis of a child's fear(s). More specifically, he stated that the difference was related to the tendency of younger children to use iconic (pictorial) representation of stimuli in contrast to the tendency of older children to use more verbal representations.

Sipes, Rardin, and Fitzgerald (1985) endeavored to establish which fears were normal or typical for adolescents to recall and report in order to discern which fears were associated with the normal maturation process. In this way, they could make it easier to detect the aberrant or rare ones. Examiners asked 2,728 ninth-grade students to write an essay about their childhood fears. Fear (anxiety) of the dark was the most common. Other categories of fears (anxieties) commonly reported were people, spooks, being alone, and animals.

In contrast to these reported developmental differences in fears (anxiety), it has been reported by Miller, Barrett, Hampe, and Noble (1972) that the fear of (anxiety about) physical harm and "psychic stress" appear to remain throughout one's life. It is interesting to speculate on the rational nature of these fears (anxieties) and to suggest that the fear of or anxiety about physical harm and psychic stress are more realistic than many other fears and anxieties. However one wonders if the fear (anxiety) of psychic stress is not a more important fear (anxiety) in advanced civilizations than in underdeveloped ones. For example, Hesse (1986) reports that there has been an increase in the fear of or anxiety about nuclear war in children. It would appear rather unlikely that this fear (anxiety) would occur without children's increased exposure to the possibility of such an event and that children in less developed countries probably have limited fear or anxiety associated with this possibility. On the other hand, the fears and anxieties of children from less developed countries are likely to be very different from those of the more developed ones. In addition, it is likely that these fears are likely to be more basic in nature, such as the fear of or anxiety about not having enough to eat, disease, loss of parent, and so on.

Another early study by Lapouse and Monk (1959) attempted to assess the influence of age, gender, race, and socioeconomic status (SES) on the reporting of fears and anxieties. The investigators interviewed the parents of 482 children between 6 and 12 years of age. Girls were found to report more fear and anxiety than boys and nonwhite children's parents reported more fears (anxiety) experienced by their children than did white parents. However, there were no differences observed for SES. To assess the accuracy of the parent's report, a subsample of 193 children was interviewed and the percentage of agreement between fears (anxieties) reported by parents and children was calculated. Agreement between parent and child report was not high, with the majority of the interview items having only moderate agreement.

The results of these studies illustrates the importance of obtaining children's reports of their subjective experiences and perceptions of their fears. It is obvious that relying only on the reports of parents may result in a different set of fears being obtained and reported than when the children's reports are obtained. Likewise, when only self-reports of fears and anxieties are employed, the effects of the individual's ability and willingness to report actual experienced fears and anxieties cannot be determined. Consequently, researchers in the area need to be careful to clearly state the source of the reported fears and anxieties. Moreover, the use of multiple sources of information would appear warranted.

In contrast to Lapouse and Monk (1959) who did not find any difference in fears associated with SES, Poznanski (1973) found that poorer children had a greater number of fears and were more likely to fear supernatural events, punishment, or parental discord. Similarly, Croake and Knox (1973) also found that children from higher SES levels reported lower rates of fears. These results would suggest the possibility that the less secure environment frequently associated with lower SES status may result in a higher rate of fears (anxieties) in children.

Gender has been found to be an important determinant in the reporting of fear and anxiety. Boys consistently have been found to report fewer fears than girls (Bauer, 1976; Croake, 1969; Lapouse & Monk, 1959; Wilson, 1967) and to report lower levels of anxiety (Reynolds & Paget, 1983; Spielberger, 1973). In addition to differences in the number of fears reported, there are differences in the types of fears reported by boys and girls. Girls report being afraid of being alone, physical harm, and their fathers. Whereas boys report being afraid of animals and heights (Sipes, et al., 1985). Wilson (1967) found that those fears which were judged as the "silliest" (e.g., spiders, worms, or moths) were reported almost exclusively by females whereas males more often reported more "reasonable" (e.g., heights and sharks) fears. Whether or not these findings reflect actual differences in fears and anxieties or variations in the willingness and/or ability of males and females to report "weaknesses" is open to debate. However, one suspects that these findings reflect a social desirability component to the reporting of fears. This hypothesis about the role of social desirability in the reporting of fear and anxiety is supported by the findings of Bamber (1974) who reported that boys admit fearing stimuli which are more socially acceptable.

SELF-REPORT MEASUREMENT OF ANXIETY

In this section we will discuss various self-report measures of anxiety in children and adolescents. Particular attention will be paid to psychometric issues to aid the reader in selecting appropriate measures. In addition, a brief discussion of the clinical usefulness of each of the measures will be given. This clinical discussion about each scale will be subjective and based purely on clinical observations. Table 8.2 presents a summary of the various measures of anxiety and fears.

Revised Children's Manifest Anxiety Scale (RCMAS; Reynolds & Richmond, 1978)

The RCMAS is a revision of the Children's Manifest Anxiety Scale (CMAS; Castenada, McCandless, & Palermo, 1956) which was a downward extension of the Taylor Manifest Anxiety Scale (Taylor, 1951) used with adults. Upon revising the CMAS, Reynolds and Richmond also gave the scale the nonthreatening title of "What I Think and Feel." Revision of the CMAS was done to improve the psychometric properties of the CMAS and lower the required reading level so that it was applicable to children in the first through the twelfth grades. The revision resulted in a

TABLE 8.2 Anxiety and Fear Self-Report Measures

Measure	Age Range	Reliability	Validity	Norms
Revised Children's Manifest Anxiety Scale (RCMAS)	1st–12th grades	Internal consistency Test-retest	Concurrent	Age by gender by race
State-Trait Anxiety Inventory for Children (STAIC)	K–6th grade (individual administration at early age levels K-2nd)	Internal consistency Test-retest	Construct Concurrent Discriminant	Gender by race
State-Trait Anxiety Inventory (STAI)	High school students	Internal consistency Test-retest	Construct Concurrent Discriminant	——
Affective Adjective Check List (AACL)	4th–6th grades	Internal consistency Test-retest	Construct	——
Youth Self-Report (YSR)	11–18 years old	Internal consistency Test-retest	Construct	Age by gender

(continued)

TABLE 8.2 (Continued)

Measure	Age Range	Reliability	Validity	Norms
Social Avoidance and Distress (SAD)	12–14 years old	Internal consistency	Construct	Age by gender
Fear of Negative Evaluation (FNE)	12–14 years old	Internal consistency	Construct	Age by gender
Social Anxiety Scale for Children (SASC)	2nd–6th grades	Internal consistency Test-retest	Construct	Grade by gender
Fear Survey Schedule for Children (FSS-FC)	9–12 years old	Split-half Internal	Face validity	——
Louisville Fear Survey for Children	4–18 years old	Internal consistency	Face validity	——
Fear Expression and Research Survey (FEARS)	Children/ adolescents	Internal consistency	Convergent Discriminant	——

37-item scale that contains 28 anxiety items and 9 Lie scale items. Items are presented as short sentences to which the youngster is asked to answer "Yes" if he or she thinks it is true for him or her or "No" if he or she thinks the item is not true of him or her. Anxiety items on the scale sample physiological, cognitive, and behavioral manifestations of anxiety. In addition, Lie scale items tap a tendency to respond in a socially desirable manner (e.g., "I like everyone I know").

Extensive normative data for the RCMAS are available and broken down by age, gender, and race, since multivariate analyses indicated that there were significant differences in scores for these variables (Reynolds & Paget, 1983). Anxiety scores were higher for females than for males; for blacks than for whites; and for younger than older children (Reynolds & Richmond, 1978).

Kuder-Richardson reliability was estimated at .85 for the RCMAS and test-retest reliability coefficients were reported to be in the .90s for a period of three weeks. Nine month test-retest correlations were reported to be .68 (Reynolds & Paget, 1983).

Concurrent validity was demonstrated by the high correlation (r=.85, p<.001, N=42) obtained between the State-Trait Anxiety Inventory for Children (STAIC; Spielberger, 1973) trait anxiety scale and the RCMAS. There was a nonsignificant (r=.24, p>.05, N=42) correlation with the State scale of the STAIC.

Reynolds, Plake, and Harding (1983) investigated the potential racial and sex bias of items on the RCMAS. Their results indicated a race by sex interaction. Although there were items which appeared to be biased, no consistent trend or type of item appeared to be able to account for the bias. The only characteristic that appeared to represent these items was that they were the items with the poorest psychometric properties and the most ambiguous wording. Hence, the researchers concluded that there was not evidence to support claims of cultural bias with the RCMAS.

In a study designed to determine whether the factors found by Finch, Kendall, and Montgomery (1974) on the original CMAS were still valid for the revised scale, Reynolds and Paget (1981) factor analyzed the responses of the normative sample (n=4,972) children ranging in age from 6 to 19 years old). Results indicated that the three previous anxiety factors of physiological, worry/oversensitivity, and concentration were essentially intact. However, the items that were included in the Lie scale emerged as two separate factors. The different response pattern for the Lie scale was suspected to result from several of the items that contained potentially confusing concepts. Since the major factors of the RCMAS were parallel to those obtained with the CMAS, the original factor names were retained.

We have employed the RCMAS extensively in our clinical assessments. Its true-false format seems to be easily understood by children and its factors have been valuable on occasions. In addition we have found the Lie scale very helpful in evaluating the openness of the child to admitting faults and have used this to evaluate the meaningfulness of the child's response to other self-report measures. The Lie scale appears to provide an indication of how open the youngster is to revealing weaknesses and shortcomings. One concern that we have had in the clinical usefulness of the RCMAS centered around the names of the subscales based on the factors. At times we have been concerned about the use of factor names without examining the actual items that make up the factors. It is not clear whether or not the content of these factor labels accurately reflected the emotional state that they purport to measure. For example, there are a number of items on the Physiological factor which have nothing to do with physiological manifestations of anxiety. For example, "I have trouble making up my mind," is one item subsumed under the physiological factor that is more representative of concentrational anxiety factor.

State-Trait Anxiety Inventory for Children (STAIC; Spielberger, 1973)

The State Trait Anxiety Inventory for Children (STAIC) is a 40-item self-report measure which assesses State and Trait anxiety. State items begin with the stem "I feel" and are followed by three response choices containing a verb in three forms i.e., "I feel . . . very upset . . . upset . . . not upset." On the other hand, trait items are statements such as, "I worry about making mistakes," followed by the choices of "sometimes" . . . "often" . . . "frequently." The state anxiety portion of the scale appraises the anxious feelings of the child at any given moment while the trait portion assesses generalized feelings of anxiety. Instructions for the state anxiety items ask the child to "find the word or phrase which best describes how you feel right now, at this very moment." Trait instructions tell the youngster to "choose the word that seems to describe how you usually feel." Both the state and trait portion of the STAIC are scored on a 3-point metric scale with a rating of 1 being the least degree of emotional arousal and a rating of 3 being the greatest degree. Raw scores are converted to corresponding T-scores and percentile ranks.

Reliability and validity data of the STAIC generally support the construct validity of this measure. Spielberger (1973) reported test-retest reliability coefficients of .65 and coefficients of .82 for internal consistency. Another reliability study, however, reported somewhat lower coefficients (r=.44; Finch, Montgomery, & Deardorff, 1974). Validity studies provide more consistent results supporting both construct and concurrent validity of the measure. These studies found that the trait scale of the STAIC correlated well with the Children's Manifest Anxiety Scale and General Anxiety Scale for Children (Spielberger, 1973), that the scale could discriminate emotionally disturbed children from normal children

(Montgomery & Finch, 1974), and that the state scores in normal and emotionally disturbed children increased when the subjects were exposed to stressful situations (Newmark, Wheeler, Newmark, & Stabler, 1975; Finch, Kendall, Dannenburg & Morgan, 1978).

Although the STAIC was developed and normed for use with fifth- and sixth-grade children, Papay and Spielberger (1986) investigated the possibility that the scale could be applicable with children as young as kindergarten. A sample of 948 kindergartners, first-, and second-graders were administered the STAIC individually and in group form. Alpha reliability coefficients for this sample ranged from a low of .70 to a high of .92, all of which are within the acceptable range. No significant differences in T-scores were noted for the second-graders according to whether the children had been administered the test individually or in a small group. However, there was a significant difference between the individual and group administration for female kindergartners and first-graders. Consequently, the authors recommended individual administration of the scales with these younger age groups. Overall, results from this study demonstrated that the STAIC was potentially applicable to young children.

Papay and Hedl (1978) examined the psychometric characteristics of the STAIC utilizing a sample of 1,522 disadvantaged black third- and fourth-grade students to determine whether the measure was reliable and valid for this population. Means and standard deviations were computed and compared to Spielberger's (1973) normative sample. Internal consistency reliability coefficients for the two samples were remarkably similar. Results also indicated that trait scores for the urban disadvantaged black students were significantly higher than the normative sample. Although differences in trait scores were obtained, the authors of the study concluded that the differences were attributable to the samples rather than the STAIC. The authors recommended employing different norms for disadvantaged children.

From a clinical point of view, we have used the STAIC with our inpatient psychiatry and pediatric populations. Its format is sometimes confusing to our more psychiatrically disturbed children who tend to respond with the middle choice on the state portion of the scale. However, we have had some interesting observations with this scale. Some of our children who have come from chaotic home environments have reported less state anxiety after being admitted to the hospital while their levels of trait anxiety have remained high. On the other hand, children with separation anxiety have shown an increase in state anxiety following admission while reporting stable levels of trait anxiety.

State-Trait Anxiety Inventory
(STAI; Spielberger, Gorsuch, & Luchene 1970)

The STAI is Spielberger's original anxiety measure of state versus trait anxiety and was designed for use with adults. The major difference between the STAIC and the STAI is the fact that the STAI contains four choices for each statement while the STAIC has three. The STAI is of potential use with adolescents. However, normative data are not available for this age group. Most clinicians and researchers who employ the STAI with adolescents utilize the data that are available for college students. Normative and psychometric data for an adolescent population are badly needed.

With our clinical populations we have used the STAI with adolescents. Many of our concerns with and observations about the STAIC hold with the STAI. The increase to four items confuses some of our more psychiatrically disturbed adolescents. At times we have been forced to use the STAI with these adolescents and have been confronted with the problem of inadequate norms for this age group.

Affective Adjective Check List
(AACL; Price, 1976)

The Affective Adjective Check List was developed as an alternative measure of state and trait anxiety in children. Price developed the scale because of his concern about the potential effects of the different wording of the state and trait scales. On the STAIC all of the state scale items have the stem "I feel" followed by three choices of intensity. On the other hand, all of the trait items are statements followed by choices of frequencies. Price doubts that children can understand the concepts of intensity and frequency to the degree that adults do, making the downward extension of the STAI inappropriate.

The Affective Adjective Check List is designed for use with fourth- to sixth-grade children and contains a "general" scale (trait) and a "now" scale (state). The 20 items on each scale are rated for intensity on a 4-point Likert scale with "not at all"=1, "a little bit"=2, "quite a bit"=3, and "very much"=4. Alpha coefficients were found to be .79 and .82 for the state and trait scales, respectively. Test-retest coefficients indicated higher trait than state reliability (.94 versus .68) supporting the more variable nature of the state scale. Validity was investigated by pre- vs. post-testing around a classroom examination. The results supported the validity of the measure by indicating increases in state anxiety immediately prior to the exam without increases in trait anxiety.

This scale needs additional research examining its utility with a wider age range of children as well as with children of different socioeconomic backgrounds. In addition, discriminant validity data are needed. However, the scale would appear to have potential as another measure of state and trait anxiety in children.

Clinically, the four item format of this scale would be expected to confuse some children and adolescents. However, the consistent wording of the scales might make it easier to compare scores on the state and trait portions of the test. It would be interesting to compare the scores of the STAIC and the Affective Adjective Check List under standard manipulations to determine if the two scales reflect the same degree of increase in state anxiety.

Youth Self-Report
(YSR; Achenbach & Edelbrock, 1987)

Achenbach and his colleagues have developed several behaviorally based inventories. The Child Behavior Checklist (CBCL) and the Child Behavior Checklist-Teacher Report Form (CBCL-TRF) are probably the most frequently employed and cited of these inventories. The CBCL and CBCL-TRF were designed to assess behavioral problems and social competencies of children utilizing parent and teacher reports. To complement the parent and teacher versions of the CBCL (Achenbach & Edelbrock, 1983), Achenbach and Edelbrock developed the Youth Self-Report (YSR).

The YSR is designed to be filled out by youngsters aged 11 to 18 years and requires fifth-grade reading skills. The YSR contains 17 items that measure the youngsters' reports of their social competencies. The form asks the child to list sports, hobbies, involvement in social organizations, and daily chores and estimate the amount of time spent engaging in each and the level of skill at which the social task is executed. There are also 103 items designed to assess behavioral problems (e.g., "I have nightmares," "I am nervous and tense"). Each of the behavioral problem items are rated on a 3-point Likert scale with "not at all"=0, "somewhat or sometimes true"=1, and "very true" or "often true"=2. The YSR contains most of the same social competence items as the CBCL parent version except the items are worded in the first person. However, there are some items from the CBCL that were deleted or were altered slightly due to their inappropriateness for the age range or that were unlikely to be self-reported (e.g., bowel movements outside the toilet).

Through factor analysis Achenbach and his colleagues determined which behavior problem items tended to arise conjointly to form behavioral syndromes. Their analyses demonstrated six narrow band groupings of syndromes for girls and seven for boys. In addition, Achenbach derived broad band groupings of problem behaviors which he identified as internalizing and externalizing factors. The internalizing broad band appears to contain many items which assess fear and anxiety.

In a study examining the test-retest reliability of the YSR over a one-week period, Achenbach and Edelbrock (1987) reported a reliability of .81 with 50 nonreferred adolescents, with older adolescents 15 to 18 years old having a higher reliability than for 11- to 14-year-old youngsters. With a group of referred adolescents, they reported a test-retest reliability of .69 for total problem scores over six months while a group of nonreferred adolescents had a test-retest reliability of .67 over eight months.

In examining validity, Achenbach and Edlebrock (1987) found significantly higher scores for a group of psychiatrically referred adolescents than for a group of nonreferred adolescents. In another validity study, Shoemaker (1987) found that with a group of 98 hospitalized emotionally disturbed children and adolescents, the internalizing portion of the YSR form correlated significantly with the RCMAS, the STAIC, and the Psychasthenia (anxiety) scale of the MMPI suggesting the potential utility of this measure for assessing anxiety in children and adolescents.

Clinically we have found it really worthwhile to have a self-report measure that has a parallel form which can be completed by teachers and parents. The differences in what the various observers report can frequently provide the clinician with very meaningful information for diagnosis and treatment planning. The different factors on the various forms can be confusing initially but the information from the different sources is invaluable. In particular, it can be quite important to compare the perceptions of the child, his or her parents, and his or her teacher to obtain a better understanding of how a child's anxious or fearful response is manifested.

Social Avoidance and Distress and Fear of Negative Evaluation (SAD; FNE; Watson & Friend, 1969)

Social-evaluative anxiety is, in essence, evaluation of anxiety experienced in social situations. SAD and FNE are examples of scales used to measure this phenomenon in adults. The Social Avoidance and Distress Scale purports to measure the degree of distress or discomfort that an individual experiences while in social situations and the degree to which the individual avoids these situations due to distressing, anxious feelings. The FNE scale was designed to assess the individual's fear of negative evaluation. This fear of evaluative situations is reportedly different from test anxiety in that it does not just apply to one specific event (i.e., test taking) rather it applies to the fear that results from evaluation whether it be in social, interpersonal, or work circumstances. The SAD scale contains 28 true-false items whereas the FNE scale contains 30 true-false items.

Watson and Friend (1969) report Kuder-Richardson-20 reliability coefficients for both scales to be .94. In addition, they report two experimental studies were designed to test the validity of the two scales. In the first study it was hypothesized that persons who scored high on the SAD would be more uncomfortable in social situations. Subjects were divided into low anxiety and high anxiety groups based on their scores on the SAD. Next subjects were asked to either write an essay alone or participate in a group discussion. As predicted, subjects with high scores on the SAD scale were more uncomfortable in the discussion group than when they were asked to write an essay alone. These results suggested that the SAD was a valid measure of social anxiety.

In the second study reported by Watson and Friend (1969), they addressed the validity of the FNE scale. Forty-eight adult subjects with high scores on the FNE scale were compared to 48 subjects with low scores. Subjects were then given four minute letter-substitution tasks and told either that a group leader would examine their work and approve but never disapprove (approval group) their work, or that the leader would examine their work and disapprove, but never approve (disapproval group). After completing the task, subjects completed questionnaires about how nervous or uneasy they felt during the task. Again, as was predicted, the results indicated that subjects with high fear of negative evaluation scores were more uncomfortable than those with low scores.

Adolescents would appear to be extremely vulnerable to social anxiety and commonly are evaluated by others. Therefore, these scales or similar ones designed especially for adolescents, might prove useful in allowing researchers and clinicians to investigate these constructs within an adolescent population. Furthermore, the assessment of these aspects of anxiety in adolescents would allow us to determine the developmental influences which may occur by comparing the findings with adults and adolescents.

While Watson and Friend (1969) did not initially develop norms for adolescent populations, Warren, Good, and Velten (1984) provided some initial normative and validity data on the SAD and FNE scales with junior high school students. Their initial findings indicated the potential research and clinical value of these scales with adolescent populations. However, the sophisticated wording of both scales' items suggests that attempts to use the current forms of the SAD and FNE with younger children would be inappropriate.

The clinical utility of the SAD and FNE scales has not been explored. However, it would appear to us that these scales might be useful in working with fairly normal adolescents. It is possible that the information provided by the two scores might be helpful in counseling students who are having social difficulties. On the other hand, many of the more severely disturbed adolescents (e.g., psychiatrically hospitalized) who would be expected to have more severe levels of anxiety producing pervasive difficulties, might find the wording of the scale too difficult. However, the clinical usefulness of these scales would appear to be worth exploring.

Social Anxiety Scale for Children (SASC; La Greca, Dandes, Wick, Shaw, & Stone, 1988)

La Greca et al. (1988) developed the Social Anxiety Scale for Children (SASC) and examined its reliability and concurrent validity with a group of 287 second- through sixth-graders using peer status variables and a measure of trait anxiety. Factor analysis produced a 10-item scale with two factors, fear of negative evaluation (FNE) and social avoidance and distress (SAD), which corresponded with those reported by Watson and Friend (1969). These factors were found to have moderate internal consistency (alphas of .83, .63 for the FNE and SAD, respectively) and test-retest reliability ($r=.70$, .39, .67 over two weeks for the FNE and SAD, respectively). Consistent with other studies of anxiety, girls and younger children were found to report more anxiety. However, this was only true for the FNE scale for girls and for the SAD scale for younger children. With regard to validity, the FNE and SAD factor scores were found to correlate significantly with anxiety scores on the Revised Children's Manifest Anxiety scale ($r=.52$, .36, .57 for FNE and SAD, respectively) and children of different peer status were found to report different levels of social anxiety. The preliminary data on this scale would suggest that it may prove to be useful in assessing social anxiety in children.

This scale is new and its clinical usefulness has not been explored. However, it would appear to have some potential as a brief screening instrument with more normal populations. Again, with clinical populations a broader measure of anxiety might be more appropriate.

SELF-REPORT MEASUREMENT OF FEAR

Fear Survey Schedule for Children
(FSS-FC; Scherer & Nakamura, 1968)

The Fear Survey Schedule for Children consists of 80 items which were selected on a conceptual basis to reflect fears frequently reported by children and adolescents. The format of the scale was patterned after the several fear surveys which had been developed previously for use with adults (Wolpe & Lang, 1964; Greer, 1965). The items selected were chosen to sample fears that fell into the following eight categories: (1) school fears, (2) home fears, (3) social fears, (4) physical fears, (5) animal fears, (6) travel fears, (7) classical phobias, and (8) miscellaneous fears. Each item is rated on a 5-point scale with none=1, a little=2, some=3, much=4, or very much=5. Both intensity of fears and frequency of fears scores are tabulated. Intensity scores are obtained by summing the ratings, and the frequency scores are the number of specific fears reported. The scale was developed for both clinical and research purposes for children from 9 to 12 years of age.

The scale has good split-half reliability (Spearman-Brown r=.94). The authors support the scales validity by pointing to the moderate correlation with the Children's Manifest Anxiety Scale (total sample r=.55, boys r=.44, girls r=.61) and the fact that those subjects who were high on anxiety reported more fears than those who were low or moderate. Establishing the validity of a measure of children's fears by comparing it with children's scores on a measure of anxiety clearly illustrates the interrelatedness of these two constructs. Consistent with other research, girls in the normative sample scored significantly higher than did boys. Factor analysis of the FSS-FC revealed eight factors which were labeled: (1) fear of failure or criticism, (2) major fears, (3) minor fears, (4) medical fears, (5) fear of death, (6) fear of the dark, (7) home-school fears, and (8) miscellaneous fears.

Ollendick (1983) revised the Fear Survey Schedule for Children to develop a response format that took into consideration the developmental and cognitive limitations of young, as well as of mentally retarded and psychiatrically impaired, children. Ollendick changed the original 5-point scale to a 3-point one (none, some, a lot). Specific items were not altered. Ollendick (1983) reported good internal consistency with the revised version of the scale as well as good short-term test-retest reliability. However, there was a reduction of reliability over longer periods of time—a not uncommon finding. In addition, he found evidence for the validity of this measure by comparing normal and school phobic children, finding significant correlation with anxiety measures. In a later study, Ollendick, Matson, and Helsel (1985) examined the normative data on the revised version of the scale and found the data very consistent with the original version.

In a later study, Ollendick and King (1988) collected normative data on American and Austrian Children on the Fear Survey Schedule for Children—Revised and found that younger children exhibited more fears than did older ones. In addition the authors reported some minor changes in the factor structure of the scale across the different ages. However, they did not feel that these variations were significant enough to warrant employing different factors at different ages. It would appear to us that the revised version of the FSS-FC may be particularly useful with younger children and with children who are more intellectually limited. The 3-point response format would appear to be more consistent with the cognitive abilities of these groups.

Louisville Fear Survey for Children
(Miller et al., 1972)

The Louisville Fear Survey for Children is an 81-item self-report inventory which samples a wide range of potentially fearful stimuli. The scale is designed for use with children and adolescents in the 4- to 18-year-old age range. Each item is rated on a 3-point Likert-type scale: 1=no fear, 2=normal or reasonable fear, and 3=unrealistic fear. Scores on the Louisville Fear Survey for Children are calculated by summing the ratings for each item.

Miller et al. (1972) asked 179 parents to rate their children's fear behavior at home utilizing the Louisville Fear Survey for Children. A factor analysis of the ratings disclosed three factors: (1) physical danger or injury, (2) natural or supernatural dangers, and (3) psychic stress.

Staley and O'Donnell (1984) factor analyzed the responses of 977 mothers to the Louisville Fear Survey (Form B), which is an expanded version of the original scale, and found five factors: (1) fear of physical injury, (2) fear of animals, (3) fear of public places, (4) night fears, and (5) school-related fears. This group of factors had good internal consistence and would appear to have considerable clinical utility, but their stability has not been evaluated.

Fear Expression and Research Survey
(FEARS; Davies, 1982)

The Fear Expression and Research Survey is a 34-item scale that was developed for use in researching the fears of children and adolescents. It is purported to sample four different fear components: (1) death and destruction, (2) social acceptance, (3) social conflict, and (4) imagination. Each fear item is rated on a 5-point Likert type scale with 1=not at all, 2=a little bit, 3=some, 4=much, and 5=very much. Scores are calculated by summing the item ratings to get a measure of intensity.

Internal consistency coefficients (Alpha) reported by the author are good, ranging from a high of .92 for death and destruction to a low of .80 for social conflict. Validity and reliability of the four components were examined employing factor analysis. Each scale item met statistical criteria for inclusion in the scale component.

Convergent and discriminant validity studies have yet to be reported with the FEARS. Experimental studies also need to be conducted to determine the possible clinical utility of this scale. Questions addressing whether the scale differentiates between clinically fearful and "normal" children are also of importance. Much of the present research regarding the psychometric properties of this scale suggests that it may have promise as a research tool for investigating specific fears in children related to the four separate scale components. However, further psychometric evaluation of this scale wll be important.

Other Fear Surveys for Children

In addition to the more general fear surveys discussed above, there are a number of specific fear measures designed to measure narrowly defined fears such as the fear of spiders (Lang, Melamed, & Hart, 1970), the fear of tests (Sarson, 1957), etc. A number of such scales are available and are potentially useful with limited fears. In addition the Fear Thermometer (Walk, 1956) offers a methodology that has been found to be reliable and valid with children as young as three years of age for measuring pain (Belter, McIntosh, Finch & Saylor, in press).

CONCLUSIONS

The assessment of anxiety and fears in children is an area that lends itself well to the integration of clinical practice and research since children are frequently seen in clinical practice for these problems. However, it is evident from the above discussion that there remains considerable confusion in the area. Beginning with the confusion which exists between the distinction of the terms and continuing through the available measures for the two constructs, it is obvious that there is considerable overlap between the two. Frequently the literature has employed the terms interchangeably and a number of scales designed to measure one construct have been validated against measures of the "other" construct. Systematic research needs to be conducted to determine the limits of the two terms as well as their overlap before our knowledge in the area can be advanced.

The assessment of fears and anxieties in children and adolescents has resulted in the development of some interesting and potentially useful measures. However, many of these scales are in the early stage of development and there is considerable work to be done on their psychometric usefulness. A number of the measures that were discussed have had limited reliability and validity data collected. In addition, there needs to be additional research into the relationship between the various measures as well as research investigating the relationship between the cognitive, behavioral, and physiological responses associated with fear and anxiety in children and adolescents. In addition, research into the relationship between self-report measures of fear and anxiety and other psychological measures needs to be explored. There is a growing body of research suggesting that children, and possibly adults, tend to report general negative affectivity rather than specific types of distress (Finch, Lipovsky & Caset, in press). It may be that the confusion that exists concerning the distinction between the terms is due to the inability of children to differentiate between anxiety and fear. Finch et al. present a fairly strong argument that children cannot differentiate between anxiety and depression. The same may be true for anxiety and fear. Certainly this area would appear to be a potentially very fruitful one.

Clinically a number of the measures have proven useful while others have received limited clinical evaluation. This lack of clinical evaluation appears to be particularly true of the fear measures. The exact reason for this is not clear, but may be related to the fact that children with severe fears of specific objects or events may not have the same degree of adjustment problems as do children with high levels of generalized anxiety. In addition, many of the fear measures are very specific and the average clinician may see few patients with any particular fear.

REFERENCES

Achenbach, T.M. & Edelbrock, C. (1983). *Manual for the Child Behavior Checklist and Revised Child Behavior Profile*. Burlington, VT: University of Vermont Department of Psychiatry.

Achenbach, T.M. & Edelbrock, C. (1987). *Manual for the Youth Self-Report and Profile*. Burlington, VT: University of Vermont Department of Psychiatry.

Bamber, J.H. (1974). The fears of adolescents. *Journal of Genetic Psychology, 125,* 127–140.

Bauer, D.H. (1976). An exploratory study of developmental changes in children's fears. *Journal of Child Psychology and Psychiatry, 17,* 69–74.

Belter, R.W., McIntosh, J.A., Finch, A.J. Jr., & Saylor, C.F. (in press). Preschooler's ability to differentiate levels of pain. *Journal of Clinical Child Psychology.*

Castenada, A., McCandless, B., & Palermo, D. (1956). The children's form of the Manifest Anxiety Scale. *Child Development, 27,* 317–326.

Croake, J.W. (1969). Fears of children. *Human Development, 12,* 239–247.

Croake, J.W. & Knox, F.H. (1973). The changing nature of children's fears. *Child Study Journal, 3,* 91–105.

Davies, M.H. (1982). *Children's fears: The development of a new measure and preliminary findings regarding age & sex differences.* Unpublished doctoral dissertation, University of Rhode Island.

Finch, A.J., Jr., Kendall, P.C., & Montgomery, L.E. (1974). Multi-dimensionality of anxiety in children: Factor structure of the Children's Manifest Anxiety Scale. *Journal of Abnormal Child Psychology, 2,* 331–336.

Finch, A.J., Jr., Lipovsky, J.A., & Casat, C. (in press). Anxiety and depression in children and adolescents: Negative affectivity or separate constructs? In P.C. Kendall and D. Watson (Eds.) *Anxiety and depression: distinctive and overlapping features.* Orlando, FL: Academic Press.

Finch, A.J., Jr., Montgomery, L.E., & Deardorff, P.A. (1974). The Children's Manifest Anxiety Scale: Reliability with emotionally disturbed children. *Psychological Reports, 34,* 658.

Graziano, A.M., DeGiovanni, I.S., & Garcia, K.A. (1979). Behavioral treatment of children's fears: A review. *Psychological Bulletin, 86,* 804–830.

Greer, J.H. (1965). The development of a scale to measure fear. *Behavior Research and Therapy, 3,* 45–53.

Grossberg, J.M. & Wilson, H.K. (1965). A correlational comparison of the Wolpe-Lang Fear Survey Schedule & the Taylor Manifest Anxiety Scale. *Behavior Research and Therapy, 3,* 125–128.

Hesse, P. (1986). Children's and adolescents' fears of nuclear war: Is our sense of the future disappearing? *International Journal of Mental Health, 15,* 93–113.

Jersild, A.T. & Holmes, F.B. (1933). A study of children's fears. *Journal of Experimental Education, 2,* 109–118.

Johnson, S.B. & Melamed, B.G. (1979). The assessment and treatment of children's fears. In B. Lahey & A. Kazdin (Eds.) *Advances in Child Clinical Psychology.* Vol. II, New York: Plenum, 107–139.

Kratochwill, T.R. & Morris, R.J. (1985). Conceptual and methodological issue in the behavioral assessment and treatment of children's fears and phobias. *School Psychology Review, 14,* 94–107.

La Greca, A.M., Dandes, S.K., Wick, P., Shaw, K., & Stone, W.L. (1988). Development of the Social Anxiety Scale for Children: Reliability and current validity. *Journal of Clinical Child Psychology, 17,* 84–91.

Lang, P.J., Melamed, B.G., & Hart, J. (1970). A psychophysiological analysis of fear modification using an automated desensitization procedure. *Journal of Abnormal Psychology, 76,* 220–234.

Lapouse, R. & Monk, M.A. (1959). Fears and worries in a representative sample of children. *American Journal of Orthopsychiatry, 29,* 803–818.

Lick, J.R. & Katkin, E.S. (1976). Assessment of anxiety & fear. In M. Hersen & A. Bellack (Eds.) *Behavioral assessment: A practical handbook.* New York, Pergamon, 175–206.

Meichenbaum, D. (1977). *Cognitive-behavior modification.* New York: Plenum.

Miller, L.C., Barrett, C.L., Hampe, E., & Noble, H. (1972). Factor structure of childhood fears. *Journal of Consulting and Clinical Psychology, 39,* 264–268.

Montgomery, L.E. & Finch, A.J., Jr. (1974). Validity of two measures of anxiety in children. *Journal of Abnormal Child Psychology, 2,* 293–298.

Newmark, C.S., Wheeler, D., Newmark, L., & Stabler, B. (1975). Test induced anxiety with children. *Journal of Personality Assessment, 39,* 409–413.

Ollendick, T.H. (1983). Reliability and validity of the Revised Fear Survey Schedule for Children (FSSC-R). *Behavioral Research and Therapy, 21,* 685–692.

Ollendick, T.H. & King, N.J. (1988). Fears in children and adolescents: Reliability and generalizability across gender, age, and nationality. Manuscript submitted for publication.

Ollendick, T.H., Matson, J.L., & Helsel, W.J. (1985). Fears in children and adolescents: Normative data. *Behavioral Research and Therapy, 23,* 465–467.

Papay, J.P. & Hedl, J.J. (1978). Psychometric characteristics and norms for disadvantaged third and fourth grade children on the State-Trait Anxiety Inventory for Children. *Journal of Abnormal Child Psychology, 1,* 115–120.

Papay, J.P. & Spielberger, C.D. (1986). Assessment of anxiety and achievement in kindergarten and first- and second-grade children. *Journal of Abnormal Child Psychology, 14,* 279–286.

Poznanski, E.O. (1973). Children with excessive fears. *American Journal of Orthopsychiatry, 43,* 428–438.

Price, J.R. (1976). *The development and evaluation of an affect adjective checklist for the measurement of anxiety in children.* Unpublished doctoral dissertation, University of Windsor.

Reynolds, C.R. & Paget, K.D. (1981). Factor analysis of the Revised Children's Manifest Anxiety Scale for blacks, whites, males, and females with a national normative sample. *Journal of Consulting and Clinical Psychology, 49,* 352–359.

Reynolds, C.R. & Paget, K.D. (1983). National normative and reliability data for the Revised Children's Manifest Anxiety Scale. *School Psychology Review, 12,* 1983.

Reynolds, C.R., Plake, B.S., & Harding, R.E. (1983). Item bias in the assessment of children's anxiety: Race and sex interaction on items of the Revised Children's Manifest Anxiety Scale. *Journal of Psychoeducational Assessment, 1,* 17–24.

Reynolds, C.R. & Richmond, B.O. (1978). What I Think and Feel: A revised measure of children's manifest anxiety. *Journal of Abnormal Child Psychology, 6,* 271–280.

Sarson, I.G. (1957). Test anxiety, general anxiety, and intellectual performance. *Journal of Consulting Psychology, 21,* 485–490.

Scherer, M.W. & Nakamura, C.Y. (1968). A Fear Survey Schedule for Children (FSS-FC): A factor analytic comparison with manifest anxiety (CMAS). *Behavior Research and Therapy, 6,* 173–182.

Shoemaker, O.S., III (1987). *Concurrent validity of the Youth Self-Report version of the Child Behavior Checklist Profile.* Unpublished manuscript, Medical University of South Carolina.

Sipes, G., Rardin, M., & Fitzgerald, B. (1985). Adolescent recall of childhood fears and coping strategies. *Psychological Reports, 57,* 1215–1223.

Spielberger, C.D. (1973). *Preliminary manual for the State-Trait Anxiety Inventory for Children ("How I Feel Questionnaire").* Palo Alto, CA: Consulting Psychologists Press.

Spielberger, C.D., Gorsuch, R.L., & Luchene, R.E. (1970). *Manual for the State-Trait Anxiety Inventory (self-evaluation questionnaire).* Palo Alto, CA: Consulting Psychologists Press.

Staley, A.A. and O'Donnell, J.P. (1984). A developmental analysis of mother's reports of normal children's fears. *Journal of Genetic Psychology, 144,* 165–178.

Swinn, R.M. (1969). The relationship between fear & anxiety: A further study. *Behavior Research and Therapy, 7,* 317–318.

Taylor, J.A. (1951). The relationship of anxiety to the conditioned eyelid response. *Journal of Experimental Psychology, 42,* 183–188.

Valentine, C.W. (1930). The innate bases of fears. *Journal of Genetic Psychology, 37,* 394–420.

Walk, R.D. (1956). Self-ratings of fear in a fear-invoking situation. *Journal of Abnormal and Social Psychology, 52,* 171–178.

Warren, R., Good, G., & Velten, E. (1984). Measurement of social-evaluative anxiety in junior high school students. *Adolescence, 19,* 643–648.

Watson, D. & Friend, R. (1969). Measurement of social-evaluative anxiety. *Journal of Consulting and Clinical Psychology, 33,* 448–457.

Wilson, G.D. (1967). Social desirability and sex differences in expressed fear. *Behavior Research and Therapy, 5,* 136–137.

Wolpe, J. & Lang, P.J. (1964). A fear survey schedule for use in behavior therapy. *Behavior Research and Therapy, 2,* 27–30.

CHAPTER 9

Assessment of Children's Social Status and Peer Relations

STEVEN LANDAU
RICHARD MILICH

INTRODUCTION

Clinical Importance of Children's Peer Relations

Clinical interest in peer relations has been an enduring one even though the attending research activity regarding the implications of disturbed relations has emerged only more recently. The classic 11- to 13-year follow-up study of third-grade children undertaken by Cowen, Pederson, Babigian, Izzo, and Trost (1973) represents an important hallmark in this area, as it demonstrates the compelling link between early peer problems and later maladjustment. Specifically, these investigators were attempting to isolate significant predictors of later breakdown as defined by a listing on the county psychiatric register. Of particular interest was the finding that negative nominations on Bower's Class Play (1969) by third-grade peers was by far the best predictor of later psychiatric problems. This result was striking when one considers the fact that the predictive utility of this measure exceeded all other collected data, including teacher ratings, self-report data, psychometric results, achievement scores, and evaluations conducted by mental health professionals.

This often cited investigation and others (e.g., Roff, 1963; Roff & Sells, 1968; West & Farrington, 1973) highlight a relationship that is impressive in the clinical outcome literature; that is, negative peer reputation is strongly related to later maladaption. For one, the predictive utility endures over relatively long periods of time and across different developmental periods. Second, even though most longitudinal investigations depend on the design model that "like predicts like" —for example, early aggression predicts later aggression (Huesmann, Eron, Lefkowitz, & Walder, 1984)—these investigations have demonstrated that peer problems predict across a broad spectrum of adaptational and outcome measures. In fact, peer rejection has been shown to relate to most accepted measures of adolescent and adult mental health as employed in the clinical outcome research. These include premature dropping out of school, later juvenile delinquency, job terminations and poor military performance, police contacts, and psychiatric hospitalizations (see Parker & Asher, 1987, for an extended review). As such, these follow-up studies suggest that early peer problems, defined in terms of rejection scores, not only indicate concurrent difficulty for the child but also seem to be a significant "at risk" marker for those children who will later present emotional and behavioral disturbance (Hartup, 1983).

Why Are Peer Relations Predictive of Clinical Outcomes?

When examining the results of these investigations, it would be tempting to infer that early problems with the peer group serve to cause this ultimate maladaptive outcome. In fact, many social skills treatment programs are promoted on the premise that a negative outcome can be prevented if the child's rejected status is eliminated or reduced (Combs & Slaby, 1977). Unfortunately, an attempt to target this inferred cause of bad outcome may represent one explanation for the disappointing results attributable to many of these social skills treatment studies (Krehbiel & Milich, 1986). Instead, it is more likely that peer problems exist as a correlate, rather than as a cause of later difficulties, and, thus, result from some early disturbance, be it behavioral or organismic. This other problem may be responsible for both the concurrent difficulties with peers and the later negative outcome (Putallaz & Gottman, 1983). A salient example of how this may operate can be found in cases of children who are at risk for the later onset of schizophrenia (Milich & Landau, 1982). These children are known to experience peer problems (Ledingham, 1981; Roff, 1963), although few would argue that the ultimate development of schizophrenia is the result of these earlier social difficulties.

A second explanation for the obtained correlations between early peer problems and later maladjustment is that the negative outcome is due to the reciprocal influences between behavior disturbance and social problems that may evolve over time (Barkley & Cunningham, 1979). For example, Dodge (see Dodge & Richard, 1985) has developed an elaborate theory to explain how the misperceptions and misattributions of aggressive children can escalate into significant peer difficulties. In addition, Landau and Milich (1988) recently found support for the importance of a reciprocity perspective by examining the social communications of attention difficulties with peers (Milich & Landau, 1982). By the use of a role-playing procedure in which one boy was to interview his partner regarding favored television programming, it was found that ADD boys can have a deleterious influence on the communication patterns of normal partners with whom they are paired, causing the normal boys, and thus the dyad, to behave in a role-inappropriate way. It is reasonable to conceive of how this type of bidirectional disturbance can evolve into other forms of social deviance as communication deficits are known to relate to interpersonal problems (Hartup, 1983).

A third, although untested, hypothesis worthy of consideration is that peer problems may serve as an "early stressor" to preexisting subclinical problems. In this case, disturbed peer relations could exacerbate latent difficulties, ultimately causing their overt manifestation. Whatever the explanation for the established relationship between early peer problems and later difficulties, an important caveat is that the mediating mechanisms accounting for this phenomenon are yet to be identified (Putallaz & Gottman, 1983), thereby making attempts at the prevention of a negative outcome an elusive endeavor.

Developmental Importance of Successful Peer Relations

Another major reason for the clinical interest in peer relations results from the well-established body of literature demonstrating that the ability to effectively relate to others is a fundamental contributor to the growth of the child (see Hartup, 1983). It is both empirically and intuitively compelling that the concept of developmental mastery is inextricably linked to status and competence within the peer group. In this context, Putallaz and Gottman (1983) provide a poignant anecdote (with spelling errors present) exemplifying the stress and pain experienced by a second-grader who is not liked by his peers.

> I can hide. i am a little boy. i don't have friends but i have som friends but win i wait at the busstop som people haet me and some like me . . . one day i was moveing so people would not tesz me in ne mor but again they tesz me. (p.13)

It is not surprising to discover that rejected children (i.e., those frequently nominated as not liked) report significantly greater feelings of loneliness and dissatisfaction than children in other status groups (Asher & Wheeler, 1985) and that popular children (i.e., those frequently nominated as most liked) engage in and receive significantly more positive social exchanges (Gottman, Gonso, & Rasmussen, 1975). Thus, the ability to get along with peers will influence the degree to which the peer group can contribute, through both reinforcement and modeling, to the social development of the child. As Hartup (1983) suggests, learning in the context of successful peer relations represents a unique medium for the child as it provides the only opportunity for the development of an egalitarian perspective and the learning of inhibition of inappropriate responding through rough-and-tumble play, among others. There is widespread and well-accepted evidence that demonstrates the importance of peer influences on the development of prosocial behavior. Evidence also suggests that rejected children experience a very different form of social feedback from both peers (e.g., Cunningham, Siegel, & Offord, 1985) and teachers (e.g., Whalen, Henker, & Dotemoto, 1981) than their accepted agemates.

Besides being essential for the child's social development, successful peer relations also seem to have obvious implications for affective aspects of functioning. The presence of friends represents an important source of emotional support and security for children. Friendships seem to neutralize the deleterious effects of stress and they can contribute significantly to the child's sense of self-esteem by documenting that he or she is valued. In fact, it has been suggested that close friendships serve as the primary source of support when emotional ties to the family become gradually weakened during adolescent development (Price & Ladd, 1986).

In this regard, having friends and being well liked may have important implications for the child's quality of life. One example of this comes from the outcome research of attention deficit disorder (ADD) children. These children, when followed into adolescence and adulthood, report that they experience a significant degree of loneliness and sadness and that they have few friends, even though many of their other symptoms have attenuated or completely remitted (Weiss & Hechtman, 1986). Thus, even if the long-term outcome measures do not reveal significant problems, one is left wondering whether children with early peer problems enjoy the same quality of life as those who do not experience such difficulties.

A final reason for clinical interest in the child's social status difficulties is that, even though these social problems are not considered a distinct diagnostic entity per se, they tend to characterize most children seen in mental health settings. Specifically, the presence of social deficits and negative peer reputation transcend a variety of special populations such as learning disabled, attention deficit disordered, conduct disturbed, schizoid, and autistic (Hops, Finch & McConnell, 1985). In fact, most recent attempts at an empirical definition of maladaptive behavior and psychopathology include reference to problems in social functioning. The fact that the widely used Child Behavior Checklist (CBC: Achenbach & Edelbrock, 1983) involves a Social Competence scale exemplifies the research and clinical interest in this area.

Purpose of this Chapter

Since there are no accepted diagnostic criteria nor standardized assessment guidelines established to date, clinicians need to know how to operationalize the social status construct and how to assess problems in social status. This is of particular concern as the clinical practitioner will most likely be faced with cases that are parent-referred and parents are not known to be reliable informants of their child's social status (Glow & Glow, 1980). Additionally, there is presently available a plethora of social skills treatment literature intended to address the remediation of social problems. Unfortunately, this body of knowledge is large, albeit nonsystematic, and pervaded by inconsistencies of definition and practice (see Krehbiel & Milich, 1986, for a discussion). Therefore, the purpose of this chapter will be to clarify these issues for the clinician and clinical researcher in order to assist in the development of a systematic assessment strategy that will have direct implications for social skills treatment. As such, this chapter will examine the issue of social status classification, especially as it relates to the development of treatment plans, and will review the measurement properties of social status constructs that result from children's reports. Additionally, this chapter will describe methodological issues and specify how best to collect social status and social competence data by reviewing procedural and ethical concerns that are embedded in such undertakings.

DEFINITION OF SOCIAL STATUS TERMS

The issue of precise and valid definition of social status is especially critical when one attempts to interpret the social skills treatment literature. It is evident that some of the equivocal results attributable to many social skills treatment programs can be explained by the fact that these regimens were designed to treat the socially withdrawn/isolated child but have been indiscriminately applied to the rejected child (cf. Krehbiel & Milich, 1986). As such, these interventions have been prescribed for children who were extremely heterogeneous with regard to the nature of their social problem or who have nonspecific social problems. This is a serious oversight as it is clear that rejected children differ in many significant ways from isolated children, including patterns of social behavior, rates of interaction, and long-term outcome, among others (Parker & Asher, 1987).

Efforts to operationalize children's social relations and peer problems reflect an extensive array of variables. These have ranged from sociometric nominations of peer reputation (i.e., acceptance and rejection), to peer nominations of disordered social behavior (e.g., aggression and withdrawal), to simple frequency counts of interaction rates, to observations of specific social behaviors that may be setting-specific (e.g., parallel play), to analog measures of social perspective-taking and role playing. Unfortunately, the literature that addresses social problems is yet to offer a systematic organization of these issues, so that an examination of obtained results across domains of performance and across studies does not yield a meaningful interpretation. There is a good deal of evidence to support the notion that significant correspondence does not exist among these variables and that they may, in fact, represent very distinct and, occasionally, contradictory aspects of the child's social functioning. Interpretation of the literature is further confounded by the fact that most investigations are limited to the use of only one or a few of these variables, thereby making the task of direct comparison even more difficult. Unfortunately, the field lacks semantic precision as there are a number of terms to describe the child's social functioning but each seems to represent a slightly different aspect of performance or development. These include friendship, social status, social skills, social competence, and social adaptation or adaptive behavior.

Social status is generally defined in terms of sociometric nominations of acceptance and rejection. In the context of the query "Is the child liked?" versus "What is the child like?" (Parker & Asher, 1987), status is represented by the former and does not, in any way, reveal anything about the latter. It is simply the personal appeal of the individual to the rest of the group. As such, social status represents how popular (accepted) or rejected (disliked) that child is.

In contrast to social status, *social skills* are considered a behavioral construct specifying a collection of discrete molecular social behaviors (Gresham, 1986). For example, giving positive reinforcement to peers, a known correlate of popularity (Hartup, Glazer, & Charlesworth, 1967), operates as an important social skill. *Social competence*, on the other hand, represents an evaluative term reflecting the application of external criteria in order to assess level of development or performance in social behavior (Gresham, 1986). Many consider it synonymous with *social adaptation* or adaptive behavior. As such, it represents the degree to which the child has been able to succeed in fulfilling developmentally appropriate role expectations precribed by the community (Walsh-Allis & Orvaschel, 1986). Its application is most evident in the context of state and federal definitions of mental retardation and, in this regard, represents the manner and degree by which the impact of cognitive impairment can be operationalized. Social competence also has relevance for evaluating children who present other clinical problems as it represents "adaptive fit" and thus serves as a statement denoting relative mental health versus deviance (Walsh-Allis & Orvaschel, 1986).

CLASSIFICATION OF SOCIAL STATUS

Even though sociometric research has a 50-year history, only more recently have there been systematic attempts to classify the social status of children. The early conceptions of peer reputation considered acceptance as a unidimensional construct in which children ranged from high to low popularity with low scores representing the interchangeable terms of unpopularity or rejection (e.g., Bower, 1969). However, most investigations have supported the contention that unpopularity and rejection are indeed different phenomena (e.g., Goldman, Corsini, & de Urioste, 1980; Landau, Milich, & Whitten, 1984) and that social status is a complex construct deserving of a multidimensional classification perspective (Gottman, 1977). As such, there have emerged several schemes for describing peer relations and each has used scores from both popularity and rejection dimensions.

Gottman (1977) employed a precedent-setting multivariate approach by the application of cluster analysis to observation categories, plus scores on acceptance and rejection scales, in order to identify five groups of children: stars (high on peer acceptance and low on peer rejection), rejectees (high on peer rejection and low on peer acceptance), teacher negative (high on observed teacher negative but also high on peer acceptance), tuned out (low on both peer acceptance and rejection), and mixers (high on both peer acceptance and rejection).

Like Gottman, Peery (1979) proposed a typology based upon the independent dimensions of popularity and rejection but, instead, developed classification from two newly derived continua of social impact and social preference. In this case, children would be asked to nominate classmates for a number of positive (e.g., "whom do you like to play outside with?") and negative (e.g., "whom don't you sit next to for stories on the rug?") activity questions in order to determine status. For each child, the number of positive nominations (P) and negative nominations (N) are summed to yield a social impact score (P + N), while social preference is determined by the difference between positive and negative nominations (P − N). From this classification model, four categories of social status are evident: popular (high social impact, positive social preference); rejected (high social impact, negative social preference); amiable (low social impact, positive social preference); and isolated (low social impact, negative social preference).

Subsequent to the appearance of Peery's (1979) model, Coie, Dodge and Coppotelli, (1982) used standardized scores derived from direct preference questions to create five social status groups: popular, rejected, average, neglected, and controversial. In an effort to offer differential validity for the status groups represented by this perspective, Coie et al. solicited "liked most" and "liked least" nominations, plus a variety of behavioral descriptors, from 537 third-, fifth-, and eighth-grade children. Planned comparisons (with the neglected group excluded) indicated that popular children were described in prosocial terms, as they were nominated most often as those who cooperate and are leaders while receiving low scores on the disruptive descriptor. In contrast, rejected children were considered most likely as ones who fight and are disruptive, and most often as those who sought help while not being considered a leader or cooperative. Of particular interest were the descriptions attributed to controversial children who seem to display features of both popular and rejected classmates. Similar to rejected children, they were perceived as disruptive and as starting fights and were nominated as frequently seeking help. However, like popular children, they were considered leaders of the peer group and were the only children who earned scores below the mean on the shyness descriptor, thereby suggesting that this group is visible, assertive, and active (Coie et al., 1982). Based upon the preceding review and other research, some of the distinctive features of these four social status groups (excluding those of average status) are summarized in Table 9.1.

TABLE 9.1   Characteristic Profiles of Popular, Rejected, Neglected, and Controversial Children

	Social Status Group			
Variable	Popular	Rejected	Neglected	Controversial
Liked most	High	Low	Low	High
Liked least	Low	High	Low	High
Social preference	High	Low	Average	Average
Social impact	Average	Average	Low	High
Cooperates	High	Low	Low	Average
Disrupts group	Low	High	Low	High
Acts shy	Low	Low	High	Low
Fights	Low	High	Low	High
Seeks help	Low	High	Low	High
Leads peers	High	Low	Low	High
Loneliness	Low	High	Low	Low
Makes social overtures	High	High	Low	High
Receives social overtures	High	Low	Low	?
Task inappropriate behavior	Low	High	Low	?

Adapted from Flicek & Landau (1985).

Another interesting perspective applied to the controversial group, and one that supports the impression that their social status is heterogeneous or variable, has been suggested in a study by Bukowski and Newcomb (1985). Due to the findings, as cited above, that controversial children present many features of those in other status groups and because controversial status has shown limited stability (Newcomb & Bukowski, 1984), these investigators attempted to clarify the nature of controversial status by examining variability scores. Third-, fourth-, and fifth-grade boys and girls were requested to nominate three same-sex classmates as best friends and least-liked playmates and, secondly, to rate each classmate on a number of behavioral descriptors relevant to social reputation. Next, in a manner consistent with Coie et al. (1982), children were assigned to one of five social status groups as a result of the nominations, and variability scores for each child (i.e., standard deviations were computed on the behavior ratings of aggression, prosociability, and withdrawal). When contrasted with those in the other status groups, results indicated that children who earn controversial status have significantly greater variability in the behavioral descriptors attributed to them. These findings indicate that peers show significantly less accord in their impressions of controversial children, thereby providing a new connotation to this social status term. As Bukowski and Newcomb (1985) suggest, these children are unique in that they apparently behave in highly prosocial ways with some peers at some times and in negative ways with others, thus accounting for their concurrent characterization as likable and dislikable.

The results of the Coie et al. (1982) and Bukowski and Newcomb (1985) investigations are noteworthy in that they, among others, indicate that status should be considered a bidimensional construct and that valuable social information may be lost if assessment of peer reputation was limited to a single acceptance dimension. The principle significance of these various classification schemes is that they separate two previously confounded types of unpopular children (Parker & Asher, 1987). One group receives few popularity nominations because they are openly disliked (i.e., rejected) whereas the other receives few popularity selections as they are neither likable nor dislikable (i.e., they are neglected).

The distinction between these two groups has been demonstrated in terms of behavioral observations and seems to have important clinical implications. Dodge, Coie, and Brakke (1982) present two studies in which third-, fourth-, and fifth-graders were observed on various behavioral categories including prosocial approaches, task appropriate and inappropriate, adult-child interaction, and aggressive behaviors. Rejected children were found to engage in less solitary task appropriate behavior than popular or average status children and were significantly more aggressive. Additionally, these children attempted significantly more social approaches in the classroom but significantly fewer approaches on the playground than children in all other status groups. This pattern of results indicates that rejected children do not successfully modulate their interactive behavior as a function of changes in setting expectations. In addition, rejected children engaged in significantly more adult-child interactions than children in the other groups. Neglected children, on the other hand, manifested few aggressive and task-inappropriate behaviors and did not approach peers at inappropriate times. However, when social approaches would have been appropriate, such as during recess, the neglected children could be distinguished from popular and average status classmates by their failure to approach others.

In an effort to determine the direction of influence in the relationship between social status and social behavior, Coie and Kupersmidt (1983) studied the interaction of unacquainted children who were placed in groups composed of four boys representing the array of a popular, rejected, neglected, and average status. Each group met for six weeks and all interactions were videotaped for subsequent coding. Not surprisingly, popular boys were found to engage in more active social interaction, neglected boys were the most solitary, and average and rejected boys were intermediate on these dimensions. Additionally, neglected boys engaged in the least amount of aversive behavior while rejected boys were observed to be the most aversive. These findings support the contention that rejected children can be distinguished from those who are neglected by virtue of qualitative aspects of their approach behaviors, in that the former are significantly more aversive in their social contacts. Both groups spend little time in appropriate and cooperative play but rejected children are hostile and intrusive and neglected children seem to engage in more appropriate solitary, albeit parallel, activities (see also, Dodge, 1983).

In summary, the data are quite consistent in demonstrating that neglected children are rarely disruptive or aggressive but they are clearly less socially interactive than other children (Coie et al., 1982; Coie & Kupersmidt, 1983; Dodge, 1983). Rejected children seem to readily reacquire their previous social status following interactions with unfamiliar playmates (Coie & Kupersmidt, 1983), and once earned, their status seems quite stable over time (Coie & Dodge, 1983). These findings have important clinical implications and may explain why it is the rejected child, but not the neglected child, that is known to be at significant risk for an unfavorable adult outcome (see Parker & Asher, 1987, for a review of this literature).

SOCIAL STATUS MEASURES

Positive and Negative Nominations

Social status is typically derived from peer sociometric procedures that have their origin in the "positive nomination technique" (Moreno, 1934) in which children are asked to nominate or identify the names of classmates that would most closely correspond with a positive interpersonal item (e.g., "whom do you like the most?"). Each child's status score would then be the total number of nominations that he or she receives.

For literate subjects, these nominations can be collected by the use of an item-by-peer matrix (Pekarik, Prinz, Liebert, Weintraub, & Neale, 1976) in which all of the names of potential nominees are listed across the top of the page and all social status items are listed in the left margin (see Fig. 9.1). Children are instructed to place an "x" under the name of each child to whom the item applies (e.g., "with whom would you like to play after school?"; ". . . sit next to in class?") and encouraged

MY TEACHER'S NAME IS _____

I AM IN GRADE (circle one): 3 4 5 6

I AM A (circle one): Boy / Girl

DIRECTIONS (read orally): I am interested in finding out how well children can notice other children's behaviors. I would like you to help me by answering some questions about your classmates. You may follow along as I read each question to the class and then answer each question as well as you can. There are no wrong or right answers, and the answers you give will not affect your grade. Neither your teacher nor your classmates will know how you have answered. If you have any questions or don't understand a word, you may raise your hand for help. Please turn the page now and wait for further directions.

With whom would you
choose to do things?

At whom does the
teacher smile?

Who never seems to be
having a good time?

At whom does the
teacher get mad?

Who can't wait his
turn?

Whom would you choose
to invite to your house
after school

FIGURE 9.1   The item-by-peer matrix for a group-administered sociometric assessment

to nominate as many as they feel best fit the item. This procedure also represents an efficient and effective way to collect peer group impressions of symptomatic behaviors, many of which have relevance for an understanding of the social status problems under investigation (Pelham & Bender, 1982; Landau & Milich, 1985).

However, there are many researchers and clinicians who are also interested in examining negative nominations of those who are "least liked" or "disliked." In these cases, the child's rejection status is determined by the sum of negative items.

Picture Sociometrics

A variant of the item-by-peer matrix is a picture sociometric technique, first developed by McCandless and Marshall (1957), that can be used by preliterate subjects. In this case, each child is presented with a random array of photographs of his or her classmates and asked to point to the picture of the boy or girl, for example, ". . . who is your best friend" or ". . . with whom do you most like to play." Following administration, each child's score for each item represents the total number of times he or she was nominated by classmates. Milich, Landau, Kilby, & Whitten (1982) successfully used this procedure to collect social status information on attention deficit disordered and aggressive boys from preschool classmates in daycare and Headstart programs who were as young as three years of age. This tends to be the procedure of choice for preschool children and should be used until second grade, at which time a group administered technique becomes feasible. This picture technique has shown acceptable levels of interrater reliability using boy versus girl nominations and significant one week retest reliability for popularity ($r=.76$) and rejection ($r=.82$) scores (Milich et al., 1982). Other investigations using this procedure have established retest reliabilities ranging from $r=.83$ to .96 after one week (Horowitz, 1962), and from .53 to .56 after one year (Roff, Sells & Golden, 1972).

Milich and Landau (1984) have used this procedure to determine if it is feasible to employ social status as a means of discriminating among subgroups of aggressive boys. This study divided 49 kindergarten boys into groups of Aggressive (A), Withdrawn (W), Aggressive/Withdrawn (A/W), and normal controls (C) based upon peer nominations of inappropriate behaviors. Social status nominations and playground observations over a six-week period were collected on each boy. Results indicated that both Aggressive and Aggressive/Withdrawn groups were significantly rejected by their classmates but Aggressive boys also earned a high degree of popularity, in fact earning greater scores than boys in the W or C groups. This study was noteworthy in that it demonstrated that the picture sociometric procedure was able to reveal a finer discrimination of social status than that provided by teacher information (see also Landau et al., 1984).

The Class Play Procedure

A frequently used and enduring version of the sociometric nomination procedure is The Class Play, first described by Bower (1969), in which children are requested to assign their classmates to different roles in a hypothetical play (e.g., "someone who could play the part of a true friend"). This particular procedure has some appealing advantages over the other sociometric approaches (Masten, Morison, & Pellegrini, 1985). For one, elementary children seem to enjoy casting their classmates as imaginary characters in the play and teachers, school administrators, and parents tend to consider this type of data collection less objectionable than asking direct social preference questions. As such, this technique may more likely gain research approval and parental consent than other more potentially provocative procedures. Further, due to the variety of roles needed for the play, there is a reduced likelihood of a negative labeling by peers (Masten et al., 1985).

In the original Class Play there are both negative (e.g., "someone who is too bossy") and positive (e.g., "someone who will wait their turn") roles to which the child may be assigned. Children receive only a single score designated as "negative peer reputation." This score represents a ratio that equals the number of negative selections received divided by the total number of roles attributed to that child. Bower (1969) argued that large percentages indicate a high degree of rejection whereas low percentages suggest that the child is held in relatively high regard. As such, Bower makes the assumption that popularity and rejection are bipolar opposites or endpoints on the same social acceptance dimension; that is, being unpopular is the same as being rejected. Unfortunately, this perspective has not earned empirical support as most investigations find that these two constructs are orthogonal or only marginally inversely related, with coefficients ranging from $r=-.04$ to $-.40$ (Gottman, 1977; Hartup et al., 1967; Hymel & Asher, 1977; Moore & Updegraff, 1964). In any case, The Class Play has a popular history with social status investigators and is responsible for a substantial contribution to the outcome research that has examined the implications of early peer problems (e.g., Cowen et al., 1973).

Roster Rating Method

Another means of collecting sociometric information is with the use of peer ratings, or the "roster rating method," in which all children are rated by all members of the group. For example, all students may be asked to rate each classmate on a 1- (frowning face) to 5- (smiling face) point scale in terms of "How much do you like to play with this person at school?" (Singleton & Asher, 1977). In this case, a child's sociometric score is the average of the ratings he or she receives from the entire group. When more than one peer group (classroom) is assessed, rating scores are typically standardized within each group to insure comparable weighting for differences in class size (Asher & Dodge, 1986).

When contrasted with nomination procedures, peer ratings offer greater reliability because each child is rated by all classmates (Asher & Hymel, 1981). As such, ratings can represent a more comprehensive index of the child's degree of acceptance to the peer group because only a few children are identified by each classmate with the nomination procedure. In fact, it has been suggested that the rating procedure will offer scores that are more sensitive than nominations to changes in social status (Asher & Hymel, 1981; Cole & Krehbiel, 1984) and, because this task insures that each child is rated by all peers, it reduces the possibility that neglected children are ignored by classmates during the sociometric assessment. This latter point may be an important consideration as it has been shown that different social competence information can accrue as a function of continuous versus dichotomous methods of measurement (Foster & Ritchey, 1979). Hymel and Asher (1977) found the roster rating method to correlate r=.63 with the positive nomination technique and to have a six-week retest reliability of r=.82, a stability coefficient greater than those typically attributed to the nomination method (Oden & Asher, 1977). A final advantage, and one that is relevant for securing parental consent and school administrator's approval, is the fact that ratings do not necessarily require negative nominations or involve negative criteria for selection. Instead, each scale will reflect both positive and negative poles on a neutral question or dimension.

An Alternative to Negative Nominations

Recently, Asher and Dodge (1986) examined the utility of a rating procedure to determine if a rating could, in fact, be used instead of negative nominations for sociometric assessment. These investigators requested that third- through sixth-grade children rate all classmates in terms of play preferences on a one (i.e., "I don't like to") to five ("I like to a lot") scale. Additionally, each child was asked to identify the names of three classmates that they liked most and liked least. For the purposes of determining the suitability of the use of low play ratings as an alternative to negative nominations, Asher and Dodge examined the correspondence between a play rating of "one" and "least liked" nominations and found them to be strongly related (r=.80, p<.001), thereby suggesting that the two methods produced similar rejected status information. Additionally, five-month stability was established at r=.69 for the standardized average play rating and r=.65 for the standardized frequency of one ratings, compared to r=.55 for the positive nomination technique. Unfortunately, this rating procedure produced a relatively high misclassification rate for children who were identified as neglected by the more traditional nomination technique. In summary, the Asher and Dodge investigation offers support for the notion that ratings can be a feasible means to identify rejected, but not necessarily neglected, children without the application of negative test items during data collection.

In summary, there presently exists a variety of procedures that can be employed to assess children's social reputation. However, since these do not represent traditional norm-referenced assessment techniques, it would be inappropriate to think in terms of the availability of standardized procedures. Most researchers and clinicians want to determine how well liked (and disliked) is the particular child and therefore tend to ask questions pertaining directly to the status constructs of popularity and rejection. To accomplish this, the most frequently employed group-administered sociometric procedures have been Bower's (1969) Class Play and the Peer Evaluation Inventory (PEI; Pekarik et al., 1976). The PEI, which uses the previously described item-by-peer matrix, reflects the three empirically derived factors of Aggression, Withdrawal, and Likability and is, therefore, suitable to assess the relationship between social status and other relevant social behaviors (see, for example, Serbin, Lyons, Marchessault, Schwartzman, & Ledingham, 1987). However, in order to meet their specific research needs, many investigators have modified the PEI by adding questions that pertain to other specific behaviors under study (e.g., Landau & Milich, 1985).

The determination of the most appropriate procedure must first depend upon the age and reading ability of respondents. If preliterate children constitute the peer group, an individually administered sociometric interview must be attempted. However, most second-graders are able to comprehend written social status questions in a group-administered sociometric inventory. With subjects this young, it is advisable to have the examiner or teacher read the questions out loud as children follow along. In terms of format, the rating procedure seems to have sound measurement properties and may be the method of choice, especially since it seems to preclude the possibility that the withdrawn or socially isolated child is ignored during data collection. In addition, most rating scales avoid the use of negative and pejorative terms. In any case, instrument selection is a function of the objectives of the assessment and the particular research and clinical questions under consideration.

RELIABILITY OF SOCIAL STATUS ASSESSMENT

Stability Over Time

The reliability of sociometric assessment has been demonstrated in several ways, and each suggests that the clinician or investigator should be able to collect consistent and repeatable social status information. For one, the research has shown acceptable levels of stability for periods up to three years (e.g., Roff et al., 1972). However, most reviews of the stability research (Hartup, 1983; Milich & Landau, 1982) report that stability is greater for positive nominations or popularity than for negative nominations or rejection.

Interestingly, Cole and Dodge (1983) discovered a different pattern of results over a five-year retest interval in which yearly sociometric data were collected on a sample of third- and fifth-graders. "Liked most" and "liked least" nominations were transformed into social preference and social impact dimensions and children were assigned each year to groups of popular, rejected, neglected, controversial, and average status. Stability results indicated that social preference scores were highly correlated across all years for both cohorts, whereas social impact scores were not significantly correlated across a period greater than three years. A child's social status in any given year was highly predictive of status the subsequent year. However, for the older cohort, there was significant continuity only for rejected status for the entire five-year period, but for only three years for the younger sample of children. Thus, "liked least" nominations and rejection status were found to be significantly more enduring. It was interesting to discover the pattern of status change. Children who earned neglected status in elementary school almost never became rejected or controversial in junior high school, whereas rejected elementary age children ran a high risk of subsequent neglected status in junior high school. As Cole and Dodge (1983) suggest, this pattern indicates that being neglected by the elementary school peer group means something quite different than being neglected five years hence.

Hartup (1983) has provided a comprehensive review of the social status stability research. That literature can be summarized as follows: As expected, test-retest reliability will be a function of the length of the retest interval with stability declining with increasing time between administrations. Second, stability seems to be a direct function of the age of the child participating in the sociometric procedure, with older children providing more stable nominations than younger ones. In addition, stability of status seems directly related to the degree of acquaintanceship among children such that the greater the familiarity with the nominated or rated child, the more stable the score. Thus, social status will be more stable in the context of established, as opposed to recent, group membership. A corollary finding is that when status fluctuations are evident, these are more likely to be attributable to those of moderate status than those who have earned extreme placement on the status dimensions. Consistent with conventional psychometric theory, Hartup (1983) reports that stability of status will be positively related to the number of sociometric criteria being assessed, the number of sociometric items used, and the size of the sample providing the sociometric information.

Interrater Correspondence

A second measure of reliability of assessment is by means of cross-source or interjudge reliability. For example, boy versus girl classroom nominations can be compared to establish interrater agreement. The typical classroom sociometric assessment has the entire class participating in the procedure but the scores are derived as the sums or averages from the same-sex classmates. This approach is employed due to the consistent evidence that both play and reputation patterns differ as a function of same-sex versus opposite-sex classmate pairings (see Hartup, 1983, for a review). Further support for this practice was recently reported by Asher and Dodge (1986) who found a strong sex bias for a sample of 200 third- through sixth-grade youngsters. These children were significantly less likely to attribute positive, and more likely to attribute negative, nominations to their opposite sex classmates. The effect of sex is an important issue that demands further investigation; much that has been learned from the social status research is based only on the use of same-sex nominations.

There are various other ways to demonstrate cross-source reliability including self-reports, parent ratings, and role-playing procedures. However, since tests of validation for these procedures have, at times, proven disappointing (Glow & Glow, 1980; Ledingham, Younger, Schwartzman, & Bergeron, 1982; Van Hasselt, Hersen, Whitehill, & Bellack, 1979), they will not be considered here. Thus, the primary alternative to peer nominations is teacher evaluation of social status and peer relationships.

Moderate correspondence has been reported between teacher and peer assessments, with coefficients ranging from .40 to .70 (Milich & Landau, 1982). This has been established for specific ratings of peer relations as well as for assessment of behavioral adjustment. Butler (1979), for example, found a correlation of −.67 between peer nominations from Bower's (1969) Class Play and teacher ratings of adjustment. Matson, Esveldt-Dawson, and Kazdin (1983) found that teacher and peer rankings of popularity were significantly related, r=.62, p<.001, but La Greca (1981) found, when examining the correspondence between teacher ratings of the three Pupil Evaluation Inventory (PEI) factors and peer ratings, that the strength of the relationship was much greater for boys than for girls.

In summary, results indicate that, at least from a broad perspective, peer and teacher assessment of social relationships and behavioral adjustment show significant convergence. When comparing these sources, however, several investigators have argued, especially with preschoolers, that teachers are the more reliable informants regarding the child's social status (Connolly & Doyle, 1981; Greenwood, Walker, Todd, & Hops, 1979). For example, Greenwood et al. developed a procedure in which teachers would rank all students in terms of the degree to which other children would most like to play with them. This procedure was shown to exhibit greater retest reliability than a comparable peer measure of popularity and seemed more sensitive for identifying the socially isolated preschooler. In a similar vein with another preschool sample, Connolly and Doyle (1981) found this same teacher popularity ranking procedure to better predict observed social behavior than positive peer nominations. In fact, to the surprise of those who advocate the use of peers as informants, the positive nominations supplied by peers did not offer any unique information (i.e., no incremental validity) in the prediction of social behavior beyond that supplied by the simple teacher rankings.

The above investigations indicate that, at least in the prediction of prosocial and appropriate behaviors, teachers and peers provide essentially redundant information, thereby suggesting that the more time-efficient teacher ranking could be considered preferable to the more cumbersome sociometric procedure for preschoolers. However, teacher information may not be as effective in predicting inappropriate or maladaptive social behavior. Landau et al. (1984) replicated the Connolly and Doyle study but this time also included peer nominations of rejection plus a variety of observed inappropriate playground behaviors. In comparison to the teacher ranking of popularity, peer nominations of both popularity and rejection made significant and unique contributions to the prediction of observed solitary play and negative interactions. This pattern of findings indicates that peers are able to improve upon the prediction made by teachers, especially if inappropriate social behaviors are of interest. The fact that the teacher ranking was only weakly related to observed negative interactions does not mean that teachers are insensitive to inappropriate social behaviors. However, it does suggest that a teacher ranking of popularity may not be sufficiently sensitive or comprehensive to assess all aspects of social relations.

Ledingham and Younger (1985) argue that the failure to establish high correspondence between teachers and peers should not be unexpected. Instead of dismissing the dissonance in data as a nuisance factor due to method variance, these researchers present findings that demonstrate that teachers and peers may, in fact, elicit different aspects of the target child's repertoire, that children manifest quantitatively and qualitatively different behaviors in the presence of teachers versus peers. As such, evaluator or informant differences should be considered a predictable characteristic of social behavior assessment, and one that can be adequately addressed by the use of a planned combination of teacher and peer data (cf. Ladd, 1983).

VALIDITY OF SOCIAL STATUS ASSESSMENT

Validation of the social status constructs has been a veritable challenge for researchers since a suitable criterion may be difficult to identify. In fact, it can be argued that peer nominations are by definition valid measures since no one knows better than children themselves whom they do and do not like. Unfortunately, there has been a paucity of research designed to clarify the social status construct and few demonstrations of both convergent and discriminative validity (see Campbell & Fiske, 1959). Instead, most efforts have simply focused on an examination of the correlates of social status.

As discussed previously, social status, and peer rejection in particular, has proven to be an excellent predictor of a variety of unfavorable adult outcome measures (e.g., Cowen et al., 1973). This phenomenon has been widely accepted as a compelling demonstration of the predictive validity of peer sociometric measures although, as Parker and Asher (1987) caution, these findings have been accepted without adequate regard for the implications that different methodological designs have on a meaningful interpretation of obtained findings.

Second, there is an abundance of research examining both the organismic and behavioral correlates of social status. In terms of the former, popular children differ from their disliked classmates in terms of intellectual potential, academic achievement, physical attractiveness, appeal of first names, athletic ability, presence of handicapping condition, and possibly, social class (Hartup, 1983). Regarding overt behavioral correlates, social status groups differ in terms of friendliness and sociability (e.g., dispensing positive reinforcement to peers or friendly approaches to peers), compliance with rules and peer perceptions of conformity, demonstrations of social knowledge or social perspective-taking, and aggressive and other aversive deviant behaviors (see Hartup, 1983, for a comprehensive review). In spite of the fact that an examination of correlates has been the focus of much research, the findings tend to reflect only modest relationships between measures of status and child attributes, with no single characteristic emerging as the comprehensive explanation for the child's popularity or rejection status (Hartup, 1983).

As such, the challenge for future researchers in this area is not to further determine the distinctive characteristics of children of different status groups but, instead, to begin to understand the causal mechanisms involved with the emergence and maintenance of a child's social status. For example, there is consistent evidence that off-task classroom behavior is significantly related to peer rejection (e.g., Gottman, 1977). However, we need to determine whether it is off-task behavior, per se, that leads to peer rejection, whether it is the correlates of being off-task in the classroom (e.g., deficient academic performance, disruptive behavior, negative teacher attention) that cause rejection, or whether some other mediating process is accounting for the coincidental development of both off-task behavior and peer rejection (Milich & Landau, 1982). Only in this way can we be confident that social skills treatment will be focused upon the genuine cause of the child's skill deficit. The alternative has been to target for treatment identified correlates of social status (Combs & Slaby, 1977); this may account for the modest and disappointing results reported by many of these studies (cf. Krehbiel & Milich, 1986). Despite these limitations, it is clear that the social status groups previously described do differ in reliable and predictable ways among themselves.

ETHICAL AND PRACTICAL CONSIDERATIONS

Not only because of the established longitudinal implications of early peer difficulties, but also because so many referred children also present with disturbed peer relations as a concomitant to their primary problem, sociometric data can represent a necessary component in the clinical child assessment battery. Even so, some attempts to collect these data have met with resistance from public school personnel. Concerns have focused on the potential harm that may accrue when children are asked to "evaluate" each other and to identify whom they do and do not like. From the lay perspective, it is hypothesized that children will become sensitized into thinking about and discussing their social preferences as they compare, after testing, whom each nominated (Asher, 1983). This concern is especially salient for negative items, with the anticipated effect that disliked and unpopular children will be further ostracized by the use of these sociometric procedures.

Although easily understood from an intuitive perspective, there has never been any empirical support for such fears. Several high risk longitudinal investigations (e.g., Pekarik et al., 1976; Serbin et al., 1987) have collected literally thousands of sociometric nominations without any reports of deleterious consequences to the children who participated. In addition, these clinical impressions have been examined in an important investigation by Hayvren and Hymel (1984). The social interactions of preschool children were observed and their verbatim comments recorded for 10 minutes immediately following individually administered sociometric assessment in which each child was requested to make both positive and negative nominations. Even though half the children made verbal reference to the procedure following return to the classroom, not one of the 27 children commented upon or identified their negative choices. Second, for the 10 minutes immediately following the procedure, preschoolers did not relate differently to identified preferred versus nonpreferred classmates. Lastly, when contrasted to observational data that were collected prior to sociometric testing, children's interactions had not changed as a result of testing. These findings are encouraging but should be interpreted with caution. For one, they may have little relevance for older children who, for developmental reasons, better understand the purposes of assessment. Additionally, the reactive effects might have been subtle and, thus, not captured by the measures, or the effects may not present immediately but, instead, have a more insidious onset. In any case, more investigations of this sort should be attempted to generate the necessary data to dissuade school administrators and university institutional review boards from attributing deleterious consequences to sociometric assessment.

As long as parents and school personnel express concerns about the use of negative nominations, sociometric testing may be limited to positive items. Even though there is evidence that valuable information may be lost if negative nominations are excluded (cf. Landau et al., 1984), the Asher and Dodge (1986) method of play preference ratings can provide a means to identify rejected children without the use of pejorative sociometric items.

A second methodological issue that must be addressed deals with the bias that may result from parental nonconsenters who do not permit their children to participate in sociometric procedures. In other words, one wonders if there is something sociometrically distinctive about those children whose parents exclude them from testing. This is an important question as it has been reported that children who are not permitted to participate are more likely to be teacher-rated as withdrawn or aggressive (Beck, Collins, Overholser, & Terry, 1984). In a series of recent studies, Foster, Bell-Dolan, and Berler (1986) examined the issue of selection bias resulting from parental nonconsent. Using three samples, consenters to participate in sociometric testing were compared with nonconsenters in terms of teacher ratings of the child's popularity with classmates. For two of the samples, the consenters were teacher-rated as significantly more popular than nonconsenters. Regarding a fourth sample, Foster et al. sent home parent consent forms to conduct a social observation study of fourth- and sixth-grade children after sociometric data had already been collected. Consenter differences for like-most and like-least peer nominations were examined. No significant consenter group differences were found. Taken together, these results offer only tentative support for the notion that a selection bias for nonconsenters does exist, when defined by teacher ratings. However, consistent with other investigations (e.g., La Greca & Santogrossi, 1980), no evidence has been found to support a selection bias when peer evaluations are used.

SELF-REPORT MEASURES OF SOCIAL STATUS

It has been suggested throughout this chapter that, if one is interested in understanding the nature of children's social status and peer relations, one must go directly to the peer group and conduct some form of sociometric assessment. The resulting sociometric data are known to be reliable and valid and may offer information regarding aspects of the child's functioning not available from other informants or procedures. However, there can be practical reasons why the clinician may feel compelled to collect children's self-reports of their social status. For one, many clinicians may not have access to their client's classmates for the more conventional form of sociometric assessment (Bierman & McCauley, 1987). Second, the need for self-report information may be enhanced by the fact that parents, who serve as principal informants regarding their child's presenting problems, are not known to be well informed regarding the nature of peer relations (Glow & Glow, 1980; Graham & Rutter, 1968). Finally, even when sociometric data are available, it may be important for the clinician to establish how problems in social relations impact the referred child. It is therefore assumed that although self-reports of social problems may not reflect a veridical view of the child's situation, they may provide insight into the child's feelings and attributions for their difficulties (cf. Dodge & Richard, 1985). Therefore, interest is emerging to establish the means by which children can reliably report the nature of their own social relations. In fact, self-reports of social status were, until not long ago, considered rare and of little utility. For example, as Green and Forehand (1980) note, "evidence for concurrent validity of children's self-report is meager at this time, especially for children younger than twelve years of age" (p. 150). Fortunately, although these measures are still in their infancy, recent work may not support such a pessimistic perspective.

Social Goals and Strategies

Renshaw and Asher (1983) developed an interview procedure to examine hypothetical social situations in order to ascertain children's goals and social strategies. It was hypothesized that popular and unpopular children not only would differ in terms of important behaviors, but also may cognitively differ in terms of social objectives and social problem-solving techniques. Third- through sixth-grade children were requested to rank order the propriety of interpersonal goals and also generate social strategies in response to these situations. Results indicated that sociometric status, based upon classmate nominations, did not distinguish children in terms of ranked goals, thereby suggesting that unpopular children are able to select the appropriate goal when offered a clear choice. However, when children's spontaneous social strategies were coded for content, high status children provided significantly more friendly and positive/outgoing goals than low status children. Age was more potent than status as a mediating variable in the creation of children's sophisticated social strategies, and this may qualify the clinical utility of obtained findings.

This significant age effect should not be surprising. Bierman and McCauley (1987) examined the correspondence between children's self-reports of their peer relations and actual social status and found that older subjects provided more accurate reports of their status. Consistent with other results (e.g., Asher, Hymel, & Renshaw, 1984), Bierman and McCauley discovered that socially adjusted youngsters tend to describe themselves as having satisfactory peer relations whereas those with peer problems may or may not report such difficulties. In a similar vein, Hymel (1983) found that popular children tend to underestimate their positive reputation with peers while unpopular ones tend to overestimate this reputation.

Loneliness

Asher and colleagues (Asher et al., 1984; Asher & Wheeler, 1985) have established a means to assess self-reports of lonelineness/social dissatisfaction and have examined this in the context of social status. A 24-item questionnaire that addressed children's feelings of loneliness (e.g., "I have nobody to talk to in class"), feelings of social adequacy (e.g., "I'm good at working with other children in my class"), and an estimation of social status (e.g., "I have lots of friends in my class") was administered, along with a sociometric inventory, to third- through sixth-grade children. Results indicate that those children considered least popular by peers or nominated as having the fewest friends do, indeed, report significantly more loneliness and social dissatisfaction (Asher et al., 1984) and that rejected and neglected children differ in terms of expressed loneliness, with rejected, but not neglected, children experiencing significantly greater loneliness (Asher & Wheeler, 1985). Consistent with the Bierman and McCauley (1987) findings, if children do admit to the negative attribute of loneliness, this admission probably represents a valid characterization of peer problems. However, some children who are known to experience relationship problems will deny such feelings, thus possibly reducing the utility of the loneliness measure as a means to rule out social difficulties.

Social Anxiety

The final area of interest pertains to self-reports of social anxiety, a construct that has been, until recently, virtually ignored while investigating social skills deficits in children. Borrowing from the adult conception of social-evaluative anxiety (see Watson & Friend, 1969), La Greca, Dandes, Wick, Shaw, and Stone (1988) developed a 10-item scale to measure children's anxiety with respect to peer relations. When applied to 287 second- through sixth-grade children, the Social Anxiety Scale for Children (SASC), which reflects the empirically derived factors of Fear and Negative Evaluation (FNE; e.g., "I worry about being teased") and Social Avoidance and Distress (SAD; e.g., "I get nervous when I talk to new kids"), was found to have adequate retest reliability and concurrent validity when compared with a measure of trait anxiety. In addition, La Greca et al. found that girls seem to report significantly greater social anxiety than boys, especially in terms of greater fear of negative peer evaluation and that younger children admit to greater anxiety than older children. Also of interest was an examination of the relationship between social anxiety and peer nominations of social status. Based upon the Cole et al. (1982) classification scheme, popular, rejected, controversial, neglected, and average status children were found to report significant differences in their feelings of social concerns. Both in terms of total and FNE scores, neglected children seemed to be the most socially anxious and to have the greatest fear of peer evaluation. Controversial children, in contrast, were found to have the least concern for social evaluation. In conclusion, the La Greca et al. procedure offers promise as a means to assess the cognitive and affective aspects of impaired social functioning.

SUMMARY AND CONCLUSIONS

Throughout this chapter, we have attempted to portray the peer group as the preeminent source of information if data are needed regarding children's peer relations and social status. Peers provide information with more apparent sensitivity and precision than other sources, including parents and teachers. In the context of comprehensive child clinical evaluations, assessment of the social domain is considered a critical undertaking, as it has become widely accepted that relationship problems are predictive of, and may even contribute to, many concurrent and later difficulties.

To date, there is a plethora of research suggesting that sociometric data are reliable, stable, and valid. In fact, some demonstrations have been so widely accepted that many investigators fail to employ a critical perspective to the procedures used to establish these "at-risk" findings (Parker & Asher, 1987). Also unfortunate is the fact that the present state of social skills research offers little to assist our understanding of the causal mechanisms regarding the child's peer status, as the necessary and sufficient ingredients of social competence are yet to be identified. In spite of these limitations, the child clinical practitioner remains well advised to develop a working familiarity with the various sociometric procedures presently available and to collect such information when appropriate. In this regard, most children seen in mental health settings, even when referred for a variety of other disorders, present with significant social competence and peer reputation problems.

However, as previously noted, there may be practical and ethical concerns that can arise when attempts are made to collect such social status information. In response to these potential challenges, alternative approaches are being developed that may overcome some of these difficulties. For example, Asher and Dodge's (1986) play-preference rating procedure has the obvious benefit of avoiding the pejorative terms associated with assessing negative peer reputation. Second, La Greca et al. (1988), among others, are exploring the means by which one can employ the children's self-reports of social functioning. This emerging area has the potential to become especially important under those circumstances when clinicians are denied access to the peer group.

Even though it has been our objective to offer the clinician and researcher a current overview of social status assessment, we would like to close with a cautionary note. It is anticipated that major developments in alternative procedures, such as highly refined self-reports, will be accomplished within the next few years so that assessment of peer relations will experience dramatic methodological changes. Not only will these improvements contribute to the technology of measurement but they are also expected to enhance our understanding of the determinants and dynamics of peer relations. Thus, professionals may be well advised to pay careful attention to this burgeoning body of research.

REFERENCES

Achenbach, T.M., & Edelbrock, C. (1983). *Manual for the Child Behavior Checklist and Revised Child Behavior Profile*. Burlington, VT: University Associates in Psychiatry.

Asher, S.R. (1983). Social competence and peer status: Recent advances and future directions. *Child Development, 54,* 1427–1434.

Asher, S.R., & Dodge, K.S. (1986). Identifying children who are rejected by their peers. *Developmental Psychology, 22,* 444–449.

Asher, S.R., & Hymel, S. (1981). Children's social competence in peer relations: Sociometric and behavioral assessment. In J.D. Wine & M.D. Smye (Eds.), *Social competence*. pp. 125–157 New York: Guilford.

Asher, S.R., Hymel, S., & Renshaw, P.D. (1984). Loneliness in children. *Child Development, 55,* 1456–1464.

Asher, S.R., & Wheeler, V.A. (1985). Children's loneliness: A comparison of rejected and neglected peer status. *Journal of Consulting and Clinical Psychology, 53,* 500–505.

Barkley, R., & Cunningham, C. (1979). The effects of methylphenidate on the mother-child interactions of hyperactive children. *Archives of General Psychiatry, 36,* 201–208.

Beck, S., Collins, L., Overholser, J., & Terry, K. (1984). A comparison of children who receive and who do not receive permission to participate in research. *Journal of Abnormal Child Psychology, 12,* 573–580.

Bierman, K.L., & McCauley, E. (1987). Children's descriptions of their peer interactions: Useful information for clinical child assessment. *Journal of Clinical Child Psychology, 16,* 9–18.

Bower, E. (1969). *Early identification of emotionally handicapped children in school,* (2nd. ed.). Springfield, IL: Charles C. Thomas.

Bukowski, W.M., & Newcomb, A.F. (1985). Variability in peer group perceptions: Support for the "controversial" sociometric classification group. *Developmental Psychology, 21,* 1032–1038.

Butler, L.J. (1979, April). *Social and behavioral correlates of peer reputation.* Paper presented at the meeting of the Society for Research in Child Development, San Francisco, CA.

Campbell, D., & Fiske, D. (1959). Convergent and discriminant validation by the multitrait-multimethod matrix. *Psychological Bulletin, 56,* 81–105.

Coie, J.D., & Dodge, K.A. (1983). Continuities and changes in children's social status: A five-year longitudinal study. *Merrill-Palmer Quarterly, 29,* 261–282.

Coie, J.D., Dodge, K.A., & Coppotelli, H. (1982). Dimensions and types of social status: A cross-age perspective. *Developmental Psychology, 18,* 557–570.

Coie, J.D., & Krehbiel, G. (1984). Effects of academic tutoring on the social status of low-achieving, socially rejected children. *Child Development, 55,* 1465–1478.

Coie, J.D., & Kupersmidt, J.B. (1983). A behavioral analysis of emerging social status in boys' groups. *Child Development, 54,* 1400–1416.

Combs, M., & Slaby, D. (1977). Social skills training with children. In B. Lahey & A. Kazdin (Eds.), *Advances in clinical child psychology.* (pp. 161–203) New York: Plenum.

Connolly, J., & Doyle, A. (1981). Assessment of social competence in preschoolers: Teachers versus peers. *Developmental Psychology, 17,* 454–462.

Cowen, E., Pederson, A., Babigian, H., Izzo, L., & Trost, M. (1973). Long-term follow-up of early detected vulnerable children. *Journal of Consulting and Clinical Psychology, 41,* 438–446.

Cunningham, C.E., Siegel, L.S., & Offord, D.R. (1985). A developmental dose-response analysis of the effects of methylphenidate on the peer interactions of attention deficit disorder boys. *Journal of Child Psychology and Psychiatry, 26,* 955–971.

Dodge, K.A. (1983). Behavioral antecedents of peer social status. *Child Development, 54,* 1386–1389.

Dodge, K.A., Coie, J.D., & Brakke, N.P. (1982). Behavior patterns of socially rejected and neglected preadolescents: The roles of social approach and aggression. *Journal of Abnormal Child Psychology, 10,* 389–410.

Dodge, K.A., & Richard, B.A. (1985). Peer perceptions, aggression, and the development of peer relations. In J.B. Pryor and J.D. Day (Eds.), *The development of social cognition* (pp. 35–58). New York: Springer-Verlag.

Flicek, M., & Landau, S. (1985). Social status problems of learning disabled and hyperactive/learning disabled boys. *Journal of Clinical Child Psychology, 14,* 340–344.

Foster, S.L., Bell-Dolan, B., & Berler, E.S. (1986). Methodological issues in the use of sociometrics for selecting children for social skills research and training. In R.J. Prinz (Ed.), Advances in behavioral assessment of children and families, Vol. 2 (pp. 227–248). Greenwich, CT: JAI Press.

Foster, S., & Ritchey, W. (1979). Issues in the assessment of social competencies in children. *Journal of Applied Behavior Analysis, 12*, 625–638.

Glow, R.A., & Glow, P.H. (1980). Peer and self-rating: Children's perception of behavior relevant to hyperkinetic impulse disorder. *Journal of Abnormal Child Psychology, 8*, 471–490.

Goldman, J.A., Corsini, D.A., & de Urioste, P. (1980). Implications of positive and negative sociometric status for assessing the social competence of young children. *Journal of Applied Developmental Psychology, 1*, 209–220.

Gottman, J. (1977). Toward a definition of social isolation in children. *Child Development, 48*, 513–517.

Gottman, J., Gonso, J., & Rasmussen, B. (1975). Social interaction, social competence, and friendship in children. *Child Development, 46*, 709–718.

Graham, P., & Rutter, M. (1968). The reliability and validity of the psychiatric assessment of the child: II. Interview with the parent. *British Journal of Psychiatry, 114*, 581–592.

Green, K.D., & Forehand, R. (1980). Assessment of children's social skills: A review of methods. *Journal of Behavioral Assessment, 2*, 143–158.

Greenwood, C.R., Walker, H.M., Todd, N.M., & Hops, H. (1979). Selecting a cost-effective screening measure for the assessment of preschool social withdrawal. *Journal of Applied Behavior Analysis, 12*, 639–652.

Gresham, F.M. (1986). Conceptual and definitional issues in the assessment of children's social skills: Implications for classification and training. *Journal of Clinical Child Psychology, 15*, 3–15.

Hartup, W.W. (1983). Peer relations. In E.M. Hetherington (Ed.), *Handbook of child psychology* (Vol. 4): *Socialization, personality, and social development* (pp. 103–198). New York: Wiley.

Hartup, W., Glazer, J., & Charlesworth, R. (1967). Peer reinforcement and sociometric status. *Child Development, 38*, 1017–1024.

Hayvren, M., & Hymel, S. (1984) Ethical issues in sociometric testing: Impact of sociometric measures on interaction behavior. *Developmental Psychology, 20*, 844–849.

Hops, H., Finch, M., & McConnell, S. (1985). Social skill deficits. In P.H. Bornstein and A.E. Kazdin (Eds.), *Handbook of clinical behavior therapy with children* (pp. 543–598). Homewood, IL: Dorsey.

Horowitz, F.D. (1962). The relationship of anxiety, self-concept, and sociometric status among fourth, fifth, and sixth grade children. *Journal of Abnormal and Social Psychology, 65*, 212–214.

Huesmann, L.R., Eron, L.D., Lefkowitz, M.M., & Walder, L.D. (1984). Stability of aggression over time and generations. *Developmental Psychology, 20*, 1120–1134.

Hymel, S. (1983). *Social isolation and rejection in children: The child's perspective.* Paper presented at the biennial meeting of the Society for Research in Child Development, Detroit, MI.

Hymel, S., & Asher, S.R. (1977, March). *Assessment and training of isolated children's social skills.* Paper presented at the meeting of the Society for Research in Child Development, New Orleans. (ERIC Document Service No. ED 136 930).

Krehbiel, G., & Milich, R. (1986). Issues in the assessment and treatment of socially rejected children. In R.J. Prinz (Ed.), *Advances in behavioral assessment of children and families* (Vol. 2, pp. 249–270). Greenwich, CT: JAI Press.

Ladd, G.W. (1983). Social networks of popular, average, and rejected children in school settings. *Merrill-Palmer Quarterly, 29,* 283–307.

La Greca, A.M. (1981). Peer acceptance: The correspondence between children's sociometric scores and teachers' ratings of peer interactions. *Journal of Abnormal Child Psychology, 9,* 167–178.

La Greca, A.M., Dandes, S.K., Wick, P., Shaw, K., & Stone, W.L. (1988). Development of the Social Anxiety Scale for Children: Reliability and concurrent validity. *Journal of Clinical Child Psychology, 17,* 84–91.

La Greca, A., & Santogrossi, D. (1980). Social skills training with elementary school students: A behavioral group approach. *Journal of Consulting and Clinical Psychology, 48,* 220–227.

Landau, S., & Milich, R. (1988). Social communication patterns of attention deficit disordered boys. *Journal of Abnormal Child Psychology, 16,* 69–81.

Landau, S., & Milich, R. (1985). The social status of aggressive and aggressive/withdrawn boys: A replication across age and method. *Journal of Consulting and Clinical Psychology, 53,* 141.

Landau, S., Milich, R., & Whitten, P. (1984). A comparison of teacher and peer assessment of social status. *Journal of Clinical Child Psychology, 13,* 44–49.

Ledingham, J. (1981). Developmental patterns of aggressive and withdrawn behavior in childhood: A possible method for identifying preschizophrenics. *Journal of Abnormal Child Psychology, 9,* 1–22.

Ledingham, J.E., & Younger, A.J. (1985). The influence of evaluator on assessments of children's social skills. In B.H. Schneider, K.H. Rubin, & J.E. Ledingham (Eds.), *Children's peer relations: Issues in assessment and intervention* (pp. 111–124) New York: Springer-Verlag.

Ledingham, J.E., Younger, A., Schwartzman, A., & Bergeron, G. (1982). Agreement among teacher, peer, and self-ratings of children's aggression, withdrawal, and likability. *Journal of Abnormal Child Psychology, 10,* 363–372.

Masten, A.S., Morison, P., & Pellegrini, D.S. (1985). A revised class play method of peer assessment. *Developmental Psychology, 21,* 523–533.

Matson, J.L., Esveldt-Dawson, K., & Kazdin, A.E. (1983). Validation of methods for assessing social skills in children. *Journal of Clinical Child Psychology, 12,* 174–180.

McCandless, B., & Marshall, H. (1957). A picture sociometric technique for preschool children and its relation to teacher judgments of friendship. *Child Development, 28,* 139–148.

Milich, R., & Landau, S. (1984). A comparison of the social status and social behavior of aggressive and aggressive/withdrawn boys. *Journal of Abnormal Child Psychology, 12,* 277–288.

Milich, R., & Landau, S. (1982). Socialization and peer relations in hyperactive children. In K.D. Gadow & I. Bialer (Eds.) *Advances in learning and behavioral disabilities*, Vol. 1 (pp. 283–339). Greenwich, CT: JAI Press.

Milich, R., Landau, S., Kilby, G., & Whitten, P. (1982). Preschool peer perceptions of the behavior of hyperactive and aggressive children. *Journal of Abnormal Child Psychology, 10*, 497–510.

Moore, S.G., & Updegraff, R. (1964). Sociometric status of preschool children as related to age, sex, nurturance-giving, and dependence. *Child Development, 35*, 519–524.

Moreno, J.L. (1934). *Who shall survive?* Washington, DC: Nervous and Mental Disease Publishing.

Newcomb, A.F., & Bukowski, W.M. (1984). A longitudinal study of the utility of social preference and social impact sociometric classification schemes. *Child Development, 55*, 1434–1447.

Oden, S., & Asher, S. (1977), Coaching children in social skills for friendship making. *Child Development, 48*, 495–506.

Parker, J.G., & Asher, S.R. (1987). Peer relations and later personal development: Are low-accepted children "at risk"? *Psychological Bulletin, 102*, 357–389.

Peery, J. (1979). Popular, amiable, isolated, rejected: A reconceptualization of sociometric status in preschool children. *Child Development, 50*, 1231–1234.

Pekarik, E., Prinz, R., Liebert, D., Weintraub, S., & Neale, J. (1976) The Pupil Evaluation Inventory: A sociometric technique for assessing children's social behavior. *Journal of Abnormal Child Psychology, 4*, 83–97.

Pelham, W.E., & Bender, M. (1982). Peer interactions in hyperactive children: Description and treatment. In K.D. Gadow and I. Bialer (Eds.), *Advances in learning and behavioral disabilities*, Vol. 1 (pp. 365–436). Greenwich, CT: JAI Press.

Price, J.M., & Ladd, G.W. (1986). Assessment of children's friendships: Implications for social competence and social adjustment. In R.J. Prinz (Ed.), *Advances in behavioral assessment of children and families* (Vol. 2, pp. 121–149). Greenwich, CT: JAI Press.

Putallaz, M., & Gottman, J. (1983). Social relationship problems in children. In B.B. Lahey & A.E. Kazdin (Eds.), *Advances in clinical child psychology* (Vol. 6, pp. 1–39). New York: Plenum.

Renshaw, P.D., & Asher, S.R. (1983). Children's goals and strategies for social interaction. *Merrill-Palmer Quarterly, 29*, 353–375.

Roff, M. (1963). Childhood social interactions and young adult psychosis. *Journal of Clinical Psychology, 19*, 152–157.

Roff, M., & Sells, S. (1968). Juvenile delinquency in relation to peer acceptance-rejection and sociometric status. *Psychology in the Schools, 5*, 3–18.

Roff, M., Sells, S.B., & Golden, M.M. (1972). *Social adjustment and personality adjustment in children*. Minneapolis, MN: University of Minnesota Press.

Serbin, L.A., Lyons, J.A., Marchessault, K., Schwartzman, A.E., & Ledingham, J.E. (1987). Observational validation of a peer nomination technique for identifying Aggressive, Withdrawn, and Aggressive/Withdrawn children. *Journal of Consulting and Clinical Psychology, 55*, 109–110.

Singleton, L.C., & Asher, S.R. (1977). Peer preferences and social interaction among third-grade children in an integrated school district. *Journal of Educational Psychology, 69,* 330–336.

Van Hasselt, V.B., Hersen, M., Whitehill, M.B., & Bellack, A.S. (1979). Social skills assessment and training for children. *Behavior Research and Therapy, 17,* 413–437.

Walsh-Allis, G.A., & Orvaschel, H. (1986). Multidimensional assessment of social adaptation in children and adolescents. In R.J. Prinz (Ed.), *Advances in behavioral assessment of children and families,* Vol. 2 (pp. 207–226). Greenwich, CT: JAI Press.

Watson, D., & Friend, R. (1969). Measurement of social-evaluative anxiety. *Journal of Consulting and Clinical Psychology, 33,* 448–457.

Weiss, G., & Hechtman, L.T. (1986). *Hyperactive children grown up: Empirical findings and theoretical considerations.* New York: Guilford.

West, D., & Farrington, D. (1973). *Who becomes delinquent?* London: Heinemann.

Whalen, C.K., Henker, B., & Dotemoto, S. (1981). Teacher response to the methylphenidate (Ritalin) versus placebo status of hyperactive boys in the classroom. *Child Development, 52,* 1005–1014.

CHAPTER 10

Issues in the Assessment of the Self-Concept of Children and Adolescents

SUSAN HARTER

INTRODUCTION

The 1980s have witnessed a resurgence of interest in the self. The self-concept has come to occupy a prominent role in numerous theories of human behavior. At a more applied level, practitioners have come to appreciate the fact that a positive self-image is central to the adaptive functioning and everyday happiness of the individual. A meaningful analysis and documentation of the significance of the self, however, requires a thoughtful approach to issues in assessment. The present chapter will explore those issues that are paramount in the assessment of child and adolescent self-concept.

The chapter will begin with an exhortation that we not put the methodological cart before the conceptual horse. Self-concept can assume many different definitions, and thus it is critical that one be clear about the particular framework one wishes to adopt. How one defines self-concept will in turn dictate the particular assessment strategy one adopts. Thus, one wants to begin with a particular *model* of self-concept, not a measure. Several models of self-concept will be reviewed in this chapter, indicating how each, in turn, dictates a particular measurement strategy. One theme in this regard involves the degree to which the self-concept is considered to be a global, unitary construct versus a more differentiated, multidimensional aggregate of self-evaluations.

Any sensitive analysis of the self-concept of children and adolescents must also take into account developmental changes in the structure and content of the self. Such differences result from cognitive-developmental changes as well as from shifts in the salient concerns associated with particular periods of development. Within this context, issues involving the nature of the self-concept in special populations will also be considered, since differences in the structure and content of the self among such groups will have implications for assessment.

A number of psychometric issues will also be discussed, including such topics as reliability, validity, the impact of socially desirable responding, and the use of self-concept instruments to compare children at different developmental levels, e.g., in either cross-sectional or longitudinal research. Implications for program evaluation will also be explored. In addition, issues involving both the *accuracy* and the *stability* of the self-concept will be addressed.

Finally, issues concerning the understanding and assessment of both the *determinants* and the *functional role* of the self-concept will be examined. One's interest in the self-concept presumably involves a concern with what factors are responsible for the range of positive to negative evaluative judgments that are observed in the assessment of the self-concept. Moreover, it behooves us to give thoughtful attention to the role that these self-evaluations play in affecting other areas of the individual's life. That is, does one's self-concept affect the day to day functioning of children or adolescents? If one's cognitive construction or reconstruction of the self has little functional value, then the flurry or activity in recent years may well be misguided. This issue is raised to highlight the fact that the zeal with which the self has been embraced in the past decade has not been matched by a thoughtful consideration of the precise role that the self may play. Therefore, it will be argued that our interest in self-evaluation should naturally extend to an assessment of the causes and the effects of the self-concept. In this section, we will also consider the extent to which children and adolescents are aware of these potential influences and links. These issues have important implications for our models of self-concept change, both at the theoretical level as well as at the level of clinical intervention.

MODELS OF SELF-CONCEPT

At the outset it is critical to appreciate the fact that the self-concept, like any psychological construct, can assume many different definitions. Which model one adopts will depend upon one's particular purpose or goal. However, the selection of a model or measure will seem distressingly arbitrary if one is not clear about one's own conceptual framework and the precise meaning one wishes to assign to the self. Clarity of purpose, therefore, is the major prerequisite for determining which model of self-concept will best meet one's needs. In this section we will review the essential features of several models, mentioning representative instruments. In the following section, we will review each measure in more detail.

Models of self-concept within the literature can be distinguished along a number of dimensions, the most important of which is whether the self is best viewed as a unidimensional construct or as self-evaluations that are more multidimensional in nature. Each of these models dictates a related measurement strategy. The prevailing models of the late 1960s were unidimensional in nature. Coopersmith's (1967) model best represents this tradition, although the Piers-Harris (1969) self-concept scale was originally based on a model in which the self was also considered to be unidimensional. These models are based on the assumption that the self-concept is a unitary construct best assessed by presenting the child subject with items tapping a range of context, e.g., the child's sense of self in school, with friends, and with family. Such a model dictates that one sums the child's responses across items tapping these different content areas, giving them equal weight. It is assumed that the single score resulting from such a combination will adequately reflect an individual's sense of self across the various areas of his/her life. The unidimensional nature of the self-concept has been challenged by recent theorists who have argued that such an approach masks important evaluative distinctions that children make about their adequacy in different domains of their lives. Proponents of this multidimensional perspective have put forth models and adopted measurement strategies that identify particular domains of self-evaluation, assessing each separately (see Mullener & Laird, 1971; Harter, 1985a, 1986; L'Ecuyer, 1981; Shavelson, Hubner, & Stanton, 1976; Marsh, 1984, 1987; Marsh, Barnes, Cairns, and Tidman, 1984).

Two of these approaches have resulted in instruments that have now met with considerable empirical support for an underlying multidimensional model. Harter's (1985b; 1986a) Self-Perception Profile for Children delineates five specific domains each of which define a separate subscale: scholastic competence, athletic competence, physical appearance, peer social acceptance, and behavioral conduct, Marsh's (Marsh, 1987; Marsh, Barnes, Cairns, & Tidman, 1984) Self-Description Questionnaire identifies seven separate domains: scholastic, math, reading, physical, peer, and parent dimensions of self-evaluations. For both these instruments, factor-analytic studies have revealed the existence of these separate components of the self-concept, justifying a multidimensional approach in which one examines a profile of scores across the designated domains.

An alternative approach to the self-concept can be found in the work of Rosenberg (1979) who has sought not to polarize the issue in the form of a unidimensional versus a multidimensional model of the self. He has argued that individuals possess a general sense of self-esteem or feelings of worth as a person, in addition to those evaluations of one's adequacy across the specific domains of one's life. However, with regard to assessment, Rosenberg has focused primarily on global self-esteem, namely the general regard that one holds for the self as a person.

It is critical to distinguish Rosenberg's model and measurement of self-esteem from Coopersmith's. Rosenberg is not suggesting that one's sense of global self-worth is a simple, additive combination of responses to discrete items on a measure such as Coopersmith's Self-Esteem Inventory. He has cogently argued that, in all likelihood, the various discrete elements of the self are weighted, hierarchized, and combined according to an extremely complex equation of which the individual is probably unaware. For this reason, he has chosen not to assess the specific bases underlying judgments of one's global self-esteem. Rather, he has opted to assess one's evaluation of self-esteem directly, based on his assumption that such a judgment is a phenomenological reality for adults as well as for adolescents. Thus, he has constructed a unidimensional measure that taps the degree to which one is satisfied with one's life, feels one has good qualities, has a positive attitude toward oneself, or, alternatively, feels useless, desires more self-respect, or thinks one is a failure. This measure, therefore, yields a single score representing the level of an individual's overall self-esteem and does not assess the specific dimensions that might underlie such a global judgment.

A fourth approach to the self-concept (Harter, 1985b; 1986) represents an integration of both the multidimensional and unidimensional themes, at the level of both model and measurement. The model underscores the importance of global judgments of esteem or self-worth, in addition to the evaluation of domain-specific competencies. Thus, global self-worth is assessed directly and independently by a set of items tapping one's overall judgment of worth as a person (similar to Rosenberg's conceptualization). These items inquire about the extent to which the individual likes oneself as a person, likes the way one is leading one's life, is happy with the way one is, etc. Separate subscales tapping domain-specific evaluations provide a multidimensional profile as well, e.g., scholastic competence, athletic competence, peer social acceptance, physical appearance, and behavioral conduct on the Self-Perception Profile for Children. (Across our various instruments, the particular domains included vary depending upon the particular developmental period assessed, e.g., middle to late childhood, adolescence, college age, and adulthood.)

By conceptually and empirically separating domain-specific judgments of competence or adequacy from the more global judgment of one's worth as a person, we are able to determine the relationship that specific competencies bear to global self-worth. That is, we have sought to specify the manner in which domains are weighted and combined to produce one's overall sense of self-worth. This larger model will be presented in a subsequent section of the chapter that deals specificially with self-worth. The point to be emphasized here, however, is that the self-concept can be conceptualized along a continuum of very specific to very global judgments about the self and that these approaches are not necessarily mutually exclusive.

MEASURES OF SELF-CONCEPT

In this section we review the particular features and psychometric properties of five self-concept measures: (a) The Coopersmith Self-Esteem Inventory (Coopersmith, 1967); (b) the Piers-Harris Children's Self-Concept Scale (Piers & Harris, 1969; Piers, 1984); (c) Rosenberg's Self-Esteem Scale (Rosenberg, 1979); (d) Harter's Self-Perception Profile for Children (Harter, 1985b); (e) Marsh's Self-Description Questionnaire (Marsh, in press). All are paper-and-pencil self-report questionnaires that tap individual evaluative attitudes that respondents are able and willing to reveal.

The Coopersmith Self-Esteem Inventory. This inventory, appropriate for children ages 8 through 15, is a 58-item questionnaire, tapping content from four areas of the child's life: school-academic, social-peers, home-parents, and general self. The original item pool was drawn from an adult scale (see Rogers & Dymond, 1954) and items were adapted for children. Items are worded as short statements, e.g., "I do well at my classwork," "I am easy to like," "I get along with my parents," "I often feel ashamed of myself," and the respondent is provided with a two-choice response format in which he/she answers either "Like me" or "Unlike me." Typically, a total score is calculated across all items, and this total score, ranging from a high of 58, if all items are answered in a positive direction, to zero, if all are answered negatively, is considered to reflect the child's overall self-esteem. Internal consistency reliabilities range from .87 to .92 for grades four to eight (Coopersmith, 1967). Adequate validity data are reported by Coopersmith (1967) as well as by Kokenes (1974; 1978). Test-retest correlations over a six-week period for grades four to seven range from .73 to .85 (Chiu, 1988). Over a three-year interval, for ages 9 to 12, they range from .42 to .64 (Coopersmith, 1967).

Initially, it was suggested by Coopersmith that separate scores for the four subscales could be calculated. However, the evidence (Coopersmith, 1967; Harter, 1983; Kokenes, 1974) reveals that such subscale scores are not sufficiently reliable, nor do they emerge as discrete factors when factor-analyzed. Unfortunately, Coopersmith concluded, therefore, that children in this age range do not make distinctions among these domains. However, it now appears that inadequacies in the construction of this instrument have led to this erroneous conclusion since recent, more carefully constructed measures clearly reveal that children of this age make clear distinctions among such domains. Thus, the Coopersmith Inventory total score will provide a general estimate of self-esteem that may be fruitfully used as a first screening assessment, but will not provide a meaningful profile of domain-specific self-evaluations. This instrument also correlates moderately with the Lie scale embedded in the measure as well as with independent assessments of social desirability indices (see Harter, 1983; Robinson & Shaver, 1973), suggesting that it is tapping some combination of a child's actual as well as idealized self-image. (For other limitations, see Wylie, 1979.)

The Piers-Harris Children's Self-Concept Scale. The Piers-Harris instrument, appropriate for children grades 4 to 12, is an 80-item instrument constructed under the assumption that the self-concept was relatively unidimensional. Items were adapted from a pool of statements collected by Jersild (1952) who asked children to comment on features about themselves that they liked and didn't like. Items are worded as first-person declarative statements, e.g., "I can be trusted," "I worry a lot," "I do well at schoolwork," and the student can respond with either "yes" or "no." Although the scale was originally conceived of as unidimensional, item content taps six domains: behavior, intellectual and school status, physical appearance, anxiety, popularity, and happiness/satisfaction. A total score, from 80 to 0, can be calculated.

Internal consistency reliabilities for the total score range from .89 to .93. Test-retest correlations range from .42 to .90 over intervals of one year to a few weeks. Convergent validity in the form of correlations with other self-concept measures range from .32 to .85.

There is some evidence for the factorial validity of the six clusters of items identified, although only three factors—behavior, intellectual status, and physical appearance—consistently emerge. The remaining three subscales appear to be much weaker factors; moreover, cross-loading suggest that most of the factors are entirely pure. Nevertheless, this instrument does suggest the value of more multidimensional approaches and generally receives higher marks from reviews than the Coopersmith Inventory as a psychometrically sound instrument providing an assessment of children's self-esteem (see Buros, 1970; Hughes, 1984; Robinson & Shaver, 1973; Wylie, 1974).

Rosenberg's Self-Esteem Scale. Rosenberg's intent has been to directly tap one's phenomenological experience of global self-esteem (rather than inferring it from an aggregate of items tapping heterogeneous content as in the Coopersmith and Piers-Harris measures). Thus, the measure is truly unidimensional given that items ask about the one dimension of self-esteem. It was initially intended for use with adolescents, although it has been used with children as well as adults. Items consist of 10 first-person statements, e.g., "I have a number of good qualities," "I am satisfied with my life," "I certainly feel useless at times." "I think I am a failure," that are responded to on a four-point scale ranging from "Strongly agree" to "Strongly disagree." Item scores are summed to produce a total score.

Internal consistency is high (rs in the high .80s and .90s), and test-retest correlations over several week periods are in the .80s. With regard to validity, Rosenberg has devoted primary attention to construct and predictive validity, demonstrating that self-esteem correlated well with other psychological and clinically relevant constructs such as depression. Rosenberg has also documented predicted effects for ethnicity and social class on self-esteem. Others (see Chiu, 1988) have demonstrated the convergent validity of this instrument. The scale is particularly recommended for those who wish a brief, but psychometrically sound, index of self-esteem, tapped directly (see Wylie, 1974).

Harter's Self-Perception Profile for Children. This multidimensional instrument was constructed to tap the dimensions of the author's theoretical model of self-concept that postulates both domain-specific evaluations as well as an overall judgment of one's self-worth (Harter, 1985b). Designed for children ages 8 to 15, it taps five specific domains: scholastic competence, athletic competence, social acceptance, physical appearance, and behavioral conduct, in addition to global self-worth. The 36 items, six for each subscale, are constructed according to a structured alternative format designed to offset children's tendency to give socially desirable responses. Children are presented with an item such as "Some kids are popular with others their age BUT Other kids are not very popular." Respondents must first decide which of the two statements are most like the self and then, for that statement, rate whether it is *really true* or just *sort of true* for the self. Each item is scored along a four-point scale, and these scores are averaged within each subscale to provide a profile of six subscale scores, each ranging from a mean of four to one.

Internal consistency reliabilities range from .80 to .90 across a large number of samples of children from third to eighth grades. Test-retest correlations range from .40 to .65, across the various subscales, over from one-month to one-year intervals. A major assumption of this instrument is that the specific domains demonstrate factorial validity. Across numerous samples, it has been demonstrated that the factor structure is very clean, with high factor loadings (.45 to .75) and virtually no cross-loadings. Predictive, convergent, discriminant, and construct validity (Harter, 1982, 1986) provide strong evidence in support of the structure underlying the model of self-concept. This instrument has been found to be useful in testing predictions derived from theory, in program evaluation, and for individual clinical and diagnostic purposes.

The version described above is appropriate for children ages eight and above. There are separate versions for younger children (The Scale of Perceived Competence and Social Acceptance for Young Children, Harter & Pike, 1984), for adolescents (The Self-Perception Profile for Adolescents, Harter, 1988c). (Less relevant to the purposes of this chapter are versions for both college students and for adults in the world of work and family.)

Marsh's Self-Descriptive Questionnaire. This instrument is the most recent multidimensional self-concept measure, designed for children ages 6 to 11 (Marsh, in press; Marsh, Barnes, Cairns, & Tidman, 1984). It is derived from Shavelson's model of the self-concept that postulates theoretically derived components (Shavelson, Hubner, & Stanton, 1976). On an a priori basis, eight subscales were identified: physical abilities, physical appearance, relationship with peers, relationship with parents, reading, math, all school subjects, and general self-concept. Respondents rate eight items per subscale on a five-point scale from "Mostly false" to "Mostly true." The majority of items are worded positively, e.g., "I make friends easily," "My parents like me." Twelve of the items are worded negatively, e.g., "I do not like mathematics." Since these negatively worded items have been found to attenuate reliability, particularly at the younger ages, they are not included in the scoring. Internal consistency reliabilities without these negative items are adequate (typically between .80 and .90 across the various subscales) although somewhat lower for second- and third-graders.

Factor analyses of the first seven subscales (see Marsh, Barnes, Cairns, & Tidman, 1984) reveal that each define their own factor with negligible cross loadings. Findings also provide evidence for the construct validity of this instrument. Evidence for the hierarchical nature of the self-concept, including the construct of general self-concept at the apex of the hierarchy in this model, is less conclusive. Nevertheless, findings on this instrument confirm recent approaches that emphasize the need for a multidimensional look at the self-concept. Moreover, this instrument contains distinctions, e.g., math versus verbal self-concept, that are not represented in other measures.

On the Choice of Molar Versus Molecular Levels of Measurement

Often those in search of self-concept instruments ask: Which instrument is best? A careful consideration of the issues will lead one to conclude that this is not the most appropriate form of the question. Rather, one needs to ask: Which instrument is best given one's specific interests and purposes? What level of the self-concept is most appropriate to one's particular concerns? The answer to this question will transcend the context of the inquiry, for example, whether one is primarily interested in theory-building, the demonstration of empirical relationships, clinical diagnosis, educational assessment, program evaluation, etc.

Consider the following examples. If one is interested in evaluating the effect of a new math curriculum on student's self-concept, one may well opt for a more molecular measure such as the math self-concept subscale on the Self-Description Questionnaire (Marsh, in press; Marsh, Tidman, Cairns, & Barnes, 1984), since presumably this facet of the self-concept would be most directly affected. If one's purpose is to document the relationship between a child's intrinsic motivation for schoolwork and his or her overall feelings of scholastic competence, assessment would more reasonably proceed at the level of the Scholastic Competence subscale of the Self-Perception Profile for Children (Harter, 1985a).

Toward other goals or ends, a more global index may be desirable. For example, if one was intrigued by the notion that positive regard from significant others influences the overall positive regard that one has for the self, then either the Rosenberg Self-Esteem Scale (1965) or the self-worth subscale from the Self-Perception Profile for Children

(Harter, 1985b) or the Self-Perception Profile for Adolescents (Harter, 1988c) would be the most appropriate. These instruments may also be useful if one wishes to examine the contention that overall self-esteem has an impact on children's or adolescent's mood state or general level of motivation, for example (see Harter, 1986).

There may also be certain circumstances in which, for general screening purposes, one wishes to obtain an initial index of a child's self-concept summed across domains, to be followed by further testing or interview procedures. The Self-Esteem Inventory (Coopersmith, 1967) or the Piers-Harris (1969) Self-Concept Scale may be useful in this regard. Many more examples could be given. The underlying dictum, however, is that the particular research and evaluation questions of interest dictate the choice of instruments and the level of measurement. The selection of an assessment device does not come first.

The Desirability of Predicting a Pattern of Scores

Another consideration in selecting the level of measurement involves the greater power in predicting a pattern across several scores, rather than an outcome based on a single score. Consider the example in which one wishes to evaluate the effectiveness of a remedial math program on children's math self-concept. As noted earlier, one would ideally select a measure specific to math self-concept. However, one may want to include other subscales, predicting that math self-concept should change as a result of the intervention, whereas other dimensions of the self-concept, for example self-concept in the area of reading, or one's perceived physical appearance, would not be expected to change. To the extent that one can predict a differentiated pattern of scores, one is in a better position to draw conclusions about the impact of a particular intervention.

In other cases, one may predict that an intervention in one domain would have an effect on another dimension of the self-concept. For example, if one's conceptual framework included the assumption that physical appearance was a critical dimension on which one's feelings of global self-worth were based, one would predict that an intervention specifically designed to enhance one's perceived appearance should impact not only this domain-specific subscale but one's global sense of self-worth, as well. To the extent, then, that one can specify an a priori network of relationships involving a pattern of predictions across the dimensions tapped by different subscales, one will be more likely to enhance one's understanding of the self-concept.

DEVELOPMENTAL DIFFERENCES IN THE STRUCTURE AND CONTENT OF THE SELF-CONCEPT

A meaningful approach to the assessment of the self-concept in children and adolescents must necessarily be sensitive to developmental changes in the very nature of how the self is constructed see Damon & Hart, 1982; Harter, 1983, 1986; in press c; Montemayor & Eisen, 1977; Rosenberg, 1986). These differences can be characterized along two major dimensions, the structure as well as the content of the self-concept (also see Chapter 2 for a discussion of developmental aspects of the self-system). The structural dimension primarily speaks to underlying cognitive-developmental changes that affect the self-concept as a cognitive construction. A central theme in the developmental literature involves the extent to which psychological systems undergo ontogenetic change that can be conceptualized in terms of the processes of differentiation and integration. The self-concept can be considered within such a structural framework. Both theory and research have revealed that with development, an increasing number of self-concept domains can be articulated as well as differentiated. (In a subsequent section we will return to the issue of how they are integrated into an overall judgment of self-worth.)

In our own development of the Pictorial Scale of Perceived Competence and Social Acceptance for Young Children (Harter & Pike, 1984), for example, we have demonstrated that four- to seven-year-olds can make reliable judgments about the following four domains: their cognitive competence, physical competence, social acceptance, and behavioral conduct, if they are pictorially depicted as concrete, observable behaviors. Thus, these four self-evaluative dimensions are meaningful to young children in that they can articulate their evaluations about the self. Interestingly, however, judgments across these four domains are not yet clearly *differentiated*. Factor analyses reveal that the cognitive and physical items combine into one competence factor, suggesting that young children do not make a clear distinction between their cognitive and their physical skills. Moreover, social acceptance and behavioral conduct items also combine into a second factor, suggesting that these dimensions are not yet differentiated.

Another structural limitation is evidenced by the fact that young children are incapable of making judgments about their self-worth. Here it needs to be clear that we are making reference to the conscious, verbalizable concept of one's worth as a person. This cognitive construction, as tapped by those items designed to assess self-worth (e.g., liking oneself as a person), is not available to the young child. Our findings reveal that it is not until middle childhood that one can make meaningful and reliable judgments about this global construct, a finding that is consistent with the developmental literature on children's ability to form concepts.

This does not mean, however, that young children do not possess a sense of self-worth or self-esteem. We have been misunderstood on this point, in part because in previous writings we have not been sufficiently clear. It is our conviction, bolstered by recent empirical work (Halti-wanger & Harter, 1988), and young children "exude" a sense of overall self-esteem as manifest in certain behaviors within their repertoire. (See Harter, in press a, for a description of the particular behaviors that have been identified as manifestations of "presented self-worth".) The point to be made here is that young children do not have a verbalizable concept of their self-worth, as tapped by self-report measures. It represents a cognitive limitation of young children, just as does their inability to differentiate many discrete domains of the self-concept, structural features that have implications for assessment.

During middle childhood, the structure of the self-concept changes in that not only are more domains differentiated, but the ability to make meaningful and reliable judgments about one's self-worth emerges. Factoring procedures applied to our Self-Perception Profile for Children (Harter, 1985b) reveal that children between the ages of eight and 12 clearly differentiate the five specific domains now included on this instrument: scholastic competence, athletic competence, peer social acceptance, behavioral conduct, and physical appearance. On the Self-Description Questionnaire (Marsh, in press; Marsh, Barnes, Cairns, & Tidman, 1984), it has now been demonstrated that the following domains can be differentiated, as revealed through factor-analytic procedures: academic self-concept, math self-concept, reading self-concept, peer relations, physical skills, physical appearance, and self-concept in relation to the family.

During adolescence, there is further articulation and differentiation. Our instrument, the Self-Perception Profile for Adolescents (Harter, 1988c), includes not only the five domains represented on the children's instrument just described, but three additional domains: close friendship, romantic appeal, and job competence. All eight of these subscales define separate factors for adolescents. Of particular interest is the finding that although close friendship items are comprehended by children (ages 8 to 12), they are not differentiated from more general peer acceptance items, suggesting that the distinction between popularity and close friendship does not emerge until early adolescence.

The distinctions that emerge at adolescence not only reflect developmental advances in underlying cognitive structures, but shifts that reflect the salient concerns of this new period, namely content differences. Certain developmental theories of the self have postulated such shifts. For example, the model proposed by Damon and Hart (1982) suggests that there are broad developmental shifts in the salience of particular dimensions, e.g., from a focus on one's physical and active self to one's social and psychological self. The emergence of the importance of the domains of close friendship and romantic appeal attest to the increasing salience of more differentiated dimensions of the social self, although it should be noted that the other dimensions do not lessen in importance. Our own findings suggest that the articulation of a greater number of dimensions that define the self represents an acquisition sequence in which new dimensions emerge, rather than an acquisition-deletion sequence in which earlier dimensions are eliminated or become less salient. (It should be noted that from a life-span developmental perspective, there is a further proliferation of domains during both the college years and the subsequent period of adulthood, although a discussion of these changes is beyond the scope of this chapter. The interested reader is referred to Harter, in press c.)

Implications for Assessment

Changes in both the structure and content of the self-concept have obvious implications for assessment. Specifically, they dictate that the instruments designed to tap the dimensions of the self-concept must necessarily change as a function of developmental level. In our own work, for example, we have now constructed three separate measures to assess the self-concept at different developmental periods between the ages of four and 18. The Pictorial Scale of Perceived Competence and Social Acceptance for Young Children covers the periods from four through seven, although two separate versions, one for preschool and kindergarten children and one for first- and second-graders, are needed to reflect content differences and skill acquisitions within this age span (see Harter & Pike, 1984).

For middle to late childhood, the Self-Perception Profile for Children (Harter, 1985b) is appropriate, although it should be noted that this instrument not only reflects changes in structure and content, but changes in item format. This instrument utilizes a questionnaire format, whereas the instrument for younger children necessitates a pictorial format in which children identify the picture that is most similar to the self.

The Self-Perception Profile for Adolescents (Harter, 1988c) follows the same questionnaire format as the Self-Perception Profile for Children, although three additional domains are included, as described above. In addition, the wording of the five comparable subscales changes somewhat, to reflect developmental changes in the level of verbal descriptions appropriate to the two age periods. In general, changes across this overall age span (4 to 18) are consistent with the findings revealing that the language of self-description shows a gradual shift from concrete, observable behaviors to more trait-like generalizations about the self (see Harter, 1983; in press a; Rosenberg, 1986).

While changes in the structure, content, and question format of self-concept measures that are sensitive to developmental level may be viewed as desirable in order to capture qualitative differences in self-concept formation, they also pose certain problems. Paradoxically, such sensitivity to developmental level makes it difficult to examine developmental changes in the self-concept at the individual level, where either longitudinal or cross-sectional designs are employed. If one is interested in longitudinal self-concept change among individuals who grow older and, as a result, cross over into the period necessitating a different version of an instrument, one may have difficulty determining whether any change in scores reflects true self-concept change or differences based on the fact that the instrument changed. This problem is particularly troublesome when one is interested in assessing the self-concept among young children, using our pictorial instrument, and then following them into middle childhood during which period the questionnaire version becomes appropriate. Despite the attempt to retain the conceptual similarity of certain domains, and to utilize a four-point scale for both instruments, changes in the structure, content, and question format make it difficult to assess whether differences obtained across the two instruments represent changes due to the instrument or real changes in the child's self-evaluations.

Such problems are not restricted to longitudinal studies, but may occur in cross-sectional research, as well. For example, if one is interested in certain *correlates* of the self-concept at different developmental periods, namely whether they bear the same relationship at different ages, any interpretation of the pattern of scores may be confounded by changes in the very nature of the instrument. These problems are not unique to the assessment of self-concept but reflect a general measurement issue when one attempts to assess the same construct across different developmental levels. In our own research on the self-concept we have tried to deal with this problem by designing instruments that are as similar as reasonably possible across adjacent age periods, but that are also responsive to major developmental changes. Nevertheless, there are obvious trade-offs that the users of such instruments must be sensitive to, particularly if one is examining the self-concept at different developmental levels.

THE ASSESSMENT OF SELF-CONCEPT IN SPECIAL POPULATIONS

A similar set of issues can be raised with regard to the assessment of the self-concept among special populations of children and adolescents. In recent years there has been increasing attention devoted to the assessment of the self-concept of children with a variety of intellectual, emotional, behavioral, and physical deficits. Typically, there is a concern with the *level* of the child's self-concept, given the implicit assumption that children with deficits should report more negative self-evaluations. The findings, however, do not unequivocally support this assumption. Yet there is a more basic issue to be considered before one is in a position to interpret self-concept or self-esteem scores in special populations, namely whether such scores are even meaningful or reliable (see Chapter 3 for a further discussion of these issues). Our own work with certain groups, e.g., mentally retarded as well as learning disabled children, suggests considerable caution in this regard. These studies reveal that the very structure of self-concept is different among these groups, for reasons having to do with either cognitive-developmental level or the unique environment that such children experience.

Cognitive-developmental level would appear to play the major role in influencing the structure of the self-concept among mentally retarded children. Our findings with educable, mentally retarded children, ages 9 to 12, with IQs between 50 and 75, have revealed that the factor structure of our own self-concept instrument is different from that of normal IQ children (Silon & Harter, 1985). In this study, we administered an earlier version of our instrument, one that contained only four subscales, scholastic competence, athletic competence, peer social acceptance, and global self-worth. Our previous normative work had consistently revealed a clear four-factor solution among normal IQ children (Harter, 1982).

However, among our sample of mentally retarded children, an interpretable two-factor solution was obtained. The peer acceptance subscale defined its own factor. However, the scholastic and athletic competence subscale items did not define separate factors but combined to form one factor. These findings suggest that retarded children at this mental age level (approximately four to seven) do not discriminate between different types of competencies, just as younger normal IQ children at these mental age levels do not differentiate these two domains, as revealed on our pictorial scale described earlier. Interestingly, the global self-worth factor did not emerge as a separate factor, nor did it represent a reliable composite that could be meaningfully interpreted. Here again, consistent with our findings with young normal children, it would appear that at these mental ages, the concept of one's worth as a person has not yet been cognitively constructed in a manner that is accessible through self-report assessment procedures. Thus, our self-concept scale in its original form is inappropriate for use with mentally retarded populations in this mental age range.

A quite different picture emerges with learning disabled children, defined in our samples as students within the normal range of intelligence who have specific deficits in the area of information processing, reading, writing, and the manipulation of symbols (Renick, 1985; Renick, 1988). Not only is scholastic competence clearly differentiated from athletic competence, as well as from social acceptance, appearance, and behavioral conduct (on our most recent version), but the learning disabled child makes further distinctions within the scholastic domain. Most interesting is the differentiation of descriptions of general intellectual ability, e.g., being smart or bright, from those more specific skills involved in particular school subjects, e.g., doing well at reading, writing, spelling, and math. Our initial discovery of this pattern led to the construction of a version specifically designed for learning disabled children (see Renick, 1988; Renick & Harter, 1988). In addition to a general intellectual ability subscale, separate subscales were constructed for each of the four academic school subjects listed above. Our most recent findings reveal that among elementary school age learning disabled children, general intellectual ability forms a separate factor from these school subjects, each of which, in turn, define their specific own factor.

The most appropriate interpretation for these findings seems to hinge on certain experiences that learning disabled children encounter within both the educational and home environment. Typically, teachers and parents emphasize the fact that these children do not lack intellectual ability, per se, but have difficulty with specific skills that involve the manipulation of symbols, in particular. It would appear that this distinction is being communicated directly to learning disabled children, a message that in turn fosters a more differentiated self-concept within the intellectual/scholastic domain. Interestingly, not only is the learning disabled child's concept of general intellectual ability differentiated from competence at more specific school subjects, but the level of the former score is often higher. Thus, such a distinction may serve to provide a mechanism whereby the learning disabled child can protect his/her self-image, a strategy that is apparently reinforced by benevolent adults within the child's environment.

Another contrast between the self-concept structure of the mentally retarded and the learning disabled involves their response to the self-worth items. Unlike the mentally retarded, learning disabled have a concept of their worth as a person that can be reliably assessed. Of further interest is the finding that global self-worth bears a larger relationship to general intellectual ability than to specific competencies at school subjects. Moreover, this relationship is more substantial among learning disabled children compared to our normal samples, suggesting that one's self-worth is more intimately linked to one's intellectual capabilities among the learning disabled. Given their history of educational identification and placement, it is not surprising that the domain of intellectual ability should be particularly salient for these students, impacting, in turn their overall level of self-worth.

From the standpoint of assessment, these findings alert us to the possibility that the structure of the self-concept may be different among special populations. There is certainly cause for psychometric concern in this regard, since measures standardized for use with normal populations may not be appropriate. Yet the implications are more promising if one strives to reveal the underlying structure of the self-concept of special groups, recrafting instruments to meaningfully assess the manner in which their self-evaluations are organized. The potential disadvantage of such an approach, however, is that there will be a proliferation of population-specific instruments, so unique that one cannot make meaningful comparisons across groups. Here there are parallels to the problem of assessing self-concept at different developmental levels, to the extent that the measure must be altered to preserve the integrity of the self-concept for a given group or level. The optimal strategy, therefore, would be one in which instruments are kept as similar as possible, for purposes of comparison, but also include modifications where necessary, e.g., the deletion or addition of subscales, in order to most meaningfully tap the structure of the self-concept for a given population.

ON THE RELATIONSHIP BETWEEN PSYCHOMETRIC AND SUBSTANTIVE ISSUES

The typical treatment of issues in assessment, especially when wedded to the use of particular instruments, includes relatively isolated discussions of such psychometric concerns as reliability and validity. Yet these topics cannot be treated that discretely, since they are intimately related to issues of more substantive interest. Nor can psychometric and substantive issues be confused. For example, in the preceding section, it was pointed out that anomalies in the factor structure of an instrument or the internal consistency of a given subscale may provide clues to the underlying structure of the self-concept, rather than merely indicting the instrument on psychometric grounds. Test-retest reliability as well as the validity of self-report measures, can be viewed through a similar lens, since test-retest reliability is often confused with the issue of the *stability* of the self-concept, and validity is typically confounded with the issue of the *accuracy* of self-evaluations (also, see chapter 3 for further discussion of these issues).

Test-Retest Reliability Versus the Stability of the Construct

In considering whether test-retest reliability is an appropriate criterion for judging a given instrument, one must first thoughtfully ascertain whether the construct itself is expected to change over time. How stable, for example, should we expect the self-concept to be over time? If we have reason to believe that the self-concept is subject to legitimate and meaningful change, then test-retest reliability is inappropriate as an index of the merit of the instrument. Under these circumstances, one may well wish to examine change, however it becomes an issue of the stability of the construct and not a cause for psychometric concern. If, on the other hand, one considers the self-concept to be stable, then test-retest reliability can be justified.

Unfortunately two trends in the literature may have served to obscure these points and to lead to the erroneous conclusion that the self-concept is more stable than recent findings now indicate. The first trend involved conclusions based on the use of self-concept instruments such as the Coopersmith Self-Esteem Inventory. The second trend involves an overemphasis on the trait-like nature of the self-concept, beginning in middle childhood, due to a failure to distinguish between several meanings of the term trait.

In his seminal work on self-esteem in older children, Coopersmith (1967) administered his Self-Esteem Inventory at several time periods, discovering that the total score that resulted from this instrument did not undergo major change. Recall, however, that this overall score represents the sum of responses to items tapping the self-concept in a number of different domains, e.g., school, peers, and family. Thus, if the self-concept in one domain increased over time, whereas self-judgments in a different domain decreased over this same time period, such changes would be masked through the procedure of calculating a total score. Such a procedure, therefore, would lead to the erroneous conclusion that the self-concept is stable, when in fact there may have been considerable change at the level of the components of the self that were combined to produce a global score. Instruments based on a model of aggregating responses across diverse domains are, therefore, insensitive to self-concept change at the level of domain-specific self-evaluations. More recent findings (e.g., Harter, 1988d, in press a) reveal that on domain-specific measures, considerable change over time can be documented, even within a period of days or weeks. In fact, during development, self-concept change appears to be more the rule than the exception (see also, Harter, 1983; Rosenberg, 1986).

Such an assertion may appear to fly in the face of literature suggesting that as one moves into middle childhood and beyond, there is a shift to self-descriptions in the form of *trait* labels. To clarify this apparent paradox, it is critical to distinguish between several uses of the term "trait." A trait can refer to a higher-order conceptualization about the self, or it can refer to consistency over situations or time. From a cognitive-developmental perspective, the shift to self-description in the form of "trait labels" represents a *conceptual* advance in that the older child becomes capable of organizing his/her observable, behavioral attributes into higher-order generalizations about the self. For example, one's prowess at soccer, tennis, and gymnastics can be combined into the concept that one is athletic, as a trait. Similarly, one's mastery of a number of school subjects, e.g., science, social studies, language arts, may lead the child to conclude that he/she is smart. In the realm of one's peer relationships, the perceived ability to listen, to offer assistance, and to share one's possessions may lead one to see the self as friendly, a social trait.

However, the ability to conceptualize the self in terms of such trait labels does not necessarily imply that these attributes are consistent or stable across situations or time. As noted above, we need to distinguish between the cognitive-developmentalist's use of the term trait as a higher-order generalization about the self and the personality theorist's use of the term trait to connote stability or consistency. The ability to cognitively construct trait labels does not imply that such evaluations are stable self-attributes. The need for this distinction becomes apparent when we consider the fact that older children, adolescents, and adults can consider themselves to be smart, athletic, popular, etc. in some contexts or periods of time, but not others. Given that one's self-concept, so defined, changes in this manner, test-retest paradigms should be directed toward an examination of those factors producing self-concept change as a substantive (rather than a psychometric) issue. It is inappropriate, under these conditions, to interpret test-retest findings as demonstrations of the reliability or unreliability of the instrument.

Given the focus on assessment issues, a discussion of those factors producing self-concept change is beyond the scope of this volume. However, there are two general thrusts in the literature, one emphasizing environmental factors that influence self-concept change, and one emphasizing cognitive-developmental shifts that produce changes in the nature and level of self-evaluations. In our own work (see Harter, 1988a, 1988d) we have metaphorically referred to cognitive-developmental as well as environmental factors that lead to "lack of conservation of self." Rosenberg (1986) has employed a similar metaphor in his analysis of the "barometric self-concept" of the adolescent. These recent trends make it clear than any comprehensive model of the self must give thoughtful attention not only to the determinants of one's pattern of self-evaluations but to their potential for change.

Considerations in the Assessment of Self-Concept Change

Often the researcher, educator, or clinician interested in the self-concept will have, as a specific goal, the assessment of change over time. Toward this end, the following suggestions may be useful:

(a) Select an instrument that *specifically* taps the *dimensions* of interest. Often, investigators do not select measures that are sensitive to the dimensions that have piqued their interest. For example, investigators often express their desire to assess self-concept in children. However, upon further reflection, it becomes evident that they are actually interested in such constructs as creativity, ego strength, fine-motor competence, social skills, resiliency, nurturance, discipline, etc., that may bear a *relationship* to self-concept but are not its defining features. It is critical, therefore, that one be as precise as possible about the particular construct under scrutiny, in order to be able to select an instrument that specifically taps that construct. Failure to be clear about one's formulation will inevitably lead to the choice of instruments that will be insensitive to potential hypotheses that may well have considerable merit.

(b) Attempt to specify a *pattern* of predictions. The investigator interested in potential self-concept change will gain increasing predictive power to the extent that he/she can anticipate what facets of the self-concept not only should change, but should be unaffected by a particular manipulation or treatment. As noted in an earlier section, this frame of reference leads to the inclusion of measures that will be expected to be influenced, as well as measures that should yield no change over time. To the extent that the predicted pattern is documented, one has greater confidence in the specific links between a given intervention and its outcome.

(c) Include measures of the *processes* thought to be responsible for self-concept change. Too often, pre-post designs focus exclusively on the potential product of a given intervention and do not directly assess those processes thought to be responsible for self-concept change. Thus, there is no way of knowing whether the postulated reasons for such change are in fact the actual factors that produced the differences observed. One cannot simply infer that one's hypotheses have been supported. Positive self-image changes as a result of a remedial educational program, for example, may have as much to do with the individualized attention given to the student as with the particular academic content that has been selected. In therapy, to take another example, the regard that the therapist communicates by thoughtfully listening to the client may be just as critical to self-concept change as the more direct suggestions that the therapist may make about changing certain behaviors or attitudes. Thus, it becomes critical at the outset to attempt to identify the mechanisms thought to be responsible for self-concept change in order to include measures that will tap these processes, as well as the potential outcome.

(d) Clarify your expectations about the *directionality* of change. Often the investigator interested in self-concept change begins with an implicit, benevolent hope that all subjects will manifest gains, defined as enhanced self-concept. In fact, much of the self-concept intervention research of the 1960s was based on such a vision that reflected the general Camelot-like optimism that pervaded this period of history. The notion that a very positive self-image might be unrealistic was far from the forefront of our thinking. From a mental health perspective, however, a more worthy goal may be the establishment of a relatively realistic self-concept. One's expectations in this regard have implications for one's measurement strategy and anticipated outcome. For example, an orientation designed to instill realistic self-judgments would lead to the expectation that subjects with an inflated sense of self might report less positive judgments at the end of a given intervention. If one adopted such a framework, one would not employ a single group design with the expectation that all scores would show gains. Rather, one would want to identify subgroups of subjects at the outset, where the goal would be increases in self-concept for some, as well as lowered scores for others, as a function of the intervention.

Another implication here is that one may be less interested in the actual level of the self-concept score, in favor of a score that tapped the *discrepancy* between perceived competence, for example, and actual competence assessed independently. A focus on the establishment of a realistic self-concept, therefore, would lead to the expectation that, in a pre-post design, such a discrepancy score would be reduced as a result of the particular treatment. Thus, clarity about the anticipated directionality of change scores will allow one to more meaningfully interpret the pattern of findings.

(e) Single group versus subgroup designs. The preceding discussion implied that in certain cases one may wish to examine self-concept change within particular subgroups of interest. Three different strategies may be suggested in this regard. One possibility is to identify subgroups of subjects on an a priori basis given their particular psychological characteristics, for example, children who tend to overestimate versus underestimate their self-concept, to pursue the previous discussion. There may well be other psychological dimensions of interest on which subjects are selected, dimensions independent of self-concept itself. One may, for example, be interested in academic self-concept change among children who are identified as intrinsically versus extrinsically motivated. Alternatively, subjects may be identified based on group membership, e.g., mainstreamed versus nonmainstreamed learning disabled children. One is then in a position to advance hypotheses about how an intervention may differentially affect the groups selected.

Often one may not have a clear pattern of a priori predictions, although there may be the general expectation that not all subjects will show equal gains. For example, self-concept change may partly be a product of where one started initially. Thus, a second strategy would be to identify subgroups based upon intial self-concept scores, e.g., high, medium, and low. One possible pattern is that subjects at the pretest with relatively high scores cannot realistically be expected to show gains since there is little room for improvement. Subjects with extremely low scores may not be expected to show gains, since often psychological factors contributing to such a pattern initially may mitigate against their responsiveness to intervention. For example, it may be very difficult to increase the academic self-concept of a child's whose educational history has repeatedly conveyed the message that he/she is intellectually inadequate. An intervention designed to improve the perceived behavioral conduct of delinquent adolescents may have little impact on those who have a stake in maintaining their images as troublemakers if it provides them with peer acceptance or other forms of secondary gain. It may well be, therefore, that the investigator would anticipate that subjects whose scores fall within some midrange, initially upon pretest, will have the greatest potential for self-concept gain.

A third strategy may involve the identification, upon *post-test*, of those subjects who actually did manifest increases, decreases, or no change in self-concept. One may then be in a position to determine what might have been different about these subjects initially, factors causing certain subjects to be more or less receptive to change in a particular direction. Such a strategy would be more appropriate in the exploratory phases of a project when one was not yet in a position to make explicit hypotheses about conditions under which self-concept change might be expected to occur. Thus, findings based upon such a strategy could be employed to design more prospective studies in which factors expected to influence self-concept change could then be selected or manipulated.

(f) Statistical considerations such as *regression to the mean*. The strategies suggested above represent various logical alternatives to understanding differential patterns of self-concept change. However, there are statistical considerations of which one must also be aware, for example, regression to the mean, or the use of difference scores, to name but two common concerns. Detailed discussions of these issues can be found in most textbooks on statistical issues in assessment and should be consulted accordingly. Regression to the mean is particularly problematic given the suggestion above that self-concept change be examined as a function of whether one's pretest scores were high, medium, or low, as one possible subgroup strategy. Statistically, it would be anticipated that those with high scores at the pretest should manifest decreases upon a second testing, whereas those with low scores initially should show gains. To the extent that a different pattern was evidenced, based on an alternative set of a priori hypotheses, one would be in a much stronger position to interpret data supporting that pattern.

In our own work, where we have been concerned about regression to the mean effects in examining scholastic self-concept change as a function of the transition from elementary to junior high school, we have employed one statistical procedure that attempts to control for such effects. Our design is one in which we have sought to identify three subgroups of students, those whose perceptions of scholastic competence (a) increase, (b) decrease, or (c) remain the same across this transition. We first determine the correlation between perceived scholastic scores at the two time periods, sixth-grade elementary school and seventh-grade junior high school. We then calculate what level of perceived competence would be predicted for each individual student in the seventh grade, based on the regression line established for the group as a whole. Increasers are defined as those students whose scores increased (more than the standard error of measurement) above the predicted value; by the same logic, decreasers are those whose scores decreased in relation to the predicted value. No change was defined as seventh-grade scores that were consistent with the prediction equation. This procedure controls for regression to the mean since increases or decreases in the seventh grade are rendered independent of the student's level of perceived scholastic competence in the sixth grade (see Harter, in press a). This is but one possible procedure that deals with certain, though by no means all, of the statistical concerns in dealing with score-change data. In implementing any of the strategies suggested above, careful consideration should be given to such issues in the analysis and interpretation of one's results.

Validity Versus the Accuracy of Self-Concept Judgments

The preceding section sought to clarify the distinction between test-retest designs as an index of the reliability of an instrument versus an index of the stability of the construct itself. A similar source of confusion is possible in dealing with issues of validity, since often validity is not clearly distinguished from the question of the *accuracy* of self-judgments (see chapter 3 for a further discussion of this issue). Consider the following types of comparisons. Perceived scholastic competence is correlated with teachers' judgments of the students' scholastic competence, with GPA, or with achievement test scores. Perceived social acceptance is correlated with sociometric ratings of popularity. Perceived physical appearance is correlated with independent judges' ratings of attractiveness, based on concurrent photographs taken of students. On the surface, these all seem like legitimate comparisons. But comparisons designed for what purpose? Are such relationships to be taken as evidence for the *validity* of the instrument? Or do they say more about the *accuracy* of children's judgments of their competence or adequacy in these domains?

The most reasonable interpretation is that such data speak to the accuracy of self-judgments and not the validity of the instrument. That is, subjective self-judgments that do not correspond to an external criterion that may be viewed as more objective become interesting in their own right. They suggest that subjective and objective judgments may rely on different sources of information. If one places one's faith in the credibility of the objective indices of competence or adequacy, then one may consider the child or adolescent to be inaccurate in their appraisals. However, it does not follow that the instrument itself is invalid. Validity is a psychometric property of an instrument and speaks to the issue of whether an instrument taps the construct it purports to measure. If the construct in question is subjectively perceived competence or adequacy, then any score that reflects such a self-judgment is, almost by definition, valid.

One cannot be content with such a seemingly circular definition, however. The logic of the argument suggests that the demonstration of the validity of a measure of self-concept must hinge on concurrent measures that also rely on self-judgments, as one possible strategy. Interview techniques, alternative self-report instruments, more projective measures may well represent psychometric avenues to the documentation of the validity of a given self-concept scale. More complex approaches involving a pattern of predictions in spite of construct validity can also be utilized. However, a direct comparison with some external index designed to represent "objective reality" does not speak to the issue of validity.

Such comparisons are intriguing, since they do alert us to the possible bases on which children and adolescents are making judgments about the self. Moreover, they may be interpreted within a framework emphasizing the accuracy of self-evaluations. Our own work, for example, has documented a very interesting developmental pattern in the relationship that perceived judgments of scholastic competence bear to more objective indices. The correlation between perceived scholastic competence and such external criteria as grades, teachers' evaluations, or achievement scores, increases from third to sixth grade (within the elementary school setting) and then plummets in seventh grade when children shift to the junior high school setting. The correlation recovers in the eighth and ninth grades, in that students seem to become more accurate, as assessed by the relationship between their judgments and the more objective indices.

Our interpretation of this pattern of relationships is that certain experiences within the educational setting impact the degree to which the child's judgments will correspond to more objective indicators. For example, the transition to junior high school seems to disrupt the bases on which students make such judgments. They encounter new standards of evaluation, multiple judges of their competencies across different school subjects, and new social comparison groups, all of which require the establishment of a new internal set of criteria by which to judge one's competence. Until such an evaluative system is cognitively put in place and tested, one's judgments are likely to be inaccurate, when compared to objective indices of one's performance. These findings suggest that an intriguing avenue for study is the basis on which children and adolescents make judgments about the self, and possibly the confidence they place in such judgments, rather than considering discrepancies between subjective and objective evaluations to be evidence that a self-report instrument, itself, is invalid.

SUPPLEMENTAL INFORMATION ABOUT
SELF-CONCEPT SCORES

In the previous section, the congruence or discrepancy between self-reported judgments of competence and more objective indices of performance was recast as an interesting substantive issue, rather than one that bears on the validity of a given instrument. The grade-related changes in the magnitude of the relationship between perceived scholastic competence and teacher judgments of competence represent but one example. There are also revealing individual differences in the extent to which perceived competence is congruent with external indicators across students. The pattern of findings suggests that we not necessarily regard children as "accurate" or "inaccurate" in their judgments, but rather consider the possible bases on which children are making judgments of competence or adequacy. What sources of information are children utilizing in coming to conclusions about themselves? Evidence in the literature has revealed several potential sources. These include social comparison, comparison with one's past performance, comparison with one's ideal self, and the feedback received from significant others in one's life.

The literature suggests that social comparison becomes increasingly salient as a basis on which children make judgments about their competence or adequacy, particularly with regard to their academic competence (see Ruble & Rholes, 1981; Eccles, Midgley, & Adler, 1984; Suls & Sanders, 1982). Our own studies with special groups (Renick & Harter, in press; Silon & Harter, 1985) have revealed that the particular social comparison group will have a major impact on the child's level of perceived competence. The majority of mainstreamed learning disabled children, for example, spontaneously compare themselves to regular classroom students, judging their competence to be significantly lower than this comparison group. However, when learning disabled children are asked to compare themselves to their learning disabled (resource room) peers, their perceived scholastic competence is considerably higher.

There are other possible interpretations concerning the bases on which children make self-judgments. Comparisons with one's own past performance, where one feels one has improved, may well result in higher judgments of competence than if one is comparing the self to a normative sample of children as one's reference group. Conversely, comparison between one's perceived *real* self and one's *ideal* self, may yield judgments that are more negative in nature. Feedback from significant others represents another source of information concerning one's competence or adequacy, although there are multiple others to whom one might turn, e.g., parents, teachers, peers. Too often, it would appear that testers interpret such discrepancies between the child's responses and an "objective other" as evidence that the child is "distorting" his/her self-evaluations, either consciously or unconsciously. Yet such interpretations may be unwarranted, if the child is relying on a source of information that is unknown to the tester.

These considerations lead to the suggestion that in our assessment procedures we do not merely administer self-concept instruments, and then make post hoc inferences about the bases on which children are making their evaluations. Rather, it would be more fruitful to examine these bases directly. There are several possible procedures that may be employed, some of which are described in the Self-Perception Profile for Children manual (Harter, 1985b). Through open-ended questions, one can ask the child on what basis he/she made his/her judgments on specific items of interest. One can also inquire about the social comparison group employed by the child. Inquiries about the child's ideal self in a given domain may also provide useful information, as well as inquiries into the use of the opinion of significant others as a source of feedback. Utilizing such procedures, one will be in a much better position not only to interpret the scores yielded by a self-concept instrument, but to understand the actual processes that underlie self-evaluative judgments.

THE FUNCTIONAL ROLE OF THE SELF-CONCEPT

The various suggestions in this chapter are based on the assumption that the self-concept is worthy of study. Yet why are we even interested in obtaining such judgments? In all likelihood, assessments of self-concept alone are not that interesting, nor are the correlations of self-concept with other variables in the absence of any thoughtful set of hypotheses about the underlying nature of such relationships. All too often, however, measures of self-concept are included in research studies or in clinical and educational assessment batteries without any clear rationale. Presumably, self-concept is not an epiphenomenon, but rather a construct that we feel is important because it has some impact on the child's life. It behooves us, therefore, to make our models of the self-concept as explicit as possible in order that they can be examined directly. On what specific aspects of the child's life do we think self-concept has an impact and why? What role does it play? How can these effects be directly documented? If we feel that self-concept does play a role in mediating other behaviors of interest, such an underlying model implies that we also be interested in the historical determinants or antecedents of a child's self-concept and the concurrent bases on which one is making self-evaluative judgments.

To exemplify such an approach, our own research has been directed toward an examination of the causes or determinants of global self-worth and its mediational role in influencing the child's affective state, as well as its motivational orientation. Specifically, we have put forth a theoretical model that specifies two major sources of self-worth, one derived from William James, and one derived from Charles Horton Cooley. James contended that one's global sense of self-esteem resulted from his/her level of success in domains deemed important. In contrast, Cooley's looking-glass self-formulation emphasizes the role that the opinions of significant others play in shaping the self.

We have operationalized James' formulation by calculating the discrepancy between how competent a child feels he/she is across the various self-concept domains and how important it is to be successful in those domains. Cooley's model has been translated into our measure of the social support and positive regard which significant others hold for the self. We have examined the relationship between the discrepancy score and self-worth as well as the correlation between positive regard and self-worth. Our findings (see Harter, 1986; in press b) have revealed support for both determinants, demonstrating that an additive model incorporating both sources of self-worth best explains the data.

We have also been concerned with the mediational role that self-worth may play in impacting both affective state, along a dimension of depressed to cheerful, and motivation, along a dimension of low to high energy. Our studies provide strong support for the impact that self-worth has on affect, which in turn influences the child's energy level. The implications of these findings for childhood depression as well as adolescent suicide have also been explored within this context. The point here is not to describe these efforts in detail, but to illustrate the need for investigators to be clear about their purposes in assessing the self-concept. In her several comprehensive reviews of the self-concept literature, Wylie (1974, 1979) has lamented the fact that the vast majority of studies have done little to inform us about the nature of the self and its role in human behavior. The challenge, therefore, will be for researchers, educators, and clinicians to be as thoughtful as possible about formulating and documenting the precise function that the self-concept plays in the lives of children and adolescents.

CHILDREN'S AWARENESS OF SELF-PROCESSES

From an applied perspective, the implicit, if not explicit, goal of most investigators is to promote a positive self-concept in order to enhance the functioning or happiness of the individual. Thus our own interest in both the causes and correlates of the self typically implies interventions in the lives of children. A thoughtful analysis of the causes of self-worth, for example, may provide the basis for a particular intervention program, e.g., reducing the discrepancy between the importance of success and a child's level of competence, or increasing the level of positive regard that a child receives from significant others. However, to what extent should such interventions be predicated on the assumption that the child understands these causal links and underlying mediational processes? How much awareness or insight do we require on the part of the child?

Our assumptions in this regard need to be carefully examined against a backdrop of knowledge about the developing child's interest in, and awareness of, self processes. From both a cognitive-developmental and psychoanalytic perspective, there is evidence that children have little interest in, or capacity for, an analysis of their own attributes (see Harter, 1988d). Anna Freud (1965) has written cogently on this topic, pointing out that children naturally direct their interest toward the outer world of events rather than the inner world of intrapsychic experiences. She notes that children do not naturally take themselves as the object of their own observation, they do not normally engage in introspection. As a result, psychological issues and/or conflicts are externalized, and environmental solutions are preferred to internal or intrapsychic analysis and change.

Cognitive-developmental theory and evidence provide a complementary perspective in alerting us to factors that mitigate against the child's ability to engage in self-observation. Among young children, their confounding of wishes and reality, their inability to engage in logical thinking, and their egocentrism all mitigate against any thoughtful reflections on the self. With the emergence of concrete operational thought, there are newly developed capacities that assume the guise of forces making it unlikely that the child will engage in self-observation. The new-found logical abilities that emerge during this period are directed toward an analysis of concrete events in the external world, as the title of this stage implies. Thus, children show little interest in analyzing internal events such as self-attributes, their causes, and their potential impact on affective and motivational processes. The ability to treat one's own thoughts as objects of reflection, to introspect about one's attributes or personality, is not fully developed until adolescence.

Selman's (1980) analysis of the developmental emergence of self-awareness is consistent with these observations in that only gradually does the child develop the ability to observe and critically evaluate the self. For Selman, the child must first acquire those perspective-taking skills necessary to appreciate the fact that others are observing and evaluating the self. This realization, in turn, sets the stage for an internalization process whereby one comes to be able to observe, evaluate, and criticize the self, a process that is necessary in order for children to adopt the opinions of significant others, the basis of Cooley's looking-glass self-formulation.

There is a paradox, therefore, in that while the self-concept would appear to be a fruitful avenue for intervention, given its impact on the child's affective, motivational, and coping processes, developmental limitations preclude the child's ability to analyze, understand, or be interested in pursuing this path. For example, children appear to have little awareness of the links between the positive regard from significant others and their feelings of self-worth, despite the impressive correlations that can be documented between these two constructs assessed separately.

Elsewhere I have discussed some potential solutions toward resolving this paradox in our intervention efforts with children (Harter, in press a). There, it was pointed out that we need to make the distinction between the *goal* of treatment, e.g., enhanced self-concept or self-worth, and the *target* of our interventions. Thus, while our goal may be enhanced self-worth, our intervention strategies may necessarily require an attempt to influence those factors that represent the *determinants* of self-worth. By addressing these causal antecedents directly, as the targets of our intervention, we can hopefully influence the self-system indirectly, which in turn will result in enhanced functioning on the part of the child. We may be much less successful if we attempt to alter children's self-concepts directly.

SUMMARY AND CONCLUSIONS

Recent years have witnessed increasing interest in the self-concept and self-esteem of children and adolescents, which in turn has dictated a need for adequate assessment procedures. Several models of self-concept were presented, indicating how each implies a particular measurement strategy. For example, models that consider the self to be unidimensional will lead to the choice of measures that are different from instruments derived from models that emphasize the multidimensional nature of the self-concept. However, the issue needs to be polarized in that older children not only make judgments about their adequacy in particular domains of the self-concept but can also evaluate their global self-worth as a person. Five self-concept measures, representing a range of models, were described in detail.

It was also suggested that the sensitive assessment of the self-concept will require an appreciation for developmental changes in the structure and content of self-evaluations. Moreover, there may well be differences in the nature and organization of the self-concept among special populations that will require somewhat different assessment strategies.

Psychometric considerations, including the need to differentiate the *reliability* of an instrument from the *stability* of the construct, as well as the need to distinguish the *validity* of the instrument from the *accuracy* of children's judgments, were discussed. Suggestions for the use of self-concept measures in developmental and program evaluation research were offered.

Finally, it was argued that our interest in the self will only be fruitful to the extent that we not only identify the antecedents of self-judgments, but their *function* in the lives of children. Such an orientation requires, therefore, that we pinpoint the determinants of the self-concept as well as those factors that we believe the self-concept, in turn, impacts. Moreover, it necessitates an assessment strategy in which we not only measure the self-concept, but include instruments that tap other constructs within the causal network as well. Thus our conceptual model, assessment methodology, and intervention strategies all need to be intimately linked, and firmly grounded in an understanding of the nature of children's self-evaluations. This is the challenge for those interested in the self-concept, a challenge that extends far beyond, but must include, an appreciation for issues in assessment.

REFERENCES

Buros, O. (1970). (Ed.), *Personality tests and reviews.* Highland Park, NJ: Gryphon Press.

Chiu, L. (1988). Measures of self-esteem for school-age children. *Journal of Counseling and Development, 66,* 298–301.

Coopersmith, S. (1967). *The antecedents of self-esteem.* San Francisco: W.H. Freeman.

Damon, W. & Hart, D. (1982). The development of self-understanding from infancy through adolescence. *Child Development, 53,* 841–864.

Eccles, J., Midgley, C., & Adler, T.F. (1984). Grade-related changes in the school environment: Effects on achievement motivation. In J.G. Nicholls (Ed.), *The development of achievement motivation.* (pp. 283–331), Greenwich, CT.: JAI Press.

Freud, A. (1965). *Normality and pathology in childhood.* New York: International Universities Press.

Haltiwanger, J. & Harter, S. (1988). *A behavioral measure of young children's presented self-esteem.* Unpublished manuscript, University of Denver.

Harter, S. (1982). The perceived competence scale for children. *Child Development, 53,* 87–97.

Harter, S. (1983). The development of the self-system. In M. Hetherington (Ed.), *Handbook of child psychology: Social and personality development.* (Vol. 4, pp. 275–385), New York: Wiley.

Harter, S. (1985a). Competence as a dimension of self-evaluation: Toward a comprehensive model of self-worth. In R. Leahy (Ed.), *The development of the self.* New York: Academic Press.

Harter, S. (1985b). *The Self-Perception Profile for Children: Revision of the Perceived Competence Scale for Children.* Manual, University of Denver.

Harter, S. (1986). Processes underlying the construct, maintenance and enhancement of the self-concept in children. In J. Suls and A. Greenwald (Eds.), *Psychological Perspectives on the self,* (Vol 3, 137–181), Hillsdale, NJ: Lawrence Erlbaum.

Harter, S. (1988a). The construction and conservation of the self: James and Cooley revisited. In D.K. Lapsley & F.C. Power (Eds.). *Self, ego and identity: Integrative approaches.* New York: Springer-Verlag, 43–70.

Harter, S. (1988b). Self-esteem and self-concept. In T.D. Yawkey & J.E. Johnson (Eds.), *Integrative processes and socialization: early to middle childhood.* Hillsdale, NJ: Lawrence Erlbaum, 45–78.

Harter, S. (1988c). *The Self-Perception Profile for Adolescence.* Unpublished Manual, University of Denver.

Harter, S. (1988d). Developmental changes in self-concept and emotional understanding: Implications for psychotherapy. In S. Shirk (Ed.), *Cognitive development and child psychotherapy.* New York: Plenum, 119–160.

Harter, S. (1988d). The relationship between perceived competence, affect, and motivational orientation within the classroom: Processes and patterns of change. In A.K. Boggiano & T. Pittman (Eds.), *Achievement and motivation: A social-developmental perspective.* Cambridge University Press.

Harter, S. (1988d). Causes, correlates and the functional role of global self-worth: A life-span perspective. In J. Kolligian and R. Sternberg (Eds.). *Perceptions of competence and incompetence across the life-span.* New Haven, CT: Yale University Press.

Harter, S. & Pike R. (1984). *The pictorial perceived competence scale for young children. Child Development, 55,* 1969–1982.

Hughes, H.M. (1984). Measures of self-concept and self-esteem for children ages 3–12 years: A review and recommendations. *Clinical Psychology Review, 4,* 657–692.

Jersild, A.T. (1952). *In search of self: An exploration of the role of the school in promoting self-understanding.* New York: Teachers College.

Kokenes, B. (1974). Grade level differences in factors of self-esteem. *Developmental Psychology, 10,* 954–958.

Kokenes, B.A. (1978). A factor-analytic study of the Coopersmith Self-Esteem Inventory. *Adolescence, 13,* 149–155.

L'Ecuyer, R. (1981). The development of the self-concept through the life span. In M.D. Lynch, A.A. Norem-Hebeison & K. Gergen (Eds.), *Self Concept: Advances in theory and research.* (pp. 203–210), Cambridge, MA: Ballinger.

Marsh, H.W. (1984). Relationships among dimensions of self-attribution, dimensions of self-concept and academic achievements. *Journal of Educational Psychology, 76,* 1291–1308.

Marsh, H.W. (1987). The hierarchical structure of self-concept: An application of hierarchical confirmatory factor analysis. *Journal of Educational Measurement, 24,* 17–39.

Marsh, H.W. (in press). *The Self-Description Questionnaire (SDQ): A theoretical and empirical basis for the measurement of preadolescent self-concept: A test manual and research monograph.* San Antonio, TX: The Psychological Corporation.

Marsh, H.W., Barnes, J., Cairns, L., & Tidman, M. (1984). Self-Description Questionnaire: Age and sex effects in the structure and level of self-concept for preadolescent children. *Journal of Educational Psychology, 76,* 940–956.

Montemayor, R. & Eisen, M. (1977). The development of self-conceptions from childhood to adolescence. *Developmental Psychology, 13,* 314–319.

Mullener, N. & Laird, J.D. (1971). Some developmental changes in the organization of self-evaluations. *Developmental Psychology, 5,* 233–236.

Piers, E. & Harris, D. (1969). *The Piers-Harris Children's Self-Concept Scale.* Nashville, TN: Counselor Recordings and Tests.

Piers, E.V. (1984). *Revised manual for the Piers-Harris Children's Self-Concept Scale.* Los Angeles: Western Psychological Services.

Renick, M.J. (1988). Examining the self-perceptions of learning disabled children and adolescents: Issues of measurement and a model of global self-worth. Doctoral dissertation, University of Denver.

Renick, M.J. (1985) *The development of learning disabled children's self-perceptions.* Unpublished master's thesis, University of Denver. Denver, CO: Author.

Renick, M.J. & Harter, S. (1988). *The Self-Perception Profile for learning disabled students: Manual.* University of Denver.

Renick, M.J. & Harter, S. (in press). A developmental study of the perceived competence of learning and disabled children. *Journal of Educational Psychology.*

Robinson, J.P. & Shaver, P.R. (1973). *Measures of social psychological attitudes.* Ann Arbor, MI: Institute for Social Research.

Rogers, C. & Dymond, R. (1954). *Psychotherapy and personality change.* Chicago: University of Chicago Press.

Rosenberg, M. (1979). *Conceiving the self.* New York: Basic Books.

Rosenberg, M. (1986). Self-concept from middle childhood through adolescence. In J. Suls & A.G. Greenwald (Eds.), *Psychological perspective on the self.* Hillsdale, NJ: Lawrence Erlbaum. (Vol. 3), 107–136.

Ruble, D. & Rholes, W. (1981). The development of children's perceptions and attributions about their social world. In J. Harvey, W. Ickes, & R. Kidd (Eds.), *New directions in attribution research.* Hillsdale, NJ: Lawrence Erlbaum. (Vol. 3), 3–36.

Selman, R. (1980). *The growth of interpersonal understanding.* New York: Academic Press.

Shavelson, R.J., Hubner, J.J., & Stanton, G.C. (1976). Self-concept: Validation of construct interpretations. *Review of Educational Research, 46,* 407–441.

Silon, E. & Harter, S. (1985). Perceived competence, motivation orientation, and anxiety in mainstreamed and self-contained educable mentally retarded children. *Journal of Educational Psychology, 77,* 217–230.

Suls, J. & Sanders, G. (1982). Self-evaluation via social comparison: A developmental analysis. In L. Wheeler (Ed.), *Review of personality and social psychology* (Vol. 3), Beverly Hills, CA: Sage. 171–197.

Wylie, R. (1974). *The self-concept: A review of methodological considerations and measuring instruments,* (Rev. Ed., Vol. 1). Lincoln, NE: University of Nebraska Press.

Wylie, R. (1979). *The self concept,* (Vol. 2). *Theory and research on selected topics.* Lincoln, NE: University of Nebraska Press.

PART IV

Special Topics

CHAPTER 11

The Child as Witness: Experimental and Clinical Considerations

KAREN SAYWITZ

INTRODUCTION

Increasingly, children are called to the stand to report about events they have witnessed or experienced. They can be involved in both criminal and civil litigation. The types of crimes that involve children vary widely from accidents and burglaries to kidnapping and molestation. Civil cases can involve family law, dependency, and other civil courtrooms. The innovative efforts of legal and mental health professionals as well as of researchers are converging to meet the needs of both the children and the system. Initially, this chapter will review research relevant to children as participants in the legal system. Then it will discuss how clinicians apply research findings and clinical expertise in child witness cases. But first, it is necessary to provide a context for understanding the controversies in a field fraught with the drama of conflicting needs of defendants and children.

The Child in the Legal System

The occurrence of children in the legal system presents a dilemma for both the children and the legal professionals involved. When children come in contact with the system, they typically follow a path of repeated contacts with strangers, in strange situations, governed by a set of unfamiliar rules. Although the process varies from jurisdiction to jurisdiction, child victim-witnesses whose safety may be at issue follow a similar course. An adult reports his or her suspicions to the authorities. Law enforcement and/or a child welfare agency initiate an emergency response. Representatives of these two agencies go out to interview the child in order to determine whether protection and removal from the home is necessary. If so, they transport the child to either a foster home or children's hall. In some cases, parents are not notified until after the children are placed.

In the days or weeks that follow, children may undergo a medical examination, investigative interviews by police, and psycho-social evaluations by mental health professionals. Then, children may be interviewed by a district attorney to determine if criminal charges will be filed, and by county counsel or private attorneys from the juvenile or family courts to determine placement and custody issues. Next, there are a string of depositions, hearings, and continuances, eventually a trial, with direct and cross-examination, and a sentencing hearing. Children may find themselves simultaneously involved with several sets of legal proceedings and attorneys in dependency, criminal, and family law courtrooms. This process can take a relatively short time if no charges are filed or years to complete if it is a criminal case.

Children can become involuntary participants in a complex network of people, places, and situations that are admittedly difficult even for adult witnesses to comprehend. Moreover, there is growing concern regarding the emotional impact of the legal process on children. Are children secondarily victimized by criminal justice procedures, such as cross-examination designed to defame a witness' character? Child witnesses are interviewed repeatedly, reliving the trauma in each retelling, without being able to put it behind them and move on with their lives and development. There are those who wonder whether the emotional cost is too great for some children (Avery, 1983; Weiss & Berg, 1982).

The Legal System and the Child

Although the system by its very nature causes difficulties for the children, the children by their very nature cause difficulties for the system, giving rise to confusing legal, constitutional, and ethical dilemmas. The judicial system finds itself laboring to balance the rights of the victim with the rights of the accused. In each case, legal practitioners must decide the extent to which the system can accommodate the needs and limitations of young children. Child victims are often the only witnesses to crimes that leave little physical evidence (e.g., oral copulation), yet their competence and credibility are often in question (Kerns, 1981). Over the years many authors have cautioned against convicting an adult on the word of a child alone (Holdsworth, 1944 as cited in Myers 1987; Stern, 1910).

Very often there are competing choices between the best interest of the child and the constitutional rights of the accused. For example, decisions regarding whether to close the courtroom to the press when children testify, in an effort to reduce public humiliation and protect children from adverse publicity, have already reached the Supreme Court (Globe Newspaper Co. v. Superior Court, see Melton, 1984). At issue are protecting the defendant's sixth amendment right to a public trial and the public's first amendment right to access to the trial process through the press. In an effort to balance their priorities, legal practitioners have become interested in what child psychology has to offer.

Historically, the law has been skeptical of children. While research on jurors' perceptions of children is still quite new, studies generally indicate that a majority of adults believe children to be less credible witnesses than adults (Yarmey & Jones, 1983; Goodman, Golding & Haith, 1984; Leippe & Romanczyk, 1987). (However, it is not clear how this view influences conviction rates [see Ross, Miller, & Moran, 1987]). Case precedent is clear that age alone does not preclude someone from offering testimony (Rex v. Brasier, 1779; Wheeler v. United States, 1895). Instead, competency to testify is determined on a case by case basis through judicial examination. In some states, children under 10, while in others children under 14, years of age are presumed incompetent unless the judge determines otherwise after interviewing the child (i.e., a process termed voir dire). Yet, children as young as four have qualified to testify (see Myers, 1987, for discussion).

Case law indicates that judges decide competency before hearing the case on the basis of whether a child can: (1) perceive a just impression of the event, (2) remember the event without coaching, (3) describe the event in court with sufficient verbal skills to be understood, and (4) understand the oath to tell the truth (Wheeler v. U.S., 1895). However, the training typically afforded judicial officers does not provide guidelines on how to determine whether a child of a given age is competent in these areas. As a result, competency criteria vary from courtroom to courtroom, and attorneys take it upon themselves to support or impeach children's competency by questioning them on the stand to underscore their strengths or weaknesses.

Nurcombe (1987) suggests that children under eight years of age be clinically evaluated for competency to testify by mental health professionals before trial. Myers, Bays, Becker, Berliner, Corwin, & Saywitz, (1989) recommend that child development experts, as friends of the court, advise judges of relevant data on children's cognitive, memory, language, and moral development to aid judges in competency determinations. Some states have passed laws enabling the judge to hear a child's entire testimony before determining competency (e.g., California). At the federal level, there is a trend toward considering all children competent to testify, leaving it to the trier of fact (judge or jury) to evaluate an individual child's competency and credibility (Federal Rules of Evidence 601).

A REVIEW OF RESEARCH RELEVANT TO CHILD WITNESS CASES

With these controversies in mind, three areas of research will be reviewed: applied developmental research on children's testimony; clinical research on traumatized children; and studies of normal development.

Research on Children's Testimony

Courtroom testimony by children has a history of empirical research dating back to the late 1800s. Goodman (1984) provides an excellent historical review. As in any period of history, early researchers approached the object of their study with the cultural stereotypes of the day. The notion that children were incompetent undersized adults generalized to the hypothesis that children were also incompetent witnesses. The early studies served to document the numerous errors children made in testimony, but comparative groups of adults were not included (Varendock, 1911/1984). More recent research into adult eyewitness testimony suggests that it is also replete with errors and distortions (Loftus, 1979; Yarmey, 1979). Moreover, suggestive questions can alter adults' reports. Adults will report having seen objects at the scene of a simulated crime that were not present but had been suggested by the interviewer (e.g., broken glass at an automobile accident, Loftus & Palmer, 1974). From these early studies it is not clear how the testimonies of children and adults differ.

In the 1980s, there has been a resurgence of research on children's testimony which can best be described as a hybrid of developmental and forensic investigation. These researchers strive to control confounding variables, include appropriate control groups, and enhance ecological validity. (Ceci, Toglia, and Ross, 1987). For the most part, these studies address children's competence and credibility. These studies focus on children's memory for real live events, the effects of stress on children's performance, how suggestible children are, their ability to distinguish fact from fantasy, and jurors' perceptions of child witnesses.

Memory

Children (like adults) present both strengths and weaknesses in memory. They perform like adult witnesses under certain conditions when testifying about certain kinds of information, but not in other conditions regarding other types of information.

By the age of three, children are quite adept at narrating autobiographical events from memory (e.g., eating lunch at MacDonalds) (Nelson, 1979; Nelson & Gruendel, 1979, 1981; Nelson, Fivush, Hudson, & Lucariello, 1983; Todd & Perlmutter, 1980). Although their accounts are skeletal outlines, children provide accurate information about the main events that would be meaningful to criminal investigations or to decisions about their custody and placement. In other cases, a skeletal outline may not be sufficient. Recall of peripheral details, which a three-year-old would have difficulty providing (e.g., exact time or location), could be crucial to the filing of charges or determination of guilt. Surprisingly, there are experimental situations where young children have performed better than adults, remembering details adults overlooked (Chi, 1978; Neisser, 1979). On the whole, children are more accurate about core, central events (actions) than about peripheral details (room decor, physical characteristics) (Goodman & Reed, 1986). They are most accurate about familiar, salient, and personally meaningful encounters in comparison to events they perceive to be unimportant and unfamiliar (Bjorklund & Muir, 1988; Lindberg, 1980; Perlmutter, 1980).

In general, children provide accurate reports when asked to "tell what happened" without further questioning, but these accounts are less complete than adult reports. As a result, adults are prompted to ask children more specific questions to elicit further information. If these questions are concrete, understandable, and objective, five-year-olds tend to respond as accurately as adults (Goodman & Reed, 1986; Marin, Holmes,

Guth, & Kovacs, 1979). Children's errors tend to be errors of omission rather than commission. Thus, they are more likely to forget information than to fabricate events that did not occur. However, when children are asked suggestive questions by authority figures about peripheral details, they demonstrate a greater degree of errors than adults. While children can recall simple familiar events in correct chronological order, they may have difficulty with the order of complex, unfamiliar events (Brown, 1975, 1976; Myles-Worsley, Cromer, & Dodd, 1986; Stein, 1978). Inconsistencies due to difficulty with peripheral details and chronological order, however, do not imply that the rest of children's reports are inaccurate (Goodman & Hegelson, 1986).

Suggestibility

Legal practitioners fear that children's memories are influenced by "leading" questions asked over the course of multiple interviews. There is concern that children's reports will become a blend of the initial memory plus information suggested by interviewers or parents about what took place. Questions that are termed leading, misleading, or suggestive have been variously defined by different authors. These types of questions lie on a continuum in terms of the degree to which they imply the answer in the question. A question which states what the questioner thinks happened and then tags, "Isn't that right?" on to the end would certainly be referred to as leading (e.g., "It was Mr. Jones you saw leaving that night, wasn't it?"). In other questions, generally considered suggestive, information gathered from sources other than the witness (e.g., parents) is inadvertently embedded in the question, providing the witness with information not previously possessed (e.g., "What color was the old man's car?" would be suggestive if the witness had not yet mentioned the man's age).

In studies of suggestibility, researchers make an objective record of the original event (e.g., videotape) and then suggest misleading information to children in later questioning. After some time period, memory for the original event and the suggested information is tested. These studies have varied greatly in their method of suggesting information, retention interval, type of stimuli, and relevance to crimes. Consequently, results are difficult to compare and integrate. Overall, studies have not converged on a simple relation between age and suggestibility (Cole & Loftus, 1987; Loftus & Davies, 1984; Zaragoza, 1987). Suggestibility depends on cognitive, social, and situational factors. Results vary depending on level of interest, salience of the event, as well as on the emotional state and knowledge base of the witness, and the type of test.

In general, researchers consistently find that children 10 to 11 years of age are no more suggestible than adults. Findings from traditional memory experiments have been inconsistent regarding the suggestibility of younger children five to nine years of age (Cohen & Harnick, 1980; Dale, Loftus, & Rathbun, 1978; Duncan, Whitney, & Kunen, 1982; Marin, Holmes, Guth, and Kovacs, 1979; Saywitz, 1987; King and Yuille, 1987). However, these studies typically examine children's memories for unfamiliar, innocuous stimuli (words, pictures, stories, or videotapes) after a single exposure reported under nonstressful conditions. In court, children typically report about traumatic real-life events, repeated over and over by familiar people under stressful courtroom conditions (e.g., incest). The experimental questions are rarely important to the child's life and are not about physical acts perpetrated upon them. Goodman and Hegelson (1986) caution against generalizing from such studies to court cases.

More recently, researchers have taken advantage of children's memories for naturally occurring stressful events (e.g., visit to doctor for injection or to have blood drawn). Researchers have also staged live events resembling criminal situations (e.g., playing with a strange man in a trailer or witnessing a theft). Afterwards, children as young as three years of age are asked questions that resemble highly suggestive sex abuse interviews (e.g., "He took your clothes off, didn't he?" "He put something in your mouth, isn't that right?" "Did he kiss you?") (Goodman, Aman, & Hirschman, 1987; Goodman, Hirschman, & Rudy, 1987; Goodman & Reed, 1986). In one study, results indicated that three- to six-year-olds' memories were unaffected by the stress. Moreover, four- to seven-year-olds were not more easily misled to make false reports of abuse than older children and even remained resistant one year later (Goodman et al., 1987). While four- to nine-year-olds were more suggestible about unfamiliar, peripheral details, they were not more suggestible about central or familiar information than older children (Yuille, Cutshall, & King, 1986 as presented in King & Yuille, 1987).

In one study, three-year-olds were found to be more suggestible than four- to six-year-olds, even in response to abuse-related questions. For example, a few three-year-olds agreed that the man in the research trailer had touched their private parts by nodding yes. However, follow-up questioning revealed that they did not know what "private parts" meant (Goodman & Aman, 1987). Overall, children 4 to 16 years of age seem able to resist suggestions about matters that are memorable, salient, and important to them. Three-year-olds seem to be most at risk for providing testimony that is difficult to interpret (Goodman & Hahn, 1987).

There are also fears that children are susceptible to social pressures to say what they think adults want to hear. Recently, there have been a few studies of demand characteristics, that is, social pressures to go along with suggestions in the context of the interview (Ceci, Ross, & Toglia, 1987; Baxter & Davies, 1985, 1987). When a child, instead of an adult authority figure, presented the misleading information, the effect of misleading questions decreased, although it did not disappear completely (Ceci, Ross, & Toglia, 1987). This suggests that at least some of the suggestibility effect is due to demand characteristics where children go along with what they perceive to be the adult's expectations. However, this study dealt with recall of peripheral detail for innocuous stories, limiting the generalizability of the findings. Until such findings are replicated with memory for real live events and dependent measures more closely resembling forensic interviews, it would be premature to generalize to actual legal cases. There is some evidence that although children may go along with certain suggestions in the moment of the interview, their original memory for the event is not actually changed by the suggested information and can be accessed with a different type of task (Popp & Zaragoza, 1987; Zaragoza, 1987). Other researchers believe that the original memory is replaced by the misleading information (Cole & Loftus, 1987). More research is needed to clarify the issue.

In summary, there is evidence to suggest that children four years of age and over are no more suggestible than adults regarding central aspects of real live events that are salient and meaningful, well understood, and directly experienced (Melton & Thompson, 1987). In particular, attempts to lead four- to six-year-olds to make false reports of abuse have been unsuccessful. Many of the events children testify about in legal proceedings (someone burglarizing the home, assaulting the parent, or kidnapping and abusing the child) are the types of events about which children four years of age and older are best able to resist suggestion. Yet, there are some situations in which four- to nine-year-olds are less able to resist suggestions about peripheral details than older children and adults. The testimony of three-year-olds is difficult to interpret and further research with three-year-olds using ecologically valid paradigms is necessary.

While the results of recent ecologically valid studies are optimistic about the role children can play in court cases, these findings are still based on group statistics. In a court case we deal with only one child. There will always be individual variations among children of all ages. There will be some children who do not adhere to predictions based on group statistics. Each child witness's strengths and weaknesses must be evaluated on a case by case basis. (A method for doing so is discussed further in the final section of this chapter.) In addition, the results of studies vary depending on the specificity of retrieval cues, salience of the information in question, response mode, type of suggestion, type of information suggested, and so forth. The circumstances surrounding a particular case may resemble one type of experimental paradigm (e.g., bystander witness) more than another type (e.g., participant witness). Generalizing from a global review of the literature may not always be appropriate in a particular case. On the other hand, it is only through the converging operations of many studies that consensus in the field regarding children's suggestibility will develop.

Differentiating Fact from Fantasy

Legal practitioners are also concerned that child victims will confuse fantasies with real events. They are especially concerned that children concurrently involved in play therapy (most often to treat symptoms of Post-Traumatic Stress Disorder [PTSD]), will be conditioned to associate the event with a playful atmosphere that displaces the seriousness of the situation and encourages children to commingle fantasy with reality.

I am aware of no studies of the effect of play therapy on memory, although developmental theorists, including Freud (1911/1958) and Piaget (1951), have suggested that children routinely confuse reality with fantasy. Currently, researchers do not find evidence for Freud's notion of infantile hallucination nor the notion that children are so egocentric as to routinely fail to distinguish between reality and fantasy (Flavell, 1977; Miller, 1983; Lindsay & Johnson, 1987). While children use pretend in their play, they seem to know when they are pretending. Preschoolers will play tea party with empty cups, but never try to take a bite from a "pretend" piece of cake when they are hungry (see Garvey, 1977, on the development of play). It is misleading to say that children cannot distinguish what is real from what is not; however, researchers have identified situations where young children are less likely to differentiate fact from fantasy on some laboratory tasks (Lindsay & Johnson, 1987).

Researchers studying reality monitoring and external-source monitoring have examined children's and adults' ability to discriminate between fresh memories of an event itself, memories of one's later thoughts about the event, and memories of what other people have said about the event. Johnson and her colleagues (Foley & Johnson, 1985; Foley, Johnson, & Raye, 1983; Johnson & Foley, 1984; Foley & Aman, 1987; Lindsay & Johnson, 1987) have reported that young children (i.e., six-year-olds) show a deficit in some types of reality monitoring, but not in others.

In Johnson's studies, children's memories were no more confused than adults in discriminating what they saw someone else do or say from what they themselves did or said; children were no more confused between memories of what two other people did or said. In other words, children accurately remembered who said and did what. Eight- through ten-year-olds made no more errors than adults in estimating the number of times they actually saw something from the number of times they only imagined seeing it (Johnson, Raye, Hasher, & Chromiak, 1979). However, six-year-olds had more difficulty than adults in discriminating memories of what they themselves had said or done from what they had only imagined themselves saying or doing. While adults also showed confusions on this latter task, children did so to a greater degree (Foley, Johnson, & Raye, 1983).

The authors note that the relevance of these findings for children's testimony may be limited by the fact that the stimuli are artificial and not embedded in any context that is meaningful to children's lives. In contrast, crimes are likely to be compelling, vivid, and important. Children in research studies, who were instructed to imagine an event or object, may be performing different mental processes than children spontaneously fantasizing about an event. Although this is an innovative and promising line of research, generalization to court cases may be premature until results are replicated with more ecologically valid paradigms.

In conclusion, as studies become more ecologically valid, results seem to suggest children are more competent witnesses than previously assumed. The application of experimental results to child witness cases entails matching what a particular case requires from a given witness to what a child of a given phase of development can be reasonably expected to provide under given circumstances. Also, one must keep in mind the fact that, under stress, individuals of all ages may not be able to function at their optimal level of performance. Certain child witnesses, under the stress of courtroom formality or police authority, may not be able to utilize strategies for resisting suggestion or retrieving detailed memories that subjects in experimental studies can employ. On the other hand, in some cases the seriousness of the occasion may promote enhanced performance by certain children. More research on their individual differences is needed.

Clinical Research

Studies of Traumatized Children
Clinical studies concerning diagnosis and treatment of traumatized children are also pertinent to child witness cases (Eth & Pynoos, 1985; Pynoos & Eth, 1984; Terr, 1981, 1983). In general, studies suggest that after

a single incident, victimized children exhibit symptoms similar to adult victims, including nightmares, phobias, emotional instability, regression, anxiety reactions, and psychosomatic complaints.

Browne and Finkelhor (1986) have reviewed the research on the impact of sexual abuse in particular. Empirical studies indicate short-term reactions of fear, anxiety, depression, anger, hostility, aggression, and sexually inappropriate behaviors. Long-term effects reported in the literature include depression, self-destructive behavior, anxiety, feelings of isolation, depreciated self-esteem, substance abuse, difficulty trusting others, and sexual maladjustment. Additionally, Conte (1987) found that 20% of child sexual abuse victims display no short-term symptoms.

Browne and Finkelhor caution that this body of research is still in its infancy and most of the studies possess sample, design, and measurement problems that could compromise the findings. While there are no studies of the impact these symptoms could have on a child's performance in the legal setting, one can speculate that symptoms such as dissociation, regression, poor concentration, and self-defeating behavior might profoundly influence a child's behavior on the stand.

The Effects of the System on Child-Participants

Clinical research is also being conducted to explore the emotional effects of testifying on children. Weiss and Berg (1982) have argued that court proceedings interfere with children's resolution of emotional reactions to the trauma because they prolong and intensify emotional reactions as well as prevent the children from putting the trauma behind them and moving along in their development and growth. In contrast, it has also been suggested that the opportunity to openly declare the injustices done to children could give them a sense of control over their previously helpless role as the victim (Pynoos & Eth, 1984).

The potential for further injury to victimized children has been discussed by experts before the United States Senate and in articles by legal practitioners and mental health professionals alike (Avery, 1983; Claman, Harris, Bernstein, & Lovitt, 1986; Roberts, 1985). Many have mentioned the multiple interviews by untrained and insensitive personnel, removal from home and placement with strangers, separation from nonoffending parents, lengthy delays, demoralizing cross-examination, and being directly confronted by the offender in court, after he or she threatened the child with bodily harm if the child ever told anyone about the event, to be potentially injurious.

There are few empirical studies of this issue. Two early studies reported harmful effects on children of participating in court, but both studies possess methodological flaws compromising their conclusions.

Gibbens and Prince (1963) found that child victims who went to court had greater psychological disturbance than those who did not. However, the authors pointed out that the children who went to court were likely to be those with the most serious charges, from the more dysfunctional families. Thus, these children may have been more emotionally disturbed before entering the court system and not due to the effects of the system. DeFrancis (1969) described the stress and tension children experienced with the legal system. However, there was no comparison group, making it difficult to determine whether the court or the initial trauma was the cause of the stress.

More recently, Tedesco and Schnell (1987) conducted a retrospective survey of 48 child witnesses. Forty-eight percent of the children surveyed felt the questioning and investigation in their case had been helpful; 19% felt it had been harmful. For the most part, treatment workers and parents felt the process was harmful (71% and 83%, respectively). The researchers isolated two factors associated with children perceiving the process as harmful: (1) number of interviewers was negatively correlated with perceived helpfulness, and (2) subjects who actually testified in court rated the procedure as significantly less helpful. Although there were problems with the design and implementation of this study, and findings require replication with a larger sample, the results highlight the fact that while some children may be at risk for harmful effects of litigation, others feel they have benefited from the experience.

Two well-controlled studies were recently completed in Colorado and North Carolina. Goodman, Pyle, Jones, Port, England, Rudy, and Prado (1988), studied 218 child victims of sexual abuse, 4 to 17 years of age. Each child victim who testified was paired with another child victim who did not testify. Pairs were matched on age, SES, sex, severity of the abuse, relationship to the accused, and initial score on the Achenbach Child Behavior Checklist (CBCL-R) (a parent report measure of behavioral disturbance). When tested seven months after the "testifiers" took the stand, children who testified demonstrated significantly more symptoms of emotional disturbance than matched child victims whose cases did not involve testifying ("controls"). When tested after the final disposition of their cases (e.g., dismissal, sentencing), the difference between the groups was reduced, although a subgroup of testifiers was still more distressed than the matched controls.

These findings reflect parents' impressions of their children's psychiatric symptomology. Results from interviewing 110 of the children about their concerns, not their symptomology, suggested that the majority expressed negative affect about testifying in general and about testifying in front of the defendant in particular. The children felt positive about talking to the prosecutor and about the possibility that their nonoffending parent might be in the courtroom with them.

Runyan, Everson, Edelsohn, Hunter, and Coulter (1988) conducted a prospective cohort study with a follow-up at five months to examine the psychological risks of court involvement in North Carolina. They used structured diagnostic child interviews (Child Assessment Schedule [CAS]) as well as parent report measures (CBCL-R) to study 79 sexually abused children, 6 to 17 years of age. Mathematical modeling controlled for type and duration of abuse, counseling, relationship to perpetrator, and estimated IQ. The results suggest that children showed clinically significant mental health problems at referral. Children with lengthy delays in prosecution were only one-twelfth as likely to improve in depression as children uninvolved in the court process. The authors conclude that children involved in protracted cases suffered from the experience. In contrast, children testifying in juvenile court (n=12) resolved their anxiety more rapidly than peers who did not testify in juvenile court. The authors conclude that juvenile court testimony may be therapeutic for child victims. However, they caution against generalizing from such a limited sample to criminal cases, cases in other states, or with younger children.

When studying the effects of the system on child witnesses, it is very difficult to control for all potentially confounding variables. It is also difficult to sort out whether effects are due to the abuse, events that took place after disclosure, or the effects of the system. These studies are the first of their kind: promising, but not definitive. They indicate a need for reforms in criminal proceedings that would reduce the stress placed on child witnesses (e.g., limiting continuances and delays). They also highlight the fact that the most fruitful direction for research in this area will not be the global documentation of harmful effects of legal intervention. Instead, studies are needed that identify the specific characteristics of the child (and the system) that lead to a child either being harmed or helped by the process. Studies are needed that focus on identifying the strengths that make some children resilient in the face of stress, as well as the factors that place other children at risk for harmful effects. More sensitive measures of impact must be developed to reveal both positive and negative effects that are not measured by standard measures of psychopathology and psychiatric diagnosis.

False Allegations of Abuse

Recently, legal and mental health professionals have become involved in cases where intrafamilial sex abuse charges arise in the context of custody and visitation disputes (Benedek & Schetky, 1985; Corwin, Berliner, Goodman, Goodwin, & White, 1987; Green, 1986). There are those who believe that this subgroup of cases has the highest number of unverifiable reports of abuse because one parent pressures the child to falsely accuse the other parent of abuse in order to obtain sole custody or to limit visitation. Alternatively, others believe that it is only after the parents separate and the perpetrator moves out of the home, that children feel safe to disclose the abuse that was genuinely occurring while the family was intact. In these difficult cases, legal practitioners have turned to mental health professionals. Guidelines for assessing such allegations at the request of family law courts have become the subject of much debate in the mental health field (Bresee, Stearns, Bess, & Packer, 1986; Corwin et al., 1987; Green, 1986).

Clinical studies of large numbers of children referred to agencies or emergency rooms for evaluation and treatment of abuse have shown very low rates (2% to 7%) of false allegations by children (Goodwin, Sahd, & Rada, 1979; Horowitz, Salt, Gomez-Schwartz, & Sanzer, 1984). Rates reported by individual practitioners who specialize in forensic evaluation are much higher (Benedek & Schetky, 1985; Green, 1986). However, their samples are much smaller and may reflect only a subset of the most ambiguous and difficult cases. These cases are unlikely to be representative of the general population.

Recently, archival studies have emerged to indicate that even in custody cases, reports fabricated by children are rare (Jones & McGraw, 1987; Theonnes & Pearson, 1988). For example, Jones & McGraw (1987) examined all 576 cases of abuse reported to the Denver Department of Children's Services and found only 7.56% fictitious, with 6.25% fictitious allegations by an adult, and only 1.56% by the children. Everson and Boat (in press) examined the rate of false allegations of abuse in a large sample of Child Protective Services cases in North Carolina. They conclude that many professionals in the field are more skeptical of children's claims than available research suggests is warranted. A study of 103 cases where perpetrators confessed or acknowledged their abuse suggests that clinical indicators of abuse commonly used by mental health professionals are valid determinants of abuse. Only six children (5.8%) failed to demonstrate descriptions or behaviors commonly considered indicative of abuse (Faller, 1988). Studies regarding false allegations and clinicians' abilities to diagnose symptoms consistent with abuse are rapidly increasing in rigor and validity. Yet, at present much controversy remains surrounding these issues. Again, predictions from group statistics to individual cases can be problematic in the legal context.

Normative Developmental Research with Forensic Application

A review of the entire literature on normal child development is beyond the scope of this chapter. Instead, this section highlights sample areas of the literature that demonstrate problems arising as a function of the legal system's insensitivity to issues of normal development. For example, legal practitioners typically are not aware of the norms of cognitive and language development. As a result, child witnesses are often asked questions about abstract concepts they do not understand, in language too complex for them to comprehend. Research results can be applied to aid legal practitioners in determining what they can reasonably expect from children in given age ranges with respect to skills that are needed to testify competently (Melton, 1981; Saywitz & Jaenicke, 1987; Saywitz, 1989, Tapp & Levine, 1974).

For example, child victims, as young as three years old, are typically asked how many times someone did something, without regard to whether or not children this age can count. Normative data on the development of number concepts, disseminated to legal practitioners, can guide their expectations and avoid damaging children's fragile self-esteem when they are continually asked questions they inherently cannot answer.

In addition, paradigms from developmental research can be consulted to develop methods for assessing whether a particular child possesses a skill necessary to testify. For example, armed with the knowledge that prepositions develop gradually, a questioner assesses children's understanding of locative prepositions before inquiring about locations. Before asking children whether they were standing "beside" a lamppost when the event took place, the interviewer would ask them to "put the blue block 'beside' the red block," checking their comprehension of "beside." Several areas of the developmental literature are particularly relevant for forensic application: This section illustrates examples from studies of cognitive, language, and moral development.

Cognitive Development

One is hard pressed to find an area of cognitive development that would not be relevant to children's ability to testify. Knowledge of Piaget's stage theory and the status of replication studies, as well as of more recent neo-Piagetian theories of information processing are all germane (Brainerd, 1978; Case, 1985; Siegler, 1986). It is nearly impossible to recognize and explain sources of inconsistency and confusion in children's reports without knowledge of the underlying developmental processes. Preoperational reasoning, which is transductive, syncretic, animistic, artificial, and egocentric, lies at the base of many of the inconsistencies in preschoolers' testimony that are misconstrued by adults as lies, denials, recantations, and evidence of fantasizing.

For example, questioning a four-year-old about family members who were allegedly present when a crime occurred can be a formidable task. In one case, the crime ostensibly took place at the paternal grandmother's sister's house. Thus, very complicated kinship relations were involved. The child's sister, father, grandmother, and grandmother's sister were allegedly present. Although she could identify them by name, she was unable to answer whether her Grandma Ann was her father's mother or her Aunt Jan was her grandma's sister.

Studies of children's understanding of kinship relations indicate that young children have a different understanding than adults (Elkind, 1962; Haviland & Clark, 1974; Piaget, 1928). To this four-year-old, the name Grandma Ann is no different from the name Mary Jo. Knowing the name her grandmother is called by does not imply she can imagine that her father was once a baby and that he had a mother, just as she does, and that this older woman is that person. This would require the mental operation of reversibility, the ability to change direction of thought. For the same reason, she knows she has a sister, but denies that she is a sister to her sister. Her credibility is compromised by developmentally inappropriate questioning and her subsequent inability to state that her grandmother is her father's mother and that she is her sister's sister.

Juries and judges are often baffled by a few unbelievable comments that tend to invalidate the rest of what a child may have to offer. Preschoolers may reason from one idea to another without logically connecting them. They may generalize in illogical ways as they go about creating explanations for what they observe. For example, after visiting a farm for the first time, Mary insists that she has seen a doggie, when the adults know for a fact that it was a cow. Such insistence is unlikely to increase her credibility in the eyes of a jury. Yet, in her limited experience around her home, all large, four-legged animals have been doggies, leading her to overgeneralize that all four-legged animals are called doggies. In another example, a preschooler comments that a train went by because a dog barked, rather than understanding that the dog barked because the train went by. This child witness is mistaken about the causal relation, not about the fact that he saw a train going by and a dog barking (Singer & Revenson, 1978). Illogical comments from children using preoperational reasoning can be misconstrued as lies, unless one refers to the child development literature for an alternate explanation.

The cognitive capacities necessary to testify differ from case to case, depending on what information can be provided by other witnesses, the parameters of the original event, and the amount of corroborating physical evidence. In order to determine whether or not to file charges, district attorneys must establish the time and place something occurred, as well as the people and actions involved. If it is crucial to a case that a young witness estimate the perpetrator's age in years and height in inches, the time the event occurred in hours and minutes, and the date in terms of the calender month, then normative studies show young children would not be able to estimate time, age, height, and weight in this manner (Davies, Stevenson-Robb, & Flin, in press; Friedman, 1982). However, children can give concrete pieces of information that can help an adult reconstruct the time or date. For example, children do not fully master telling clock time until about second grade (Singer & Revenson, 1978). Rather than asking a preschooler, "What time was it when Jim came into the room?," one would ask about something meaningful to the child, such as, "What television show were you watching when Jim came into the room?" then reconstruct from the TV Guide what time it must have been.

While young children may not be able to state someone's age in years, they may be able to tell whether someone was old enough to be a grandparent, a mommy, a babysitter, or to drive a car. The Piagetian concept of "centering" is also relevant here. In certain situations, preoperational thinkers tend to focus (center) on one aspect of information at a time. They may think the tallest person in the room is the oldest person. They may focus on height to indicate age and not yet process information about hair color, wrinkles, etc., as indications of age as well (Singer et al., 1978). Knowledge of this aspect of normal development would lead an interviewer to surmise that when children say someone was old, follow-up questions must be asked to determine why they think the person was old (e.g., "What makes you think he was old?," "Did he have any hair?," "What color was his hair?"). These examples provide the reader with a flavor for the varied ways in which findings and theories of cognitive development pertain to children's competence and credibility as witnesses and adults' ability to interpret children's reports.

Communicative Competence

The ability to communicate what one remembers in a fashion that is understood by adult listeners is a critical component of participating in the legal process. Successful communication is an interaction between what the speaker (child) and the listener (adult) bring to the context (courtroom) in which the interchange occurs. For successful testimony, children must have developed a certain level of intelligibility, vocabulary, grammar, and conversational skill. Adults must ask questions that are matched to the children's stage of comprehension and interpret children's responses in light of their developmental level of functioning. It does little good to ask children who only understand simple sentences six to eight words long, questions that are 30 words long, involving embedded clauses and double negatives. Children are left feeling inadequate for not being able to answer something an adult expects them to know.

Studies indicate that children learn to communicate through a gradual sequence of phases. It behooves practitioners trying to elicit information from children to be familiar with these phases. Consider a child trying to tell his mother that he just saw a car and a truck in a collision and it was the truck's fault (deVilliers & deVilliers, 1979). At the telegraphic phase of early word combinations, a child might know all the component words "truck," "car," "bump," but his mother would have to guess which vehicle caused the accident because he is not yet at the phase where he understands the rules of word order (grammar) which indicates that the first word is the agent (initiator of action) in "truck bump car."

Even when young children have mastered the basics of simple sentences, they remain unfamiliar with most legal terminology. Studies of semantic development suggest that even when children think that they understand a word, they may not have the same meaning in mind as the adult (see Dale, 1976; Clark & Clark, 1977 for elaboration). For example, young children are unlikely to understand the concept of "jury" until about 10 to 11 years of age (Saywitz, 1989). They frequently mistake the unfamiliar word jury for the familiar word jewelry. To young children, a case is something you carry papers in, charges are something you do with a credit card, court is a place you play basketball, a minor is someone who digs coal, and parties are for getting presents (Saywitz & Jaenicke, 1987). Much confusion arises when adults misjudge children's level of knowledge.

During their third year, children learn the "wh-questions"—where, what, when, who, why, which, and the question how—in a particular order. Initially, children can only answer questions about information that they use in their own speech. "What," "who," and "where" questions are the first learned because this is the kind of concrete information they understand—agents, objects, and locations. In contrast, "why" questions develop much later and are not mastered until kindergarten or first grade. "Why" questions require a certain level of understanding causality and also tend to take on a confusing negative connotation because they are frequently used to reprimand children (e.g., "Why did you do that?"). Knowledge of the norms for the ages at which children master various interrogatives can help ensure that children are answering the questions that were asked.

Norms for the acquisition of certain words are highly relevant to interpreting reports from children. For example, children may not use "frontwards," "sideways," or "backwards" to indicate movement accurately until about seven years of age (Taylor & Purfall, 1987). Yet these words are used frequently in court to describe accidents, body positions, and so forth. Relational terms are common in describing the sizes and shapes of people and things, but they are difficult for young children to use because they have different meanings at different points in time and when referring to different objects (e.g., more/less, fat/skinny, wide/narrow, thick/thin, and deep/shallow). Initially, children may not use them the way adults do.

For example, with familiar objects, three-year-olds know whether a ball is big or little in relation to balls in general. However, if given an unfamiliar object, the child begins to use himself as the standard; if it is small enough for him to hold, it is little, but if too big for him to pick up, it is big. At times, a child of three will be unsure about whether tall refers to the height or the width of an object (Carey, 1978; Clark, 1972). When two things vary only in height, he can pick out the taller. However, if they also vary in width, he may be confused (deVilliers & deVilliers, 1979).

Children's pragmatic skills, (i.e., the functional use of language) develop gradually. It is not until three years of age that children are typically adept at taking turns with an adult in conversation and understanding that they are supposed to keep their responses relevant to the topic being discussed by the adult (Bloom, Rociassano, & Hood, 1976). Children often fail to monitor how well they understand messages from adults (Flavell, Speer, Green, & August, 1981; Ochs & Schiefflin, 1979). They tend not to treat messages or memories as analyzable cognitive objects. They do not critically evaluate their own messages or the incoming messages of others for possible errors, omissions, inconsistencies, or contradictions (Singer & Flavell, 1981; Flavell, 1981). For example, in one study, children listened to instructions on how to perform a magic trick. Despite omissions of vital information, six-year-olds claimed to understand the instructions. Eight-year-olds were likely to ask for more information, recognizing that they didn't understand (Markman, 1977, 1979). In another study, young children served as listeners and were told that they were permitted to ask questions when necessary. Nevertheless, they almost never spontaneously questioned the speaker or requested more information, even when the messages were completely uninformative (Cosgrove & Patterson, 1977; Patterson, Massad, & Cosgrove, 1978).

Children's difficulty assessing what they don't understand limits their ability to request clarifications from adults and may often lead children to try to answer questions they do not comprehend. They may not understand the question, but they are aware that it is time to take their turn in the conversation and that an entire room of adults are waiting for an answer. This often results in irrelevant responses which compromise their credibility as witnesses. They may be responding to a small piece of the question that they did understand, ignoring other parts that may be critical to an adult's understanding of the answer. Unfortunately, very young children rarely announce that they don't understand; they are not aware of what it is that they do not know (Dickson, 1981).

One consequence of children's limited comprehension monitoring and referential listening skills is that they may be unable to protect themselves from appearing inconsistent the way an adult would be able to. When adults realize their message is being misunderstood, they can stop and reiterate that this is not what they meant. Children's limitations in taking another person's perspective may prevent them from recognizing they are misunderstood. In sum, their limitations in monitoring their own comprehension prevent them from recognizing and correcting inconsistencies in their reports. The foregoing examples demonstrate the vital role language development research can play in evaluating children's reports and assessing their ability to participate in the processes of investigation and litigation.

Moral Development

The legal system is concerned with children's understanding that they must tell the truth and avoiding the possibility that they will perjure themselves. Although a child's level of moral reasoning can be assessed according to Kohlberg's stage theory, controversy remains regarding the relationship between moral reasoning and moral behavior.

It is common to assume that honesty is a developmental variable; that it is highly correlated with age. However, research findings suggest that we do not grow more honest as we grow older (Hartshorne & May, 1975; McClelland, 1976; Walsh, 1967). Studies have examined children's tendencies to cheat, lie, and resist temptation. In one representative study, children were warned not to play with some irresistible new toys. Then the adult left the room to watch from behind a one-way window. Resisting temptation was not correlated with age (Walsh, 1967). Instead, honesty seems to be both an individual difference and a situationally dependent variable. Even a relatively honest person will tell a lie in a certain situation and a relatively dishonest person may frequently tell the truth (see Burton, 1976, for a thorough review of research on children's honesty and dishonesty.) In addition, researchers have distinguished "altruistic" lying from "selfish" lying (Greenglass, 1972). In cases where child witnesses may want to protect someone, studies of this distinction require attention.

Asking a child to describe the difference between the truth and a lie is a common courtroom practice to determine children's competency to testify. However, recent research has failed to find a correlation between the ability to provide this description and the accuracy of children's memories for real live events (Goodman, Aman, & Hirschman, 1987). Very young children know that it is wrong to lie, before they can define "to lie" accurately or articulate the differences between two concepts (Wimmer, Gruber, & Perner, 1985). Piaget (1932) found that for six-year-olds, naughty words, deliberately misleading comments, and unintentional errors were all construed as lies. By 10 to 11 years of age, mistakes were still labeled as lies. Wimmer, Gruber, and Perner (1985) found that four- to five-year-olds could discriminate between someone intending to be truthful but unintentionally saying something false, and someone saying something false intentionally; however, they may be confused as to whether or not these are both called lying. This confusion is commonly the source of difficulty in qualifying children to testify on the basis of their ability to describe the difference between truth and a lie.

CLINICAL CONSIDERATIONS AND APPLICATION OF RESEARCH

With the preceeding review of research in mind, we consider the application of these findings to child witness cases. Clinicians and researchers can advise legal practitioners of research findings relevant to the management of child witness cases in several ways: clinical evaluation and treatment of child witnesses; out of court consultation to and education of attorneys, judges, and parents; expert testimony in individual court cases; expert testimony to legislative bodies regarding public policy reforms. The content of consultation, evaluation, and expert testimony ranges from the discussion of the capabilities and limitations of children in given age ranges or diagnostic categories to discussion of methods to make testifying less stressful for children. The following section addresses clinical considerations and controversies in evaluation of individual cases, and consultation/education of legal practitioners.

Evaluation and Assessment

At the time of referral, a clinician may or may not be aware that a case will involve legal consultation. A child may be referred who exhibits sexual precociousness, sudden school failure, social withdrawal, fearfulness, and repetitive nightmares. During the course of the evaluation, the child discloses a sexual encounter with an adult caretaker. In combination with symptoms of Post-Traumatic Stress Disorder and additional samples of behavior from parent and teacher reports, the clinician reports his suspicions of sexual abuse to the appropriate agency. This can mark the beginning of many interactions with the legal system.

In another case, a clinician may be asked to assist police or attorneys with a forensic investigation to determine whether a child who witnessed one parent murder the other parent is competent to testify. Or the clinician may be asked to describe the child's strengths and weaknesses in order to help the attorney infer the child's likely credibility (i.e., whether the child will be a "good" witness). The court may need to determine if the child is "medically unavailable" to testify due to mental illness or if testifying against his only living parent will result in "serious psychological harm."

When children are victimized by strangers, parents may ask a clinician to recommend whether they should press charges and put their child through what they perceive to be the "ordeal" of testifying. Parents may request recommendations regarding modifications of standard legal procedures that would reduce the stress on their child or request preparation for court appearance.

Interviewing Child Witnesses

Forensic decisions about a child's competence, credibility, treatment needs, and placement are routinely based on interview results. While the interview is considered one excellent source of information, several psychometric issues have arisen in the literature that are important for understanding the use of interview data in the forensic context.

Early studies indicated that, in general, inter-interviewer reliability was poor. However, reliability has been shown to be adequate when (1) efforts are made to use clearer diagnostic systems, such as DSM-III; (2) interviewers are well trained in the systematic use of diagnostic categories; and (3) statistics take the base rates of diagnoses into consideration (Matarazzo, 1978). Yet research concerning the use of child interviews for forensic purposes is in its infancy. With regard to the legal context, decision-making criteria are not well developed, often interviewers are not well trained, and base rates are rarely considered. Structured or standardized protocols are virtually nonexistent, except for two concerning the use of anatomically detailed dolls that are limited to sex abuse cases (Boat & Everson, 1985; White, Strom, & Santilli, 1985). Moreover, the reliability and validity of these two has not been empirically tested or documented. (See Chapter 12 for a discussion of child interviews in cases of sexual abuse.) One can use the structured diagnostic interviews (e.g., CAS; see chapter 5) available to diagnose disorders that are common among traumatized children (Post-Traumatic Stress Disorder, Overanxious Disorder, Depression, etc.), so as not to rely solely on parents' and teachers' reports.

Clinicians and researchers typically view the interview process as a benign diagnostic tool. This is not the case in the legal context. The clinician is confronted with choices in conducting the interview which juxtapose what is traditionally thought to be best for the patient with what will be best for the court case. Consider whether play therapy encourages confusion between fantasy and reality; do children intermix wishes and fears with actual memories as they attempt to resolve traumatic experiences? The significance of this concern is that some legal practitioners believe child victims should not begin psychotherapy until their legal case is closed. In some cases this may be months or years after the trauma occurred. From this perspective, the preservation of the evidence (a child's testimony), critical to a conviction, is pitted against the child's immediate mental health needs. Yet, at times, what is best for the court case may also be in the best interest of the child. A conviction may validate the child's sense of reality, while acquittal due to a child's credibility being compromised by clinical interventions may return the child to a potentially dangerous situation with the stigma of having not been believed.

There is marked controversy in the field of mental health regarding the degree to which clinicians ought to modify their procedures in order to avoid certain trial ramifications. Common clinical occurrences (e.g., offering a sticker or cookie at the end of the interview) can be construed by the court as coercion. A clinician may choose instead to verbally praise children for their effort, noting what a good job they are doing of talking about something that is hard for them to talk about. This kind of comment is used because it has less problematic trial consequences than reassuring children each time they disclose information that is in the direction of the interviewer's expectations. A clinician may decide arbitrarily to praise children for every nth verbal response to avoid accusations in court that reinforcement biased the witness. Conscious choices must be made at various points in the interview regarding whether or not to modify a procedure because of implications for the court case. However, this is not to say that one should abandon sound clinical practice in favor of tiptoeing around legal professionals' concerns.

There can be landmines at many turns in the course of this work. Choosing to videotape an interview and preserve a child's statement may reduce the number of interviews a child must endure; it also limits confidentiality since the clinician has no control over whether the tape is later duplicated and distributed to attorneys and experts on both sides, as well as to the media. Later, the tape may be used to impeach the child as evidence of prior inconsistant statements. It also preserves the interviewer's techniques and questions for later scrutiny.

Information gathered originally from other children or adults may be inadvertently embedded into questions, suggesting that the child answer in a particular direction. As a result, some authors recommend that clinicians avoid suggestive questions at all cost because they will compromise the child's credibility in court. Others believe that the mental health field should be dictated by the clinical needs of the patient, irrespective of legal system concerns, erring on the side of offering treatment if responses to suggestive questions indicate a need.

The research reviewed earlier indicates that children under 10 years of age can be more influenced by leading questions from authority figures about peripheral details than adults (e.g., room decor). These details can be vital to some cases and superfluous to others. Novice interviewers who use leading questions concerning such details could compromise the child's credibility regarding these pieces of information. However, the work of Goodman and her colleagues suggests that these questions would be unlikely to invalidate the rest of the child's report. Her work also suggests that interview questions would be unlikely to lead a child four years of age or older to falsely report an abusive event. In either case, the impact of differential phrasing of questions on children's reports has become the object of much controversy and study. Clinicians ought to consult this literature and be cognizant of the legal ramifications of their clinical choices.

The purpose of this discussion is not to provide the reader with the "right" way to conduct a child interview for forensic purposes, but to highlight some of the problems that arise when standard diagnostic techniques are applied to the legal context without caution. As a general guideline, authors tend to agree that questioning should start by trying to elicit the most general, spontaneous descriptions in response to an open-ended inquiry, such as, "Tell me what happened?" Over the course of questioning, the interviewer gradually moves toward more direct and specific questions. In this fashion, a hierarchy of reliability of information is created. Information provided at the beginning is less influenced by parent, police, and attorney reports, or the preconceived notions of the interviewer, than information that is disclosed at the end.

After the child offers the spontaneous narrative, the interviewer moves into open-ended questions, starting with when, where, how, who, and how many times. Then, the interviewer asks open-ended questions about specific categories of information. For example, rather than asking a leading question, such as, "It was raining outside that night, wasn't it?" one says, "Tell me about the weather that night." Finally, the interviewer may use multiple choice or yes/no questions, but should follow them with further questions to clarify the answer and insure that the child's "yes" means what the interviewer thinks it means. Much of the inconsistency in children's reports stems from the inferences adults draw from children's yes/no responses.

Self- and Parent-Report Measures

How useful are the more common psychological assessment techniques in forensic evaluations? For the most part, interpretations of specific test results (e.g., Rorschach responses) as indicative of a particular trauma, (e.g., abuse) are based primarily on clinical experience and not rigorous research efforts. The field has not devised any single reliable and valid "test" specific to child witnesses that can assess: (a) a child's competence to testify, (b) whether the child was involved in a criminal event, or (c) what the effect of a particular legal proceeding will be on a particular child. The state of the art is such that psychologists are able to state only that test results are consistent with a child having been abused or having witnessed a horrifying event, rather than proof of that fact. Test results are also useful to help rule out alternate explanations for children's behavior.

Attempts have been made to develop diagnostic measures for specific types of cases, such as sexual abuse. Friedrich, Urquiza, and Beilke, (1986) have developed a behavioral checklist and are conducting reliability and validity studies which are very promising. Others have attempted to establish a specific disorder of sex abuse that could be used in court to "prove" that children with those symptoms have been abused. However, such a disorder also runs the risk of being used to "prove" that children without the full cluster of symptoms have not been abused. Referring to the research discussed previously, such a use of clinical diagnosis is complicated by the fact that many of the symptoms abused children display are nonspecific (anxiety, dissociation) and not necessarily pathognomonic to having been sexually abused. Some children who have genuinely been abused do not demonstrate short-term effects. On the other hand, when three-year-olds with limited language skills are involved, the only evidence that a child is in danger and in need of intervention may be his or her psychiatric symptomatology.

Much confusion exists concerning the relationship between the diagnosis of psychiatric disorder and the proof that a crime has been committed. A dilemma the clinician will encounter in forensic work is determining the boundaries between the psychological evaluation and the forensic investigation. One must think carefully about the wisdom of using psychiatric diagnoses to prove that a crime took place. Psychiatric diagnoses employ a different criteria for determining the need for treatment than the legal system's criteria for determining guilt beyond a reasonable doubt in a criminal case, or by a preponderance of the evidence in a dependency court case.

One might assume that when eliciting a child's report of a traumatic event, self-report measures could be very valuable. However, their use has been limited. Reliable and valid objective measures of children's perceptions of their problems specifically related to traumatic events do not yet exist. While there are no self-report measures designed specifically to evaluate children's reports of traumatic events, self-report measures of anxiety, depression, personality characteristics, and self-esteem can be very useful in considering forensic referral questions. The same can be said for parent-teacher report measures (e.g., CBCL-R) and tests to assess developmental delays. Overall, standard batteries are very helpful clinical tools for answering forensic referral questions, but are limited in their role as proof that a crime occurred.

Legal Consultation Regarding Child Witnesses

Traditionally, clinicians are called to take the stand in order to discuss the results of an evaluation of a child after the fact or when a child is in treatment and psychotherapy records are subpoenaed. Another traditional role of the clinician has been to assist children through the legal process. This may involve preparing children for court appearance, accompanying them to the courtroom to become desensitized to the setting or role-playing the court experience. Intervention is also common to help children cope with the often traumatic experiences of separation, foster placement, guilt over their role in the outcome of the trial, and humiliation after critical media exposure. Clinicians are often involved in supporting the family so that they can in turn support the child. More recently, clinicians and researchers have become involved in educating legal practitioners, juries, and legislators through consultation and expert testimony.

Education of Legal Practitioners

On a case by case basis, judicial discretion determines whether children are competent to testify and whether modifications of legal proceedings to reduce stress on child witnesses are necessary. The dissemination of research findings to legal decision-makers could be influential in these determinations. Recently, child psychologists have begun to consult directly with judges as "friends of the court," hired by neither side, as well as with attorneys when hired by one side or the other. Consultation ranges from telephone conversations on the memory capacity of the average four-year-old, to reviewing transcripts to help make sense of a child's inconsistencies or behaviors on the stand. Consultation may focus on the dynamics of intrafamilial abuse or symptoms of Post-Traumatic Stress Disorder. Child development experts have been consulted to insure that questions asked of children are developmentally appropriate. They have begun to educate judicial officers to recognize behaviors that might indicate when children are fatigued or distressed on the stand. Mental health professionals are asked to make suggestions concerning appropriate judicial intervention, perhaps in the form of an empathic comment from the bench or simply a break from the process. In a recent book on the impact of child development research and the law, Melton (1987) discusses additional routes for educating the judiciary, such as appellate briefs and disseminating information to legislators and the media.

Expert Witness

In some jurisdictions, expert testimony by mental health professionals in criminal and civil cases can be provided on the principles of child development and the dynamics of intra-familial child sexual abuse (Berliner, Blick, & Bulkley, 1981). Testimony in some states can also be provided on the "child sexual abuse accommodation syndrome" described by Summit (1983) to aid juries in understanding children's delayed disclosures and recantations. Specific clinical conditions (e.g., PTSD) are described to the court, as are research findings on children's memory and suggestibility. However, there is an increasing number of conflicting legal decisions regarding the proper uses of such expert testimony (Myers, 1987). Myers et al. (1989) describe eight different uses of expert testimony in child sexual assault cases. It is important for each professional to inquire as to the areas about which expert testimony is admissable in his or her jurisdiction and for what purposes (e.g., on rebuttal after a witness' credibility is impeached).

In the courtroom, a mental health professional is qualified as an expert on the basis of both education and professional experience in the field, although both are not always necessary. The expert is expected to present information about which there is consensus in the field, going beyond the lay knowledge of the jury without invading its decision-making province. The ideal expert is someone who can integrate relevant research findings with clinical experience working with children. Clinicians who form opinions on the basis of their own private practice alone must acknowledge that it may be a biased and unrepresentative sample of children. Researchers who form opinions on laboratory studies alone must consider the limits on generalizing to the legal setting and acknowledge the early stage of research in this field. It is best to integrate both clinical experience and experimental research in forming expert opinions about child witnesses.

At the peak of research on adult eyewitness testimony, a debate began to rage among experts regarding testimony requested by defense counsel to make juries aware of factors affecting the accuracy of adult eyewitness identification (Loftus, 1983; McCloskey & Egeth, 1983). Differences of opinion focused on how much empirical support for a conclusion is necessary in order to testify to that fact in a court of law. How much evidence and consensus in the field is enough to warrant application to the legal setting? Prospective expert witnesses were warned that applying research findings to real-world problems may be premature. There was also concern that the inevitable "battle of experts" who interpret the data differently would foster a negative reputation for the field of psychology and the experts would ultimately be ignored.

These concerns are equally relevant for experts who testify about child victim-witnesses. Some conclusions possess greater empirical support, are based on more ecologically valid studies, and are more consistent with the clinical literature than others. At this stage in the development of forensic child psychology, each mental health professional must decide individually which conclusions can be testified to comfortably and with what degree of qualifications, despite potential pressure and seduction from the legal system to offer specific opinions. Maintaining one's integrity is paramount. There is no guarantee that the impact of expert testimony will always result in acquitting the innocent and convicting the guilty. One's professional identity is constantly challenged and redefined in this type of interdisciplinary venture.

A FRAMEWORK FOR INTEGRATING RESEARCH INTO CLINICAL WORK

A heuristic framework for conceptualizing child witness cases and making forensic recommendations is presented. Child witnesses and legal cases vary on a number of dimensions important to making forensic recommendations. A useful heuristic device is to evaluate each case in terms of its developmental, individual, clinical, and situational dimensions. The interactions of these four dimensions must be simultaneously considered in making recommendations regarding child witnesses.

Developmental Differences

Consideration of the child's developmental level of functioning will be critical to any recommendation or expert testimony. Consider the different renditions one might obtain from a preschooler and an adolescent who had both witnessed or participated in the same event. These two witnesses would likely differ in their initial perception of the event due to differences in perceptual development, perspective-taking skills, egocentrism, contextual knowledge, phase of cognitive developent, and so forth. Their performance on the stand might also be influenced by differences in verbal skills to articulate the event, language comprehension of questions asked, memory strategies available for recalling the event, knowledge of the legal system itself, and level of emotional maturity with which to put their feelings in perspective. In short, children's phases of development in different domains will greatly influence the different kinds of information they can testify to and the different conditions under which they can provide meaningful testimony in an adult setting.

Each case must be analyzed in terms of the task demands placed on the child and whether the child's developmental capabilities match task requirements. If the case will require a child to order complex, unfamiliar events chronologically, very young children may be inherently unable to provide this type of information. On the other hand, if the case requires ordering of familiar, concrete events, young children are likely to be quite accurate. Recommendations regarding children's capabilities will depend on an analysis of the task of testifying in a particular case as well as the strengths and weaknesses of a given child.

Individual Differences

Two children of the same age or stage of development will still present individual differences in temperament, premorbid personality characteristics, or social skills that will likely influence forensic recommendations. For example, a generally shy, anxious, insecure, and withdrawn child may perform quite differently on the stand than an outgoing, friendly, and self-confident child. The adult eyewitness literature has revealed a number of individual differences that affect a witness' credibility (e.g., attractiveness, consistency, confidence, likability, intelligence, etc.,) (Loftus, 1979; Yarmey, 1979). We do not yet know which factors are relevant for children. However, despite the lack of rigorous experimental data, it is essential to consider individual differences as they interact with a child's developmental level in recommendations about child witnesses.

Clinical Conditions

Consider the differences between child witnesses in terms of psychiatric diagnosis or the manner in which they cope with the stress of the initial event and the stress of testifying. For example, if a child witness is demonstrating symptoms of depression, including poor concentration, psychomotor retardation, social withdrawal, and anhedonia, then he or she is likely to demonstrate these on the stand, resulting in a withdrawn, unmotivated witness who offers only one word responses. One would want to consider whether an initial trial of antidepressant medication and/or psychotherapy would enable this child to provide a richer and more elaborate report at a later date.

Alternatively, for children without a psychiatric diagnosis, one would want to consider how they are coping with the trauma, be it molestation, kidnapping, or divorce. For example, if coping with abuse by denial or repression, the likelihood of a recantation may be higher. If coping with a desire for mastery and control, testifying may be experienced as a cathartic, empowering, and positive experience. Overall, implications of the child's clinical condition can be as important to consider in forensic recommendations as accuracy of memory for the event.

Situational Factors

Situational factors include a broad array of variables related to (1) the initial event about which the child may testify and (2) the particular path a child is likely to take through the legal process. For example, the literature on adult eyewitness testimony has identified several factors that affect eyewitness accuracy (Loftus, 1979; Yarmey, 1979). One would want to consult this literature and consider characteristics of the event, such as the lighting, duration of exposure, retention interval, whether the person to be identified was a stranger or a familiar person, how many times the witness was exposed to the perpetrator, whether a weapon was involved that could have become the focus of the witness' attention, and so forth.

In determining whether to recommend to a family that their child testify, it would be important to consider the likelihood of winning the case (e.g., Is there any corroborating evidence?), the nature of the crime itself (e.g., What was the level of violence involved? Was the child threatened not to tell what happened?), the role of the child in the event (e.g., Was the child a victim, bystander, or participant?), the relationship of the accused to the child (e.g., parent, teacher or stranger), and the support system available to the child. There are also psychological barriers to testifying that should be considered (Berliner & Barbieri, 1984). A child who must testify against her father, knowing that her mother and siblings do not believe her, and that she may cause the break-up of the family, will likely have mixed feelings about testifying when compared to a child who is testifying against a stranger and has the support of her entire family.

Characteristics of the legal process itself may affect a clinician's recommendations regarding child witnesses. One must consider the research on the effects of the system on young children. In addition, consider the likelihood of numerous interviews and interviewers, the possibility that support persons can be present during testimony, the likelihood that a child will be given breaks when fatigued or upset, the use of closed circuit television, the degree of confrontation by defendant, the use of videotaped interviews, the extent of character defamation; all of these vary from case to case.

To summarize, it is important to keep in mind the way in which the child witness' stage of development interacts with individual differences in personality, clinical diagnosis, and coping strategy, as well as with situational factors relevant to the event and the legal process. This heuristic framework can be extremely helpful in the adversarial context to balance the needs of the child with the needs of the system. Sound objective forensic recommendations are based on empirical findings, tempered by consideration of the limitations on generalization, as well as attention to clinical consensus, techniques, and sensitivity.

SUMMARY AND CONCLUSIONS

The goal of this chapter has been to familiarize readers with the wide range of controversies surrounding child witnesses. To further this goal, discussions have centered on the following:

- Experimental research on children's testimony;
- Clinical research on traumatized children and the effect of the system on children;

- Studies of normal child development;
- Clinical considerations in evaluation, treatment, and expert testimony.

The review of research and clinical application underscores the following recommendations:

- To integrate relevant empirical findings with clinical considerations in this interdisciplinary context;
- To design more ecologically valid investigations;
- To consider developmental, individual, clinical, and situational differences in making forensic recommendations regarding child witnesses;
- To determine under what circumstances it is appropriate to disseminate research findings and clinical consensus to a wider audience as public policy reforms regarding the treatment of child witnesses are debated and instituted across the country.

REFERENCES

Achenbach, T. M., & Edelbrock, C. (1983). *The Child Behavior Checklist and Revised Child Behavior Profile.* Burlington, VT: Department of Psychiatry, University of Vermont.

Avery, M. (1983). The child abuse witness: Potential for secondary victimization. *Criminal Justice Journal, 7*(1), 1–48.

Baxter, J., & Davies, G. (1985). *The suggestibility of child witnesses.* Unpublished manuscript.

Baxter, J., & Davies, G. (1987, April). *Conformity and the child witness.* Paper presented at the meeting of the Society for Research in Child Development, Baltimore, MD.

Benedek, E., & Schetky, D. (1985). Allegations of sexual abuse in child custody and visitation disputes. In D. Schetky & E. Benedek (Eds.), *Emerging issues in child psychiatry and the law* (pp. 145–156). New York: Bruner/Mazel.

Berliner, L., & Barbieri, M.K. (1984). The testimony of the child victim of sexual assault. *Journal of Social Issues, 40,* 125–138.

Berliner, L., Blick, L., & Bulkley, J. (1981). Expert testimony on the dynamics of intra-family child sexual abuse and principles of child development. In J. Bulkley (Ed.), *Child sexual abuse and the law* (pp. 166–183), Wasington, D.C.: American Bar Association National Legal Resource Center for Child Advocacy and Protection.

Bjorklund, D., & Muir, J. (1988). Children's development of free recall memory:

Remembering on their own. In R. Vasta (Ed.), *Annals of Child Development*, Vol. 5, Greenwich, CT: JAI Press.

Bloom, L., Rociassano, L., & Hood, L. (1976). Adult-child discourse: Developmental interaction between information processing and linguistic knowledge. *Cognitive Psychology, 8*, 521–552.

Boat, B., & Everson, M. (1985). *Using anatomical dolls: Guidelines for interviewing young children in sexual abuse investigations.* Chapel Hill, NC.: University of North Carolina.

Brainerd, C. (1978). *Piaget's theory of intelligence.* Englewood Cliffs, NJ: Prentice-Hall.

Bresee, P., Stearns, G., Bess, B., & Packer, L. (1986). Allegations of child sexual abuse in child custody disputes: A therapeutic assessment model. *American Journal of Orthopsychiatry, 56*, 561–569.

Brown, A. (1975). The development of memory: Knowing, knowing about knowing, and knowing how to know. In H. Reese (Ed.), *Advances in child development and behavior, 10*, (pp. 103–152). New York: Academic Press.

Brown, A. (1976). The construction of temporal succession by the preoperational child. In A. Pick (Ed.), *Minnesota symposium on child development, 10*, (pp. 28–83). Minnesota: University of Minnesota Press.

Browne, A., & Finkelhor, D. (1986). Impact of child sexual abuse: A review of research. *Psychological Bulletin, 99*, 66–77.

Burton, R. (1976). Honesty and dishonesty. In T. Lickona (Ed.) *Moral development and behavior.* (pp. 173–197), New York: Holt Rinehart & Winston.

Carey, (1978). The child as word learner. In M. Halle, J. Bresnan, & G. Miller (Eds.), *Linguistic theory and psychological reality*, Cambridge, MA: MIT Press.

Case, R. (1985). *Intellectual development: A systematic reinterpretation.* New York: Academic Press.

Ceci, S., Toglia, M., & Ross, D. (1987). *Children's eyewitness memory.* New York: Springer-Verlag.

Ceci, A., Ross, D., & Toglia, M. (1987). Age differences in suggestibility: Narrowing the uncertainties. In S. Ceci, M. Toglia, & D. Ross (Eds.), *Children's eyewitness memory.* (pp. 79–91). New York: Springer-Verlag.

Chi, M. (1978). Knowledge structures and memory development. In R. Siegler (Ed.), *Children's thinking: What develops?* (pp. 73–96). Hillsdale, NJ: Erlbaum.

Claman, L., Harris, J., Bernstein, B., & Lovitt, R. (1986). The adolescent as a witness in a case of incest: Assessment and outcome. *Journal of the American Academy of Child Psychiatry, 25*, 457–461.

Clark, E. (1972). On the child's acquisition of antonyms in two semantic fields. *Journal of Verbal Learning and Verbal Behavior, 11*, 750–758.

Clark, H., & Clark, E., (1977). *Psychology and language.* New York: Harcourt Brace Jovanovich.

Cohen, R., & Harnick, M.A. (1980). The susceptibility of child witnesses to suggestion. *Law and Human Behavior, 4*, 201–210.

Cole, C., & Loftus, E. (1987). The memory of children. In S. Ceci, M. Toglia, & D. Ross (eds.), *Children's eyewitness memory.* (pp. 178–208). New York: Springer Verlag.

Conte, J. (January, 1987). *The effects of sexual abuse: Results of a research project.* Paper presented at Human Sexual Aggression: Current Perspectives, The New York Academy of Sciences, New York.

Corwin, D., Berliner, L., Goodman, G., Goodwin, & White, S. (1987). Allegations of child sexual abuse in custody disputes—No easy answers. *Journal of Interpersonal Violence, 2,* 91–105.

Cosgrove, M., & Patterson, C. (1977). Plans and the development of listener skills. *Developmental Psychology, 13,* 557–564.

Dale, P. (1976). *Language development: Structure and function.* New York: Holt Rinehart & Winston.

Dale, P., Loftus, E., & Rathbun, L. (1978). The influence of the form of the question on the eyewitness testimony of preschool children. *Journal of Psycholinguistic Research, 7,* 269–277.

Davies, G., Stevenson-Robb, Y., & Flin, R. (in press). Tales out of school: Children's memory for an unexpected event. In M. Grunenberg, P. Morris, & R. Sykes (Eds.), *Practical aspects of memory.* Chester, PA: Wiley.

DeFrancis, V. (1969). *Protecting the child victim of sex crimes committed by adults.* Denver, CO: American Humane Association.

deVilliers, P., & deVilliers, J. (1979). *Early language.* Cambridge, MA: Harvard University Press.

Dickson, W.P. (1981). *Children's oral communication skills.* New York: Academic Press.

Duncan, E., Whitney, P., & Kunen, S. (1982). Integration of visual and verbal information in children's memories. *Child Development, 53,* 1215–1223.

Elkind, D. (1962). Children's conceptions of brother and sister: Piaget replication study V. *Journal of Genetic Psychology, 100,* 129–136.

Eth, S., & Pynoos, R. (1985). *Post-traumatic stress disorder in children.* Washington, D.C.: American Psychiatric Press.

Everson, M., & Boat, B. (in press). False allegations of sexual abuse by children and adolescents. *Journal of the American Academy of Child and Adolescent Psychiatry.*

Faller, (1988). Criteria for judging the credibility of children's statements about their sexual abuse. *Child Welfare, 67,* 389.

Flavell, J. (1977). *Cognitive development.* Englewood Cliffs, NJ: Prentice-Hall.

Flavell, J. (1981). Cognitive monitoring. In P. Dickson (Ed.), *Children's oral communication skills* (pp. 35–60). New York: Academic Press.

Flavell, J., Speer, J., Green, F., & August, D. (1981). The development of comprehension monitoring and knowledge about communication. *Monographs of the Society for Research in Child Development, 46*(5) (Serial No. 192).

Foley, M., & Aman, C. (1987, April). *Remembering actions: An analysis of the sources of children's confusions.* Paper presented at the meeting of the Society for Research in Child Development, Baltimore, MD.

Foley, M., & Johnson, M. (1985). Confusions between memories for performed and imagined actions: A developmental comparison. *Child Development, 56,* 1145–1155.

Foley, M., Johnson, M., & Raye, C. (1983). Age related changes in confusions between memories for thoughts and memories for speech. *Child Development, 54,* 51–60.

Freud, S. (1958). Two principles of mental functioning. In J. Strachey (Ed. and Trans.), *The standard edition of the complete psychological works of Sigmund Freud.* (Vol. 12, pp. 218–226). London: Hogarth Press (Original work published 1911).

Friedman, W.J. (1982). *The developmental psychology of time.* New York: Academic Press.

Friedrich, W., Urquiza, A., & Beilke, R. (1986). Behavior problems in sexually abused young children. *Journal of Pediatric Psychology, 11*(1), 47–57.

Garvey, C. (1977). *Play.* Cambridge, MA: Harvard University Press.

Gibbens, T., & Prince, J. (1963). *Child victims of sex offenses.* London: Institute of Psychiatry.

Goodman, G. (1984). The child witness. *Journal of Social Issues, 40,* 1–175.

Goodman, G., & Aman, C. (1987, April). Children's use of anatomically correct dolls to report an event in evaluation of suspected child abuse: Developmental, clinical, and legal perspectives on the use of anatomically correct dolls. Symposium presented at the Society for Research in Child Development convention, Baltimore, MD.

Goodman, G., Aman, C., & Hirschman (1987). Child sexual and physical abuse: Children's testimony. In S. Ceci, M. Toglia, & D. Ross (Eds.), *Children's eyewitness memory* (pp. 1–23). New York: Springer-Verlag.

Goodman, G., Golding, J., & Haith, M. (1984). Juror's reactions to child witnesses. *Journal of Social Issues, 40,* 139–156.

Goodman, G., & Hahn, A., (1987). Evaluating eyewitness testimony. In I. Weiner & A. Hess (Eds.), *Handbook of Forensic Psychology* (pp. 258–292). New York: Wiley.

Goodman, G., & Hegelson, V. (1986). Child sexual assault: Children's memory and the law. In J. Bulkley, (Ed.), *Papers from a National Policy Conference on Legal Reforms in Child Sexual Abuse Cases* (pp. 41–60). A report of the American Bar Association.

Goodman, G., Hirschman, J., & Rudy, L. (1987, April). Children's testimony: Research and policy implications. Paper presented at *Children as witnesses: Research and social policy implications,* S. Ceci (Chair). Symposium of the Society for Research in Child Development meetings, Baltimore, MD.

Goodman, G., Pyle, E., Jones, D., Port, L., England, P., Rudy, L. & Prado, L. (1988). The emotional effects of criminal court testimony on child sexual assault victims: A preliminary report. In G. Davies & J. Drinkwater (Eds.), *Proceedings from the International Conference on Child Witnesses: Do the courts abuse children?* Oxford: British Psychological Association.

Goodman, G., & Reed, R. (1986). Age differences in eyewitness testimony. *Law and human behavior, 10,* 317–332.

Goodwin, J., Sahd, D., & Rada, R.T. (1979). *Bulletin of American Association of Psychiatry and Law, 5,* 269, 275.

Green, A. (1986). True and false allegations of sexual abuse in child custody disputes. *Journal of the American Academy of Child Psychiatry, 25,* 449–456.

Greenglass, E. (1972). Effects of age and prior help on "altruistic lying." *Journal of Genetic Psychology, 121,* 303–313.

Hartshorne, H., & May, H. (1975). *Studies in the nature of character: Vol 1 Studies in deceit.* New York: Arno Press.

Haviland, S., & Clark E. (1974). This man's father is my father's son. *Journal of Child Language, 1,* 23–47.

Horowitz, J., Salt, P., Gomes-Schwartz, Z., & Sanzer, M. (1984). *Unconfirmed cases of sexual abuse.* Unpublished Manuscript. Division of Child Psychiatry, Tufts Medical Center, Boston, MA.

Johnson, M., & Foley, M. (1984). Differentiating fact from fantasy: The reliability of children's memory. *Journal of Social Issues, 40,* 33–50.

Johnson, J., Raye, C., Hasher, L., & Chromiak, W. (1979). Are there developmental differences in reality monitoring. *Journal of Experimental Child Psychology, 27,* 120–128.

Jones, D.P.H., & McGraw, J.M. (1987). Reliable and fictitious accounts of sexual abuse in children. *Journal of Interpersonal Violence, 2,* 27–45.

Kerns, D.L. (1981). Medical assessment in child sexual abuse. In P.B. Mrazek & C.H. Kempe (Eds.), *Sexually abused children and their families.* (pp. 126–141). Oxford: Pergamon.

King, M., & Yuille, J. (1987). Suggestibility and the child witness. In S. Ceci, M. Toglia, & D. Ross (Eds.), *Children's eyewitness memory* (pp. 24–35). New York: Springer-Verlag.

Leippe, M., & Romanczyk, A. (1987). The child in the eyes of the jury: A communication/persuasion analysis of juror's reactions to child witnesses. In S. Ceci, M. Toglia, & D. Ross (Eds.), *Children's eyewitness memory.* (pp. 155–177). New York: Springer-Verlag.

Lindberg, M. (1980). The role of knowledge structures in the otogeny of learning. *Journal of Experimental Child Psychology. 30,* 401–410.

Lindsay, D.D., & Johnson, M. (1987). Reality monitoring and suggestibility. In S. Ceci, M. Toglia, & D. Ross (Eds.), *Children's eyewitness memory* (pp. 92–117). New York: Springer-Verlag.

Loftus, E. (1979). *Eyewitness Testimony.* Cambridge: Harvard Univ. Press.

Loftus, E. (1983). Silence is not golden. *American Psychologist, 41,* 564–572.

Loftus, E., & Davies, G. (1984). Distortions in the memory of children. *Journal of Social Issues, 40,* 51–68.

Loftus, E., & Palmer, J. (1974). Reconstruction of automobile destruction: An example of the interaction between language and memory. *Journal of Verbal Learning and Verbal Behavior, 13,* 585–589.

Marin, B., Holmes, D., Guth, M., & Kovacs, P. (1979). The potential of children as eyewitnesses. *Law and Human Behavior, 3,* 295–306.

Markman, E. (1977). Realizing that you don't understand: A preliminary investigation. *Child Development, 48,* 986–992.

Markman, E. (1979). Realizing that you don't understand: Elementary school children's awareness of inconsistencies. *Child Development, 50,* 543–655.

Matarazzo, J. (1978). The interview: Its reliability and validity in psychiatric diagnosis. In B.J. Wolman (Ed.), *Clinical diagnosis of mental disorders: A handbook* (pp. 47–96). New York: Plenum Press.

McClelland, N. (1976). Character development in children: Correlates of honesty behavior in 4th, 5th, and 6th grade children. *Dissertation Abstracts, 3494-A–3495-A.*

McCloskey, M., & Egeth, H. (1983). What can a psychologist tell a jury? *American Psychologist, 41,* 550–563.

Melton, G. (1981). Children's competency to testify. *Law and Human Behavior,* 5(1), 73–86.

Melton, G. (1984). Child witnesses and the first amendment: A psycholegal dilemma. *Journal of Social Issues, 40* (2), 109–124.

Melton, G. (1987). *Reforming the law: Impact of child development research.* New York: Guilford Press.

Melton, G., & Thompson, R. (1987). Getting out of a rut: Detours to less traveled paths in child-witness research. In S. Ceci, M. Toglia, & D. Ross (Eds.), *Children's eyewitness memory* (pp. 209–229). New York: Springer-Verlag.

Miller, P. (1983). *Theories of developmental psychology.* New York: W.H. Freeman.

Myers, J. (1987). *Child witness law and practice.* New York: Wiley.

Myers, J., Bays, J., Becker, J., Berliner, L., Corwin, D., & Saywitz, K. (1989). Expert testimony in child sexual abuse litigation. *University of Nebraska Law Review,* Lincoln, NE.

Myles-Worsley, M., Cromer, C., & Dodd, D., (1986). Children's preschool script reconstruction: Reliance on general knowledge as memory fades. *Developmental Psychology, 22*(1), 22–30.

Nelson, K. (1979). How children represent their world in and out of language: A preliminary report. In R. Siegler (Ed.), *Children's thinking: What develops?* (pp. 255–273). Hillsdale, NJ: Erlbaum.

Nelson, K., & Gruendel, J. (1979). At morning it's lunchtime: A scriptal view of children's dialogues. *Discourse Processes, 2,* 73–94.

Nelson, K., & Gruendel, J. (1981). Generalized event representations: Basic building blocks of cognitive development. In M. Lamb & A. Brown (Eds.), *Advances in developmental psychology Vol. 1* (pp. 131–158). Hillsdale, NJ: Erlbaum.

Nelson, K., Fivush, R., Hudson, J., & Lucariello, J. (1983). Scripts and the development of memory. In Chi, M. (Ed.), *Current trends in memory development research* (pp. 52–69). New York: Karger.

Neisser, U. (1979). The control of information pickup in selective looking. In A. Pick (Ed.), *Perception and development: A tribute to Eleanor Gibson* (pp. 210–219). Hillsdale, NJ: Erlbaum.

Nurcombe, B. (1987). The child as witness. In L. Lipsitt (ed.), *When children need help.* Providence, RI: Manisses Communications Group.

Ochs, E., & Schiefflin, B. (1979). *Developmental pragmatics.* New York: Academic Press.

Patterson, C., Massad, C., & Cosgrove, M. (1978). Children's referential communication: Components of plans for effective listening. *Developmental Psychology, 14,* 401–406.

Perlmutter, M. (1980). *Children's memory: New directions in child development,* No. 10. San Francisco: Jossey-Bass.

Piaget, J. (1928). *Judgement and reasoning in the child.* London: Kegan-Paul

Piaget, J. (1932). *The moral judgement of the child.* London: Kegan-Paul

Piaget, J. (1951). *Play, dreams, and imitation in childhood.* New York: Norton.

Popp, J., & Zaragoza, M. (1987, August). *Suggestibility of eyewitness memory in preschoolers.* Paper presented at the meeting of the American Psychological Association, New York.

Pynoos, R., & Eth, S. (1984). The child as witness to homicide. *Journal of Social Issues, 40,* 87–108.

Rex v. Brasier 11 Leach 199,168 Eng. Rep. 202 (1779).

Roberts, M. (1985, September). Testimony before the United States Senate Subcommittee on Juvenile Justice pertaining to The Child Victim Witness Protection Act of 1985.

Ross, D., Miller, B., & Moran, P. (1987). The child in the eyes of the jury: Assessing mock juror's perceptions of the child witness. In S. Ceci, M. Toglia, & D. Ross (Eds.), *Children's eyewitness memory* (pp. 142–154). New York: Springer Verlag.

Runyan, D., Everson, M., Edelsohn, G., Hunter, W., and Coulter, M. (1988). Impact of legal intervention on sexually abused children. *Journal of Pediatrics,* 647–653.

Saywitz, K. (1987). Children's testimony: Age-related patterns of memory errors. In S. Ceci, M. Toglia, & D. Ross (Eds.), *Children's eyewitness memory* (pp. 36–52). New York: Springer-Verlag.

Saywitz, K. (1989). Children's conceptions of the legal system: "Court is a place to play basketball." In S. Ceci, D. Ross, & M. Toglia (Eds.), *Perspectives on children's testimony.* New York: Springer-Verlag.

Saywitz, K., & Jaenicke, C. (1987, April). Children's understanding of legal terminology: A preliminary report of age-related trends. Paper presented at the meeting of the Society for Research in Child Development, Baltimore, MD.

Siegler, R. (1986). *Children's thinking.* Englewood Cliffs, NJ: Prentice-Hall.

Singer, J., & Flavell, J. (1981). Development of knowledge about communication: Children's evaluations of explicitly ambiguous messages. *Child Development, 52,* 1211–1215.

Singer, D., & Revenson, T. (1978). *How a child thinks.* New York: Plume.

Stein, N. (1978). *How children understand stories: A developmental analysis* (Report No. 69). Cambridge, MA: Bolt Beranek Newman, Inc.

Stern, W. (1910). Abstracts of lectures on the psychology of testimony. *American Journal of Psychology. 21,* 273–282.

Summit, R. (1983). The child sexual abuse accommodation syndrome. *Child Abuse and Neglect, 7,* 177–193.

Tapp, J., & Levine, F. (1974). Legal socialization: Strategies for an ethical legality. *Stanford Law Review, 27,* 1–72.

Taylor, M.G., & Purfall, P.B. (1987, April). *A developmental analysis of directional terms frontwards, backwards, and sidewards.* Paper presented at the meeting of the Society for Research in Child Development, Baltimore, MD.

Tedesco, J., & Schnell, S. (1987). Children's reactions to sex abuse investigation and litigation. *Child Abuse and Neglect, 11,* 267–272.

Terr, L. (1981). Psychic trauma in children: Observations following the Chowchilla schoolbus kidnapping. *American Journal of Psychiatry, 138,* 14–19.

Terr, K. (1983). Chowchilla revisited: the effects of psychic trauma four years after a schoolbus kidnapping. *American Journal of Psychiatry, 140,* 1543–1550.

Theonnes, N., & Pearson, J. (1988). *The Sexual Allegations Project* (final report). The Association of Family and Conciliation Courts Research Unit. Denver, CO.

Todd, C., & Perlmutter, M. (1980). Reality recalled by preschool children. In M. Perlmutter (Ed.), *Children's memory: New directions in child development,* (pp. 69–85). No. 10. San Francisco: Jossey-Bass.

Varendock, J. (1911). Les termoignages d'enfants dans un proces retentissant. *Archives de Psychologie, 11,* 129–171. (C. Hazan, R. Hazan, & G. Goodman Trans., 1984).

Walsh, R. (1967). Sex, age, and temptation. *Psychological Reports, 21,* 625–629.

Weiss, E., & Berg, R. (1982). Child victims of sexual assault: Impact of court procedures. *Journal of the American Academy of Child Psychiatry, 21,* 513–518.

Wheeler v. United States, 159 U.S. 523 (1895).

White, S., Strom, G., & Santilli, G. (1985). *Clinical protocol for interviewing preschoolers with sexually anatomically correct dolls.* Unpublished manuscript. Case Western Reserve Univ., School of Medicine, Cleveland Metropolitan Hospital, Cleveland, OH.

Wimmer, H., Gruber, S., & Perner, J. (1985). Young children's conception of lying: Moral intuition and the denotation and connotation of "to lie." *Developmental Psychology, 21*(6), 993–995.

Yarmey, A. (1979). *The psychology of eyewitness testimony.* New York: Free Press.

Yarmey, A., & Jones, H. (1983). Is the psychology of eyewitness identification a matter of common sense? In S.M. Lloyd & B.R. Clifford (Eds.), *Evaluating witness evidence* (pp. 13–40). New York: Wiley.

Zaragoza, M. (1987). Memory, suggestibility, and eyewitness testimony in children and adults. In S. Ceci, M. Toglia, & D. Ross (Eds.), *Children's eyewitness memory* (pp. 52–78). New York: Springer-Verlag.

12

The Investigatory Interview with Suspected Victims of Child Sexual Abuse

SUE WHITE

INTRODUCTION

This volume concerns itself with interviewing of children from the child's point of view. The field of interviewing child sexual abuse victims has yet to consider fully the child's viewpoint. This chapter addresses factors which may influence the information a child brings to the evaluation.

Until relatively recently, suspected victims of child sexual abuse did not receive much special consideration with reference to how they should be interviewed. Because of subsequent judicial involvement of the interviews, as the 1980s have progressed, much more attention is now being paid to this unique group of individuals, especially those children under the age of eight years. Older victims who have no disability (e.g., mental retardation, communication problems) have not been targeted for special consideration in interviewing situations. These older victims are usually deemed competent by the court to testify in their own behalf. Thus the data from their interviews are not subject to hearsay rules

(Myers, 1986). Younger victims may testify for themselves (*Commonwealth v. Reid,* 1987; *People v. Draper,* 1986; *State v. Harmening,* 1985), but corroborating testimony of those who interview the younger children is frequently offered. Regardless of the type of proceedings (juvenile, family, criminal), this testimony should be based on data obtained in an investigatory interview. Herein lies the crux of the problem.

Techniques of interviewing these young children have been based on practical experiences and are only now beginning to receive any research attention. To date, pertinent research has been related to how the children are best to be interviewed in court proceedings (Dent, 1982; Goodman, 1987) and how they respond to anatomical dolls (Jampole & Weber, 1987; White, Strom, Santilli, & Halpin, 1986). While a number of authors have detailed suggestions of how best to interact with a child suspected of being a victim of sexual abuse (Flammung, 1980; Jones & McQuiston, 1985; MacFarlane & Waterman, 1986; Sgroi, 1982), interviewers have been forced to discover clinical techniques which work best in their particular situation. The results of such interviews are then subjected to legal system proceedings and may be found lacking (*Idaho Department of Health and Welfare v. Syme,* 1986; *In re J. H.,* 1987). Presented here are some suggestions relative to investigatory interviewing of the young suspected sexual abuse victim and some problems that arise which may compromise the results of such an interview. While the issues discussed are pertinent to all ages of abuse victims, they are most applicable to the young victim who may not prove to be competent enough to protect or testify for himself.

THE SPECIAL NATURE OF INTERVIEWING A SUSPECTED ABUSE VICTIM

While evaluating a child for evidence of a mental health disturbance requires specialized training, interviewing a suspected child abuse victim carries with it the additional responsibility of recognizing that the information gathered in the interview may result in legal proceedings. These legal actions include the temporary or permanent removal of a child from a parent, a custody hearing between parents, civil litigation seeking monetary damage settlements, and/or felony charges against an individual. Acknowledging that these possibilities exist should guide evaluators to utilize techniques which result in the material's being acceptable by the legal system.

Because we cannot wait until research data become available to answer the multitude of questions being posed by the court system about child sexual abuse interviews, the following concepts and interviewing suggestions provide a format which offers a very conservative and, hopefully, legally acceptable approach. These concepts are a result of clinical and forensic experiences of the sexual abuse team at Cleveland Metropolitan General Hospital. Research is underway to evaluate these postulated concepts. As research data become available, it is anticipated that some of these suggestions will be modified. Until then, however, we must offer the best to the children by interviewing them in a way so as to allow for their protection and advocacy in the legal system. By following these guidelines, we also are providing more equitable treatment to the alleged perpetrator.

THE GOAL OF THE INVESTIGATORY EVALUATION: UNCONTAMINATED DATA

The first goal in investigatory interviewing must be the gathering of data which are as true as possible a representation of the child's experiences and which are not subject to charges of being contaminated (e.g., *Idaho Department of Health and Welfare v. Syme*, 1986; *In re J. H.*, 1987). Contamination occurs when the source of the child's memory of the events supporting the allegation becomes ambiguous or confounded. Contamination may take the form of poor interview techniques, an adverse interview environment, the interviewer's inappropriate behaviors, or influences outside the interviewer's control (e.g., family pressures). As a child's reflection of an actual experience may well be altered by his/her being questioned or talking about the incident (White & Quinn, 1988), care must be taken to minimize the possibility of changing the data which the child carries with him/her. This type of contamination is discussed later in this chapter as well as in Chapter 11.

External Independence

The constant companion of child sexual abuse evaluators in minimizing contamination of a suspected victim's memory is the adherence to *independence* or objectivity, both externally and internally. *External independence* is "the evaluator's objective stance of not allying him/herself with any particular individual involved in the investigation of the allegation" (White, Santilli, & Quinn, 1988, p. 94). All parents, lawyers, and other interested individuals are dealt with on an equal basis regardless of whether the evaluator is legally mandated (department of human service, police) or not (mental health professionals).

The legally mandated agencies do not have a choice in investigation. Thus, whether or not the workers obtain cooperation from all sides and their lawyers, the evaluation must proceed. Yet these investigators can still demonstrate independence by their objective interactions with all parties.

Until recently, evaluations by someone other than a legal authority were quite common as mental health professionals often completed the first assessment of a parent's allegation that the child was being abused. Such initial evaluations by nonlegally mandated agencies are decreasing as it is becoming standard procedure to minimize the number of evaluations a child has. If an allegation is initially presented to a mental health professional, it is recommended that the case be immediately referred to the local legal authority for the initial evaluation. Mental health professionals may, however, become involved by court order, in a request for a second opinion, or under agreement by a department of human service (DHS).

Under either of these types of evaluations, practical aspects of maintaining external independence may take several forms. Foremost is the requirement that all referral motives be evaluated in any abuse allegation. Motives other than the child's best interests include a wish to have visitation or custody modified, harassment of an individual, or the need for attention by the referrer.

If there is any hint of a custody and/or visitation dispute, extra care must be taken to maintain external independence. As sexual abuse allegations are becoming more frequently seen in custody disputes (MacFarlane, 1986), these referrals should be accepted by nonlegally mandated evaluators if, and only if, there is agreement that both sides accept independent evaluation criteria (White et al., 1988). Working through the parties' lawyers is the most advantageous method. While this recommendation does not appear to have anything to do with interviewing, the lack of obtaining such an agreement by all parties will quite frequently negate any information gathered as it will not be presented to a judicial system as independently gathered material. Only in rare circumstances of documented threat of harm should an evaluation be done if independence cannot be agreed upon by all involved.

External independence may also be tested when a parent presents a child's specific behavior (e.g., excessive masturbation) as a basis for suspicion of abuse. If no specific disclosure has been made, the evaluator must decide if it is best to collect additional preliminary data on which to make a decision for referral to a DHS office. If further information is gathered, care must be taken that the interviewer not ally with the individual (e.g., mother) with whom he/she has the most contacts.

Freedom from alignment with one side will allow for maintenance of external independence.

In cases in which the clinician is asked to provide a second opinion regarding the allegation, external independence requires that the issues of contamination be evaluated prior to accepting the case. Especially important is information concerning the earlier prior interviews of the child. Details of previous evaluations should include location, those present, interviewers, techniques employed, frequency of contacts between child and interviewer, dates of the interviews, and any intervening events (such as physical examinations). Any original disclosure information that was given to the caregiving parent(s) or other professionals about the child's story at the time of the first evaluation also needs to be clarified.

If the interviewer concludes that the first evaluation was a good assessment with little or no contamination, there should be strong consideration given not to reinterview the child. Explanations about how a child can freeze and/or recant because of emotional issues (Sgroi, 1982; Summit, 1983) or subtle or explicit pressure by a seemingly cooperative parent (Jones & McQuiston, 1985) can be discussed with the referrer.

If there were a number of confounding factors in the original evaluation, the decision to reinterview should be made if, and only if, there is reason to believe that the present evaluation may result in more reliable information. If the contamination is judged to be severe, it may be recommended that nothing further be done as it will only result in additional problems.

External independence is also tested when a suspicion of abuse is raised in an ongoing therapeutic situation. There are several reasons for the therapist not to be the one to provide the abuse evaluation, especially in the cases of young children. First, the confidential relationship that has developed will no longer be in effect and future therapeutic progress may then be in jeopardy. Second, the therapist's emotional relationship with the child would change as he/she must interact in a less empathic manner. Third, in many therapeutic cases, there is a strong alliance between the therapist and the parent bringing the child. If the allegation is against the other parent, interviewer independence will never be achieved. A fourth consideration is that the investigatory interviewer may testify regarding the child. Should this be done, the relationship with the child may well suffer. Thus, for the sake of the child's well-being, the therapist who suspects an allegation of abuse arising should have the child seen by an investigatory interviewer before a great deal of information is imparted to the therapist.

Internal Independence

Once a decision to interview a suspected victim of sexual abuse has been made, the evaluator must then adopt the concept of *internal independence*, or *neutrality*, i.e., "the internal ability not to be biased relative to the allegations..." (White et al., 1988, p. 95). Maintaining internal independence mandates that the interviewer must be extremely careful not to influence or change the data the child brings to the interview. For instance, if the allegation had been presented to the interviewer as, "Her father has been messing with her on visitations," the biased interviewer may then present only an adult male doll and label it "Daddy." The interviewer asks the child to show what "daddy" did to her without evaluating the possibility that the child may call more than one man "daddy," that another individual may be responsible for the abuse, or that the child has been programmed to make such a statement implicating the father. Assumptions of veracity of the allegation should not be incorporated into the interview (Benedek & Schetky, 1987; Goodwin, Sahd, & Rada, 1982; Jones & McQuiston, 1985).

THE INVESTIGATORY INTERVIEWER

Investigatory interviewing may be done by anyone with appropriate child interviewing experiences provided that he/she approaches the case with at least the following particular skills. *Comfort in interacting with children* and the *ability to manage a wide range of children's behaviors* are prerequisites. *Knowledge of basic child development principles* and *familiarity with child witness issues* are critical as is *knowledge of sexual abuse dynamics* (Boat & Everson, 1986; Friedemann & Morgan, 1985; MacFarlane, 1986; Sgroi, Porter, & Blick, 1982; Schetky et al., 1988; White et al., 1988). Quality investigative interviewing can be done by mental health practitioners, protective service workers, and police detectives. Allied professionals, such as pediatricians, gynecologists, pediatric nurses, prosecuting and defense attorneys, and judges, should all be aware of basic guidelines for investigatory interviews. Unless they are adequately trained in child development, these individuals should be cautious about performing investigatory interviews so as not to disturb the data that the trained interviewer may obtain from the child. It is important for all individuals, including mental health professionals, to know if, and when, to choose *not to do* an investigatory interview.

THE EVALUATION

The investigatory evaluation consists of at least two major parts: *history taking* and *interviews of the child* (Jones & McQuiston, 1985; Sgroi et al., 1982; White et al., 1988). White and her colleagues suggest a two-person team: a designated intake person and an interviewer. These roles may be interchanged on various cases, but within a case remain the same. The intake person is responsible for gathering background information and for providing the referrer with the basic guidelines set by the office, including the format of the evaluation. Special attention should be paid to legal matters, such as details of the family constellation (divorced, separated, etc.), custody and visitation arrangements, any court hearings planned, attorneys involved, DHS workers assigned, and a history of any prior evaluations. The importance of knowing about prior evaluations cannot be underestimated because this information is not necessarily volunteered by a referring party who is "shopping" for the answer he/she wants. In addition, the intake person should discuss the financial considerations, take care of written arrangements (i.e., consents), and discuss the disposition of the results. It is imperative that this person document all contacts (including telephone calls) by date, person contacted, and the content of the interaction.

In this two-person approach, the child interviewer has no contact with the referrer or family until the child is brought for the evaluation. While others (Conerly, 1986; Sgroi et al., 1982) do not recommend such a stance, White et al. (1988) feel that this recommendation allows for the evaluator to be better able to maintain objectivity and to assess the facts without prior biases. An evaluator, especially one not maintaining internal independence, may be more likely to push to substantiate certain "facts" to the exclusion of other information the child may have. In settings where a two-person team is not possible or is not utilized by choice, the investigator must mentally separate various roles in order to maintain both external and internal independence. This is especially critical for DHS workers who must simultaneously fulfill several roles for the family (e.g., support for parent; investigator; liaison).

Gathering of Background Information

An evaluation of a suspected child sexual abuse victim is more than just a child's interview. It also mandates a complete psychosocial history of the family to elucidate various factors which may be important in assessing the validity of the allegation. Among the issues which should be addressed are:

1. An account of the family's daily living patterns (bathing, toileting, sleeping habits).
2. Their traditions concerning privacy and nudity.
3. Their approach to sexuality and sex education.
4. A history of exposure to sexually explicit materials and activities.
5. The child's level of development concerning sexuality.
6. The history of abuse of all parties.
7. The family dynamics, including the marital history of the parents and their sexual practices.
8. The full history of behavioral disturbances in the child.
9. The significant mental health history of primary caregivers (White et al., 1988).

A complete picture which synthesizes these data and those obtained in the child's interviews comprises the results of an investigatory evaluation.

Contacts During the Evaluation

While some evaluators only see a child once to assess the possibility of sexual abuse (e.g., data presented by Boat & Everson, 1988), most recommend seeing a child on multiple occasions (two to three times) (Boat & Everson, 1986; Conerly, 1986; Friedemann & Morgan, 1985; Schetky et al., 1988; Sgroi et al., 1982; White, Strom, Santilli, & Quinn, 1987). Multiple interviews allow for an opportunity to assess consistency of the allegation (content as well as language and emotional reaction) and issues of coaching versus the child's independent memory. This recommendation has arisen from clinical judgments as research data on this issue are not yet available.

Parent Interactions

Bringing a child for a sexual abuse evaluation is an anxiety-producing situation for a parent. To decrease this anxiety, the child's caregiver should be informed about who will be interviewing the child and what the procedures will be. Plans for dissemination of the information should have already been discussed. Particularly important is informing the parent that details from the child's interview will not be released immediately unless there is a need for protection of the child.

Who Should Participate in the Interview?

Parent or parent substitute. The presence of a parent or support-ive adult in the child's interview is a debated one. Some argue for the child's being seen alone (Schetky et al., 1988; White et al., 1988) while others allow an adult to be present if the child is unable to separate (Boat & Everson, 1986; Friedemann & Morgan, 1985; Jones & McQuiston, 1985; Sgroi et al., 1982). It must be considered that the parent's presence in the interview room with the child raises the potential of parental con-tamination of the child's data. First, even without their participation in the actual interviewing process, the presence of a parental figure allows for the expectation that the child will produce information specifically to please the parent. While the effect of this "pressure to produce" on the child's story is unknown empirically, it must be acknowledged as a distinct possibility. Second, the parent is commonly the primary com-plainant and may direct the child to produce information consistent with his/her beliefs concerning the allegations or to duplicate "what you told me at home." Third, the parent may also have "become an expert at non-verbally reminding the child to keep the secret while 'telling the truth'" (Jones & McQuiston, 1985, p. 17). Fourth, the parent may be utilized to interview the child, a practice which frequently introduces coercive and leading statements and questions into the interview.

If the parent does not know what the child has said, there is less of a chance of accusations being raised that the child's story was manipulated by the parent between sessions, even by a well-meaning parent. For example, if a parent is told that Uncle John was named as the alleged perpetrator, the mother may be quite surprised and later ask the child, "You said, 'Uncle John'? Did you really mean him?" The child may subsequently change his/her answer to suit what he/she thinks the parent wished him/her to say.

Siblings. The presence of siblings in conjoint interviews with the alleged victim should also be considered contaminatory. By using the older sibling to pressure the younger child to "tell the doctor what you told mom," the interviewer is introducing coercion to the interview. Sec-ond, in encouraging a sibling to recount his/her own experience of abuse in front of the younger child, the source of the younger child's informa-tion is then contaminated. Third, if the older sibling is to be employed as a surrogate interviewer, inappropriate interviewing techniques may be used in his/her sincere effort to have the younger child reveal infor-mation. Fourth, on top of the problems of influencing the data of the younger child, the use of the older child in the interview may in itself contaminate his/her own allegations which may arise.

Peers. The problems of utilization of peer groups to interview suspected victims in mass disclosures are similar to those which occur during sibling interviews. The source of a child's information may be confounded by his/her having heard another child's disclosure. The presence of several peers may add to the children's perceptions of their needing to give data or to agree with their peers' disclosures.

Alleged perpetrator present. The effect of the presence of the perpetrator on the child's telling his/her experiences is a debated and unresolved issue. Although Green (1986) has recommended that the child be interviewed with the alleged perpetrator present, most do so only with very cautious reasoning, such as when allegations arise during custody disputes (Schetky et al., 1988).

Evaluation Procedures

There are several suggested evaluation procedures (Boat & Everson, 1986; Jones & McQuiston, 1985; MacFarlane & Krebs, 1986; Sgroi et al., 1982; White et al., 1987). Some recommend a structured set of guidelines (Boat & Everson, 1986; White et al., 1987) while others (Conerly, 1986; Yates & Terr, 1988a,b) feel that observing the child's freeplay and following the child's lead is more appropriate. Still others (Friedemann & Morgan, 1985; MacFarlane & Krebs, 1986) recommend semistructured procedures, combining some formal questioning mixed with freeplay. The decision to utilize a particular stance is, at present, a clinical choice. It is probably advantageous to establish a systematic evaluation method as these data often find their way to the court system. If an interviewer is quite able to tell exactly what he/she did with the child and to describe the child's responses, there is a higher likelihood that the data will receive their "day in court."

Environment of the Interview

The environment should allow for a quiet, controlled interview. The room should be equipped with age-appropriate furnishings so that the atmosphere will be most conducive to the victim's feeling comfortable. For very young children, the interviewer's sitting on the floor as close to the child's eye level as possible often helps the child relax. For young children, a few suggested toys include: dollhouse, people puppets, two play telephones, markers and paper, trucks and cars, and tools for an abuse evaluation.

Free Play Period

The interview should begin with a free play period so as to: (a) relax both the child and interviewer, (b) build rapport, and (c) allow the interviewer to learn about the child's developmental levels. It is the important task of the interviewer to discover the child's general levels of abilities in the areas of cognition, speech and language, emotional development, and play skills (Jones & McQuiston, 1985; Sgroi et al., 1982; White et al., 1987). Having knowledge of these skills, the interviewer can then adjust the questions during the remainder of the interview to optimize the information gathered.

The free play period should be just that: free play. Only if the child introduces the topic of abuse spontaneously should it be discussed. The free play period may last up to 30 minutes. When the interviewer feels that he/she knows the general levels of abilities of the child, is able to communicate with him/her, and has gotten the child to interact relatively freely, it is time to move to a more formal stage of the interview relative to the allegations (White et al., 1987). Occasionally, the child will never relax, and the interviewer must decide whether to attempt the formal abuse evaluation or to have the child return at another time.

Tools

Other than verbal interviewing procedures, some suggested tools include drawings (Goodwin, 1982; Yates, Beutler, & Crago, 1985) for the child who has adequate fine motor skills and puppets (MacFarlane & Krebs, 1986). Much caution should be used with puppets as they usually include only the upper part of the body. Data resulting from their use will be difficult to generalize to situations relative to the allegations.

Likewise, materials about sexual abuse which have been designed to teach a child how to protect himself/herself from abusive situations should not be used. The goal of the investigatory interview is to obtain data from the child, not teach the child about bodily functions and what is supposed to be "good" or "bad" touching.

Dolls. Anatomical dolls are recommended by many as one of the tools for evaluating allegations of sexual abuse, but should not be considered the only tool (Boat & Everson, 1986; MacFarlane, 1986; Schetky et al., 1988; White et al., 1987). Additionally, *the doll interview should not be considered a diagnostic test.* At this time, adequate data are not available to support any interviewer's claim that the results from a doll interview definitely demonstrate sexual abuse. The dolls, as well as drawings, can be tools to obtain information from the child, information which may then be a part of the overall sexual abuse evaluation and

and be subject to judicial proceedings in which the judge or jury makes the legal determination of sexual abuse. (For a review of anatomical doll usage, see White and Santilli [1988] and White [1988]).

PROBLEMATIC INTERVIEWING TECHNIQUES

Interviewers must be aware that their interviewing techniques may have a significant impact on the results of the abuse evaluation itself as well as have repercussions on the subsequent life of the child, family, and alleged perpetrator. A number of potential problems that may be introduced by the interviewer have been proposed by White and Quinn (1988; Quinn, White, & Santilli, 1989).

Pursuit of an Agenda

From the initial contact through judicial proceedings, the foremost problem that may underlie the entire evaluation is that of the interviewer's *agenda*, that is, his/her efforts to have the child describe, confirm, or verify the assumptions the interviewer holds concerning the allegations. Either general or specific, these assumptions range from believing that all children referred for an abuse investigation have indeed been abused to the other extreme that no child is ever abused and that the allegations are false. Various possibilities fall in between these two extremes. Interviewers with an agenda are felt to be more likely to utilize some problematic interviewing techniques in their determination to prove the allegations. White and Quinn (1988) have proposed two primary categories of problematic interviewing techniques: conceptual problems and the interviewer's behaviors.

CONCEPTUAL PROBLEMS

Leading Questions

A primary controversial issue is whether interviewers should ask children leading questions during abuse investigations. Legally, *leading* is described as that ". . . which instructs the witness how to answer or puts into his mouth words to be echoed back" (Black, 1979, p. 800). White and Quinn (1988) have simplified leading to indicate the interviewer's providing of specific data for the child during the interview, information which the child has not previously revealed to that interviewer. The data being introduced may have come from legitimate sources (e.g., parents) or from the biases of the interviewer. In any case, the information is introduced by the interviewer, not by the child.

Some authors are strongly supportive of interacting with the child on a totally nonleading basis except where the child's safety is clearly in question (Friedemann & Morgan, 1985; White et al., 1988). Others allow more freedom in utilizing leading techniques (MacFarlane, 1986; Sgroi, 1982). Data on the issue are extremely scarce. A recent study by Goodman and Aman (1987) of three- and five-year-olds revealed that while the three-year-olds were more easily led in general, the effect was less so when the leading questions were of an "abuse" type (e.g., "He touched your peepee, didn't he?"). Of concern is that even the five-year-olds demonstrated some false positive answers to leading questions even though the errors tended to be ones of omission rather than commission. (See Chapter 11 for a further discussion of this issue.) While tentative, these data suggest that until further information is available, a very important factor in interviewing a child is not giving him/her any information which he/she has previously not given to the interviewer. With this in mind, White and Quinn (1988) have outlined some specific leading interviewing techniques which should be avoided until empirically shown to not change a child's information.

"Yes-no" questions. Very frequently utilized with children who are reluctant to interact freely with an interviewer, the "yes-no" question is introduced to obtain an affirmation or negation of the information presented. Such questions may appropriately be presented when an interviewer is attempting to clarify or verify information already given by the child so as to evaluate the consistency of the child's answers. When used with information introduced by the interviewer, however, such questions are problematic for at least two reasons. First, it is not known how the child's memory will subsequently utilize the introduced material. Second, although a child may respond with a "yes" or "no" which the interviewer feels is a true reflection of the child's memory, there is always a possibility that the interviewer made a wrong inference and that the child's response to the adult's question was just to move the conversation along. The interviewer must wage a guess as to the child's true intent in such situations, a guess which may not always be correct.

Multiple choice questions. When multiple-choice leading questions are introduced, the child is expected to select the "correct" answer from a set of possibilities. Such questions are often used to explore which of the interviewer-posited possibilities the child will endorse. The child may affirm items related to the allegations which are either true, partially true, or false. The possibility exists that the information given in the multiple-choice question may have some relevance to the child's life other than to the allegation. A listing of possible perpetrators might include only one name that the child knows. When the child selects it due to familiarity, the interviewer may assume that the selection is directly related to the allegation. For example, if the child is asked by the interviewer, "Has anyone ever touched you?" and responds, "Yes", the interviewer might then introduce a multiple-choice question of, "Was it someone named Dane, Russell, or Gerald?". Having a father named Gerald and never having known anyone with any of the other names, the child replies "Gerald." The interviewer then may inappropriately conclude that the person identified is the perpetrator. Alternate possibilities or explanations for why the child named that individual were not considered.

Disconfirmation. Disconfirmation is a technique adults frequently use to influence children's decisions. A mother asks, "What do you want to drink?", to which the child responds, "Coke." Dissatisfied with that answer, she then says, "You don't want Coke. How about some juice?" In an investigatory interview, disconfirmation occurs when the interviewer refuses to accept a child's answer and leads the child in a new direction (White & Quinn, 1988). Use of this technique is frequently introduced when the child's answer does not coincide with the information the interviewer is seeking to confirm. Examples of disconfirmation formats include either ignoring or leading away from the child's answer and/or telling the child he/she is wrong. For example, the interviewer asks, "Has anyone touched your bottom?" to which the child responds, "My daddy." In assuming this occurred during hygienic care activities, the interviewer proceeds to disconfirm the child's answer by ignoring it and then asks, "Yes, but who at school touched your bottom? Didn't Mr. Bob touch your penis?"

Another example of disconfirmation involves telling the child she is wrong. When asked, "Who did you go into the bathroom with?", the child may respond, "David." Avoiding the "David" response, the interviewer attempts to verify other information by stating, "But your mother told me that you went with Paul." The child responds, "No, I didn't." In a determined effort to have Paul identified as the alleged perpetrator, the interviewer then replies, "Oh, you know you did. Your mommy said so. Now when you went into the bathroom with Paul, what did he do to hurt you?" Only the child's assertiveness to correct the information will overcome this interviewer's agenda.

Children's responses to leading materials. The introduction of leading information may contribute to a number of possible outcomes, most of which should be considered detrimental to the overall evaluation. In the best instance, the information may be denied by the child as being true while he/she spontaneously provides his/her own details of the allegation. If the interviewer then pursues this newly disclosed information, then not much harm may have been done.

A serious situation may occur when the child denies the leading information, but does not provide spontaneous data in return. In such circumstances, it may be argued that this child may assimilate the leading information and may subsequently incorporate it into a statement concerning the allegation, a statement which, at a later point, might be considered a true disclosure. By that stage, tracing the path of such information from the interviewer through the child's memory is very difficult.

An even more serious problem may arise when the child affirms the leading information by answering in a positive manner (head shake or verbalization). If the interviewer then takes the child's affirmation as support for the leading material, the interviewer is compounding the error of leading with providing an interpretation of the child's behavior without supportive data supplied by the child. At that point, it may be difficult to know if some, all, or none of the affirmed information is true.

Coercion

When the interviewer has used his/her position of authority to pressure the child to provide an answer consistent with the interviewer's expectations, then coercion has been utilized (White & Quinn, 1988). The essence of this interviewing error is the manipulative or socially forceful imposition of the interviewer's beliefs on the child. Coercion is seen in several ways.

Truth-lie paradigms. While seemingly benign, the interviewer's demand that the child "tell the truth" should be considered coercive. The simplest form of this problem occurs when the interviewer provides a lesson in the general concept of truthfulness. The child is told, "Now you know the difference between the truth and a lie. Tell me the truth about . . . " In another truth-lie paradigm, the interviewer gently discusses possible true and false statements with the child, like "If I say this dress is red, am I telling the truth?" Often this occurs when the interviewer is confusing the assessment of the child's competency to be a witness with the investigation of the allegation (Quinn, 1986). A third level of the "truth/lie" paradigm is the interviewer's urging the child to tell the truth, but doing so in a gentle or pleading fashion. A fourth and more forceful type of "tell the truth" coercive technique occurs when the interviewer forcefully demands that the child tell the truth. This more frequently is seen when the child answers a question in a manner inconsistent with the interviewer's agenda, and the child is then prodded with "Now, John. You know that isn't the truth. Now, tell me the truth about . . . ". It is suggested that truth/lie paradigms such as those described here are not appropriate techniques in an investigatory interview.

Tangible rewards. Tangible rewards should be considered a coercive technique. These include items or privileges given to the child, such as stickers, food and drink, playtime, or specific toys. Even if not intended as such, offering treats during evaluation sessions may be seen as attempts to bribe or coerce the child into giving information. To maintain internal independence, such reinforcements should not be given.

Repetitive questioning. Interviewers in pursuit of confirmation of details may repetitively question a child about a specific area of content, especially when the child is not providing the "correct" answers. Such instances are considered coercive in that repetitive questions tell the child that he/she is wrong and demand the child to supply the expected information.

Threats. The most coercive interview technique occurs when the evaluator demands that a child answer questions in accordance with the interviewer's agenda and enforces this demand with a threat. For instance, in the situation in which the child has been less responsive than the interviewer wished to the questions of "Who hurt you?", the child may ask to see his/her mother in the waiting room. The interviewer then coerces the child by saying, "You can see your mother after you tell me who hurt you."

Coercion versus limit-setting. Recognizing the difference between coercive acts designed to elicit details consistent with the interviewer's agenda and limit-setting techniques instituted to establish a comfortable environment for the child is very important. For example, a child may cry to go to the toilet. The interviewer may indicate that the child will be allowed to go to the toilet only when he/she has made the request calmly. The child's request should not be used in a coercive manner to get the child to reveal information about the allegations, such as, "You can go to the toilet when you tell me who touched your peepee." The difference between these two approaches is that the second instance relates to the allegation whereas the first one allows the interviewer to communicate to the child that the adult is responsible for the control of the session.

BEHAVIORS OF THE INTERVIEWER

The degree to which specific techniques influence the results of the evaluation is determined in part by the behaviors the interviewer uses to implement the content of the agenda. These behaviors may include verbal and/or physical components and may be classified as having various emotional qualities, inappropriate interactional patterns, and/or disruptions in the continuity of the interactions (White & Quinn, 1988). Table 12.1 depicts the various influences felt to be important.

Emotional qualities. The information which the child carries with him/her may become distorted due to the interviewer's emotional behaviors. An overly solicitous voice may be used to convey a demand which is couched in a seemingly positive emotional tone. For example, the phrase, "Fred, I'm so very glad you told me about what your Aunt Marie did to you," may create several problems: (a) The voice tone, as well as the content, inappropriately demonstrates the approval of the content of the child's statements; (b) such reinforcement then provides an implicit demand for further production; (c) the interviewer's tone then provides the child with an assessment of the interviewer's value judgment concerning the statement.

The outcome of such interactions varies according to the child's characteristics. An overly dependent child may subsequently attempt to please the interviewer by producing further material of this type. On the other hand, if the child perceived the interaction as condescending, he/she may decide to inhibit further interactions.

An adult may verbally reinforce a child's statement in a positive manner, as just cited, or in a negative manner. Even with a positive statement, the negative voice tone may be perceived as unpleasant to the child. The child's response may include withdrawal, providing data inconsistent with his/her experience, or becoming oppositional. In addition, the interviewer's emotional interpretation of the event described by the child should be neutral. The evaluator must not make emotional judgments of "good" or "bad"; that value judgment is for the child to

TABLE 12.1   Interviewer's Behavioral Influences on Children's Responses in Child Sexual Abuse Interviews

	Communication of Emotions	Inappropriate Patterns	Discontinuity
Voice	Overly solicitous Inappropriate reward Harsh, cold tone	Inappropriate level	Tone change
Physical	Controlling Caressing Interfering/grabbing	Body posture Anatomy ID	Position changes

Adapted from Quinn, White & Santilli, 1989.

make. As part of the evaluation, interviewers must learn how the child interprets the incidents. It is not uncommon for young children to have perceived the experiences in a positive manner.

Negative reactions demonstrated by the child should not automatically be assumed to be directly related to an abusive situation. Fear expressed by the child before, during, or after the interview may come from several sources, some of which may be unrelated to the suspected abuse. Evaluators must try to assess the cause of the fear or anxiety and not jump to conclusions without data from the child to support such conclusions.

Nonverbal emotional communications consist of facial expressions, body language, and physical contact. The effect of such behaviors by the interviewer should be monitored closely. Of particular concern is the use of physical contact between the interviewer and the child. Touch should only be used for a legitimate purpose and never for reinforcing a response. For instance, the child may have just revealed a detail specific to the allegation and the interviewer inappropriately leans close to the child, strokes his/her head, and states, "You're talking so good today." The physical closeness and stroking of the child's head should be considered as inappropriate as is verbal reinforcement.

Inappropriate behavior patterns. Besides emotional reactions of a verbal or physical nature, there are other interviewer behaviors which may contaminate the data by influencing the child's disclosures. Included in this category are interviewer responses which are inconsistent with the child's developmental level, such as too advanced vocabulary or, on the other hand, the use of babytalk. The condescending attitude conveyed by the use of babytalk may impair subsequent interactions. Developmentally appropriate activities and interactions for each child must be utilized. The free play period provides an opportunity for the interviewer to gauge the child's developmental status, especially with respect to speech and language development, and subsequently allows him/her to interact accordingly. The interviewer's choice of activities should be based on sound developmental research data. (See Chapters 2, 4, and 11 for further suggestions.)

Inappropriate behavior patterns may also include the interviewer's posture or reference to personal body parts. While sitting on the floor (so as to be on the same level as the child), some examples of inappropriate body positions include reclining poses or sitting in a suggestive or sexually revealing manner (i.e., skirt hiked up). These behaviors may signal an atmosphere of physical permissiveness and seductiveness to the child. In addition, if the interviewer has promoted an atmosphere in which the child becomes very free with his/her physical contacts with the interviewer, the interviewer should not then further compound the problem by interpreting the child's actions as if they originated with the child and/or were based on the child's experience relative to the allegation.

The reference to personal body parts, either those of the interviewer or of the child, to evaluate the child's knowledge of anatomy is generally inappropriate. It should be acknowledged, however, that the child may spontaneously point to his/her own body parts as having been touched by someone or as a clarification of the disclosed allegation. The interviewer then may request the child to "show me where you were touched. . . " after the child has given the information voluntarily. This technique should be used for children who are unable verbally to describe what has happened.

Discontinuity. Sudden changes in tone of voice or body posture communicate an emphasis on the material which the child just presented. For example, the interviewer and child have been playing with a dollhouse, and the child is having the family members perform daily routine activities. The interviewer has been assigned the role of the mother by the child and has been using a "mother" voice during the play. Suddenly the child remarks, "Oh, mother. Did you know what Bob did to me?" The interviewer must be extremely careful to continue the play sequence without a voice change which would communicate to the child that now she is discussing very important information.

Systems Contamination

Contamination by a system consists of the external influences outside of the interviewer-child interactions which may alter or influence the child's statements. While systems contamination may arise from community hysteria, media (TV), and safety education, interviewers must be aware of such influences on the child's disclosures and use the information in assessing the child's allegations.

EVALUATION CONCLUSIONS

Report presenting clinical conclusions should include what was known prior to the evaluation, the techniques utilized, what was learned from the child and the parents, and how the clinical facts have been synthesized. Care must be taken that the conclusions drawn from the behavioral observations and the data are directly relevant to the issues at hand. Making inferential leaps without data support are not appropriate (e.g., "I just know she was abused. I can see it in her eyes.").

Some particular issues which need to be addressed in the final report include: (a) the possibility of the child's being preprogrammed (educated as to what to say), (b) the likelihood of hygienic versus abuse touching, (c) an evaluation of contamination factors, and (d) any limitations of the data.

Preprogramming of the Child

Preprogramming of the child should always be considered a possibility. The preprogramming can take the form of a conscious, willful manipulation by the parent, as is sometimes seen in custody disputes. On the other hand, an unconscious manipulation of the child may arise from an overwhelming anxiety due to a variety of reasons, including the adult's own victimization, psychiatric disturbance, or family dynamic problems.

Preprogramming should be considered a possibility when the allegations are described by the child in rote phrases without deviation and without a fuller context. A preprogrammed child may give the same rote responses to different questions or become flustered when the interviewer probes in certain unexpected areas or rephrases the questions. Such rote recitation of a coached child should not, however, be confused with a very young child's lack of extensive vocabulary. Awareness must be made of the possibility that a child who has been interviewed multiple times may have inadvertently been programmed by the interviewers themselves to respond in rote-like phrases or answers. Some children who refuse to talk without the parent in the room or who look to the parent repeatedly for cues may be giving indications that they have been coached. Care should be taken, however, to differentiate this cueing behavior from the child who may experience separation anxiety and cannot easily tolerate being away from the parent.

Asking, "Is there anything else you were supposed to tell me?" in a casual fashion at the close of the interview may help the interviewer delineate the issue of preprogramming. Some coached children will spontaneously respond with statements like, ". . . that Daddy put his penis in my vagina." When asked further, "Who told you to say that?", the child may say, "Mommy." Such a response does not conclusively point to coaching as the mother may have instructed the child to "tell the interviewer the truth." Additional inquiry about who else the child has spoken with, what that person's response was, and close questioning of the caregiver around his/her discussions with the child may provide clarification in examining this important issue.

Hygienic Touching Versus Abuse

Abuse is not always a clear-cut issue. Statements such as "he touched my peepee" should always be assessed relative to its being a description of an hygienic activity, of personal boundary issues, or of abusive problems. The question must be asked: When is cleaning a "peepee" or medicating a genital rash considered hygienic and when does it become abuse? This distinction is an especially difficult issue for determining abuse in young children as hygienic touching is a normal parenting activity. With the increasing number of divorced fathers who provide hygienic care during their time with the children, there are likely to be misinterpretations. For example, if a child returns from a visit and tells her mother, "Daddy rubbed my peepee," assessment must be made relative to the child's true reflection of an abuse or a misinterpretation of hygienic cleaning.

Contamination Assessment

Contamination assessment takes two forms. One is the evaluator's own assessment of contamination in his/her own evaluation. Each of us must continually evaluate our own interactions and interviewing techniques to maintain techniques least likely to produce contamination. The second form of contamination assessment is when the report is scrutinized by others in the case, or, more specifically, someone appointed for this task. In either case, the same issues should be evaluated.

The degree to which the child has been exposed to various contamination influences must be evaluated as well as the degree to which the techniques actually influenced the child's reporting of the experiences. The materials needed to make this assessment include a thorough review of all primary sources documenting the child's initial complaints as well as historical considerations (family history, etc.). These primary sources include data recorded at the time of the interview, audiotapes, videotapes, contemporaneous transcripts, or data sheets. The primary sources may allow evaluation of the allegation report as well as of the interactions of the child and interviewer. Secondary sources, such as reports of the interview sessions and other documents not recorded at the time of the interview (e.g., family notes), are helpful in assessing the degree of the interviewer's agenda and/or the effects of other individuals' contamination influences. For example, a parent's notes recalling his/her reflection of the child's initial statements should be helpful in this assessment. Comparing the primary sources with the secondary sources will frequently allow the assessor to judge the degree and direction of contamination.

Reports of the evaluations should reflect how contamination factors may have: (a) distorted true data, (b) allowed the child to incorporate data not originally introduced by the child, and/or (c) changed the child's memory. Figure 12.1 depicts various influences on a child's memory in child sexual abuse investigations.

Distortion of true data. The most common result of contamination influences is how the data which originally represented the child's actual experiences become distorted by various techniques, such as coercion and leading. Understanding both the nature and the degree of the evaluator's agenda and the techniques used in pursuit of the agenda is important. The independent evaluator must attempt to discover any original, uncontaminated data presented by the child in order to determine if and how these data were then distorted.

Incorporation of data. Another result of contamination is the incorporation or inclusion of data by the child from sources other than the child. This most frequently occurs as a result of leading questions. Although this result has been observed in clinical settings, the degree to which it occurs remains unknown empirically. There may be a specific age factor involved in which children are more susceptible to data incorporation.

Memory changes. When a child has either been asked to repeatedly discuss the allegation or has been exposed to repetitive leading discussions about the allegations, his/her memory may have been changed significantly so that the true sources of a child's memory may have be-

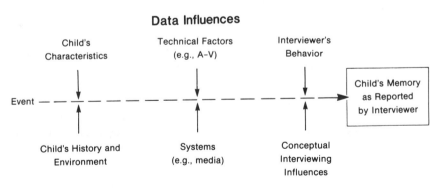

Adapted from Quinn et al., 1989.

FIGURE 12.1 Influences on the Ultimate Reporting of a Child Sexual Abuse Allegation (Quin et al., 1989).

come unclear. The child's later statements may actually come from several memory sources including the child's actual experiences, memory of his/her earlier statements, and/or memory of other experiences of the allegations' being presented (e.g., family or interviewer's statements, viewing of videotapes, exposure to media, grand jury testimony). Attempts to trace the data as they have been distorted and/or incorporated are essential in evaluating contamination of these cases.

Data Limitations

Once the data have been evaluated, the limitations of what the data allow us to say must be assessed. Limitations may arise due to the developmental status of the child, the interviewer's skills, and extraneous influences on the child (White et al., 1988). Even when an interview is conducted within optimal parameters, the results may still not support an allegation of abuse. There are instances in which data indicative of abuse may have gathered through other sources (i.e., medical exams), but could not be corroborated in the child's interview. Evaluators must be willing to admit that, regardless of interviewing techniques, further information may not be forthcoming from the child at that time. Acceptance of such data limitations and the termination of the investigative phase should be considered a viable option. Further interviewing of the child may contaminate the data. At a future date the child may feel more comfortable in disclosing details of the allegation. The investigation may then be reopened and the child's actual abuse experiences as well as the factors involved in the initial evaluation may be reflected in this second evaluation. If the initial evaluation was not contaminated, the data from the second interview are more likely to be considered valid.

Much caution should be used in making judicial conclusions (i.e., diagnosis of sexual abuse) (Melton, Petrila, Poythress, & Slobogin, 1987; Weithorn, 1987). It must be remembered that the judge or jury is to decide the case. The expert witness is to provide the trier of fact (i.e., judge or jury) the data with which the decision is then made. The expert witness should be allowed to tell what he/she did with the child and report how the child responded. If the data have been gathered with minimal contamination, then they may be useful in court proceedings.

Violating the Rules of Investigation

In certain situations, abuse allegations may not be substantiated through the child interview or medical examination, but protective service involvement may be indicated. The interviewer must be able to decide when the investigatory phase should be terminated and a protective stance begun. Many cases simply cannot be substantiated for criminal judicial involvement, but that does not preclude the necessity of protecting the child. In such cases, the interviewer may consciously and with good reason decide to use techniques not consistent with those being discussed here. If this occurs, the interviewer has a responsibility to report and document any deviations from his/her standard practice and does so with the knowledge that legal involvement may be limited or compromised. It is important that the material obtained from all investigatory interviews be preserved for assessment by other professionals in the case (White et al., 1988).

SUMMARY AND CONCLUSIONS

This chapter has presented suggestions for interviewing children alleged to have been sexually abused so as to minimize contamination of their memory for the experiences. Approaching the evaluation with a systematic plan, interviewing the child without undue influencing factors, and then presenting a report which tells all that happened, should help the evaluator feel more confident that he/she has done the best for that child.

Scientifically gathered information about interviewing children suspected of being sexually abused is just becoming available. Many questions still need to be answered, from a scientific as well as from a judicial perspective (Myers, 1987). The list of experimental factors which merit investigation is endless: the characteristics of the children being interviewed (socioeconomic status, race, type of abuse, perpetrator relationship, cultural background, emotional status, intellectual abilities), characteristics of the dolls (racial attributes, detail of characteristics, number), interview method (structured, free play, alone, dolls), characteristics of evaluator (sex, race, training level), characteristics of the interview (who is present, location), and types of interactions (e.g., nonleading versus leading). There is much to be done, but progress in this field is likely to be slow. We must be aware that the judicial process will continue to move faster and ask questions about children's interviews in more depth than we can respond for some time to come. Because of this, we must act conservatively and provide the courts only with what is truly known about our interviews and not overstep our boundaries in the judicial decision-making process. If we draw conclusions on an inadequate database, the judicial process may disallow the interview material and leave the children defenseless.

REFERENCES

Benedek, E.P., & Schetky, D. (1987). Problems in validating allegations of sexual abuse. Part 2: Clinical evaluation. *Journal of the American Academy of Child and Adolescent Psychiatry, 26*, 916–921.

Black, H.C. (1979). *Black's law dictionary*, 5th Ed. St. Paul: West Publishing Co.

Boat, B., & Everson, M. (1986). *Using anatomical dolls: Guidelines for interviewing young children in sexual abuse investigations*. Chapel Hill, NC: University of North Carolina.

Boat, B., & Everson, M. (1988). Use of anatomical dolls among professionals in sexual abuse evaluations. *Child Abuse and Neglect, 12*, 171–180.

Commonwealth v. Reid, 511 N.E. 2d 331 (1987).

Conerly, S. (1986). Assessment of suspected child sexual abuse. In K. MacFarlane & J. Waterman (Eds.), *Sexual abuse of young children: Evaluation and treatment* (pp. 30–51). New York: Guilford.

Dent, H.R. (1982). The effects of interviewing strategies on the results of interviews with child witnesses. In A. Trankell (Ed.), *Reconstructing the past: The role of psychologists in criminal trials* (pp. 279–298). Deventer, The Netherlands: Kluwer.

Flammung, C.J. (1980). Interviewing child victims of sex offenders. In L.G. Schultz (Ed.), *The sexual victimology of youth* (pp. 175–186). Springfield, Ill.: C.C. Thomas.

Friedemann, V., & Morgan, M. (1985). *Interviewing sexual abuse victims using anatomical dolls: The professional's guidebook*. Eugene, OR: Shamrock Press.

Goodman, G. (December, 1987). The child witness in court: Problems and solutions. In S. Smith (Chair), The child witness in court. Symposium conducted at California Professional Society on the Abuse of Children. Costa Mesa, CA.

Goodman, G., & Aman, C. (April, 1987). Children's use of anatomically correct dolls to report an event. In M. Steward (Chair), *Evaluation of suspected child abuse: Developmental, clinical, and legal perspectives on the use of anatomically correct dolls*. Symposium presented at the biennial meeting of the Society for Research in Child Development, Baltimore, MD.

Goodwin, J. (1982). The use of drawings in incest cases. In J. Goodwin (Ed.) *Sexual abuse: Incest victims and their families* (pp. 47–56). London: John Wright.

Goodwin, J., Sahd, D., & Rada, R.T. (1982). False accusations and false denials of incest: Clinical myths and clinical realities. In J. Goodwin (Ed.) *Sexual abuse: Incest victims and their families* (pp. 17–26). London: John Wright.

Green, A., (1986). True and false allegations of sexual abuse in child custody disputes. *Journal of the American Academy of Child and Adolescent Psychiatry, 25*, 449–456.

Idaho Department of Health and Welfare v. Syme, 714 P. 2d 13 (1986).

In re J. H., 505 N.E. 2d (1987).

Jampole, L., & Weber, M. (1987). An assessment of the behavior of sexually abused and nonsexually abused children with anatomically correct dolls. *Child Abuse and Neglect, 11,* 187–192.

Jones, D.P.H., & McQuiston, M. (1985). *Interviewing the sexually abused child.* Denver: Kempe Center.

MacFarlane, K. (1986). Child sexual abuse allegations in divorce proceedings. In K. MacFarlane & J. Waterman (Eds.), *Sexual abuse of young children: Evaluation and treatment* (pp. 121–150). New York: Guilford.

MacFarlane, K. & Krebs, S. (1986). Techniques of interviewing and evidence gathering. In K. MacFarlane & J. Waterman (Eds.), *Sexual abuse of young children: Evaluation and treatment* (pp. 67–100). New York: Guilford.

MacFarlane, K. & Waterman, J. (Eds.) (1986). *Sexual abuse of young children: Evaluation and treatment.* New York: Guilford.

Melton, G.B., Petrila, J., Poythress, N.G., Jr., & Slobogin, C. (1987). *Psychological evaluations for the court: A handbook for mental health professionals and lawyers.* New York: Guilford.

Myers, J.E.B. (1986). Hearsay statements by the child abuse victim. *Baylor Law Review, 38,* 775–916.

Myers, J.E.B. (December, 1987). How to lay a proper foundation for expert testimony in child sexual abuse cases. Paper presented at California Professional Society on the Abuse of Children. Costa Mesa, CA.

People v. Draper, 389 N.W.2d 89 (1986).

Quinn, K.M. (1986). Competency of the child witness: A major forensic issue. *Bulletin of the American Academy of Psychiatry and the Law, 14,* 311–321.

Quinn, K.M., White, S., & Santilli, G. (1989). Influences of an interviewer's behavior in child sexual abuse investigations. *Bulletin of the American Academy of Psychiatry and the Law, 17,* 45–52.

Schetky, D., Adams, C., Derdeyn, A., Green, A., Lassers, E., Nurcombe, B., Porter, S., Chadwick, D., Lloyd, D., Sauzier, M., & White, S. (1988). Guidelines for evaluation of child sexual abuse. *Journal of the American Academy of Child and Adolescent Psychiatry, 27,* 655–657.

Sgroi, S.M. (1982). An approach to case management. In S.M. Sgroi (Ed.), *Handbook of clinical intervention in child sexual abuse* (pp. 81–108). Lexington, MA: Heath.

Sgroi, S.M., Porter, F.S., & Blick, L.C. (1982). Validation of child sexual abuse. In S.M. Sgroi (Ed.), *Handbook of clinical intervention in child sexual abuse* (pp. 39–80). Lexington, MA: Heath.

State v. Harmening, 376 N.W. 2d 254 (1985).

Summit, R. (1983). The child sexual abuse accommodation syndrome. *Child Abuse and Neglect, 7,* 177–193.

Weithorn, L., (1987). Psychological consultation in divorce custody litigation: Ethical considerations. In L. Weithorn (Ed.), *Psychology and child custody determinations: Knowledge, roles and expertise* (pp. 182–209). Lincoln: University of Nebraska Press.

White, S. (1988). Should investigatory use of anatomical dolls be defined by the courts? *Journal of Interpersonal Violence, 3,* 471–475.

White, S. & Quinn, K.M. (1988). Investigatory independence in child sexual abuse evaluations: Conceptual considerations. *Bulletin of the American Academy of Psychiatry and the Law, 16,* 269–278.

White, S., & Santilli, G. (1988). A review of clinical practices and research data on anatomical dolls. *Journal of Interpersonal Violence, 3,* 430–442.

White, S., Santilli, G., & Quinn, K.M. (1988). Child evaluator's roles in child sexual abuse assessments. In E.B. Nicholson & J. Bulkley (Eds.), *Sexual abuse allegations in custody and visitation cases* (pp. 94–105). Washington: American Bar Association National Legal Resource Center for Child Advocacy and Protection.

White, S., Strom, G., Santilli, G., & Halpin, B., (1986). Interviewing young children with anatomically correct dolls. *Child Abuse and Neglect, 10,* 519–529.

White, S., Strom, G., Santilli, G., & Quinn, K.M., (1987). *Clinical guidelines for interviewing young children with anatomically correct dolls.* Unpublished manuscript, Case Western Reserve University School of Medicine, Cleveland, OH.

Yates, A., & Terr, L. (1988a). Debate forum: Anatomically correct dolls: Should they be used as a basis for expert testimony? *Journal of the American Academy of Child and Adolescent Psychiatry, 27,* 254–257.

Yates, A., & Terr, L. (1988b). Debate forum: Issue continued: Anatomically correct dolls: Should they be used as a basis for expert testimony? *Journal of the American Academy of Child and Adolescent Psychiatry, 27,* 387–388.

Yates, A., Beutler, L.E., & Crago, M. (1985). Drawings by child victims of incest. *Child Abuse and Neglect, 9,* 183–190.

CHAPTER 13

Obtaining Child Reports in Health Care Settings

LYNNDA M. DAHLQUIST

INTRODUCTION

As the field of behavioral medicine has developed over the last 15 to 20 years, psychologists, medical personnel, and the public have become increasingly aware of the interplay between psychological factors and health and illness. In the pediatric domain, in particular, there has been a dramatic increase in research and clinical efforts designed to minimize the potentially negative psychological effects of illness and stressful medical treatments on children (Elkins & Roberts, 1983; Varni, 1983).

While the progress being made in refining psychological interventions for children in medical settings is indeed exciting and important, the development of appropriate dependent measures to evaluate the effectiveness of such interventions has simply not kept pace with the increased demand for treatment. Some progress has been made in the refinement of behavioral observation tools, but the development of child self-report measures has been relatively neglected.

The objective of this chapter is to review the existing self-report measures designed specifically for children in health care settings in enough detail to guide the clinician or researcher in selecting potential

395

measures. The review will focus on children's report of pain, anxiety, and compliance as these areas are common targets for psychological intervention.

ASSESSMENT OF PAIN

Pain may well be the single most important phenomenon to evaluate in the health care setting. First, pain serves as an adaptive biological warning signal, indicating the presence of active disease or injury requiring medical treatment. Therefore, any thorough pediatric medical examination is likely to include some effort to determine whether or not the child is in pain. Secondly, many pediatric diagnostic and treatment procedures involve injections or venipunctures or other painful events. Severe anxiety reactions are common in children who must undergo these painful medical procedures, especially when the procedures are repeated. Interventions designed to decrease the child's experience of pain and anxiety during invasive medical procedures must rely on the child's self-report of pain as an important indicator of the effectiveness of the treatment program. Finally, chronic pain conditions often are associated with depression, school absences, and inactivity which can interfere with the child's psychosocial development (Varni, 1983). In order to minimize long-term impairment due to chronic pain, the child typically is taught pain management strategies, the effectiveness of which need to be monitored at least in part via self-report. Therefore, accurate assessment of the child's pain is an extremely important aspect of pediatric health care.

However, there are a number of practical problems in the assessment of pain in children. First, the very nature of pain itself poses major problems. The International Association for the Study of Pain (1979) has defined pain as "an unpleasant sensory and emotional experience associated with actual or potential tissue damage . . ." (p. 250). This definition takes into account the fact that there is not a one-to-one correspondence between physical tissue damage and the experience of pain and emphasizes that pain is a subjective, idiosyncratic phenomenon.

Because of the highly subjective nature of pain, self-report is considered "the most reliable indicator or the most valid evidence of pain" (Beyer & Byers, 1985, p. 152). Adult pain assessment typically involves asking about the nature, location, duration and intensity of pain through verbal questioning, pain rating scales, such as visual analog scales (Scott & Huskisson, 1976) or structured questionnaires such as the McGill Pain Questionnaire (Melzack, 1975).

The limited verbal abilities of children, however, complicate pain assessment considerably. Many of the structured pain measures used with adults are too complicated for children. More concrete, nonverbal assessment procedures may be needed to obtain pain information from children. In addition, different assessment strategies may be needed for children at different levels of development.

Secondly, much of the information currently available regarding valid pain measurement techniques, the relationship between pain stimuli and pain experience, and the effectiveness of pain control strategies, is the result of laboratory research involving experimental pain induction (i.e., shock, ice water, ischemic pain) in healthy adult volunteers. However, ethical considerations have limited the application of such research strategies with children (McGrath, 1987). As a result of these practical constraints, the field of pain assessment in children is quite young, and our understanding of the pain experience of children is limited.

Beyer and Byers (1985) propose that because of the limited evidence available regarding pain in children, medical practitioners have had to rely on personal beliefs and experience in making decisions regarding pain in children. They argue that the following beliefs are still prevalent among health care providers:

> "(a) children do not feel as much pain as adults; (b) children tolerate pain better than adults; (c) the neural system of infants is different from that of adults, thus they do not experience or perceive pain as acutely or meaningfully as adults; (d) children do not have past experiences with pain and, therefore, do not experience or perceive it in the same negative way as adults" (p. 154).

Important medical decisions often are made on the basis of these beliefs. For example, until recently, tonsillectomies were performed on infants and young children without anesthesia. Circumcisions are still often performed without anesthesia, although recent research on neural development and pain perception in infants has resulted in controversy regarding this practice (Beyer & Byers, 1985; Owens, 1984).

Children also receive less pain medication than adults, although it has been argued that there is little evidence that they actually need less medication. For example, Eland and Anderson (1977) studied 25 children and 18 adults after surgery. The children received 24 doses of analgesics in contrast to the 671 doses given to adults with identical diagnoses. Similar trends were found by Beyer, DeGood, Ashley, and Russell (1983) when they reviewed the charts of 50 adults and 50 children after open heart surgery. All of the adult patients received analgesic medications; 24% of the children were not medicated. The adults received 564 doses;

the children received only 237 doses. On the fifth postoperative day, 47% of the adults received analgesics, while only 12% of the children received medication, and the adults received 136 doses compared with 10 doses for the children.

The infrequent use of analgesic medication with children may reflect, in part, justifiable concerns about addiction, respiratory depression, and/or respiratory arrest resulting from narcotics. However, undermedication due to inaccurate understanding of the child's experience of pain may be causing children unnecessary pain and suffering in a variety of medical settings/situations. In this respect, accurate pain assessment strategies are crucial.

In the following section of this chapter, current strategies for assessing children's pain experiences will be reviewed. Because this is a relatively new area of research, each approach to self-report pain assessment will be described in enough detail to provide the prospective clinician or researcher with a sense of the potential strengths and weaknesses of each approach.

Drawings

Because of the limited verbal repertoire of young children, a number of researchers have attempted to develop essentially nonverbal measures to assess children's pain. For example, Jerrett (1985) gave 40, five- to nine-year-old ENT outpatients five markers (red, blue, green, yellow, and black) and instructed them to draw a picture that shows pain. The drawings were then rated by four independent judges to determine the content, location, source, and color of pain depicted. Approximately 75% of their sample drew a person or part of a person with pain. Drawings reflecting a personification of pain were obtained from 12.5% of the children. Abstract representations and inanimate objects inflicting pain were much less frequent (each category occurred in only 5% of the drawings).

The location of pain depicted in the drawings appeared to represent the child's past experience of pain; 40% of the drawings depicted ear or throat pain. Roughly 58% of the drawings reflected a health problem (internal) source of pain; 30% depicted an external source (such as a fall). Finally, 85% of the children used the colors red or black to represent pain. A few children used blue or green. Yellow was never used. Although the method of agreement calculation was not reported, percentage agreement among raters ranged from 77% to 80% for the content, location, source, and color categories.

Unruh, McGrath, Cunningham, and Humphreys (1983) used a similar drawing approach to evaluate 109 children aged 5 to 18 who were

TABLE 13.1 Pain Self-Report Measures

Measure	Aspect of Pain Assessed	Ages	Reliability	Validity	Research Use	Clinical Use
Drawings						
Jerrett (1985)	Content, location, source, color	5–9	Interrater	Yes	ENT pts.	Unknown
Unruh et al., (1983)	Content, source, location, color	5–18	Interrater	Unknown	Migraine, musculo-skeletal pain	Unknown
Projectives						
Cartoons (Scott, 1978)	Color, texture, shape, pattern, continuity	4–10	Unknown	Unknown	Healthy children	Unknown
Pediatric Pain Inventory (Lollar et al., 1982)	Duration, color, source, relief	4–19	Internal consistency	Yes	Healthy children	Unknown
Questionnaires/Interviews						
Pediatric Pain Questionnaire (Savedra et al., 1982; Tesler et al., 1983)	Cause, descriptors, color, affect, location	9–12	Test-retest	Yes	Healthy children Hospitalized pts.	Unknown
Varni/Thompson Pediatric Pain Questionnaire (Varni et al., 1987)	Descriptors	4–16	Interrater	Yes	Rheumatology pts.	Unknown
Incomplete Sentences (Gaffney & Dunne, 1986; 1987)	Cause, descriptors	5–14	Unknown	Unknown	Healthy children	Unknown

(continued)

399

TABLE 13.1 (*Continued*)

Measure	Aspect of Pain Assessed	Ages	Reliability	Validity	Research Use	Clinical Use
Questionnaires/Interviews						
Structured Interview (Ross & Ross, 1984)	Descriptors, pain relief	5–12	Interrater	Unknown	Healthy children	Unknown
Color/Intensity Matching						
Eland Color Assessment Tool (Eland, 1981; Varni et al., 1987)	Intensity (4-point)	4–5	Unknown	Yes	Injections, rheumatology pts.	Injections
Likert Scales						
Zeltzer & LeBaron (1982)	Intensity (5-point)	6–17	Interrater, under age 10?	Yes	Oncology pts, bone marrows, LPs	Oncology pts., bone marrows, LPs
Hilgard & LeBaron (1982)	Intensity (11-point)	6–adol.	Interrater, under age 10?	Yes	Oncology pts.	Oncology pts., bone marrows, LPs
Faces (LeBaron & Zeltzer, 1984)	Intensity (5-point)	6–18	Unknown	Yes	Oncology pts, bone marrows, LPs	Oncology pts., bone marrows, LPs
Headache descriptors (Richardson et al., 1982)	Intensity (6-point)	9–17	Interrater	Yes	Migraine headaches	Unknown

Measure (Author)	Description	Age range	Reliability	Validity	Population	
Headache Diary (Andrasik et al, 1985)	Intensity (5-point), frequency, duration	8–16	Interrater	Yes	Migraine headaches	Migraine headaches
Visual Analog Scales Abu-Saad (1984)	Intensity (10 segment line)	9–15	Unknown	Yes	Surgery pts.	Unknown
Pain Thermometer (Jay et al, 1983; 1987; Elliot et al, 1987)	Intensity (100 segments)	2–20	Interrater, problem under age 8?	Yes	Oncology pts, bone marrows	Oncology pts, bone marrows
Pain Thermometer Miser et al, (1987)	Intensity (100mm)	8–adol.	Interrater	Yes	Disease state, oncology pts.	Unknown
Varni et al, (1987)	Intensity (100mm line)	4–16	Interrater	Yes	Rheumatology pts.	Unknown
McGrath et al., (1985)	Intensity (150 mm line) Affect (150mm line)	3–15	Test-retest	Yes	Healthy, oncology pts.	Chronic pain, oncology pts.

being treated for migraine headaches or chronic musculoskeletal pain. The children were provided blank paper and eight markers (black, brown, blue, purple, orange, red, yellow, green) and were asked to draw two pictures: one of their pain and one of themselves while in pain.

Each of the drawings were scored by two independent raters. Pain drawings were classified into the following categories: (1) actions and instruments causing pain; (2) personification of the pain; (3) physiological representation of the pain; (4) perceptual disturbance associated with the pain, (5) abstract representation of the pain; (6) location of the pain; and (7) nonspecific representation of the pain. The drawings of the children in pain were classified according to: (1) recipient of pain; (2) agent in relieving pain; (3) emotion due to pain; (4) location of pain; and (5) nonspecific representation. Raters also determined the dominant color of each picture. Interrater agreement ranged from 73% to 80% for color, and from 81% to 84% for classification. No significant differences in categories or colors of drawings were found for sex or age (5 to 8 years versus 9 to 12 years versus 13 to 18 years). Red and black were most often dominant colors.

These studies suggest that children five years of age and older can use drawings to depict some aspects of their pain experience, and that such drawings can be classified into general content categories with moderate levels of agreement between judges. The clinical utility of children's pain drawings, however, remains to be demonstrated. Unruh et al. (1983) proposed that drawings be used to facilitate communication with children regarding pain. In the present author's clinical experience, drawings have been helpful in "breaking the ice" with some shy patients by providing a concrete stimulus about which to begin a discussion of the child's pain or other aspects of his or her medical experience. However, there have been no empirical studies to date documenting whether the use of pain drawings actually facilitates communication. In addition, the validity of drawings as sensitive indicators of changes in the child's subjective pain state also has not been investigated. For instance, further research is needed to determine whether drawings could be used to assess changes in pain status postoperatively or postanalgesic medication administration.

"Projective" Instruments

Another approach to nonverbal or at least "less" verbally based pain assessment involves presenting children with standardized visual pain stimuli to which they are asked to respond. For example, Scott (1978) used cartoon pictures depicting painful events and clever sensory stimuli to assess qualitative aspects of children's perceptions of pain. One cartoon sequence portrayed: (a) a child building something out of wood, (b) a hammer blow to the child's finger, and (c) the child with tears and a grimace. The second sequence involved: (a) a child entering a doctor's office, (b) the doctor giving the child a shot in the arm, and (c) the child with tears and a grimace.

The cartoons were shown to 58 healthy children aged 4 to 10 years. Pain sensations for each cartoon were assessed by having children pick one stimulus from each of the following pain sensation sheets: (a) nine different colored circles; (b) texture circles including a prickly plastic brush, sandpaper, corrugated cardboard, terrycloth, and cotton; (c) four shapes (two rounded and two jagged); (d) patterns (two circular and two angular or zigzag patterns); (e) a "continuity" stimulus consisting of a row of lightbulbs colored yellow to indicate "on" and a row of lightbulbs alternating "on" and "off." Although Scott's measure is a novel and intriguing nonverbal tool, efforts to validate the scale have been disappointing. Scott evaluated age and sex differences via Chi-square analyses, but the number of comparisons found to be significant was less than expected by chance alone. The most consistent finding was that the majority of children chose the color red. At the time of this review, no subsequent studies using the Scott (1978) cartoons could be found. Therefore, the potential utility of this assessment strategy remains undetermined.

More encouraging results have been obtained with the Pediatric Pain Inventory (Lollar, Smits, & Patterson, 1982), which is a structured projective instrument consisting of 24 drawings representing four different pain settings (medical, psychosocial, recreational, and activities of daily living). In a structured interview format, the child is asked questions regarding: (a) responsibility for the situation; (b) whether the child in the picture needed help with the hurt; (c) who could help; and (d) what would be done. The child is also asked how long the hurt would last (seconds, day, week, or longer). Finally, the pictures are sorted by the child into three color categories to represent pain intensity based on early work by Eland: red = much pain; yellow = some pain; green = little pain.

In a preliminary study with 240 children aged 4 to 19 years, Lollar et al. (1982) obtained internal consistency (alpha) coefficients ranging from .41 to .76 for intensity ratings, and alpha coefficients of .49 to .70 for duration ratings. The medical stimuli showed the poorest internal consistency, perhaps reflecting the variability in subjects' experience in medical settings.

They also obtained some preliminary evidence to support the validity of the subscales. The four categories did differ in mean intensity and duration ratings, and item total correlations were highest for the designated content area, compared with the other three content areas. In addition, overall intensity and duration ratings were not significantly correlated ($r=.08$), suggesting that they measure different dimensions.

The Pediatric Pain Inventory appears to show some promise in the discrimination of different pain contexts and the differentiation between intensity and duration dimensions of pain and may be useful in identifying developmental aspects of children's perceptions of pain. However, the low internal consistency of the medical subscale suggests that the test would need to be revised for use in health care settings. In addition, the stability of scores over time also should be evaluated.

Questionnaires and Structured Interviews

Pediatric Pain Questionnaire

The Pediatric Pain Questionnaire (Savedra, Gibbons, Tesler, Ward, & Wegner, 1982; Tesler, Ward, Savedra, Wegner, & Gibbons, 1983) represents one of the earliest efforts to elicit information regarding children's pain in a structured verbal format. The questionnaire was designed for children between the ages of 9 and 12 and includes the following questions, which are administered in written format:

1. List three things that have caused you to have pain. (Children's responses were then categorized according to three categories: physical external, physical internal, and psychological/miscellaneous.)
2. Circle the words that describe pain. (24 words were provided.)
3. What color is pain?
4. When I have pain I feel . . . (circle "yes" or "no" to 13 choices.)
5. Remember the worst pain you have had. What was it? Tell how it felt.
6. What helps you feel better when you have pain?
7. What is good about pain?
8. Are you having pain now? If yes mark an X on a body outline in the places where you feel pain.

The majority of the items of the Pediatric Pain Questionnaire were based on previous work by Schultz (1971) and the authors' clinical experience. Each question was then evaluated by an experienced elementary school teacher for appropriateness for 9- to 12-year-olds and then was pilot tested on 23 children. An open-ended format for question (2) was then compared with a forced-choice format of 18 descriptors adapted from Melzack (1975) with a separate sample of 46 children in grades four to six. Tesler et al. (1983) found that the forced choice format elicited more responses than the open-ended format. Therefore, this structure was retained in the final version of the scale.

Preliminary evaluation of the stability of responses to the scale over a three-day period revealed that 68% of the 12-year-old children demonstrated test-retest agreement of at least 70%, but only 38% of the nine-year-olds showed this degree of stability in responses (Tesler et al., 1983). Therefore, extensive refinements in the scale will be needed to achieve a more reliable measure before the utility of the Pediatric Pain Questionnaire for clinical populations can be determined.

Varni/Thompson Pediatric Pain Questionnaire

Varni, Thompson, and Hanson (1987) also included a list of pain descriptors as part of the structured interview format Varni/Thompson Pediatric Pain Questionnaire. Although the list of words provided by Varni et al. (1987) was larger than the 24 items used by Savedra et al. (1982), no significant differences in percent endorsement were apparent between the samples included in the two studies. At present, it is unclear whether pain descriptor checklists are reliable or valid measures for children.

Incomplete sentences

The incomplete sentences format has recently been used to assess children's understanding of different aspects of pain. Gaffney and Dunne (1986, 1987) studied 680 Irish school children between 5 and 14 years of age. Their pain questionnaire consists of 10 incomplete sentences, which are individually and verbally administered to boys under 9 years old and girls under 8 years old. Older children are typically asked to write their responses in a group assessment format.

To date, only their findings regarding children's responses to two of the questionnaire statements: "A person gets a pain because . . ." and "Pain is . . ." have been published (Gaffney & Dunne, 1986, 1987). Their data suggest that there are developmental changes in children's definitions of pain as well as in their understanding of the causality of pain. These developmental differences may be very important to take into account in designing specific pain intensity ratings to be used in clinical settings. For example, their finding that the preoperational (i.e., under age seven) child's concept of pain as concrete and limited to a part of the body has definite clinical implications. For instance, it may be pointless to ask a preoperational child to evaluate his or her general level of pain. Instead, it may be necessary to refer to a specific body part in assessing pain intensity with this age child. Similarly, retrospective recall of past pain relative to current pain (i.e., "Is your pain worse," "better," or "about the same" as it was last week?") may be far too complex for the preoperational child.

Generated versus Supplied Formats

The pediatric pain questionnaires reviewed so far should be considered exploratory, preliminary versions of measures that need substantial refinement before they can be used clinically. In particular, the relative merits of the format of the individual items need to be evaluated in light of what information is desired. Ross and Ross (1984a,b) propose that when opinions, ideas, reasons, and descriptions are sought, the child should be asked to generate information, rather than indicate whether he or she agrees or disagrees with *supplied* information. They argue that "the generate format allows complete freedom of choice of answer without biasing the direction that the answer might take. . . . By contrast, the supplied format spells out the direction that the answer *must* take and thus may be one which would *not* otherwise have occurred to the child" (Ross & Ross, 1984b, p. 73).

Their support for their argument is compelling. Ross and Ross (1984b) compared generated versus supplied formats in a study of 161 recently hospitalized children. Children were first asked what they had tried to help decrease their pain. A wide range of responses were obtained, with 5% of the sample reporting trying not to think about the pain and 4% saying that they had tried to sleep. The next two questions asked were supplied format items to which the child responded "yes" or "no" (eg., "Did you try not to think of the pain?" "Did you try to go to sleep?"). With the supplied format, 81% of the sample said they tried not to think about the pain; 60% said they tried to sleep.

A fourth question was then asked in a generate format ("Which of the things that you tried to do yourself worked best?"). Ninety-three children, who did not mention either trying not to think about pain or sleeping in the first question, now reported that one of these two strategies "worked best." Thus, the supplied format questions appeared to bias the children's responses.

They encountered similar problems when they used a checklist of pain descriptors with 20 5- to 12-year-old children. When they were interviewed after completing the checklist, eight out of the 20 subjects reported that they chose words for reasons other than to reflect their personal pain experience. For example, some children tried to figure out which were the "correct" words that they were supposed to choose;

others selected all the words so that the investigators would know how much pain they were experiencing. These sources of potential bias need to be considered in the development of pain questionnaires and in clinical interviewing, as well. In order to minimize bias, it may be most appropriate to first ask open-ended questions about the child's pain experience. Then, if comparisons across children are of interest, one would ask the child to select descriptors from a supplied list.

The projective, questionnaire, and interview methods reviewed so far appear to offer the greatest promise for the assessment of qualitative aspects of children's pain experiences. These methods may prove to be particularly useful in research investigating developmental changes in children's concepts of pain. Reliable qualitative information about children's pain also could be extremely valuable clinically. The differential diagnosis of many illnesses depends to some degree on identifying the quality of the patient's pain. For example, throbbing pain typically indicates a different underlying pathology than does sharp, searing pain. Therefore, this important aspect of pain self-report warrants considerable further study.

Color/Intensity Matching

In addition to the "quality" of a child's pain, it is often important to evaluate the "quantity" or intensity of the child's pain. Quantitative pain indices are important in monitoring disease progress, the effectiveness of medications and/or medical treatment, as well as the effectiveness of psychological pain management interventions. When quantitative, rather than qualitative self-report is desired, different scaling techniques are needed. Eland (1981) developed a unique ordinal scaling procedure involving colors to represent pain intensity, the Eland Color Assessment Tool. For this instrument, the child is shown a white felt board with eight, 1 1/2-inch colored squares placed across the bottom in the following sequence: yellow, orange, red, green, blue, purple, brown, black. The child is asked to select a colored square that is similar to the event that is most painful for him/her. The child then selects from the remaining squares a square that is "like hurt but not quite as much hurt as the event identified by the child as the most painful hurt," followed by a square for "something that hurts just a little," and finally a color like "no hurt at all" (p. 367). The resulting four colored squares serve as the child's individualized rating system, and are coded from 0 (no pain) to 3 (most painful) for use in data analysis.

The validity of the Eland Color Assessment Tool was evaluated with 40 preschool children aged 4–9 to 5–9 (Eland, 1981). Children who received an injection preceded by an application of a coolant spray reported lower levels of pain on the color scale (M=1.85, SD=1.14) than did children whose injections were preceded by aerosol air only (M=2.55, SD=.76). Twenty-two children reported that the pain they experienced during the injection was like the most severe pain color. In contrast, when asked to choose a color to reflect the way they felt when they were dressed and leaving the office, only two children chose the severe pain color. The stability of color scale choices over time, the reliability of the color scale over repeated painful stimulation, and the applicability of the measure to other pain contexts are areas requiring further study.

Varni, Thompson, and Hanson (1987) included a modification of the Eland Color Assessment Tool in the Varni/Thompson Pediatric Pain Questionnaire. Twenty-five rheumatology patients were shown four boxes labeled with "developmentally appropriate" pain intensity categories. The subjects selected colors for each box from eight standard crayons and then colored in a body outline with the four colors to represent pain intensity throughout their bodies. Red was the color most frequently selected to represent severe pain. Varni et al. (1987) did not attempt to quantify the children's color choices or the area of body outline colored in each color intensity. However, their descriptive data demonstrated significant individual differences in colors chosen to represent the four levels of pain intensity. Varni et al. (1987) argued that children can be specific in identifying pain intensities at various body sites if allowed to make their own color/intensity match.

Thus, there appears to be some preliminary support for the use of color intensity matching procedures for pain self-report. However, considerably more work is needed to determine the reliability of these procedures and to validate their applicability to clinical settings.

Likert Scales

Likert-type pain rating scales have been used with some success as outcome measures for pain management programs for children. For example, Zeltzer and LeBaron (1982) used a 5-point Likert scale (1 = none, 5 = maximum) for 45, 6- to 17-year-olds' self-report of pain during oncology medical procedures. Self-report ratings were higher (M=4.51, SD=0.68) for bone marrow pain than for lumbar puncture pain (M=3.70, SD=1.12). Self-report of pain also decreased following hypnosis.

However, some investigators appear to have encountered some difficulty using Likert ratings with younger children. For example, Hilgard and LeBaron (1982) used an 11-point Likert scale anchored 0 = no pain, 10 = the most severe pain they could think of, to assess bone marrow aspiration pain in children aged six through adolescence. However, they noted that pictures of facial expressions were needed for younger children who could not use the numerical system. Since they did not report their faces methodology in much detail, it is difficult to determine the utility of this rating scale from this study.

LeBaron and Zeltzer (1984) used a 5-point Likert-type scale to assess pain in 67 pediatric cancer patients between the ages of 6 and 18. The scale was anchored "no pain" and "extreme pain." For children under 10 (and for older children who had difficulty with the rating procedure) the numbers were accompanied by faces with expressions of increasing distress. The child was asked to point to the number or face that showed how much "hurting" he/she had felt during a bone marrow aspiration procedure. Self-report pain ratings correlated with observed distress on the Procedure Behavior Check List (Spearman rho=.26 − .44), as well as with trained observers' 5-point Likert ratings of the child's pain (Spearman rho=.39 − .59) during the preparatory period and actual bone marrow aspiration.

Two aspects of the LeBaron and Zeltzer (1984) study are encouraging. First, appropriate nonparametric statistics were used for the fundamentally ordinal 5-point scale. In addition, the scale appeared to have some validity. However, further study is needed to determine whether or not the addition of faces facilitated young children's comprehension of the measure. Also, whether or not one can equate scores on a "number only" Likert scale with a combined number and faces scale also needs to be empirically tested.

Likert-type ratings accompanied by verbal descriptors are often used with adult patients to measure headache pain intensity (Budzynski, Stoyva, Adler, & Mullaney, 1973), but have only recently been applied to children. Richardson, McGrath, Cunningham, and Humphreys (1982) compared two variations of such a Likert headache intensity scale for 16 9- to 17-year-old children with migraine headaches. All subjects completed a headache diary four times a day for four weeks. The diary included a record of symptoms experienced with each headache (nausea, etc.) as well as an intensity rating. Half of the subjects were trained to use a "behavioral" Likert scale which involved the following descriptions:

0 = No headache

1 = Headache — I am only aware of it if I pay attention to it.

2 = Headache — but I can ignore it at times.

3 = Headache — I can't ignore it but I can do my usual activities.

4 = Headache — It's difficult for me to concentrate. I can only do easy activities.

5 = Headache — Such that I can't do anything (p. 185).

The remaining subjects were trained to use a "subjective" Likert scale which was the same as the behavioral scale, but with the addition of subjective labels (slight, mild, painful, severe, very severe) for the numbers 1 through 5. The child's parent received the same headache diary format as the child and was asked to independently rate the child's headache daily.

Weighted kappa measures of concordance (which correct for chance agreement) were computed to determine the degree of correspondence between child and parent report of the child's headache. No differences were found between the "behavioral" and "subjective" Likert scales. Weighted kappas ranged from .18 to 1.00, with 88% of the values ranging from "fair" to "almost perfect" parent-child agreement. Many of the discrepancies in ratings appeared at the lower levels of headache intensity. Richardson et al. (1982) speculated that it may be too difficult to discriminate between no, slight, and mild headache when the child continues to engage in normal activities and suggested that better concordance ratings might be obtained with a condensed, 4-point scale.

More recently, Andrasik, Burke, Attanasio, and Rosenblum (1985) evaluated a Likert-type intensity scale for children's headaches similar to that employed by Richardson et al. (1982). Fifty-three children, aged 8 to 16, with migraine or tension headache and their parents were interviewed separately regarding: (a) the number of headaches the child had each month, (b) the typical duration of each headache, and (c) the mean peak intensity of each headache. Headache intensity was rated on a 5-point Likert scale ranging from 1 = slight pain, the child is only aware of pain when he or she thinks about it, to 5, where headache pain is described as "so intense that the child typically cannot complete homework, chores, play and the like, and bed rest is usually required" (p. 422). The children then completed daily headache diary recordings of the frequency, duration, and peak intensity of their headaches over four weeks. Parents also recorded the frequency and peak intensity of their child's headaches in a daily diary.

They found no difference between parent and child retrospective recall of headache frequency, duration, or intensity in the interview. However, both the child's and the parent's interview report overestimated the actual frequency, duration, and intensity of the child's daily headaches recorded over the following four weeks by 56% to 112%. When the children's diary records were compared with the parents; parents were found to have underestimated the child's headache frequency by 40%; intensity ratings were approximately congruent. The discrepancy between parent and child report of headache frequency obtained by Andrasik et al. (1985) may represent the same phenomenon observed by Richardson et al. (1982). Mild headaches which do not interfere with ongoing activity may be difficult for parents to reliably observe.

Subjects and their parents were reevaluated by Andrasik et al. (1985) following psychological treatment. Daily headache diaries were collected for four weeks after treatment, at which point another headache interview was conducted. Agreement between child and parent report was generally greater at post-testing than at baseline, although parents still overestimated the intensity of their child's headaches in the interview, compared with the child's diary data. Both parent and child interview and headache diary data reflected symptom improvement following treatment.

Several interesting issues are raised by the headache pain studies. First, the scale appears to be an ordinal scale and should be treated appropriately in statistical analysis. Secondly, the scale appears to be useful for children eight years old and over, although this should be documented with a larger sample of children. Younger children's ability to use the scale also should be evaluated.

The inflated ratings of headache frequency and intensity obtained from both parents and children in the interview setting is consistent with the behavioral assessment literature. Daily records typically are more accurate estimates of behavioral frequency than is retrospective recall (Cone & Hawkins, 1977). Therefore, if accurate, specific child self-report of pain frequency or intensity is needed, care should be taken to use daily self-monitoring records or obtain self-report ratings during the actual painful event. Finally, investigators and clinicians should be cautious in using parental retrospective recall of their child's pain experience as an indicator of the validity of child pain self-report. Parents may overestimate or underestimate the child's actual experience. The ideal validation procedure would involve (1) independent assessment by parents at the same time as the child's self-report, with both ratings occurring at the time of the painful event, accompanied by (2) concurrent independent observation of the child's overt behavior.

Visual Analog Scales (VAS)

Visual analog scales involve some sort of graphic representation, such as a line or a thermometer. Some scales are marked off in segments;

most scales are descriptively labeled at either pole. For example, Abu-Saad (1984) used a 10cm line marked off into 10 segments. The left end of the scale was labeled "0, I have no pain;" the right extreme was labeled "10, I have very severe pain." Ten pediatric surgery patients, aged 9 to 15, were evaluated while hospitalized on the first and second days after surgery. Their self-report pain ratings corresponded with observed behaviors indicating pain, but did not correlate with pulse, respiration rate, or blood pressure. However, these findings need to be interpreted cautiously, since the author was also the observer in this study and the sample size was quite small.

Jay, Ozolins, Elliott, and Caldwell (1983) used a pain thermometer based on earlier work by Katz, Sharp, Kellerman, Marston, Hershman, and Siegel (1982) to assess pain in children undergoing bone marrow aspirations. The pain thermometer is a drawing marked off in gradations from 0 ("no pain at all") to 100 ("worst pain possible"). Forty-two 2- to 20-year-old children completed the thermometer to show how much pain they expected to experience during the bone marrow aspiration; following the procedure they rated the actual pain they experienced. Both "anticipated pain" ratings and "experienced pain" ratings correlated with observed behavioral distress during the medical procedure ($r=.76$ and $.62$).

Additional support for the validity of the Katz et al. (1982) pain thermometer was obtained by Jay, Elliott, Katz, and Siegel (1987). They compared the effects of cognitive-behavioral therapy, Valium, and an attention control condition on the distress of 56 3- to 13-year-old children undergoing bone marrow aspirations. Children in the behavior-therapy condition reported 25% lower levels of pain on the thermometer after intervention than did children in the other two conditions. Lower pain self-report was accompanied by lower pulse rates and lower levels of observed distress.

In a subsequent study of 55 cancer patients, aged 3 to 13 (Elliott, Jay, & Woody, 1987), anticipated pain thermometer ratings were correlated with observed behavioral distress during a bone marrow aspiration ($r=.24$), but experienced pain thermometer ratings were not significantly related to observed distress ($r=.20$). When the results were reexamined, Elliott et al. (1987) found that experienced pain thermometer scores were significantly correlated with observed distress, but only for children older than seven ($r=.51$). They argued that younger children may not be able to rate their experienced pain reliably. An alternative hypothesis, however, is that the 0 to 100 scaling of the thermometer may have been confusing, especially for preschool-aged children.

Miser, Dothage, Wesley, and Miser (1987) used a 100mm visual analog scale without any interval divisions in the form of a thermometer to assess pain in 126 pediatric cancer patients over the age of eight. This study is unique, in that children who had received a diagnostic procedure (i.e., bone marrow aspiration or lumbar puncture) were eliminated. Thus, subjects in the sample had pain related to their disease state and/or side effects of treatment. The median pain score of the inpatients was 26mm; the median score for the outpatients was 20mm. The investigators also independently rated the subjects' pain on the same visual analog scale. Although the overall Pearson correlation between the child and investigator ratings was moderately high (r=.75), the investigators tended to underestimate the pain of children who reported moderate to severe pain (i.e., above 50mm). In addition, ratings of children under 17 with severe pain correlated most poorly with the investigator's ratings. However, it is difficult to determine from these data if the poor correspondence between the child's self-report of pain and the adults' ratings of the child's pain reflected limitations of the self-report instrument itself, or rather the previously discussed tendency for adults to underestimate children's pain in general.

Another true ratio visual analog scale (VAS) (with no actual or implied interval markings) was included by Varni et al. (1987) in the Pediatric Pain Questionnaire. Their VAS consisted of a 10cm line anchored with "developmentally appropriate pain descriptors and happy and sad faces" (p. 31) on the left and right ends. Forty rheumatology patients, aged 4 to 16 years, used the VAS to rate their worst pain intensity for the previous week as well as their present pain. Independent visual analog ratings anchored "no pain" and "severe pain" for the past week and for the child's present pain were obtained from the child's mother. The child's physician also rated the child's present pain intensity following a physical examination.

The range of scores obtained on the visual analog scales was good. Child VAS scores ranged from 0–8cm for present pain, and from 0–10cm for worst pain. Parent ratings ranged from 0–10cm. Physician ratings ranged from 0–8.5cm. Parent and child VAS scores were significantly correlated for present pain (r=.72) and worst pain (r=.54). Physician VAS scores also were significantly correlated with child self-report of present pain (r=.65) and with parent VAS scores (r=.85). Finally, child VAS present pain ratings corresponded with physician-rated disease activity, thus lending some support for the construct validity of the Varni/Thompson VAS.

One of the few studies to directly evaluate the sensitivity and reliability of children's use of visual analog scales was conducted by McGrath, deVeber, and Hearn (1985). Their methodology was based on cross modality matching procedures typically employed in sensory perception research. Because of the uniqueness of their approach, their data will be presented in some detail.

Forty children, 3 to 15 years of age, 20 of whom were healthy and 20 of whom were oncology patients, participated in the study. Subjects were presented five identical containers ranging in weight from 75 to 275 grams, in 50 gram increments. The children were asked to make a light as bright as the container was heavy. In separate trials they marked a line as long as the container was heavy. The left point of the 150mm line was labeled "not heavy"; the right end was anchored "heaviest sensation imaginable."

Seven children with an average age of 4.7 years did not complete the study. The remaining subjects were able to use both the brightness and visual analog scale in a valid manner, which corresponded to actual weights. Ratings obtained two weeks later correlated with initial ratings at about the .70 level for five- and six-year-olds. Median test-retest correlations for 13- to 15-year-olds were .99.

McGrath et al. (1985) then applied the cross modality matching procedure to determine whether brightness and visual analog scales could be used to quantify a scale of "unpleasantness" or affective magnitude. The same subjects were presented pictures of nine faces drawn to represent: a neutral face, four increasingly happy faces, and four increasingly sad appearing faces. The same brightness and visual analog line marking procedure was used. The end points of the visual analog scale were designated as the "saddest" and "happiest" faces imaginable.

Again, consistent results were obtained for both the brightness and visual analog ratings. Mean ratings for each face were then computed. Interestingly, the positive faces were rated at approximately equal intervals, but the intervals between the quantitative ratings for the negative faces were not equal. First, the "neutral" face was perceived as slightly negative. Secondly, the first and second "negative" faces were rated as only slightly increasing in negative valence.

Finally, the validity of the visual analog and facial scales were evaluated by having children rate their own pain during check-ups, finger sticks, intravenous injections, lumbar punctures, and bone marrow aspirations. Both the visual analog and faces measures varied as a function of the different medical procedures. Thus, there appears to be preliminary evidence that these two scales are sensitive to differences in pain experience.

The combined visual analog and faces scales used by McGrath et al. (1985) represent an important advance in pain assessment in children for a number of reasons. First, they documented that the visual analog scale can be used consistently across time by children over the age of five, and that the measure is sensitive to at least one dimension that can be quantified objectively, in this case, weight. This is a simple, yet elegant method for beginning to establish the reliability and validity of a child self-report pain instrument. It makes excellent sense to begin with a criterion like weight that can be reliably measured and then progress to the measurement of the more elusive phenomenon of pain, once rudimentary sensitivity and reliability properties of the measurement tool have been documented.

An additional significant contribution offered by the McGrath et al. (1985) study is their inclusion of a measure of the affective aspect of pain and the accompanying documentation that affective faces scales cannot be assumed to be equal interval scales. Their use of visual analog ratings to provide quantifications of interval scaling for faces is an exciting methodological contribution which warrants replication with a different sample of children. Similar scaling procedures could be applied to other existing faces scales, such as the pain intensity faces scale used by LeBaron and Zeltzer (1984) and Varni et al. (1987). One could then use the McGrath et al. procedure to compare the two scales and select the scale which appears to have the closest approximation of equal intervals for future research or clinical use. Finally, the relative utility of including both positive and negative faces in comparison with a restricted range of neutral to negative faces also needs to be examined further.

Summary

Although the field of pain assessment in children is relatively young, a number of the assessment approaches reviewed appear to have considerable potential. Children appear to be able to communicate qualitative aspects of their pain experience through drawings, projective instruments, such as the Pediatric Pain Interview (Lollar et al., 1982), and in structured interviews and questionnaires. Open-ended question formats appear to offer the most information, with less chance of bias than forced-choice formats. More research is needed to determine the reliability of children's qualitative reports of pain and to evaluate whether more streamlined assessment strategies, such as pain descriptor checklists, are valid for children.

Children as young as five years of age also appear to be able to reliably report the intensity of their pain experience via visual analog scales, whereas Likert scales appear to be confusing to many children, especially children under the age of 10. Although the pairing of faces or colors with numbers may improve young children's understanding of

Likert rating systems, this contention has not been documented empirically. At present, there does not appear to be any advantage in using an ordinal Likert scale over an interval visual analog scale to quantify pain intensity. However, Likert scaling of pain intensity does appear to be useful for children over the age of eight, when ratings are paired with detailed behavioral descriptors, such as the systems employed in headache studies. It should be noted, however, that such systems can only provide ordinal data and may not be sensitive to changes in mild levels of pain.

ASSESSMENT OF MEDICAL FEARS

Hospitalization, surgery, and invasive medical and dental procedures are stressful and anxiety-provoking experiences for most children. Negative reactions to medical treatment may be mild and transient and may actually serve as valuable opportunities for children to learn to cope with stress (Melamed, 1977). However, severe anxiety and distress reactions to medical treatment can result in behavior problems that interfere with medical care as well as in long-term psychological disturbances (Elkins & Roberts, 1983; Melamed, 1977). Therefore, accurate methods for assessing children's medical fears and anxiety are crucial for the identification of children in need of special preparation for medical treatment as well as for the evaluation of the efficacy of psychological interventions designed to decrease anxiety in medical settings.

Global Anxiety Measures

Global measures of child anxiety have been found to have some utility in identifying children who are anxious during medical treatment. For example, Jay et al. (1983) found that children who scored high on the trait scale of the State-Trait Anxiety Inventory for Children (STAIC) (Spielberger, Edwards, Lushene, Monturi, & Platzek, 1973) demonstrated higher levels of behavioral distress during a bone marrow aspiration than did children with low trait anxiety scores.

However, when global anxiety measures are used to assess the effects of psychological treatment for medical fears, the findings are mixed. Kellerman, Zeltzer, Ellenberg, and Dash (1983) and Zeltzer, Kellerman, Ellenberg, and Dash (1983) found lower STAIC trait anxiety scores in adolescents after hypnosis for procedural distress. In contrast, Roberts, Wurtele, Boone, Ginther, and Elkins (1981) found no changes in scores on the Children's Manifest Anxiety Scale (CMAS) after children participated in a medical fears prevention program, even though self-report of specific medical fears did decrease. Similar results were obtained by Melamed and Siegel (1975). Surgery patients who reviewed a modeling film showed decreases in behavior problems, physiological arousal and specific medical fears. However, their CMAS scores did not change.

Medical Fear Questionnaires

Melamed and Siegel (1975) modified the Fear Survey Schedule for Children (FSS-FC) (Scherer & Nakamura, 1968) to include more specific, medically related items in order to obtain a more sensitive measure of children's fears. Their new scale, called the Hospital Fears Rating Scale, consists of eight items from the medical fears subscale of the FSS-FC, plus eight items with "face validity" for assessing hospital fears, and nine filler items. Children rate their level of fear for each item on a 5-point thermometer (ranging from 1, "not afraid at all," to 5, "very afraid"). Total scores for the 16 medical fears are then computed. A test-retest reliability coefficient of .75 was reported by Melamed, Dearborn, and Hermecz (1983) with 4- to 17-year-old children. Younger children tend to score higher on this test (Ferguson, 1979; Melamed & Siegel, 1975) than do older children.

High scores on the Hospital Fears Rating Scale have been shown to be related to negative behaviors during intravenous venopunctures and disruptive behavior in the operating room (Melamed, Dearborn, & Hermecz, 1983). The measure also appears to be somewhat sensitive to interventions designed to prepare children for surgery (Faust & Melamed, 1984; Ferguson, 1979; Zastowny, Kirschenbaum, & Meng, 1986) and to medical fears prevention programs for healthy children (Roberts et al., 1981).

The FSS-FC also has been modified for dental settings. Melamed, Yurcheson, Fleece, Hutcherson, and Hawes (1978) added 15 specific dental items to the FSS-FC to assess the effects of modeling on 80, 4- to 11-year-old children's dental fears. As was true of the Hospital Fears Rating Scale, young children gave higher self-report of fear on the dental version of the FSS-FC than did older children (8- to 11-year-olds). The children in the modeling condition had lower general fears on the dental fear survey schedule than did children who viewed a demonstration. Palmar Sweat Index (PSI) measures correlated with general as well as specific fears on the FSS-FC (r=.30–31).

Siaw, Stephens, and Holmes (1986) also modified the FSS-FC. They used only the eight medical items from the FSS-FC to assess anxiety in 33 children aged 3 to 12, who were hospitalized for surgery. Each item was presented orally. Children were asked to point to one of five faces

TABLE 13.2 Anxiety Self-Report Measures

Measure	Type of Anxiety	Ages	Reliability	Validity	Research Use	Clinical Use
Global Measures						
State Trait Anxiety Inventory for Children (Spielberger et al., 1973)	General	9-adol.	Intratest, test-retest	Yes	General & medical	General & medical
Children's Manifest Anxiety Scale (Reynolds & Richmond, 1979)	General	4-12	Intratest, test-retest	General-yes Medical-unknown	General & medical	General
Medical Fears Questionnaires						
Fear Survey Schedule for Children, dental version (Melamed et al, 1978)	General & dental	5-11	Intratest, test-retest	Yes	General & dental	General & dental
Hospital Fears Rating Scale (Melamed & Siegel, 1975)	General medical	4-17	Test-retest	Yes	Surgery pts, healthy children	Surgery pts.
Hospital Fears Questionnaire (Roberts et al, 1981)	General medical	3-12	Unknown	Yes	Surgery pts, healthy children	Healthy children

Instrument	Type	Age	Reliability	Validity	Population	Population
Medical Fears						
Questionnaire (Broome, 1986)	General medical	4–7	Intratest	Yes	Healthy children	Unknown
Child Medical Fear Scale (Broome & Hellier, 1987)	General medical	5–11	Intratest, test-retest	Yes	Healthy, previously hospitalized children	Unknown
Likert Scales						
Bradlyn et al., (1986)	State (5-pt)	4–16	Unknown	Yes	Cardiac cath.	Cardiac cath.
Zeltzer & LeBaron (1982)	State (5-pt)	6–17	Unknown	Unknown	Oncology pts.	Oncology pts.
Hilgard & LeBaron (1982)	State (10-pt)	6–adol.	Poor—confused with pain	Unknown	Oncology pts.	Oncology pts.
Peterson & Shigetomi (1981)	State (5-pt)	2–10	Poor—34% did not understand	Yes	Surgery pts.	Surgery pts.
LeBaron & Zeltzer (1984)	State (5-pt, "faces")	6–17	Unknown—under age 10?	Yes	Oncology pts.	Oncology pts.
Elliott et al., (1987)	State (3-pt, "faces")	3–13	Unknown	Yes	Oncology pts.	Oncology pts.
Johnson et al., (1975)	State (4-pt, "figures")	6–11	Unknown	Yes	Cast removal	Cast removal
Nonverbal Measures						
Picture Test (Venham et al., 1977)	State	2–10	Unknown	Unknown	Dental pts., surgery pts.	Unknown

(rather than a thermometer), numbered 1 to 5 to indicate their degree of fear. Faces ranged in emotion from Face 1 (a smile, labeled "not scared at all") to Face 5 (a frown, labeled "very, very scared"). Scores on the Siaw et al. (1986) measure were positively correlated with scores on the Hospital Fears Questionnaire (HFQ) (Roberts et al., 1981).

An alternative approach to the assessment of children's medical fears involves developing lists of fears that appear face valid based on the literature and the author's experience. For example, Roberts et al. (1981) developed a Hospital Fears Questionnaire which included items such as, "How afraid are you of having an operation?" "How afraid are you of getting your blood tested?" (p.296), which are rated on a 5-point thermometer like the one used in the Hospital Fears Rating Scale (Melamed & Siegel, 1975). In a study of 36 7- to 8-year-old children, the Roberts et al. (1981) scale appeared to be sensitive to changes in fears following a fear prevention program. However, whether this scale offers any greater utility than the adaptations of the FSS-FC remains to be determined.

Broome (1986) used a similar face validity approach to develop the Medical Fear Questionnaire. The Medical Fear Questionnaire consists of 12 fear statements involving doctors, nurses, hospital settings, and procedures. The child is asked to pick one of three responses to indicate how fearful he or she is for each item (1 = not at all, 2 = a little, 3 = a lot).

In a preliminary study of 128 children, aged four to seven, who were participating in a preschool health screening, Broome (1986) obtained a Cronbach's alpha of .84, suggesting that the instrument had a high degree of internal consistency. Scores obtained on the questionnaire also varied across the entire possible range (12–36; M=17.8; SD=5.3). Children who described themselves as more fearful on the Medical Fear Questionnaire were rated by independent observers as more fearful during an interview and during a medical examination than were children who reported low medical fear.

The medical fear questionnaires presented so far all appear to have face validity and appear to have some utility, in that they appear to be sensitive to changes in self-reported fear following interventions designed to reduce children's medical concerns. However, empirical data regarding the reliability and validity of these measures are quite limited. In particular, it has been argued that these face-validity based measures may not be comprehensive enough and may not include all of the fears children may have regarding medical experiences (Broome & Hellier, 1987).

Broome and Hellier (1987) attempted to address the limitations of the existing medical fear instruments by designing an empirically based scale. In a preliminary study, experienced pediatric nurses interviewed 146 children between the ages of 6 and 11 years to determine their medical fears. The following questions were asked in taped interviews:

1. Tell me how you feel when you are sick; hurt.
2. What do you like about being sick? What don't you like?
3. Tell me how you feel when you go to see the doctor or nurse.
4. What do you like about seeing the doctor or nurse; going to his or her office? What don't you like?
5. Tell me how you feel (or would feel) about going to the hospital. What do you like about the hospital? What don't you like about the hospital? (p.79)

On the basis of the interviews, the 29 items of the Child Medical Fear Scale (CMFS) were developed and were classified into four subscales (intrapersonal fears, interpersonal fears, procedural fears, and environmental fears). The child is asked to rate each fear item on a 3-point scale (1 = not at all afraid, 2 = a little afraid, 3 = very afraid). Total and subscale scores are then computed by summing the child's ratings.

In a subsequent study, the CMFS was administered to 84 children, aged 5 to 11 years, to obtain preliminary reliability and validity data. Roughly 40% of the children in the sample had been hospitalized in the past. The resulting psychometric data were very positive. A good range of scores was obtained (30-82 out of a possible range of 29-87). Reliability indices also were good. A Cronbach's alpha coefficient of .93 was obtained for total scores. Test-retest reliability over two weeks was .84. The CMFS also was significantly correlated with the medical subscale of the FSS-FC ($r=.71$). Because the CMFS is such a new instrument, additional validity studies have not yet been conducted. Further research is needed to evaluate the appropriateness of the instrument for children currently involved in medical treatment.

Likert Scales

Likert-type rating scales of anxiety have been used as dependent measures in many medical preparation studies. These rating scales appear to correlate with observed behavioral distress and adults' ratings of children's anxiety, however there are also some conceptual and procedural problems associated with this type of scale.

For example, Bradlyn, Christoff, Sikora, O'Dell, and Harris (1986) used a graphic representation of a 5-point scale to assess anxiety in 4- to 16-year-old children. They found that younger children rated themselves as more anxious and demonstrated more anxiety behaviors during cardiac catheterization.

Zeltzer and LeBaron (1982) also found that a 5-point rating scale was useful for assessing anxiety in 45 6- to 17-year-old cancer patients undergoing painful medical procedures, in that the self-report scale was sensitive to intervention (lower scores were obtained following hypnosis). However, the obtained values were very similar to the self-report ratings of pain obtained from the same subjects, suggesting that it may be difficult for children to distinguish between pain and anxiety when asked to rate both dimensions.

Hilgard and LeBaron (1982) provided some support for this contention. They attempted to use a 0 to 10 rating scale for anxiety and for pain self-report with children aged six to adolescence. However, they eventually dropped the anxiety measure because "the young patients were confused by the request to distinguish between anxiety and pain ('being scared' and 'feeling the hurt')" (p. 422).

In addition to difficulties distinguishing between anxiety and pain, young children also may have difficulty simply using the Likert rating format to report their anxiety. For example, LeBaron and Zeltzer (1984) used a 5-point scale for anxiety assessment, which was identical to the system they used to assess pain, discussed in the preceding section of this chapter. Children were asked to pick a number from 1 (labeled "no anxiety") to 5 (labeled "extreme anxiety") to indicate how "scared" he or she had felt during a bone marrow aspiration. In a sample of 50 6- to 17-year-old cancer patients, the self-report anxiety ratings correlated positively with observed behavioral distress before and during the actual bone marrow aspiration ($r=.49 - .53$) and with trained observers' 5-point ratings of the child's anxiety during the procedure ($r=.53 - .71$). However, young subjects appeared to have some difficulty using the scale. Children under the age of ten and older children who "had difficulty with the self-rating procedure" (p. 732) were shown faces showing increasing distress above each of the numbers. Peterson and Shigetomi (1981) reported a similar experience with a 5-point Likert type anxiety rating scale. They found that 34% of their child-subjects (aged 2 1/2 to 10 1/2) did not understand the ratings. It is unclear, however, whether the pairing of faces with the numbers of the Likert scale actually improves the reliability and validity of the measures.

Nonetheless, some researchers have used Likert fear scales accompanied by drawings with some success. For example, a simple fear rating system was used by Elliott et al. (1987) to assess 55 pediatric cancer patients fear of an upcoming bone marrow aspiration. The children, aged 3 to 13, rated "how scared" they felt by selecting one of three faces "ranging from a 'happy' face indicating 'not at all scared' to a 'sad' face indicating 'very scared' " (p. 546). The self-report fear ratings correlated significantly with the children's observed distress during the actual medical procedure (r=.38).

Johnson, Kirchoff, and Endress (1975) showed 6- to 11-year-old children "stick figures of four children on an equal interval continuum," They were told that each child in the picture was having a cast removed. "One child was 'not at all afraid,' one was 'a little afraid,' one was 'quite a bit afraid,' and one was 'very, very much afraid' " (p. 406). The child was asked to pick the child that reflected how afraid they were of having their own cast removed. Children who reported no fear of cast removal showed fewer behavioral signs of distress during cast removal.

Nonverbal Anxiety Measures

Venham, Bengston, and Cipes (1977) attempted to avoid young children's comprehension difficulties by developing a nonverbal anxiety measure. The picture test consists of eight pictures, each containing two boys expressing different emotional states (e.g., crying versus laughing). The child is asked to choose the boy in each picture who feels the most like he or she feels. The number of times the child chooses the more anxious appearing child is then totalled.

Although this measure is attractive because of the simple format which may allow self-report anxiety ratings to be obtained from children as young as preschool age, the results of studies using the Venham picture test have been disappointing. Venham et al. (1977) found no changes in the picture test scores of 29 preschool children over the course of six dental visits, despite the fact that significant changes were noted in the subjects' overt behavioral distress. Similarly, Peterson and Shigetomi (1981) and Siegel and Peterson (1980) obtained no changes in picture test scores following preparation programs, again despite apparent improvements in behavioral distress and physiological arousal. Therefore, the utility of the Venham Picture Test remains highly questionable.

Summary

Global anxiety measures appear to be most useful for screening purposes, to identify children who are at risk for high levels of distress during medical procedures and may be in need of psychological intervention. However, global anxiety measures may not be sensitive enough to reflect changes in the child's specific medical fears following psychological treatment. A number of medical fear questionnaires are available, which appear to be more sensitive than the global anxiety measures. The various medical and dental adaptations of the Fear Survey Schedule for Children have been used most frequently to measure changes in fears after psychological treatment, however, the reliability of the Broome and Hellier (1987) Child Medical Fear Scale has been more extensively documented. Further research is needed to determine which medical fear scale is most appropriate as a clinical outcome measure.

Efforts to obtain state anxiety ratings from children during stressful medical procedures have been less successful. Children appear to have difficulty using 5-point Likert anxiety scales and have trouble distinguishing between anxiety and pain. It may be the case that young children simply cannot make the conceptual distinction between pain and anxiety. On the other hand, it may be necessary to use very simple rating systems like the 3-point "scared" faces scale used by Elliott et al. (1987), or to use visual analog scales similar to those used in pain intensity assessment. Further research is needed to develop valid state anxiety measures to assess the ongoing effects of medical anxiety treatment programs.

On the basis of the literature reviewed, it appears safe to conclude that children can, indeed, provide valuable information about their pain and their medical fears. Children as young as four years of age appear to be able to provide information about their pain experience in a structured interview format. Structured pain and fear questionnaires may be useful in verbal formats for children five years and older, whereas written formats may be used with older children. Visual analog scales appear to be valid for children five years of age and older and also appear to be associated with fewer comprehension difficulties than Likert scales or graphic scales involving numerical ratings.

Considerably more research on developmental issues in pain and medical fear is needed, however. More normative data for existing measures are needed. In addition, more extensive work with preschool children is necessary in order to determine the youngest age at which children can provide reliable pain and fear self-report and to identify the age at which behavioral observation and physiological arousal alone must be relied upon to infer the child's distress.

Clearly, more extensive evaluation of the reliability and validity of these relatively new self-report measures is needed. In some respects, we need to take a few steps backwards in evaluating existing instruments. Most investigators have focused on content and construct validity issues, documenting correspondence between self-report and behavioral or physiological indices of pain and fear, or on evaluating changes in self-report following psychological intervention. Although these validity issues are extremely important, they appear premature. The sensitivity and reliability of the instruments used to obtain self-reports often have not been documented. We need to return to the fundamentals of psychometrics and first document reliability for different aged children before proceeding with validity evaluation. The use of physical properties such as size or weight to first document the sensitivity of the measurement technique appears to hold considerable promise in this regard.

A final note of caution needs to be raised regarding the evaluation of child distress self-report measures in health settings. It is commonly argued that children's distress can be conceptualized as a triad involving overt behavior, physiological arousal, and cognitive-affective factors (assessed by self-report) (Jay, Elliott, & Varni, 1986). Validation of self-report, therefore, involves comparisons with behavioral and physiological indicators. However, the three systems do not necessarily vary together. For example, adolescents show fewer overt signs of distress during painful medical procedures than do younger children, yet they report significant levels of pain and anxiety (Jay et al., 1986). As one of the children in a study of relaxation and cognitive distraction during chemotherapy (Dahlquist, Gil, Armstrong, Ginsberg, & Jones, 1985) so eloquently expressed, "I know your graphs [behavioral observations] said I did better when I didn't look at the needle going in, but I didn't like not watching. I felt worse when I didn't know what was happening." This example illustrates the important information provided by child self-report.

ASSESSMENT OF COMPLIANCE

The medical treatment of many acute and chronic pediatric illnesses requires the child and/or family to follow a prescribed medical regimen at home. Such medical recommendations may be relatively simple, such as taking prescribed medications at designated times, or may involve complex daily management programs in the case of chronic illnesses. For example, children with diabetes frequently are required to follow a prescribed diet, monitor their exercise, test their urine or blood daily or more frequently, and adjust amounts of daily insulin injections accordingly. Similarly complex daily treatments are necessary for cystic fibrosis patients, which include dietary supplements, antibiotic and pulmonary medications, chest percussion several times a day, as well as pulmonary treatments. Childhood asthma, cancer, and rheumatoid arthritis also are examples of chronic illnesses which require complicated daily medical management.

The accurate evaluation of the degree to which the child and family complies with medical treatment is crucial. If the treatment is being followed accurately and the child's condition worsens or does not improve, changes in the medical treatment may be needed. However, the adequacy of the prescribed treatment cannot be evaluated if one cannot determine whether or not it is being followed. Furthermore, recent reports in the literature suggest that roughly 50% of pediatric populations do not adhere to prescribed medical treatments (La Greca, 1988). Because of the serious health consequences of noncompliance, pediatric psychologists frequently are called upon to assist in evaluating patient compliance and to design interventions to improve compliance.

Although some aspects of medical adherence can be inferred from drug assays or medical outcome measures (i.e., weight gain or pulmonary function tests), many treatment regimens cannot be reliably monitored in this manner due to cost, limited sensitivity to short-term changes in compliance, and individual variability in physical response to medical treatment (La Greca, 1988). Therefore, in most cases, the clinician must rely on child and/or parent report of compliance.

In the following section, the most common approaches to obtaining child self-report of medical compliance will be described. Because the particular details of compliance measurement vary with the specifics of the medical regimen, space considerations prohibit an exhaustive review of all available child self-report adherence measurement strategies. Therefore, each general approach will be illustrated with selected examples of compliance self-report for specific diseases.

Questionnaires

In order for a child to comply with medical treatment, he or she must understand the medical regimen and know what to do in various situations. Although accurate knowledge does not necessarily ensure adherence, inadequate or inaccurate information virtually guarantees problems with compliance. Furthermore, knowledge or skill in one aspect of disease management does not necessarily predict skill in other aspects of managing the same disease (Johnson, 1984). Therefore, it is important to assess knowledge in all aspects of disease management.

The child's knowledge of his or her medical regimen is most often assumed to be adequate or is indirectly inferred from conversations with medical staff. However, there have been some recent efforts to objectively evaluate the child's understanding via structured, criterion-based ques-

TABLE 13.3 Compliance Self-Report Measures

Type of Measure	Ages	Reliability	Validity	Research Use	Clinical Use
Questionnaires					
General Information Questionnaire (Johnson et al., 1982)	6–18	Intratest	Yes	Diabetics	Diabetics
Problem-Solving Questionnaire (Johnson et al., 1982)	6–18	Intratest	Yes	Diabetics	Diabetics
Structured Interviews					
4-point ratings (Allen et al., 1983)	8–17	Unknown	Yes	Diabetics	Unknown
24-hour recall (Johnson et al., 1986)	6–19	Unknown	Yes	Diabetics	Unknown
Projectives					
Medical Compliance Incomplete Stories Test (Czajkowski & Koocher, 1986)	13–23	Interrater	Yes	Cystic fibrosis pts.	Unknown
Self-Monitoring (Baum & Creer, 1986; Carney et al., 1983; Dahlquist & Gil, 1986; Epstein et al., 1981; Gross et al., 1985; Lowe & Lutzker, 1979; Rose et al., 1983; Schafer et al., 1982)	6–10	Interrater	Yes	Asthmatics, diabetics, pediatric dentistry	Asthmatics, diabetics, pediatric dentistry

tionnaires for some diseases. For example, Johnson and her colleagues (Harkavy, Johnson, Silverstein, Spillar, McCallum, & Rosenbloom, 1983; Johnson, 1984; Johnson, Pollack, Silverstein, Rosenbloom, Spillar, McCallum, & Harkavy, 1982) developed two tests of diabetes knowledge, the General Information and Problem-Solving Questionnaires. The General Information Questionnaire consists of multiple choice questions about the cause of diabetes, the definitions of common terminology and facts related to treatment (i.e., "What color would the Clinitest show if you had large amounts of sugar in your urine?"). The Problem-Solving Questionnaire presents situations that diabetic children are likely to encounter and asks the child to select the appropriate course of action from several alternatives.

The available psychometric data for the two questionnaires have been satisfactory. To maximize content validity, items were derived from existing diabetes educational programs. Items were then independently administered to two physicians and a nurse, and only those items to which all three respondents provided the same answer were retained (Harkavy et al., 1983). Split-half reliability quotients of .90 and .84 were obtained for the General Information and Problem-Solving Questionnaires, respectively (Johnson et al., 1982). The two scales appear to measure different aspects of knowledge, as indicated by the moderate intercorrelation between the two measures ($r=.65 - .72$) (Harkavy et al., 1983; Johnson et al., 1982). Older children tend to score higher on both tests (Harkavy et al., 1983; Johnson et al., 1982). Scores on both measures also have been found to change following a summer camp experience, but only for older children (aged 12 to 15).

As discussed earlier, a one-to-one correspondence does not exist between knowledge and skill in performing medical management tasks or between knowledge and actual daily compliance. Thus, it is not surprising that scores on the General Information and Problem-Solving Questionnaires have been shown to be related to observed skill in urine testing and self-injecting only at low levels ($r=.20 - .48$) (Harkavy et al., 1983; Johnson et al., 1982). Furthermore, changes in General Knowledge and Problem-Solving Questionnaire Scores have not been found in studies demonstrating improved accuracy and improved urine glucose levels in children following instruction and a token economy program (Epstein, Beck, Figueroa, Farkas, Kazdin, Daneman, & Becker, 1981).

Interviews

Many of the studies of children's compliance with medical treatment attempt to identify factors associated with adherence through interviews with parents and their children. Several such investigations have yielded useful information regarding critical self-management competencies, areas of relatively good versus relatively poor compliance, and factors which interfere with adherence (e.g., McNabb, Wilson-Pessano, & Jacobs, 1986; Passero, Remor, & Salomon, 1981). However, the resulting information often is collapsed into general problem areas, with no delineation of the differences in responses of children compared with their parents. Thus, one cannot determine the usefulness of the child's self-report from the findings.

Very few studies in the literature specifically focus on interview data provided by the child. However, the limited reports available offer interesting information that suggests that child interview data could be better utilized in the study of compliance. For example, Allen, Tennen, McGrade, Affleck, and Ratzan (1983) independently interviewed 34 diabetic children between the ages of 8 and 17 and their parents using a structured format. Participants were asked to rate on 4-point scales (never, sometimes, usually, always) the extent to which the child took responsibility for eight different aspects of diabetes management. They then indicated how satisfied they were with the child's level of responsibility (i.e., about right for age versus too much or too little). Finally, the children indicated how much they minded (not much, a little, a lot) these procedures as well as other aspects of medical treatment.

Although no reliability data were presented, this interview format did appear to have some utility. For instance, parent-child disagreement was apparent in specific areas of management, suggesting considerable conflict over the child's responsibility for managing these aspects of his or her care. In addition, children who were least compliant with their diets reported "minding" their diets the least. This question format (that is, asking how much the child "minds" a procedure) may provide a means by which the interviewer could avoid the social desirability issues which might keep a child from admitting he or she is noncompliant, but still gather information that would suggest areas of care to which the child may not be adhering. (Of course, this inferential approach would only be useful for presumed aversive aspects of the medical regimen). Finally, this study identified areas of care (in this case, insulin injections) where too early delegation of responsibility to the child appeared to be associated with poorer metabolic control of the disease. The interview format employed by Allen et al., appears to be applicable to a variety of illnesses and may be particularly useful in identifying "high risk" aspects of the medical regimen, where compliance difficulties are likely to occur.

An alternative interview approach for assessing compliance is the 24-hour recall interview. This procedure has been widely used to assess dietary adherence (Christensen, Terry, Wyatt, Pichert, & Lorenz, 1983), and has more recently been modified to collect information on multiple aspects of disease management. For example, Johnson, Silverstein, Rosenbloom, Carter, and Cunningham (1986) interviewed 186 diabetic children between the ages of six and 19 three times over a two-week period. The children were asked to recall the previous day's events in temporal sequence, beginning with awakening in the morning and ending with going to bed. If the child did not mention diabetes care activities, the interviewer prompted with specific questions about insulin injections, diet, etc. If the child said that an activity had taken place, the interviewer then asked for details. The child's parent also was interviewed on the same days.

Johnson et al., (1986) scored each child's interview data to indicate degree of compliance with 13 categories of diabetes management. For example, the regularity with which insulin injections were given was calculated by measuring the standard deviation of injection times across the three interviews. Reported calorie consumption was compared with calculated ideal calorie intake for each child to determine the degree to which the child consumed more or less than the ideal daily recommendation. Similar objective coding guidelines were employed to determine injection intervals and their regularity; meal timing; regularity of injection-meal timing; percentage of calories from fat, carbohydrates, and concentrated sweets; eating frequency; exercise type, duration, and frequency; and glucose testing frequency.

Correlations between parent and child report ranged from r=.42 (regularity of injection-meal timing) to r=.78 (glucose testing frequency). Children six to nine years of age showed the poorest agreement with parents for measures involving time, which may have reflected the young children's difficulty with the abstract concept of time. On simpler qualitative or frequency measures, their responses correlated well with their parents. Ten- to 15-year-old children showed the most consistent parent-child agreement, whereas the 16- to 19-year-old age group had highly variable parent-child correlations. The older subjects also reported being significantly less adherent to their regimens than did the younger subjects. Finally, Johnson et al., found that youngsters were not uniformly compliant or noncompliant. Rather, varying levels of adherence were obtained, depending on the task.

The 24-hour recall interview employed by Johnson et al., (1986) appears to have considerable potential for assessing adherence to specific aspects of disease management. The limited time span of recall and the specific details requested in the interview most likely contributed to the generally good correspondence between parents and children. Given the discrepancies between parent and child report on time dimensions for younger children, it would appear advisable to use both parent and child report to estimate compliance in younger children. For adolescents, who have greater independence in managing their daily routines, the Johnson et al. findings provide strong support for the need to obtain the youngster's report, rather than to rely solely on parent estimates, if accurate compliance data is desired.

Johnson et al. (1986) also employed some methodological approaches which may be important for clinicians and researchers alike to consider. First, they obtained multiple measurements over a limited time period which provided additional information regarding regularity in adherence behaviors, in addition to information regarding occurrence, and also minimized the chances that unrepresentative data would be obtained. Secondly, they utilized interviewers who were not associated with the clinic staff, which may have encouraged participants to be more candid. Further research is needed to determine whether reliable and valid self-report data could be obtained via 24-hour recall interviews in clinical settings. In particular it would be useful to investigate the validity of 24-hour recall data through comparison with corresponding physiological indicators of adherence.

Projectives

A unique self-report approach to predicting compliance, the Medical Compliance Incomplete Stories Test (M-CIST), was developed by Czajkowski and Koocher (1986). The M-CIST consists of five stories in which the protagonist is "confronted with a dilemma involving a decision about whether or not to follow specific medical advice. The participant is asked to complete the story and in so doing to predict the outcome for the main character . . ." (p.299). Verbatim responses are recorded.

The child's responses are scored along three dimensions: compliance/coping, optimism, and self-efficacy, and then summed across all five stimuli for the three dimensions. In a study of 40 13- to 23-year-old cystic fibrosis patients, Czajkowski and Koocher (1986) obtained good interrater agreement for the scoring categories ($r=.81$ to 1.00). In addition, M-CIST scores: (1) correlated with independent ratings of patient compliance (based on hospital records) over a seven-day period, (2) accounted for a significant portion of the variance in patient compliance, and (3) significantly discriminated compliant from noncompliant patients. Czajkowski and Koocher propose that the M-CIST could be used for the early identification of noncompliant patients and to provide information regarding differences in behaviors and beliefs of noncompliant cystic fibrosis patients. However, these clinical applications have not yet been tested empirically.

Self-Monitoring

By far the most common method for obtaining child self-report of compliance involves self-monitoring. This is a relatively straightforward approach, which simply involves asking the child to record when or if he or she performs specific management behaviors. In designing a self-monitoring system, several issues should be considered. One must first determine how compliance is to be reported. If the child is to merely indicate whether or not a prescribed behavior was performed, a clear operational definition of the behavior is needed. A good example of an operational definition of compliance is one reported by Lowe and Lutzker (1979) for a diabetic girl's skin care ("put on clean, color-fast socks each day, wash her feet with mild soap, pat them dry, and inspect them for cuts and bruises" p. 59). A time was set daily for completion of the task. Compliance was defined as completion of a task at the prescribed time or within 15 minutes before or after that time. Such a definition allows for clear determination of task completion and can be easily applied to management behaviors such as pill-taking, shot administration, blood and urine testing, or tooth brushing and flossing (e.g., Carney, Schechter, & Davis, 1983; Dahlquist & Gil, 1986; Gross, Magalnick, & Richardson, 1985; Lowe & Lutzker, 1979; Schafer, Glasgow, & McCaul, 1982).

For more complex routines, "yes"/"no" indications of compliance may not be practical. For example, to determine adherence to dietary regimens it may be most appropriate to ask children to record all food intake over a several day period. In the case of exercise programs, timing, duration, and intensity of exercise may be important to assess in addition to frequency. Similar issues in timing of behaviors are important for insulin injections or for medications which must be taken in conjunction with meals (i.e., in cystic fibrosis) or at the sign of physical symptoms (i.e., in asthma). Self-monitoring strategies for such complicated regimens typically involve daily diaries with specified blanks for monitoring events and management behaviors.

An example of a multifaceted self-monitoring system is the approach employed by Baum and Creer (1986). They asked 6- to 16-year-old asthmatic patients to record the following in daily diaries: (1) morning and evening highest peak flow values, (2) whether or not daily medications were taken on time, and (3) for every asthma attack the severity, medications taken prior to the episode, perceived precipitants, and the child's responses to the attack. The daily diaries were subsequently analyzed to identify differences in children's reliance on self-management skills rather than solely on medications.

Regardless of the format of the self-monitoring system employed, most researchers have attempted to evaluate the reliability and validity of the child's self-monitoring data. Parents frequently have been asked to informally check on the child's accuracy (e.g., Baum & Creer, 1986), independently monitor the same behaviors that the child records (e.g., Lowe & Lutzker, 1979; Rose, Firestone, Heick, & Faught, 1983), or check the accuracy of the child's records at random intervals determined by the experimenter (e.g., Rose et al., 1983; Schafer et al., 1982). However, concurrent observations by parents also present some problems. Both parents and child may distort data to present a more favorable impression (La Greca, 1988). Parents also may not cooperate with the reliability checking process. For instance, Rose et al. (1983) found that parents' cooperation with reliability checks ranged from 34.3% to 75.3%, with a mean of 55.6%. Furthermore, parents may not be able to observe many of their child's independent management behaviors (especially during adolescence), or the child may not allow the parent to observe (e.g., Schafer et al., 1982). As an alternative to requiring parents to check the child's daily test results, Lowe and Lutzker (1979) had their subject save one-half of each urine sample she collected. The experimenters then tested randomly selected samples to corroborate her data.

It is also possible to evaluate self-monitoring data through examining permanent products. For example, Carney et al. (1983) asked subjects to save all Chemstrips from blood glucose tests and staple them to a sheet on which the date, time of test, and test results were to be recorded. Dahlquist and Gil (1986) required subjects to save their dental floss after use to corroborate their self-monitored frequency of flossing. Self-monitored medication compliance can also be checked by counting remaining pills.

One can also incorporate a marking process into the task to which the patient is expected to comply. To illustrate, Epstein et al. (1981) included random amounts of placebo Clinitest tablets in subjects' weekly supplies of actual Clinitest tablets for urine testing. When the child found an inert placebo tablet, he or she was instructed to record the fact and repeat the test with a new tablet. At the end of the week, the child's parent tested the remaining tablets and added the number of placebo tablets the parent found to the number the child found. The totals were then compared with the correct number of placebos provided by the experimenter.

Further evidence for the validity of self-monitoring compliance data can be found in studies demonstrating a correspondence between self-monitoring data and physical indicators of compliance. Examples of such physiological indicators include amount of plaque on teeth in dental compliance studies (e.g., Dahlquist & Gil, 1986), and long-term metabolic control in diabetes (e.g., Carney et al., 1983; Schafer et al., 1982).

Summary

The compliance measures reviewed in this section illustrate general approaches to self-report compliance assessment, which could be applied to any pediatric medical condition. First, it is important to assess the child's understanding of what he or she is supposed to do in terms of daily medical care. All aspects of the prescribed regimen must be evaluated, since knowledge in one area does not predict knowledge or adherence for other management tasks.

If one is interested in exploring specific attitudes about adherence, structured interviews or projectives may prove useful, although very little empirical work has been done in this area, and the clinical utility of these approaches has not been determined. To obtain a relatively quick assessment of potential compliance problem areas, the 24-hour recall interview appears to offer considerable promise. By eliciting specific details of the child's behavior during the previous day, this strategy closely resembles standard behavioral interviewing techniques and should prove useful in identifying problematic compliance settings or behaviors that could become later targets for intervention. On the other hand, to assess ongoing adherence, self-monitoring appears to be the most appropriate. Of course, the complexity of the monitoring system needs to be tailored to the developmental level of the child and to the important aspects of the medical regimen (i.e., frequency versus timing).

Finally, it is consistently recommended in the literature that for any compliance assessment, care should be taken to obtain multiple measurements of adherence from as many sources as possible (Johnson, 1984; La Greca, 1988; Stark, Dahlquist, & Collins, 1987). Thus, an ideal measurement strategy might include child self-report, parent report, permanent products, physiological measures, and direct observation, in order to yield the most comprehensive picture of the child's medical compliance.

SUMMARY AND CONCLUSIONS

In evaluating the validity of self-report instruments for children in medical situations, one must consider the purpose of the assessment. If the goal is to obtain maximum, unbiased information about how children perceive their medical experiences, unbiased, open-ended interview or questionnaire strategies that can be reliably scored appear most useful. On the other hand, if it is important to identify quantifiable changes in the child's experience, visual analog scales appear to have the greatest potential reliability and sensitivity for the assessment of subjective distress, whereas self-monitoring has shown the greatest utility for monitoring changes in compliance with daily medical management. Regardless of the ultimate goal of assessment, children's self-report offers a unique source of information in the medical setting and warrants considerably more clinical and empirical attention.

REFERENCES

Abu-Saad, H. (1984). Assessing children's responses to pain. *Pain, 19*, 163–171.

Allen, D.A., Tennen, H., McGrade, B.J., Affleck, G., & Ratzan, S. (1983). Parent and child perceptions of the management of juvenile diabetes. *Journal of Pediatric Psychology, 8*, 129–141.

Andrasik, F., Burke, E.J., Attanasio, V., & Rosenblum, E.L. (1985). Child, parent, and physician reports of child's headache pain: Relationships prior to and following treatment. *Headache, 25*, 421–425.

Baum, D., & Creer, T.L. (1986). Medication compliance in children with asthma. *Journal of Asthma, 23*, 49–59.

Beyer, J.E., & Byers, M.L. (1985). Knowledge of pediatric pain: The state of the art. *Children's Health Care, 13*, 150–159.

Beyer, J., DeGood, D., Ashley, L., & Russell, G. (1983). Patterns of postoperative analgesic use with adults and children following cardiac surgery. *Pain, 17*, 71–81.

Bradlyn, A.S., Christoff, K., Sikora, T., O'Dell, S.L., & Harris, C.V. (1986). The effects of a videotape preparation package in reducing children's arousal and increasing cooperation during cardiac catheterization. *Behaviour Research and Therapy, 24*, 453–459.

Broome, M.E. (1986). The relationship between children's fears and behavior during a painful event. *Children's Health Care, 14*, 142–145.

Broome, M.E., & Hellier, A.P. (1987). School-age children's fears of medical experiences. *Issues in Comprehensive Pediatric Nursing, 10*, 77–86.

Budzynski, T., Stoyva, J., Adler, C., & Mullaney, D.J. (1973). EMG biofeedback and tension headache: A controlled outcome study. *Psychosomatic Medicine, 35*, 484–496.

Carney, R.M., Schechter, K., & Davis, T. (1983). Improving adherence to blood glucose testing in insulin-dependent diabetic children. *Behavior Therapy, 14*, 247–254.

Christensen, N.K., Terry, R.D., Wyatt, S., Pichert, J.W., & Lorenz, R.A. (1983). Quantitative assessment of dietary adherence in patients with insulin-dependent diabetes mellitus. *Diabetes Care, 6,* 245–250.

Cone, J.D., & Hawkins, R.P. (1977). *Behavioral assessment: New directions in clinical psychology.* New York: Brunner/Mazel.

Czajkowski, D.R., & Koocher, G.P. (1986). Predicting compliance among adolescents with cystic fibrosis. *Health Psychology, 5,* 297–305.

Dahlquist, L.M., & Gil, K.M. (1986). Using parents to maintain improved dental flossing skills in children. *Journal of Applied Behavior Analysis, 19,* 255–260.

Dahlquist, L.M., Gil, K.M., Armstrong, F.D., Ginsberg, A., & Jones, B. (1985). Behavioral management of children's distress during chemotherapy. *Journal of Behavior Therapy and Experimental Psychiatry, 16,* 325–329.

Eland, J.M. (1981). Minimizing pain associated with prekindergarten muscular injections. *Issues in Comprehensive Pediatric Nursing, 5,* 327–335.

Eland, J.M., & Anderson, J.E. (1977). The experience of pain in children. In A. Jadox (Ed.), *Pain: A sourcebook for nurses and other health professionals.* Boston: Little, Brown.

Elkins, P.D., & Roberts, M.D. (1983). Psychological preparation for pediatric hospitalization. *Clinical Psychology Review, 3,* 275–295.

Elliott, C.H., Jay, S.M., & Woody, P. (1987). An observation scale for measuring children's distress during medical procedures. *Journal of Pediatric Psychology, 12,* 543–551.

Epstein, L.H., Beck, S., Figueroa, J., Farkas, G., Kazdin, A.E., Daneman, D., & Becker, D. (1981). The effects of targeting improvements in urine glucose on metabolic control in children with insulin dependent diabetes. *Journal of Applied Behavior Analysis, 14,* 365–375.

Faust, J., & Melamed, B.G. (1984). Influence of arousal, previous experience, and age on surgery preparation of same day of surgery and in hospital pediatric patients. *Journal of Consulting and Clinical Psychology, 52,* 359–365.

Ferguson, B.F. (1979). Preparing young children for hospitalization. A comparison of two methods. *Pediatrics, 64,* 656–664.

Gaffney, A., & Dunne, E.A. (1986). Developmental aspects of children's definitions of pain. *Pain, 26,* 105–117.

Gaffney, A., & Dunne, E.A. (1987). Children's understanding of the causality of pain. *Pain, 29,* 91–104.

Gross, A.M., Magalnick, L.J., & Richardson, P. (1985). Self-management training with families of insulin-dependent diabetic children: A controlled long-term investigation. *Child and Family Behavior Therapy, 7,* 35–50.

Harkavy, J., Johnson, S.B., Silverstein, J., Spillar, R., McCallum, M., & Rosenbloom, A. (1983). Who learns what at summer camp. *Journal of Pediatric Psychology, 8,* 143–153.

Hilgard, J.R., & LeBaron, S. (1982). Relief of anxiety and pain in children and adolescents with cancer: Quantitative measures and clinical observations. *International Journal of Clinical and Experimental Hypnosis, 4,* 417–442.

International Association for the Study of Pain Subcommittee on Taxonomy. (1979). Pain terms: A list with definitions and notes on usage. *Pain, 6,* 249–252.

Jay, S.M., Elliott, C.H., Katz, E., & Siegel, S. (1987). Cognitive-behavioral and pharmacologic interventions for children's distress during painful medical procedures. *Journal of Consulting and Clinical Psychology, 55,* 860–865.

Jay, S.M., Elliott, C., & Varni, J.W. (1986). Acute and chronic pain in adults and children with cancer. *Journal of Consulting and Clinical Psychology, 54,* 601–607.

Jay, S.M., Ozolins, M., Elliott, C.H., & Caldwell, S. (1983). Assessment of children's distress during painful medical procedures. *Health Psychology, 2,* 133–147.

Jerrett, M.D. (1985). Children and their pain experience. *Children's Health Care, 14,* 83–89.

Johnson, J.E., Kirchoff, K.T., & Endress, M.P. (1975). Altering children's distress behavior during orthopedic cast removal. *Nursing Research, 24,* 404–410.

Johnson, S.B. (1984). Knowledge, attitudes, and behavior: Correlates of health in childhood diabetes. *Clinical Psychology Review, 4,* 503–524.

Johnson, S.B., Pollack, R.T., Silverstein, J.H., Rosenbloom, A.L., Spillar, R., McCallum, M., & Harkavy, J. (1982). Cognitive and behavioral knowledge about insulin-dependent diabetes among children and parents. *Pediatrics, 69,* 708–713.

Johnson, S.B., Silverstein, J., Rosenbloom, A., Carter, R., & Cunningham, W. (1986). Assessing daily management in childhood diabetes. *Health Psychology, 5,* 545–564.

Katz, E.R., Sharp, B., Kellerman, J., Marston, A.R., Hershman, J.M., & Siegel, S.E. (1982). B-endorphin immunoreactivity and acute behavioral distress in children with leukemia. *Journal of Nervous and Mental Disease, 170,* 72–77.

Kellerman, J., Zeltzer, L., Ellenberg, L., & Dash, J. (1983). Hypnosis for the reduction of the acute pain and anxiety associated with medical procedures. *Journal of Adolescent Health Care, 4,* 85–90.

La Greca, A.M. (1988). Adherence to prescribed regimens. In D.K. Routh (Ed.), *Handbook of pediatric psychology* (pp. 299–320). New York: Guilford Press.

LeBaron, S., & Zeltzer, L. (1984). Assessment of acute pain and anxiety in children and adolescents by self-reports, observer reports, and a behavioral checklist. *Journal of Consulting and Clinical Psychology, 52,* 729–738.

Lollar, D.J., Smits, S.J., & Patterson, D.L. (1982). Assessment of pediatric pain: An empirical perspective. *Journal of Pediatric Psychology, 7,* 267–277.

Lowe, K., & Lutzker, J.R. (1979). Increasing compliance to a medical regimen with a juvenile diabetic. *Behavior Therapy, 10,* 57–64.

McGrath, P.A. (1987). An assessment of children's pain: A review of behavioral, physiological and direct scaling techniques. *Pain, 31,* 147–176.

McGrath, P.A., deVeber, L.L., & Hearn, M.T. (1985). Multidimensional pain assessment in children. In H.L. Fields, R. Dubner, and F. Cervero (Eds.), *Advances in pain research and therapy,* Vol. 9, (pp. 387–393). New York: Raven Press.

McNabb, W.L., Wilson-Pessano, S.R., & Jacobs, A.M. (1986). Critical self-management competencies for children with asthma. *Journal of Pediatric Psychology, 11,* 103–117.

Melamed, B.G. (1977). Psychological preparation for hospitalization. In S. Rachman (Ed.), *Contributions to Medical Psychology (Vol. 1),* (pp. 43–74). Oxford: Pergamon Press.

Melamed, B.G., Dearborn, M., & Hermecz, D.A. (1983). Necessary considerations for surgery preparation: Age and previous experience. *Psychosomatic Medicine, 45,* 517–525.

Melamed, B.G., & Siegel, L. (1975). Reduction of anxiety in children facing hospitalization and surgery by use of filmed modeling. *Journal of Consulting and Clinical Psychology, 43,* 511–521.

Melamed, B.G., Yurcheson, R., Fleece, E.L., Hutcherson, S., & Hawes, R. (1978). Effects of film modeling on the reduction of anxiety-related behaviors in individuals varying in level of previous experience in the stress situation. *Journal of Consulting and Clinical Psychology, 46,* 1357–1367.

Melzak, R. (1975). The McGill Pain Questionnaire: Major properties and scoring methods. *Pain, 1,* 277–299.

Miser, A.W., Dothage, J.A., Wesley, R.A., & Miser, J.S. (1987). The prevalence of pain in a pediatric and young cancer population. *Pain, 29,* 73–83.

Owens, M.E. (1984). Pain in infancy: Conceptual and methodological issues. *Pain, 20,* 213–230.

Passero, M.A., Remor, B., & Salomon, J. (1981). Patient-reported compliance with cystic fibrosis therapy. *Clinical Pediatrics, 20,* 264–268.

Peterson, L. & Shigetomi, C. (1981). The use of coping techniques to minimize anxiety in hospitalized children. *Behavior Therapy, 12,* 1–14

Reynolds, C.R., & Richmond, B.O. (1978). What I think and feel: A revised measure of children's manifest anxiety. *Journal of Abnormal Child Psychology, 6,* 271–280.

Richardson, G.M., McGrath, P.J., Cunningham, S.J., & Humphreys, P. (1982). Validity of the headache diary for children. *Headache, 23,* 184–187.

Roberts, M.C., Wurtele, S.K., Boone, R.R., Ginther, L.J., & Elkins, P.D. (1981). Reduction of medical fears by use of modeling: A preventive application in a general population of children. *Journal of Pediatric Psychology, 6,* 293–300.

Rose, M.I., Firestone, P., Heick, H.M.C., & Faught, A.K. (1983). The effects of anxiety management training on the control of juvenile diabetes mellitus. *Journal of Behavioral Medicine, 6,* 381–395.

Ross, D.M., & Ross, S.A. (1984a). Childhood pain: The school-age child's viewpoint. *Pain, 20,* 179–181.

Ross, D.M., & Ross, S.A. (1984b). The importance of type of question, psychological climate and subject set in interviewing children about pain. *Pain, 19,* 71–79.

Savedra, M., Gibbons, P., Tesler, M., Ward, J., & Wegner, C. (1982). How do children describe pain? A tentative assessment. *Pain, 14,* 95–104.

Schafer, L.C., Glasgow, R.E., & McCaul, K.D. (1982). Increasing the adherence of diabetic adolescents. *Journal of Behavioral Medicine, 5,* 353–362.

Scherer, M., & Nakamura, C. (1968). A fear survey schedule for children (FSS-FC):

A factor-analytic comparison with manifest anxiety. *Behaviour Research and Therapy, 6,* 173–182.

Schultz, N. (1971). How children perceive pain. *Nursing Outlook, 19,* 670–673.

Scott, J., & Huskisson, E. (1976). Graphic representation of pain. *Pain, 2,* 175–184.

Scott, R. (1978). "It hurts red:" A preliminary study of children's perception of pain. *Perceptual and Motor Skills, 47,* 787–791.

Siaw, S.N., Stephens, L.R., & Holmes, S.S. (1986). Knowledge about medical instruments and reported anxiety in pediatric surgery patients. *Children's Health Care, 14,* 134–141.

Siegel, L.J., & Peterson, L. (1980). Stress reduction in young dental patients through coping skills and sensory information. *Journal of Consulting and Clinical Psychology, 48,* 785–787.

Spielberger, C., Edwards, C., Lushene, R., Monturi, J., & Platzek, S. (1973). *The state-trait anxiety inventory for children.* Palo Alto, CA: Consulting Psychologist Press.

Stark, L.J., Dahlquist, L.M., & Collins, F.L. (1987). Improving children's compliance with diabetes management. *Clinical Psychology Review, 7,* 223–242.

Tesler, M., Ward, J., Savedra, M., Wegner, C.B., & Gibbons, P. (1983). Developing an instrument for eliciting children's descriptions of pain. *Perceptual and Motor Skills, 56,* 315–321.

Unruh, A., McGrath, P., Cunningham, S.J., & Humphreys, P. (1983). Children's drawings of their pain. *Pain, 17,* 385–392.

Varni, J.W. (1983). *Clinical behavioral pediatrics: An interdisciplinary bio-behavioral approach.* New York: Pergamon.

Varni, J.W., Thompson, K.L., & Hanson, V. (1987). The Varni/Thompson pediatric pain questionnaire. I. Chronic musculoskeletal pain in juvenile rheumatoid arthritis. *Pain, 28,* 27–38.

Venham, L., Bengston, D., & Cipes, M. (1977). Children's response to sequential dental visits. *Journal of Dental Research, 56,* 454–459.

Zastowny, T.R., Kirschenbaum, D.S., & Meng, A.L. (1986). Coping skills training for children: Effects on distress before, during and after hospitalization for surgery. *Health Psychology, 5,* 231–247.

Zeltzer, L., Kellerman, J., Ellenberg, L., & Dash, J. (1983). Hypnosis for reduction of vomiting associated with chemotherapy and disease in adolescents with cancer. *Journal of Adolescent Health Care, 4,* 77–84.

Zeltzer, L., & LeBaron, S. (1982). Hypnosis and nonhypnotic techniques for reduction of pain and anxiety during painful procedures in children and adolescents with cancer. *Journal of Pediatrics, 101,* 1032–1035.

INDEX

440

INDEX OF MEASURES

Measures of Anxiety/Fear

Measures of Child Behavior Problems

Measures of Depression and Related Constructs